How a Cuban-Born, Soviet-Trained

Commando Took Down the Strip to the

Tune of Five World-Class Hotels,

Three Armored Cars, and Millions of Dollars

STORMING

JOHN HUDDY

LAS VEGAS

BALLANTINE BOOKS—NEW YORK

To my parents, Norman Walter and Anna May Huddy,

and the spirited, colorful, and multitalented tribe they

left behind, including Colonel Norman W. Huddy, Jr., USMC,

wife, Margaret, Anne, Virginia, Erica, John Trevor, Juliet,

Brentt, Kathleen, John Norman, Terri, and Bernadette

2009 Ballantine Books Trade Paperback Edition

Copyright © 2008 by John Huddy
Map copyright © 2008 by
Mapping Specialists Ltd.

Published in the United States by
Ballantine Books, an imprint of
The Random House Publishing Group,
a division of Random House, Inc., New York.

BALLANTINE and colophon are registered
trademarks of Random House, Inc.

Originally published in hardcover in the
United States by Ballantine Books, an imprint of
The Random House Publishing Group,
a division of Random House, Inc, in 2008.

LIBRARY OF CONGRESS
CATALOGING-IN-PUBLICATION DATA
Huddy, John.
Storming Las Vegas : how a Cuban-born,
Soviet-trained commando took down
the Strip to the tune of five world-class
hotels, three armored cars, and millions
of dollars / John Huddy.
p. cm.
ISBN 978-0-345-51441-7
1. Vigoa Perez, Jose Manuel.
2. Criminals—Nevada—Las Vegas—Biography.
3. Criminals—Cuba—Biography. 4. Casinos—
Nevada—Las Vegas. 5. Crime—Nevada—
Las Vegas. I. Title.
HV6795.L37H83 2008
364.15'52092—dc22   2007042769

Printed in the United States of America

www.ballantinebooks.com

1 2 3 4 5 6 7 8 9

Book design by Barbara M. Bachman

We called him the Angry Man, the victim of a random shooting in traffic when gang members sprayed his car, wife, and two young daughters with 9 mm submachine gun fire. It was the summer of 2001 in Las Vegas, the temperature was 100 degrees at midnight, and the powerfully built young father tore at his shirt as he walked in circles in the street. "My babies, my babies, the motherfuckers tried to kill my babies, tried to kill my babies!" he raged in the glow of flashing police lights, referring to the children who had been showered with glass shards but survived the unprovoked attack. Then the Angry Man, by this time bare chested and drenched in sweat, slumped to the pavement on his knees, wiped away a trickle of blood from his forehead, and began to sob.

I was directing and producing a documentary called *Vegas Cops* for the Discovery Channel and the Travel Channel. I turned to my cameraman. "Did you get that?" He shrugged. "Some of it."

"*What?*"

"Sorry, we ran out of tape."

"*You ran out of tape?*"

I was about to have my own moment of spontaneous combustion, when my cell phone rang. I would soon forget the Angry Man and the great shot we just missed and the insanity of directing a film in the middle of the summer in the brutal heat of Las Vegas, and the fact that some numb-nuts assistant forgot to load tape in the truck. Detective Sergeant Timothy Shalhoob of the police department's tourist safety unit was calling with a tip. Tim was about to open a door to a journalistic pursuit that would begin in a small village in western Cuba, move to the stark mountains of Afghanistan, then the historic Mariel boatlift, and finally the neon-lit Strip of Las Vegas.

"You gotta talk to John Alamshaw in the robbery section," Sergeant

Shalhoob said. "Forget the gangbangers, pickpockets, hookers, and hustlers. John has got the goddamnedest story you'll ever hear—*if* he'll talk to you." I thought I detected something in the sergeant's voice that you don't normally hear when macho cops talk about crime sprees and bad guys and major investigations. Was it awe? Fear? Anxiety? Or maybe the sense that even the modernized, computerized, and proper-copper Las Vegas Metropolitan Police Department had encountered something unexpectedly dark, disturbing, and perhaps, as one senior commander later suggested, a dangerous new threat almost out of its league.

Lieutenant Alamshaw did agree to see me. During the next three years, he told his remarkable story with patience and self-deprecating humor. The eerie rumors about an alarming new threat to the peace and order of Las Vegas, gleaned not only from Shalhoob but from a police captain at the training academy, various detectives, and the sheriff himself, turned out to be largely true. Thank you, Lieutenant.

Likewise, Jose Manuel Vigoa, the lieutenant's antagonist, cooperated fully and beyond my expectations. Vigoa consented not only to multiple in-person interviews, but later wrote detailed reports, complete with color sketches and blueprints, chronicling his life story, foreign adventures, arrival in the U.S., family life, and the eventual (and literal) storming of Las Vegas. Vigoa also permitted me to interview his former wife and three daughters, and authorized me, without restrictions, to view his legal records.

I am also grateful to Sheriff Bill Young and his successor, Sheriff Doug Gillespie (who originally approved the project while under sheriff), for green-lighting Metro's approval; and to Carla Alston, the department's head of public information, for her professional follow-through. Thanks as well to FBI Special Agent Brett W. Shields and his colleagues, including the legendary undercover agent Larry Brito in El Paso, Texas; Angela Bell, the FBI public information officer at headquarters; then-lieutenant Jutta Chambers of the Henderson Police Department; Al Cabrales and his crack crime scene analysis crew; Captain Leroy Kirkegard and the correctional officers at the Clark County Detention Center; Pedro Durazo of the U.S. Probation Office; Clark County Coroner P. Michael Murphy; and the firefighters and paramedics of the Henderson Fire Department.

David Roger, the Clark County district attorney, was the first senior official I met at the outset of the project. At breakfast, Roger promised his assistance. He proved to be a man of his word. The DA and his staff were unfailingly helpful and courteous. Jay Angelo, who prosecuted Vigoa during the "Tony Montana era," went above and beyond in helping me re-create the drug lord phase in the 1980s, when, as the saying went at the time, it was snowing all year long in Sin City.

I owe much to Drew Christensen, the attorney who introduced me to Vigoa. Christensen gave me fascinating and nuanced insights during our long drives to meet his client. Certainly the attorney's cache of confidential files fleshed out the reporting of *Storming Las Vegas*. Thanks, too, to E. K. McDaniel, a Nevada state official who must have winced when I first appeared on his doorstep asking for the impossible. In the end, I could not have proceeded without his help, and for that I am grateful. Vegas hotel executives are loath to talk about casino crime, especially successful robberies accompanied by gunfire. However, Yvette Monet of the MGM Mirage public relations staff, and Stephen G. Koenig, the chain's security chief, cooperated fully. Koenig and Bellagio security supervisor Brian Zinke not only consented to interviews but gave me tours of the Bellagio's gaming surveillance room and a replay of what happened the morning of June 3, 2000.

I am also grateful to the families of the victims, Gary Dean Prestidge and Richard Sosa, and to the guards who were shot but survived during one of the hotel gunfights. Thanks to Gary Prestidge Sr., Shala Premack, Norma Sosa and her children, Donald Bowman, and Chuck Fichter. Thanks also to the management of Brink's Incorporated in Las Vegas for permitting the wounded guards to talk to me.

Peggy Noonan once described an author's first book as an "exciting trauma." It is. But I had many wonderfully bright and loyal supporters to turn to during the more challenging moments, when a big story seemed almost too sprawling, and they kept me on course. Thanks to my bride of thirty-three years, Erica Trevor Huddy, who told me twenty years ago that I would someday write a book (but first I had to clean up my room). Also, thanks to Roger Ailes, William Shine, Christina Bertuca, Van Gordon Sauter, John Burrud (my original partner in the *Vegas Cops* series), Sandy Spooner, the late Gene Miller of the *Miami Herald,* other *Herald* reporters, the management of KVVU-TV, the Fox affiliate in Las Vegas, the *Las Vegas Review-Journal,* and a who's who of former CIA agents, including Peter Brookes, Brian Latell, and Robert Baer, who helped me analyze Vigoa's professed military background in the absence of official Cuban confirmation. Wayne Smith, the former U.S. Mission chief in Havana, provided keen insight into Cuban affairs and the plausibility of Vigoa's claims. Also, I appreciate the help given by Captain Ted Rose, a veteran Oxnard, California, charter boat owner; attorney Anson Whitfield; Range Master Raymond Witham Jr. of the American Shooters Gun Club in Las Vegas (who checked me out in an AK-47); and Jules Harding, the actress and motivational therapist.

And then there were those who had to put up with *me,* who helped turn a rambling initial proposal into a published work and who did so with finesse and style. Simon Green, of the POM Agency, proved smart, funny, and tough on many levels. He's as proficient at steering a paranoid, insecure writer through rough creative shoals as he is marketing the product. CAA's Matthew Snyder, unflappable and savvy, was brought into the project by fellow agent Martin Spencer and managed to option the book rights to a major studio a full eighteen months before its publication.

Mark Tavani of Ballantine Books, of The Random House Publishing Group, edited this book. In a thirty-year media career, I've worked with some of the best in the business, and even in that august company, Mark stands apart. He took an oversized first draft and with patience and care (and with occasional steel behind his courteous, encouraging e-mails), guided the author to the finish line—and we both lived to tell the tale.

There are two others close to me who contributed immensely to the book. My son, John Trevor Huddy, did the reporting relating to Vigoa's Tony Montana–like drug career, tracking down long-retired FBI agents and conducting many of the key interviews. A prize-winning newspaperman before joining WNYW-TV, the Fox flagship station in New York, John spent days sifting through old files at the FBI archives in Perris, California, and returned with invaluable grand jury records, trial transcripts, and even long-forgotten FBI wiretap material. Good job, Mr. Huddy.

And finally, a deep bow to my multitalented researcher and transcriber, Donna Jo Shatters-Pimentel. Donna was with me from the beginning, transcribed hundreds of hours of interviews, and, through a savantlike memory, kept track of thousands of details. As good hearted as she is talented, Donna Jo was the glue that held the team together, and I will be forever grateful for this young woman's loyalty, hard work, and good cheer. Hector, her massive and handsome pit bull companion, although often asleep on the job, was appreciated too.

CONTENTS

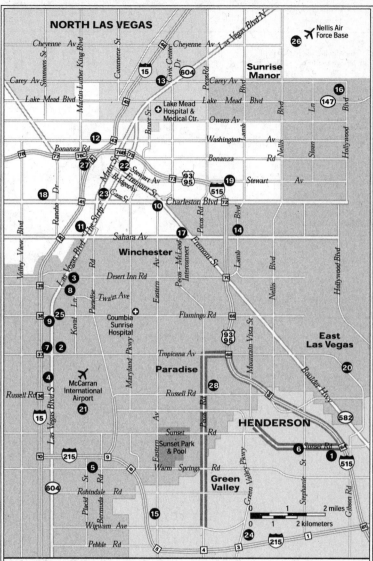

NORTH LAS VEGAS

Cheyenne Av
Cheyenne Av
Simmons St
Martin Luther King Blvd
Commerce St
Civic Center Dr
Las Vegas Blvd N

Nellis Air
Force Base
26

Carey Av
Carey Av

**Sunrise
Manor**

13
604
15

Lake Mead Blvd
Lake Mead Blvd
Lake Mead Hospital & Medical Ctr.
Bruce St
Pecos Rd
Lamb Blvd
Sloan Ln
Hollywood Blvd

16
147

Owens Av

Washington Av

12
Bonanza Rd
Bonanza Rd

76C
27
Main St
Stewart Av
22
Bridgeway
Fremont St
Cass St
73
93
95

19
Stewart Av

18
Rancho Dr
23
41
10
Charleston Blvd
515

11
Las Vegas Blvd (The Strip)
Sahara Av
17
Pecos Rd
Fremont St
Lamb Blvd
14

Hollywood Blvd

Winchester

Valley View Blvd
35
3
Desert Inn Rd
Eastern Av
Pecos – McLeod Interconnect
70

8
Koval Ln
Paradise Rd
Twain Ave

9
25
Coumbia Sunrise Hospital
Flamingo Rd
69
93
95
Mountain Vista St

**East
Las Vegas**

7 **2**
Tropicana Av
68
Boulder Hwy
20

4
Paradise
Maryland Pkwy
28
Russell Rd

McCarran International Airport
21

HENDERSON

Russell Rd
15
Eastern Av
Pecos Rd

582

10
215
9
Sunset Rd
Sunset Park & Pool
6 Sunset Rd
1
Stephanie St
515
Green Valley Pkwy

5
Warm Springs Rd
**Green
Valley**
Gibson Rd

604
Robindale Rd
Placid St
Bermuda Rd

0   1   2 miles
0   1   2 kilometers

Wigwam Ave
15
Pebble Rd
24
215
1
61

---

1. **Sunset Station Hotel in Henderson.** Jose Vigoa's aborted robbery here serves as a dress rehearsal for the onslaught to come.

2. **The MGM.** The world's largest hotel and the site of a superbly planned robbery that nearly became a disaster.

3. **The Desert Inn.** The crown jewel of Mafia-run Vegas. The occurrence of a robbery here symbolized the end of the Mafia's control of the city.

4. **Mandalay Bay.** The site of a quick, clean, and profitable robbery and an example of Vigoa's first rule: The gang will have no modus operandi because it will shift tactics with every strike.

5. **Thrifty Car Rental.** The site of a stunningly audacious robbery that left Vigoa's crew with a fleet of getaway cars and told police the worst was yet to come.

6. **Ross Dress-for-Less.** An unlikely site for a murderous robbery, but the peace of an upscale suburban shopping center was shattered when Vigoa's crew arrived there.

7. **New York-New York.** The site of a robbery that exhibited Vigoa's boldness and ended with his crew wheeling a money cart through the lobby and into valet parking.

8. **The Venetian.** The site of a robbery that never came to be, though the gang did enter the hotel before aborting the mission.
CONTINUED →

9. **The Bellagio.** Though the heat was on and casino guards were on the alert, Vigoa was undaunted. But here he made his first major mistake.
10. **Showboat Hotel & Casino.** The site of Vigoa's first employment in the United States. The building was imploded in 2006.
11. **The Naked City.** A rough neighborhood where Vigoa made his reputation as a fierce drug enforcer.
12. **The bar at Jackson and F St.** The toughest gin mill in town, which was visited by Detective John Alamshaw and fellow Metro officers.
13. **Donna St. and Carey.** The intersection where a routine drug bust became a riot, and where Alamshaw made his bones.
14. **Sahara-Lamb Storage.** It was here that Vigoa and the FBI skirmished during a federal raid.
15. **Residence at Sandy Slate Way.** Although the home was in the name of Oscar Cisneros, this was the residence of the Vigoa family after the MGM heist.
16. **Residence at 6553 Cordelle Dr.** Cisneros's home, where a startling discovery was made.
17. **1685 S. Palm St.** Main office and vault of the Armored Transport Company, the employer of Gary Dean Prestidge and Richard Sosa.
18. **Robbery section offices**
19. **Task force offices**
20. **Vigoa's "roach coach" trailer**
21. **McCarran International Airport**
22. **Police headquarters**
23. **The Clark County Detention Center**
24. **Henderson, Nevada**
25. **The Strip:** The title is somewhat misleading: The Strip is one entity; downtown, where the mayor is trying to rejuvenate a drug-ravaged high-crime area, is another. Downtown is where one finds the older hotels with penny slots and locals at the $1 blackjack tables.
26. **Nellis Air Force Base and neighborhood.** General area where Oscar Cisneros's and Gary Prestidge's families lived.
27. **The Spaghetti:** A notorious spot where the I-515, 93, 95, I-15, and other roads intersect in one ghastly snarl.
28. **The Chase**–marked in dark gray in Green Valley, Henderson, area.

BOOK ONE

GUNFIGHT ON
LAS VEGAS BOULEVARD

FIRST BLOOD

*I*t is June 28, 1999, 9:52 a.m.

Pedro Sandoval tosses his empty plastic water bottle into the wheel well and double-checks his paperwork as the moving van threads its way down the Strip to the Desert Inn Hotel and Casino at 3145 Las Vegas Boulevard. It's going to be a long, hard day. The blistering heat rises from the desert, eventually reaching 110 degrees by midday. The crew is scheduled to drop off twenty-four electronic slot machines, each costing $15,000, weighing six hundred pounds, and featuring stars like Pat Sajak whooping and hollering on the sound track. Lots of bells and sirens for the fanny-pack and flip-flop crowd.

At 9:54 the eighteen-wheeler pulls up to the south side of the hotel, next to the Desert Inn Race & Sports Book.

After manhandling five of the machines onto a forklift, Pedro wipes the sweat from his brow and glances toward the Sports entrance as an off-duty showgirl pedals by on her red bicycle. Beyond the casino doors is a strip of landscaping about thirty feet long and twenty feet wide; there, something catches Pedro's eye. On a morning devoid of breeze, it seems odd that the rosemary plants in the mini-oasis appear to be moving. Pedro looks again. The thick shrubbery shakes vigorously and then, to Pedro's amazement, expels two dark shapes. Pedro blinks. *"What the fuck?"*

As a second, smaller truck—gray and boxlike, with blue striping on its side—turns off Spring Mountain Avenue and approaches the casino entrance, the shapes from the shrubbery come into focus: two men dressed in black from head to toe. They are moving, all too quickly, toward Pedro and the eighteen-wheeler. They are armed.

Pedro Sandoval, a former paratrooper, recognizes the firearms and issues new orders to his three-man slot machine crew, perhaps the most prudent and useful instructions he has given in his twelve years as a foreman. "Fuck the slots!" he yells. *"Vamonos, vamonos, muchachos! Vete de aquí! Get out of here!"*

The movers break and run in the direction of Las Vegas Boulevard.

The gunmen are now within thirty yards of the moving van, but they have no interest in the slot machines or the laborers fleeing the scene. The men in black have been hiding in the bushes since four in the morning, sleeping, fidgeting, quarreling, dreaming of untold riches and pristine beaches in Costa Rica, beautiful women in Spain, oceanfront villas in Portugal, and leggy, bronze women in Rio. Although the desert night is balmy and the early morning uncomfortably warm, the two men wear black fatigue trousers, black boots, black sweatshirts, black hoods, black baseball batting gloves, and black ski masks. The shorter man clutches a white garbage bag. His taller, heavier partner carries a duffel bag containing hand grenades and spare ammunition magazines that rattle. The larger man has a .45-caliber Glock pistol in his right hand.

The squat gray truck that just pulled off Spring Mountain Avenue and rolled to a stop in front of the Desert Inn is the target of the gunmen. Often called an armored car, the vehicle is a 25,500-pound 1994 International Harvester 300 truck with 10-gauge galvanneal zinc-alloy steel plating, level-three window armor capable of stopping a .44 Magnum, five gun ports, and high-security six-pin key-lock cylinders. There is an emblem on the truck and the word *BRINK'S* spelled out in large blue letters. Inside are a driver and two guards. Each carries a .38-caliber pistol in a holster.

The Brink's truck, on the road since six in the morning, began the day at the Sahara Hotel and Casino, then picked up cash at hotels along the southern end of the Strip, including Circus Circus, Westward Ho, the Stardust, Treasure Island, the Mirage, Caesars Palace, Harrah's, and the Venetian. The Desert Inn will be the last stop before the armored car heads for the suburbs to make additional pickups at shopping centers.

The gunmen close in.

Pay attention to the shorter man. There is something different about him. He walks like a prizefighter on his way to the ring, witnesses will later recall. He dances, he bobs, he weaves, he's ready for action, he's ready to do damage, but now he is telling us to pay attention. *Look at me,* he is saying. *Look at how nimble I am, how strong and swift and sure. I am the leader. Look at me and do as I say.*

The second gunman, taller and heavier, is described by eyewitnesses as "lumbering," most likely because of the obvious body armor he wears and the spare ammunition and duffel bag he carries.

Now the shorter man reaches into the garbage bag and pulls out a compact black weapon with a long banana clip that curls forward. When compared to a hunter's .30-30 or a U.S. Army M16, it is stubby and compact. The gun has no wooden stock, a large front sight, and a prominent flash suppressor. Thanks to the hurried, energetic way the gunman approaches the truck, he almost seems like a casino host greeting an important arrival.

The Brink's truck is now stopped in front of the Desert Inn's south casino entrance facing Las Vegas Boulevard and the Frontier Hotel and Casino. The engine rumbles. Two thirty-six-inch-wide side doors, with continuous stainless-steel hinges, shock-absorbing nylon-web straps, and nonslip internal steps, swing open.

Chuck Fichter is the designated guard on this run. Randy Easton is the driver, and Donald Bowman will handle the money—the messenger, in Brink's terminology. Sometimes Fichter drives the truck, but today Chuck will exit the vehicle first, move into a prearranged position by the casino doors, and cover the messenger, who physically transports the money into the casino on a two-wheel metal dolly known as the money cart. At five foot eight, 180 pounds, Fichter is stocky, square jawed, gray haired, and athletic, and although he is fifty-six, he could pass for a man in his mid-forties. Despite degrees from Indiana University and Northern Arizona University, and dual careers as a high-school social studies teacher and a tennis instructor, Fichter considers himself adrift in life. A self-described hedonist, he came to Las Vegas in 1989. But now Fichter has become a drinker, a gambler, a man attracted to any female with a discernible pulse. Fichter admits he is out of control. He was once a devout Catholic, an altar boy at St. Ann's church back home in Dixon, Illinois. For two years, Fichter worked as a casino supervisor in a sports betting operation, but he grew tired of rousting angry drunks and took the Brink's job, he says, because it requires absolutely no intellect. He has never fired a gun in anger and, unlike many Brink's guards, has no military or law enforcement background. He earns $9.50 an hour.

Fichter's partner is forty-nine-year-old Donald Bowman. Other Brink's employees marvel that Fichter and Bowman are close friends. Fichter is intense and educated, a talker and a cynic, while Bowman is easygoing, a listener, a man who takes life as it comes. At six foot one and 205 pounds, Bowman has rough, calloused hands from a career in construction. He's also an ex-marine, having spent two tours in Vietnam as an ammunition handler. As a rifleman, Bowman qualified as a crack shot. Bowman tells Fichter that he was in Vietnam for two Christmases, '67 and '68, and his claim to fame was "seeing Bob Hope twice. The second time, he brought Ann-Margret."

Today the two men, between stops on the Strip before they reach the Desert Inn, talk about the amount of cash aboard the truck. They've never seen the truck so filled with money bags, and Fichter is concerned. There are so many stops and pickups now, so much cash to haul back and forth to the casinos—doesn't anybody ever *win* in this town?

Bowman grins, but Fichter is not necessarily joking. The local Brink's manager is bucking for a promotion, and the truck guys get the short end of the stick, Fichter says. He feels the manager is overloading the trucks

Nearing the end of its route on the Strip, the Brink's truck on June 28, 1999, contained more than $7 million in cash and coins, according to authorities. COURTESY CLARK COUNTY DISTRICT ATTORNEY.

with too much cash. The two men have picked up so much money today that the cash is stuffed in what the guards call body bags—sacks that when filled come up to the courier's waist.

"People think this is easy work, but it's not," Fichter says as the armored vehicle approaches the Desert Inn. "In and out of the trucks, up and down the ramps, working your way through the crowded casinos, pulling heavy loads on carts—this is hard work. If anything goes wrong, God forbid, it's *never* Brink's' fault."

Bowman smiles broadly. He's heard this before.

"The Brink's mentality is, if there's a robbery, it must be an inside job," Fichter continues. "The driver didn't do the right thing. The messenger didn't do the right thing. The guard didn't do the right thing."

The truck turns off Las Vegas Boulevard and enters the south Desert Inn parking lot. Instead of picking up money, as they have at the other casinos, Fichter and Bowman will deliver cash to the Desert Inn—and a cart loaded with heavy boxes containing $500 in nickels, dimes, and quarters.

The brakes squeal loudly. Bowman starts to load his dolly. "Well, compared to roofing work or what I did in Vietnam, I'll take this job any day," he tells his friend.

The former marine ammo loader has one more thing to say to Fichter: "Sure there's a risk to this job, and I think about it every day. When we go into a bad neighborhood, we yell out loud, 'Lock and load! Get ready! Don't be lax at *this* stop!' In L.A. we did that plenty of times. Here in Vegas, when we pull up to the check-cashing store over on Rancho, I always yell, 'Lock and load!' before we jump out. I try to get everybody fired up because there are certain areas that *are* dangerous. Of course, you can kick back and get lax in other places. Most places aren't so bad . . ." His voice trails off. This is a long speech for Donald Bowman, the quiet Marine.

Fichter reaches for his door handle. Nobody says lock and load. The Brink's men step out into the bright sunshine and gasp at the heat. "Like stepping into an oven, every fucking time," Fichter says.

It is 10:02, and the temperature is already 108 degrees.

The robbery that's about to unfold, unlike the typical Vegas 7-Eleven stickup, has been tirelessly rehearsed for four weeks at an old junkyard south of Las Vegas. It is the end of the financial quarter for casino accountants, and one well-kept Vegas secret is this: To inflate their books and show an abundance of cash, hotels move as much money as possible from the casinos to the local banks in time for the quarter's end. Once the cash is posted, the accountants return the money to the hotels at the beginning of the new accounting period.

The plan calls for the gunmen to wait until the Brink's guards exit the vehicle, enter the Desert Inn, and return to the truck an estimated fifteen minutes later, pulling behind them a dolly piled high with cash. The leader of the crew has been following the truck for months on its daily 6:00 a.m. to 3:00 p.m. route and knows its schedule, the number of stops, and the approximate arrival time at the Desert Inn.

The men in black estimate there will be $10 million in the truck, and they are nearly right. Which is why the stocky, muscular leader of the crew says over and over during the run-throughs that are choreographed like a Balanchine ballet, "We are not after the money from the Desert Inn but the money already in the truck." Nevertheless, the gunmen plan to attack when the guards return from the casino because that's when both armored car doors will pop open—and expose the driver, as well as the guards, to gunfire.

"You'll be fat and happy for the rest of your lives," the leader told his crew the day before the robbery. "Our children will go to the best schools, we will drive German-made sports cars with giant motors, and we will have houses all over the world."

"Will the guards shoot back?" one of the crew asked.

"Maybe we don't kill nobody," the leader said impatiently. "The guards have little pistols, and we have big guns. I don't want their fucking wallets or wristwatches or cheap little gold-plated wedding rings, I want the money in the truck. It's not their money. There's no reason for any hero bullshit."

If you want God to laugh out loud, tell him you have great plans.

At four in the morning, precisely on schedule in a robbery that is planned to the second, the gangsters arrive at the south end of the Desert Inn and hide in the rosemary bushes next to the Sports Book side door. At eight, two police cars pull up to the side entrance of the hotel, and the Metro officers enter the casino. The two robbers hiding in the shrubbery considered fleeing, but the police, barely thirty feet away, return and drive away. Later, a large moving van containing slot machines and fork lifts pulls up. Again the gunmen consider aborting. But then the leader realizes that the truck blocks the view of the boulevard, which is to the benefit of the robbery crew. The movers will force the armored truck to park closer to where the gangsters are hiding.

But the wait is long, and the gunmen have grown impatient. Even as the Brink's armored car comes to a stop before the casino doors, the leader of the crew, anxious to spring his ambush, calls the criminal equivalent of a quarterback's audible. Reeking of rosemary and weary from more than six hours spent crouched in the shrubbery listening to his partner belch, pass gas, and snore—and perhaps unable to delay those extravagant fantasies of wealth and travel dreamed during those long hours in the dark—the leader springs out of the bushes, followed by his confederate.

A third gunman, who serves as the getaway driver, waits in the parking lot in a bronze Isuzu Rodeo. The new plan is to take the Brink's guards as they exit the truck, and while the truck doors are still open, penetrate the interior of the vehicle and either disarm or kill the driver. Access to the truck's interior is essential to the heist in any case, but the new tactic requires two things to happen almost simultaneously: The gunmen must attack the guards before the side door closes, and they must kill or disable the guards at precisely the right instant. Too soon, and the Brink's men will reenter the armored truck, button up, and drive off. Too late, and the doors will close, with guards left outside to fire upon the robbery gang.

It is 10:03.

Swiftly, the gunmen advance to within thirty yards of the Brink's truck. The leader with the rifle approaches the right side of the truck, now parked parallel to the curb in front of the Sports Book, while the other gunman, the Glock .45 semiautomatic pistol dangling by his side, moves to the rear of the vehicle.

Time slows.

Chuck Fichter is now stepping out of the truck. He closes his front passenger door and starts to move into position in front of the casino doors. He takes three steps from the truck in the direction of the hotel doors. The Brink's vehicle is behind him, the casino doors about fifteen yards away. Fichter's pistol, a four-inch Smith & Wesson revolver with six rounds in its cylinder, is in its holster. This is casino policy.

The robbers are now within fifteen yards and advancing from Fichter's right. The second gunman, with the heavy pistol and the duffel bag, is circling behind the truck. The leader, now between the truck and casino doors, stops his advance. *"Don't fucking move, or I will blow you up!"*

Bowman, the former marine, is out of the truck now. His back is turned while he reaches for the money cart inside the vehicle, and he doesn't hear the gangster's command. He struggles with the money cart burdened with the heavy coins. *Watch out for those heavy wheels,* Bowman reminds himself, *or they'll be calling me Stumpy.*

Time stops.

Fichter, his pistol still in his holster, looks blankly at the rifleman and then smiles. *They're making another movie. Nobody told me.*

It is 10:03:27. On the boulevard, traffic is picking up.

See the rifleman. He holds his weapon casually on his right hip, almost jauntily, leaning into the weapon and bracing for the heavy recoil. Only this is not a shotgun but a high-powered military assault weapon capable of automatic fire. In a single brisk motion, the rifleman flips down the safety on the right side of the long gun, pulls back the charging lever, and lets it fly backward like an unwound slingshot. Now the weapon is live and hot.

The rifle is a short-stock Norinco 90, a Chinese-made copy of the legendary AK-47 combat rifle designed by Mikhail Kalashnikov. An unrefined but durable weapon with loose tolerances designed to survive battlefield conditions—it can be dropped in water, mud, and sand, and still operate—the AK-47 and its replicas fire a heavy 7.62 mm × 39 mm round with a practical rate of about one hundred rounds per minute automatic and sixty rounds per minute semiautomatic. In the hands of the average marksman, it is accurate up to two hundred yards. When fired, the AK-47 makes a distinctive clattering sound because of its coarse design, often described as a *clackety-clack* noise, like a train traveling on old rails and ties. Also, it is common knowledge among professional soldiers that when the enemy fires an AK-47 nearby, and you see a narrow plume of fire, the enemy is firing at someone else. But when the AK-47's fiery discharge is wide and flat, the enemy is firing at *you.*

As Chuck Fichter stares at the man in black, wondering if he too might work as an extra in a Hollywood action flick, the Brink's guard is startled to see a broad, flat flame coming from the barrel of a squat, short rifle, accompanied by a distinctive sound known on battlefields from Mozambique to Mosul.

Boom!

Clackety-clack!

There is more firing, more broad, flat bursts of flame, more sparks from the flash suppressor, more angry hornets buzzing by, the firecracker odor of cordite, the dainty tinkle of expended shell casings, and now Fichter is focused for the first time in years. The altar boy, schoolteacher, tennis pro, good student, bad husband, party animal, gambling dude, lover of all women fair and foul, proud recipient of a master's degree cum laude, middle-aged crazy, sports fan, and lapsed Catholic with tarnished dreams and no place to go but a lousy $8- to $12-an-hour job as a security guard in a money-grabbing town of exploding volcanoes, jousting knights, a fake Times Square, and a phony Eiffel Tower, where you can whistle up a $300 hooker faster than you can a Domino's pizza and play the slots for $500 a pull—well, Fichter is paying *attention*. He lives in a noisy 800-square-foot one-bedroom apartment without basic cable and spends his days lugging heavy bags of someone else's money in and out of casinos in 110-degree heat. Now some lunatic in a movie costume is firing a machine gun at him. Some lunatic is trying to *kill* Charles Leon Fichter, son of Bob and Irene Fichter of Dixon, Illinois.

The man with the smoking Chinese-made AK-47 replica moves closer.

"Welcome to the Desert Inn with five world-class restaurants," the gunman says with a Latin accent.

Fichter is amazed: *Not only is this total stranger shooting at me, he's talking to me!*

The gunman fires another volley.

By any measurement, this is not a fair fight. Fichter has no firearms training. There are fifty thousand Brink's employees, and Chuck Fichter, who used to teach American history at Lake Havasu High School in Arizona, is possibly the least qualified of all of them to be frozen in the crosshairs of a Chinese-made assault rifle. By most accounts, Fichter is a gentle man, with a dash of education and the look of a drugstore pharmacist, who is admired even by his ex-wife and former pupils. But he is so absurdly outgunned, we expect the gunman to laugh and to tell the stunned Brink's guards it's all a prank cooked up by the boys in the Race & Sports Book.

But it is not a prank. Fichter is fighting for his life and would scream in fright or panic, except there is no time. Surprising even himself, the gray-haired guard in the navy blue polyester slacks and the sky blue shirt does not lose control. As of this moment, he is no longer bored, listless, jaded, tuned out. He is fully engaged—"firing on all cylinders," as Dad used to say—and what Chuck Fichter does next would impress even a battle-hardened infantryman.

Fichter dives to the pavement on his stomach, rolls on his side, pulls his four-inch Smith & Wesson .38 from its holster in one fluid motion as though he has done so all his life, and, with more 7.62 rounds buzzing overhead and the hot concrete burning his knees and hands, Fichter rolls again, then again, and finally half-crawls, half-scampers toward the front of the armored truck.

High-velocity rounds stalk Fichter at 2,100 feet per second as he moves around the hood to the left front tire, using the armored truck as a shield even as the slugs slam into it and explode, sending slivers of metal into the air and pieces of chrome and glass flying. Other bullets ricochet across the sidewalk into the casino wall, then bounce back into the truck.

Fichter contemplates the righteousness of returning fire. He concludes that somebody is trying to kill him, so maybe he "ought to go ahead and shoot back at them." One elbow resting on the hood of the truck—Fichter notices with alarm that the engine is still running, as though the driver were ready to flee—the Brink's guard takes aim at the rifleman.

In this instinctive reaction to a professionally mounted ambush from men with superior firepower, Fichter somehow does everything right. He hits the deck, limiting his exposure from the deadly barrage of automatic gunfire. He seeks cover while drawing his weapon and preparing to fire, conserving his ammunition until he reaches a safer and more stable firing position. After all, Fichter has only twelve bullets—six in the revolver, six in his pocket. He must wait until he has a clear shot.

An army ranger, force recon marine, or navy SEAL could not have done better.

It is 10:04.

Donald Bowman is manhandling a heavy money cart at the open side door of the armored car. When Bowman hears the sharp snap of the AK-47 charging lever, he glances sideways and spots the gunman as he opens fire on Chuck Fichter. Then the gunman swivels his weapon and faces Bowman, who is close to the truck, a mere yard from the door, but in the open and completely exposed. The rifle is still smoking from the volley fired at Fichter.

The next ten seconds will decide the outcome of this battle off Las

Vegas Boulevard. The robbers must keep the truck door open if they are to take the money. Bowman is in the way.

Bowman moves first. Unlike his partner, now crouched behind the left front fender of the armored car, Bowman has been under fire in combat, having survived rocket and mortar attacks while working at the Ammunition Supply Point-1 (ASP-1) near Da Nang, Vietnam. Every marine is a rifleman, and Bowman was a good one—he earned an expert badge, the highest marksmanship rating in the corps. A marine for five years, a security guard for sixteen, six with Brink's, Donald Bowman, easygoing and laid back, has been waiting for this moment all his life.

Bowman sizes up his opponent: *He's got a shotgun—at least he's holding it like a shotgun—down at his waist, not up on his shoulder. If he holds the weapon up on the shoulder and starts to sight it, I am dead. But now he's leaning into the gun as if it was going to go off.* Bowman's mind is racing. *The gunman doesn't want to fire for some reason. I may have a chance.*

The marine, like his buddy Chuck, does something entirely out of character. His body wilts. He bows his head, almost like a shy child. His body signals surrender.

But he has a plan. *I don't want to make any quick moves. I'm relaxed, Mr. Gunman, now you relax. I'm not a threat, so don't fire your weapon.* He is playing a part, and he hopes the gunman buys it.

Snipers talk about looking through the keyhole before pulling the trigger, going deaf at the moment of execution, surrendering every brain cell, synapse, chemical, electrical, and mechanical function to that one pure and perfect act. Bowman, right now, is looking through the keyhole.

The gunman, sensing Bowman is about to give up, hesitates. Bowman dives into the doorway, sideswiping the coin cart and falling onto the floor. "Robbery!" he shouts at the driver, Randy Easton.

Now, finally, the rifleman opens fire.

Boom!

Clackety-clack!

The first round hits the door dead center and shatters. The bullet fragments shower the interior of the truck. They rattle like small stones.

Bowman is now in the vehicle. He is euphoric. He looks out the door. *Man, why aren't you shooting more? Why aren't you charging? What's wrong? Are you afraid to make some noise? Okay, now I have to close the door. I've got two arms, two hands, two chances to get that door closed.* Bowman reaches for the door with his right arm. He tugs hard on the heavy door, and it begins to swing shut, but just before it closes, a second round hits the edge of the armored door and explodes like an artillery shell. Though the momentum of the pull will shut the door, four bullet fragments tear into Bowman's outstretched arm.

Bee stings, Bowman thinks. *My arm feels like a bunch of bee stings. He got me.* A deep, sharp pain radiates from Bowman's arm, but he still believes he has been hit by slugs from a shotgun. His arm near the elbow swells up immediately. There is heavy bleeding from the entry wounds.

The driver stares at the arm. "Your elbow! They shot off your elbow!" Easton is on the edge of panic, his face turning pale as he watches the blood drip onto the plastic money bags.

Then Bowman remembers. *Chuck is still outside. We're buttoned up here, but he's out there.*

"Let's get these guys off Chuck!" Bowman yells to the driver. Easton nods. After broadcasting a brief Mayday to the Brink's dispatcher, Easton puts down the radio microphone and looks frantically for the missing guard. "I can't see him! Where is he?"

Thirty-six years earlier, a younger, leaner Donald Bowman, a raw kid from Oregon, a marine recruit, learned how to survive what is perhaps the most shocking of all combat action: the ambush. Again and again, in marine exercises from Camp Pendleton, California, to Camp Lejeune, North Carolina, Bowman's rifle company was marched into the field and surprised by an "enemy" force. The exercises were lifelike, and the marines were taught an important small-unit tactic: In such moments, no matter how great the shock and how strong the enemy, even a lowly private must know what to do, because lieutenants, the first to stick up their heads when the shooting erupts, are likely to be killed. Squad leaders may not survive the first fusillade in an ambush. Every marine is a small independent force. What do you do in an ambush? Seek cover. Maintain a line of fire. Establish fire superiority. Find a weak point. Summon help. Break out.

Randy Easton, who was in the U.S. Army, understands that doctrine but also recognizes the familiar sound of an AK-47. Then, too, he is shocked by the sight of Bowman's bloody arm and considers pulling away. Brink's teaches that in the event of an ambush, if guards are trapped outside the truck, or even wounded, the driver may choose to drive off to safety or even use the vehicle as a weapon.

The truck is a fortress. It must not be breached. The mission is to save the money.

The engine is still idling. Easton begins to push in the clutch, as if to drive away. The tempo of the motor changes. It appears that Easton intends to flee the shooting scene.

However, the marines have one other battlefield rule: Never leave your wounded or dead behind. Bowman looks up and glares at Easton, shaking his head. Despite four fragment holes in his arm—the floor now slippery with bright red blood—Bowman is in fighting mode. The firing angle is wrong through the gun port. *I shouldn't open the door, but this is the only way to take the heat off Chuck.* To the driver's dismay, Bowman pushes open the door. Now the firing angle is right. Bowman empties his pistol at the rifleman.

Crack! A loud, sharp sound inside the truck, like the sound of a bull-whip. *Crack-crack-crack!* A pause. Then, *crack-crack!* Bowman turns his revolver sideways, flipping out the cylinder and dumping spent casings into the truck's wheel well.

Outside, Fichter wonders if he will survive. The rumbling engine is ominous. Will his colleagues drive off and leave him to die?

His .38 pistol now drawn, Fichter crouches in front of the right front bumper of the armored car, takes aim, and opens fire at the rifleman just as Bowman empties *his* revolver at the assailant. Four shots are fired by Fichter, six more by Bowman. Now taking heavy fire himself, the first gunman walks backward and returns the fire as bullets whiz by his head. The AK-47 clatter is now constant.

The rifleman is a Cuban named Jose Manuel Vigoa Perez, and he too has seen combat before. An ex-convict who served more than seven years in a succession of U.S. federal prisons for assaulting two FBI agents, and for drug and weapons offenses, Vigoa has sprung his trap prematurely by mere seconds. By appearing at the truck too soon, and by not giving Bowman enough time to move away from the truck with the money cart, Vigoa has made a significant error. Instead of trapping Bowman in the clear on the sidewalk between the truck and the south doors of the Desert Inn Race & Sports Book, Vigoa has commenced the attack with Bowman standing mere feet from the open hatchway of the armored truck.

If Vigoa waits ten more seconds before confronting the guards, then Bowman will be cut off from the truck and cut to pieces if he resists. But the volatile, impatient Vigoa, anxious to leave the foul-smelling bushes and glimpsing stacks of currency inside the armored car door, cannot wait. Bowman leaps into the truck. And once Bowman is secure behind the steel-armored plates, with Fichter blazing away from behind the engine block, the caper quickly unravels. There's no way to get to the money even if Fichter, still trapped outside the vehicle, is eliminated.

The robbery has failed. There are no bugles on this battlefield to sound retreat, so the Cuban, enjoying the rattle of heavy gunfire and the thrill of the firefight, walks backward. The ten-shot barrage from the Brink's guards reminds Vigoa, too, of a swarm of "angry African bees."

Not that Jose Vigoa thinks well of the determined Brink's guards as they spoil what could have been his retirement heist. *Stupid hero bullshit!* thinks Vigoa as he takes heavy fire from the two guards and retreats to the waiting Rodeo. Vigoa is amazed that the low-paid Brink's men fight back. If not for the heavy fire now streaming toward him and the crazy American blazing away over the hood of the truck, Vigoa would tell the guards to their faces how foolish they are: *I'm not trying to take the money away from you, or disrespect you, or steal anything from your families. I want to take the money from the fat pig casino owners who have millions and millions and exploit their employees with peanut wages.*

A bullet snaps by, and Vigoa scowls. *I don't have nothing against you guards, but you're not going to shoot at me. Now you are disrespecting me. I could have killed you all.*

It is 10:05:01.

As Vigoa withdraws and moves out of visual range, Fichter senses movement to his right. The second gangster, with the .45, has circled behind the truck and is now standing about twenty yards off the left rear bumper, catching Fichter, who is crouched by the driver's door, in a crossfire. Fichter's luck holds again: The second robber is not a good shot. Glock .45s in general have a strong recoil and tend to be inaccurate. But when the second gunman empties his magazine at Fichter, the rounds chew up the truck, plow up the street, and ricochet under the vehicle itself. The bullet fragments rip into Fichter's right leg, striking the calf and puncturing the thigh. As he falls to the street, Fichter sees the rifleman on the other side of the truck reloading. The second gunman, with the .45, has a fresh magazine in his pistol and is aiming at Fichter again.

His heart closed to God for nearly forty years, Chuck Fichter believes his soul is no longer in a state of grace. The thought is jarring: *If I die now, I will not go to heaven.* He offers the Catholic Act of Contrition: *O my God, I am heartily sorry for having offended Thee, and I detest all my sins, because I dread the loss of heaven and the pains of hell* . . . The oldest of the three Brink's guards is once again taking fire from two gunmen, and there is no place to go. . . . *I firmly resolve, with the help of Thy grace, to sin no more and avoid near occasions of sin.* On his knees, Fichter crawls along the front bumper of the truck as more pistol rounds bounce off the vehicle, sending debris into the air. *We glory in tribulation because tribulation worketh perseverance and perseverance worketh trial and trial worketh hope.* For one brief instant, there is despair: *So tired . . . God, need some help down here . . .*

At this moment, there is a change within Chuck Fichter. Vigoa is wrong. It's not about hero bullshit antics or protecting fat cats who exploit poor people. Fichter does not admire Brink's management and what he considers the company's harsh policies toward its men on the front lines. But suddenly he is willing to give his life to protect the Brink's cargo. The gentle schoolteacher who wants no commitments, the lost soul who disengaged from life and shunned responsibility years ago, is now undergoing a metamorphosis in the middle of a blistering firefight. He will risk his life because of duty and pride and his own sense of honor.

He takes aim at the second gunman. *You're not getting the fucking money. Not today. And not from me.*

The second gunman is Oscar Cisneros, six foot one, two hundred pounds, a twenty-three-year-old Mexican national who will participate in every crime committed by the Vigoa crew in the years to come. Cisneros is the only non-Cuban in the gang and has no criminal history other than drunk driving and buying liquor while under age. After circling behind the armored truck, Cisneros squats behind a gray Toyota van in the parking lot. He is determined to prove himself to his older, harder associates. He fires again at Fichter.

With rounds coming from two directions, and splinters and fragments from just about everywhere, Fichter pulls himself up, hanging on to the right fender, and edges toward the front passenger door, which is now closed. He fumbles for a key. *Don't drop it, or you may die right here.* Fichter sticks the key in the door, but before he can turn it, another round hits a tire, and the door trembles. Suddenly the door pops open, and Randy Easton is there, grabbing Fichter by his shirt collar and pulling him, dragging him into the truck. Fichter closes the door. His right leg is all lumpy and mushy; his work shoes are squishy with blood.

There is absolute silence in the truck. The firing stops. Easton renews his call for help on the radio. "I say again: Robbery in progress . . . Desert Inn south parking lot . . . Sports Book . . . Shots fired . . . Chuck and Don are hit, in the arm and legs . . . We're all in the truck and will attempt to leave the area . . . I'm heading for Valley Hospital; better have some people waiting for us. I think the suspects are leaving too."

Well, almost. The gunfire from outside the truck resumes with a fury. The guards can feel the rage of the frustrated gangsters, who pour fire onto the Brink's truck.

Bowman counts his ammunition—twelve shells left. Fichter, barely conscious, has two rounds in his revolver. The guards locked in the truck are certain that the gangsters are trying to blow open the vehicle. The truck shudders from the intense barrage. The glass on Easton's side begins to crack.

It's like a hammer hitting the side of the truck over and over, Bowman thinks. He yells above the din to his fellow guards: "We've pissed these guys off,

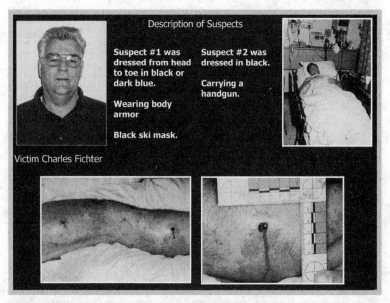

Description of Suspects

Suspect #1 was dressed from head to toe in black or dark blue.

Wearing body armor

Black ski mask.

Suspect #2 was dressed in black.

Carrying a handgun.

Victim Charles Fichter

Brink's guard Chuck Fichter recovering from his gunshot wounds at Las Vegas's Valley Hospital the afternoon following the robbery.

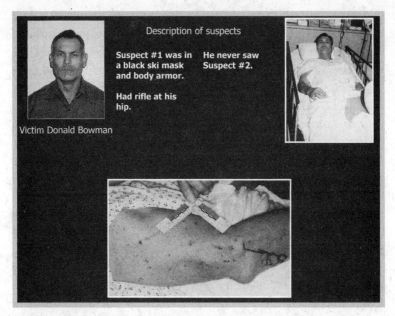

Description of suspects

Suspect #1 was in a black ski mask and body armor.

He never saw Suspect #2.

Had rifle at his hip.

Victim Donald Bowman

Donald Bowman, the Brink's messenger who initially retreated to the armored truck but then reopened the door to engage Jose Vigoa, was photographed by Metro Crime Scene Analysts (CSA) in the hospital emergency room. COURTESY CLARK COUNTY DISTRICT ATTORNEY.

and now they're coming through the windows. They're putting rounds into the tires."

"Are they trying to test the truck?" Fichter shouts. "Do they have armor-piercing rounds?"

"If they do," Bowman says. "They'll cut through these windows like butter."

It is 10:06:08.

In fact, the gunmen are retreating to a bronze-colored Isuzu Rodeo that will serve as the first of three cars used by the robbery gang in its escape. They are indeed furious, but they break off the attack and don't look back when the Brink's truck roars out of the south parking lot, squeals onto Las Vegas Boulevard, and heads for the Valley Hospital trauma center. Bowman and Fichter, who will be hospitalized with multiple gunshot wounds, recover fully.

The gunmen scramble aboard the Isuzu. One of Vigoa's more unusual innovations in planning his robberies is to place the second getaway car close to the crime scene, a practice that pays off today. Hearing police sirens approaching the Desert Inn, an excited Pedro Duarte, the third member of the gang, floors the accelerator and promptly loses control of the sport utility vehicle. At sixty-eight miles an hour, the vehicle hits a speed bump and goes airborne. "What the fuck you doing? This no fucking airplane!" Vigoa yells as his head bounces off the truck roof.

Crunch! The Rodeo returns to earth, shedding transmission parts a quarter-mile from the robbery scene. The SUV's transmission has been destroyed by the Rodeo's unexpected flight, and power can no longer be transmitted to the drive shaft. Duarte pumps the accelerator frantically but to no avail. Although the truck is effectively without power, the momentum of the high-speed escape propels the SUV across Spring Mountain Avenue, over a median, past a sidewalk, and into the Vagabond Motel parking lot. Incredibly, there's no traffic. The SUV bucks its way into a parking stall.

The sirens grow louder, and the gang scrambles to switch from the Rodeo to a cherry red 2000 Nissan pickup truck in the next parking slot. Cisneros slides behind the wheel. Duarte and Vigoa ride in the open truck bed of the pickup, gripping AK-47s and lying flat. In a near disaster, one of the spare rifles slides to the rear of the truck bed as the Nissan pulls away from the Vagabond lot. When the Nissan brakes abruptly at a stop sign, the AK-47 slams into the tailgate and discharges. A round burrows through the truck's cab, grazing the hand of Cisneros, who yelps but continues driving.

There is a second red pickup truck in the parking garage that initially will confuse the police but later will provide a forensic breakthrough.

"When I was planning our escape route, I decided to put getaway car number two, the red Nissan 2000 compact truck, in the motel parking lot," Vigoa explains. "At this point, 'Mr. X,' one of my crew, says he wants to have his own red truck there too and drive away in his truck after the robbery. 'I go separate,' Mr. X says, meaning he's going to bring his truck to the Vagabond and take off by himself after the robbery. I warned him not to do it.

" 'You know what, Mr. X? You should never involve your own car, your real car, in this stuff.' But Mr. X wants to play his way. *Coño!*[1] I say, 'Well, Mr. X, you want to play your way, go ahead, fuck you, go ahead

[1] A vulgarity that means, roughly translated, "Fuck me!" or "Oh, fuck!" Usually said in exasperation.

and use your own truck.' So Mr. X steals a license plate and sticks it on his truck with rubber bands and puts it over his real license plate. Stupid!

"Only, as it turns out, he doesn't leave the parking lot in his own car. As we pull into the Vagabond, there's a man walking his dog close to Mr. X's truck. He was a tourist, and later I find out he is a correctional officer from California. Mr. X was scared, so he winds up jumping in the back of our truck, and we take off. He leaves behind his truck, also painted red like our number two getaway vehicle. After we escape, the police come to the Vagabond and notice Mr. X's truck, the stolen license plate, and his real license plate under the stolen tag. *That's right! He leaves his own plate underneath the stolen plate!*"

At first police suspect that the gang, in its haste, took the wrong getaway vehicle. Not true, says Vigoa.

"We took our own getaway car as planned. It wasn't hot-wired. I had the keys. The DA [district attorney] said we tried to hot-wire the car and we forgot which one it was. We were not that stupid. We did not want to take the truck of Mr. X, and, as I said all along, it should not have been there to begin with. You don't use your personal car as your getaway car—it defeats the whole fucking purpose! So the Desert Inn was important for the police, and even though the police got everything wrong—so wrong I am still laughing—they managed to find and interview our getaway driver. But Mr. X don't tell them nothing, and they let him go. That's how Mr. X gets into trouble, and eventually someone notices that he is married to my sister-in-law, and now I am a suspect too."[2]

MAKING ITS GETAWAY, the bright red Nissan pickup slowly turns left onto Las Vegas Boulevard and heads north to the I-15 freeway at the speed limit. There is one more close call: A Nevada State Police car, its siren wailing and lights flashing, comes up fast behind the Nissan. It passes the truck.

Police estimate that more than fifty rounds were fired during the four-way gun battle. A second-floor Desert Inn conference room was laced

---

[2] An amusing episode on both sides of the law. Police swarm over the parking lot, find the bronze Rodeo with the broken transmission and discover 180 rounds of pistol and rifle ammunition in the cargo bed. They also discover Duarte's red truck and theorize that the gang panicked and sped off in the wrong getaway vehicle. In fact, the second getaway vehicle used by Vigoa, an extended-cab Nissan, was the intended escape truck. Duarte's blunder, which connects him to the crime scene, gives Metro its first major break.

with bullet holes, and room 4019 of the Frontier Hotel, across the boulevard, was riddled with stray rounds from the firefight. Fortunately, the fourth-floor suite was unoccupied. Pedro Duarte, who is married to Jose Vigoa's sister-in-law, decides to take up new employment and leaves the gang. Three slot machines, caught in the crossfire, were dead at the scene. It is later confirmed that more than $7 million in currency was aboard the Brink's truck.

Undaunted, Vigoa conducts a debriefing and announces a new policy: "Next time we shoot first and ask no questions of nobody. I didn't ask the guards for their fucking wristwatches and wallets. Everybody wants to be a hero in this country." Vigoa later writes in his journal: "In my world, you are either the hunter or the hunted. Vegas makes it, Vigoa takes it."

Chapter 2

VEGAS DISARMED

*T*here was a great hue and cry after the Desert Inn shoot-out. A four-way gun battle on the Strip! How could this happen? Mayor Oscar Goodman took notice: Maybe this kind of violence happened in Los Angeles—as had happened two years earlier in the famous North Hollywood bank shoot-out—but not on the Strip, for God's sake.[1] The two wounded guards survived the firefight, but the Vegas myth of invincibility was shattered.

The storming of Las Vegas lasts twenty-four months and nine days. Six (and nearly seven) world-class hotels are hit, including the Desert Inn, which is targeted a year into the crime spree. Unlike the DI, as the hotel is called by locals, the other casinos, armored car companies, and businesses suffer losses exceeding $3 million. The Vigoa crew learns quickly from the Desert Inn firefight, changes its tactics, and grows more violent. The precision raids will stun the Fortune 500 owners of the luxury hotels, threaten the resort's reputation for tourist safety, introduce a colorful new crime family to the city, and signal the end of mob-enforced order on the storied Vegas Strip. An undermanned police department, with twenty-three detectives handling more than three thousand robberies a year, will come of age as it scrambles to defend the city from well-organized, high-velocity gunmen as hard and dangerous as the mobsters ever were. Unpleasant surprises lie ahead: Las Vegas, the tough little town

---

[1] On February 28, 1997, two heavily armed men brandishing automatic rifles and wearing body armor shot it out with more than two hundred Los Angeles Police Department officers. The furious gun battle was captured on live television. Although both robbers were eventually killed, it was clear the LAPD was outgunned early in the pitched battle. The LAPD and other departments responded by upgrading the firepower of patrol officers. Vegas Metro did not.

that grew up to be the tough big city, always thought itself immune to this kind of criminal violence and casino mayhem. But the Strip's vaunted casino security force, more than six thousand strong, turns out to be as formidable as a snoozing seventy-year-old bank guard with a pacemaker, dead batteries, and an empty holster.

There are other gaping holes in the defenses: In the new hotels such as the Bellagio, MGM, New York–New York, and the Mandalay Bay, architects create a more "friendly" environment by building cashier windows without bars or bulletproof glass. Throughout the city, lawyers order casino managers to disarm their private security force to reduce liability in the event of a robbery. Brink's guards are prohibited from drawing their weapons on casino property even while hauling millions in cash on open dollies.

In military terms, Las Vegas is a soft target.

Lieutenant John Alamshaw, commander of the robbery section of the Las Vegas Metropolitan Police Department, warns his men: "These are the most dangerous criminals we have yet to encounter. They are heavily armed. They plan the robberies with skill, timing, and precision. From their initial ambush to the gang's escape, the robberies are carefully rehearsed. It's no coincidence that the robbery took place at the end of the armored car's route on the Strip, when the truck was loaded with cash. And the Desert Inn caper proves this crew is willing to kill."

What Alamshaw doesn't know at the time of the Desert Inn shoot-out is that the gangsters have a large cache of Russian-made ammunition, assault rifles, and hand grenades. The detective doesn't know that the Vigoa crew has acquired C-4 explosives and intends to use them in future heists. Alamshaw is correct when he says they have inside information and employ sophisticated planning. It will be years, however, before the police and FBI discover Vigoa's secret: The Cuban has planted electronic listening devices in the targeted armored cars, has inspected the trucks from within in search of weak points, and has followed the vehicles for weeks before striking.

Jose Vigoa, when not using an assault rifle, brandishes a heavy-caliber pistol in each hand like a nineteenth-century train robber in the Wild West. No matter how many black-and-white sector cars race to the scene after the initial 911 call, no matter how fast the first-response uniformed cops get there, the gunmen are inevitably gone, melting into the city like phantoms—all of this taking place in broad daylight before scores of witnesses who describe the men as white, black, Hispanic, short, tall, and varying sizes and shades in between.

The Metro police, the FBI, and the Henderson Police Department belatedly form a task force; it is discovered that important leads have been neglected during the first months of the investigation. Gordon Martines, the primary detective on the case, is "flopped"—police jargon for reassigned under a cloud. He later will run for sheriff and attack the department as mismanaged.

The robberies and the small-unit tactics used by the gang remind police of their own SWAT training. Marine and army veterans recognize Special Forces guerrilla warfare tactics. Special Agent Brett W. Shields of the FBI realizes that the gang uses classic commando doctrines: (1) clandestine insertion, (2) brief, violent combat, (3) rapid disengagement, and (4) swift, deceptive withdrawal. The cops realize they are up against an organized criminal as colorful and lethal as any old-school hoodlum, but one in possession of exceptional battlefield intelligence, modern-day firepower, and sophisticated small-unit tactics.

The question, then, is who are these men? And who is their leader? There are whispered theories about disaffected former police SWAT team members from other cities or rogue Arab terrorists using casino heists to build a war chest. They are dismissed by senior police officials as preposterous.

In the end, however, the wildest of speculation, the most fanciful of fantasies, do not do justice to Jose Vigoa, a Cuban defector who admires Tony Montana, the fictional Cuban portrayed by Al Pacino in the 1983 movie *Scarface*. Like Montana, Jose Vigoa comes to America on the Mariel boatlift in 1980. Like Montana, Vigoa becomes a drug lord before going to prison. But Vigoa's story will have no equal in the long and colorful history of the onetime railroad water stop in southwest Nevada. And after the Desert Inn, Vigoa will shoot to kill, something he says he has done many, many times before on battlefields far, far away.

BOOK TWO

CHILD OF THE REVOLUTION

Chapter 3

JOSE

My name is Jose Manuel Vigoa Perez. Some people call me Manolo. So, you want to know what I am doing in Las Vegas, Nevada? You want to know *why*. Why the shootings, the robberies, the raids on the famous American hotels? And *where*. Where did I get my guns, my AK-47s and Chinese copies, the hand grenades, the explosives, sniper rifles, and all of those things? Where did I come from? Where would I strike next? Where did I get my intelligence about the truck and its wonderful money?

You want to know my secrets, do you not? And you want to know who I really am?

I am Cuban. I am born a few hours before the birthday of Jesus Christ. I am a former Marxist who was trained by the communists. I am a killer, more than the police know, more than the federals[1] know. I have other secrets, but you must be patient. My story is not about one man, it is about the world and the times we live in. You should know me well and understand who I am, because there are others like me, and they will be coming soon to visit, of this I am certain. Some will be Cuban. Or Russian. Or Israeli. Or Chinese. Or Arabs. We are children not only of revolutions and violence but of history you have made yourself. It is true I organized, trained, and led the gang that robbed many hotels and many cash-filled armored trucks serving the rich casinos and the wealthy suburbs. After the Desert Inn—and especially after some of my more exciting withdrawals from the fat-cat casinos and the money I take from the homo-faced rich people—I thought about returning home to my beloved Cuba. I have so much cash, maybe I buy a hotel on the beach if they let

[1] Jose refers to the FBI as "the federals."

me. Or maybe I buy a whole town. Cuba is like the first woman you ever love. She may have a fiery temper, she may be wild and difficult, she may be flawed, she may lie, she may cheat on you, and you may lose her—but you can never forget her.

I remember my little town, Caimito del Guayabal, surrounded by beautiful green mountains, rivers, natural lakes, and the Gulf of Mexico. A paradise of flowers, fruits, sugarcane, tobacco, citrus trees of every imaginable variety—and some fruits you have never heard of but are delicious all the same. Wild, tropical birds like the tiny hummingbird, the tocororo, and the woodpecker fly everywhere in the most amazing colors. Why, you can live off the land your entire life where I grew up. It rains almost every day, and then the sun comes out brighter than ever. The air is fresh, there is no pollution, nothing is artificial, and the people are the most friendly in the world.

Cubans also are a strong and enduring people. We have to be that way after a century of colonialism, imperialism, Yanqui dictatorship, military dictatorship, fascist dictatorship, communist dictatorship, and Russian occupation. Some very bad people have ruled Cuba, and not just the communists. I do not hate Fidel. He did good things for the Cuban people. He made big mistakes, too. I have been away from Cuba for many years now. The American embargo is still in force, the people are still poor—but are they worse off than before?

My story really begins the year before Fidel Castro rolled into Havana with his bearded guerrillas from the mountains. The people were overjoyed. My mother, soon to be pregnant with me, was happy. Fidel had driven out one of the most evil men who ever lived, in Cuba or anywhere else: the worst tyrant in the hemisphere, Fulgencio Batista. Without this man, there would have been no Fidel, no revolution, no Soviet missiles, no Russians in the Caribbean, no Cuban army in Angola, Afghanistan, and elsewhere—and maybe no Jose Manuel Vigoa Perez in Las Vegas.

I think Batista was not only a very bad man, with his torture chambers and death squads, and the way he stole from everybody, Cubans and Yanquis alike, but I think he was a little bit crazy even by Cuban standards. Batista started out as a clerk in the Cuban army, and twice he overthrew our government with America's approval. You have to understand: Batista was made in the USA. Financed by the Americans. Armed by the Americans. Praised by the Americans. Condoned by the Americans.

That's part of my story too.

Chapter 4

CUBA

Jose Manuel Vigoa Perez entered the world in a home delivery by a local midwife on December 24, 1959, in the barrio of Cayaguazal, located in the village of Caimito del Guayabal, ten miles southwest of Havana. The name of the town means "the sweet dark fruit of the guava."

Cuba's politics long had been chaotic and bloody, bordering on anarchy, in part because of the brutal *gangsterismo* of Fulgencio Batista and in part because of a deepening culture of corruption.[1] Soon, however, the Republic of Cuba, small, poor, and brave, would become a symbol of resistance to neocolonialist superpowers—and a cautionary tale about the price of nonalignment and what happens when a small country seeks to wrench itself away from a powerful empire. Blood would flow in Cuba, more than ever, and Cuban politics and Cuba's relationship with the U.S. would nearly trigger World War III if not an all-out nuclear exchange between America and the Soviet Union. Jose Manuel Vigoa Perez would grow up in this undeclared state of war and what his *comandante,* Fidel Castro, in a speech condemning U.S. policy, would call "perfidious defamation and vulgar crimes."

The land itself was lush and beautiful, strewn with wild flowers, tropical fruits, and towering royal palm trees that swayed in the cool breeze. Colorful birds sang day and night. Cuba's climate, Jose remembered wistfully, was so good "no one needed air-conditioning or central heating, you just opened the windows." Cuba, then and now, was a land of pristine beaches, sparkling green water, and sun showers. Whether the rulers of Cuba were cruel and corrupt, or dedicated revolutionaries, or hard-

[1] Accused of torturing and then burying alive two hundred of his opponents, Batista protested this charge was a "filthy lie." He tortured and buried alive only *fifty* young men, the dictator insisted.

ened Marxists, the Cubans themselves were good-natured, lively people, gregarious, sensual, musical, and athletic. Cubans also were proud: Boasting Spanish, Indian, and African blood, the race was a mix of the explorer and the conqueror, the warrior and the rancher.

To understand Jose Vigoa, and the code and ferocity he would later bring to the boulevards of Las Vegas, it is important to know what it meant to be Cuban in the latter half of the twentieth century. A banana republic through virtually all of its history—and a weekend destination for many a promiscuous American tourist—Cuba would become, by 1960, a player on a world stage and the target of relentless terrorism. Cuba also would be almost ruined by possibly the longest economic siege in modern history, but the country would survive on sheer defiance. Declared Fidel in a typically fiery address: "Ninety miles away from that [U.S.] power, Cuba is committing and will continue to commit—don't let there be any doubt of this—the sin of existing."

Nineteen fifty-nine, the year of Vigoa's birth, marked two epic events in Cuban history: the fall of Batista and the victory of Fidel. Vigoa, his sister, and three brothers would become "children of the revolution," in Vigoa's words, and their world would be carried along violently and haphazardly by the forces of revolution, counterrevolution, terrorism, the Cold War, the collapse of the Soviet Union, and other adventures and mishaps, large and small. The Cuba of Vigoa's generation found itself occupying ground zero in a dirty war waged by the U.S., its intelligence services, and embittered Cuban refugees.

Vigoa never forgot those difficult years. "I remember many times saying to myself: These fucking Americans are worse than the devil. Why do they do this to us? What do they want from us? What the fuck have we ever done to them!" Vigoa remembers that when the sugarcane harvest failed, and there wasn't enough gasoline, state-controlled newspapers, radio, and TV blamed the Yanquis, since the Americans were maintaining a trade embargo in an effort to starve out the Cuban people. Shortages in food, clothing, and everyday needs? Blame the Americans. The electricity just went off for the rest of the day? Blame the U.S.

"I wanted to grow up desperately fast. I wanted to go to war with these devils, with these monster faces I saw in the cartoons, on TV, and in the newspapers. The Americans were always drawn with an evil, twisted look. I hated these fucking Americans. I wanted to kill them all. Every day there was something. You couldn't get this, you couldn't that. Or the rumor would go around that the Yanquis were going to bomb us."

These were not distant headlines or academic theories. Vigoa and his family lived through the events, scanned the horizon for American warships, looked skyward when an aircraft flew overhead. The family resided less than a mile from a large Soviet military installation near Caimito, and by Jose's tenth birthday, in 1969, Russian troops were everywhere.

Vigoa may have been bewildered in the beginning by the hostility of the American superpower, but over time he began to suspect the revolution left much to be desired as well. Vigoa wondered about all government. Were there good regimes and bad regimes? Or did it always come down to one set of power-crazed scoundrels replacing another?

But at least the revolution offered hope. The Cuban people would not soon forget Batista and his torture chambers and murder squads, as well as the thieves and thugs who came before him. Until the revolution, Cuba had been ruled for decades by corrupt politicians, political gangs, and opportunists. Havana's casinos were owned by the American Mafia; on weekends the enchanting city turned into a bordello for degenerate Americans flying in from Miami to sample underage prostitutes and watch S-M shows by overendowed performers. And the American government supported Batista because he was the perfect puppet: absolutely corrupt. Merciless in the exercise of power, shameless in allowing his beautiful Havana capital to become a center of Mafia vice. Most of all, the dictator was bought and paid for. He did what he was told.

"When Fidel came, it wasn't that the Cuban people embraced Marxism or didn't, or liked socialism or did not," Vigoa said. "All we knew is there were about eight million Cuban people during the Batista time, and more than seven million of them were poor, they could not write their own name, they had no medical or dental care, no housing, no decent clothing, no nothing. We knew Batista was responsible for some of this, but also we knew the rich imperialists—the Americans—had something to do with our plight."

The despoilment of Cuba[2] might have continued unabated but for a fiery and brilliant young Cuban lawyer named Fidel Castro Ruz, son of

---

[2] As when American sailors climbed the statue of Jose Marti in Havana and urinated on it. Marti, a poet, general, and national hero, is considered the Father of Cuban Independence.

Angel Castro, a former Spanish soldier from Galicia in northwest Spain. Angel had come to Cuba to fight on the losing side of the Spanish-American War at the turn of the century, then remained in Cuba, acquired land, and prospered. Fidel Castro, his tall, athletic, and charismatic son, would challenge not only Batista but eventually the mighty American empire itself. Fidel liked to say, "Anything is possible within the revolution, nothing without." They were ruthless men, certainly, but steadfast and fearless.

Then, in June 1960, Fidel did the unthinkable: He nationalized American property and firms. That was too much for the American government. One crazy Cuban knocking off another didn't mean much to the State Department, but appropriating U.S. factories and firms? The United States retaliated with a trade and travel embargo in 1960 that sought to bring down the Castro government within six months. It did not. Impatient for results, the Kennedy administration launched the Bay of Pigs invasion in 1961, using 1,500 poorly trained exiles who were abandoned on the beaches when President John F. Kennedy lost his nerve. The "invasion" was crushed within three days by Castro's troops. A year later the U.S. established a naval blockade during the Cuban Missile Crisis, itself a three-way horror show of cascading miscalculations starring the Soviet Union, the U.S., and Castro.

Over time, U.S. machinations against Castro, in part driven by American presidential politics[3] and militant Cuban voters in South and Central Florida who voted en masse for the most reactionary candidates on the ballot, deteriorated from the failed amateurish invasions and vicious paramilitary raids organized by the CIA, to the sordid and bizarre. Vigoa lived as a child amid this constant struggle.

By age ten, it was Jose's job to feed the family; he shined shoes and stole the occasional chicken. Food was scarce, and the Cubans might have starved but for abundant tropical fruit and fish taken from local waters. Jose began to develop newer and more cynical theories about society: Law and order was just an instrument of oppression controlled by the "wealthies." The smart man lived by his wits and made his own laws. Jose developed his theory of hard hands: Strike fast, strike often.

From the mid-1960s and well into 1970, "the entire island of Cuba was

---

[3] In population and electoral votes, Florida was one of the two fastest-growing states between 1960 and 2006. In 1960 Florida had ten electoral delegates; in 1972, seventeen; in 1992, twenty-five; in 2006, twenty-seven.

one big Soviet military camp," Vigoa later recalled. A decade after the Cuban Missile Crisis, when the Russians covertly installed long-range offensive nuclear missiles in Cuba—the original Soviet launch sites were less than ten miles from Vigoa's cement-block home—the Cold War between the U.S. and the Soviet Union remained intense in 1973. Although the Vietnam War was ending, it seemed certain that other proxy wars between the superpowers would replace it, and because of its reliance on the USSR, Cuba would have its role to play. Military service in the rapidly expanding Cuban army was now mandatory, and an ominous phenomenon—one Vigoa could hardly miss—was becoming noticeable: Cuban boys between the ages of thirteen and sixteen were rapidly disappearing.

Chapter 5

JOSE VIGOA: THE USSR
NEEDS A FEW GOOD MEN

Somehow I always will blame Jorge Guitterez for the great changes that took place when I was thirteen years old, marking the end of my childhood in Cuba, such as it was, and sending me on long journeys to strange and difficult places.

Jorge was the fattest kid in our barrio, and although we didn't see fat people too often in those days, he was *big*. I don't know nothing about no genes, or whether Jorge had a secret stash of food somewhere, but by the time he was fifteen, Jorge was five foot eight inches tall, weighed at least three hundred pounds, and when he walked across the street, he sounded like an old train with a broken boiler, huffing and puffing and making high squealing noises through his nose. We called him Gordo Guitterez, which is like calling someone Fat Freddy in English, and most of the time Gordo just smiled and rolled his eyes. Fat people often act cheerful, and Jorge did too, although in reality maybe he wasn't so happy on the inside after all.

The strange thing was that Gordo Guitterez was one of the best baseball players I ever saw, and there were many great baseball players in the Havana province where I lived. Well, maybe I should make a small correction: Gordy was one of the best *hitters* I ever saw. He looked like Babe Ruth all blown up. Other teams from outside our town would take one look at him, and they'd start to laugh and yell insults. I admit, when Gordo ran down to first base or around the bases, it was like watching a giant duck waddling down the base path in a big hurry. It was funny. Then Gordo would step up to the plate. Our hand-me-down bats were all broken many times and had more nails than a coffin, but it didn't matter to Jorge. *Bam!* He would hit the ball so hard, the infielders would dive just to get out of the way. *Bam!* Jorge would line the ball over the center fielder's head and into the saw grass, where it disappeared. *Bam!* There went one into the windshield of a passing 1950 Pontiac Chieftain.

One day we were playing a pickup game alongside a paved road from Bauta to Caimito near a Soviet army base when Gordo hit a ball real strong into right field. The ball dropped in for a hit and bounced so hard that it hit the right fielder in the chest and almost knocked him over. The right fielder then did something I had never seen before: After a clean hit he threw the ball to the *first* baseman. It was a close call, but the umpire called Gordo out. Everybody was shocked. Gordo was so fat and slow running down the line, he was thrown out! This was embarrassing to Gordo, and he went crazy.

The first baseman flipped the ball to me at shortstop, and I walked over to first base, laughing. All of a sudden Gordo started screaming, his face became all red and twisted, and he ran up to me and punched me in the forehead. Down I go. Gordo jumped on my back and started hitting me. I somehow managed to clear my head, wiggle out of his grip, and now *I* was fucking mad. I took the ball, which I still held, and *thump!*— I punched him in the nose. He went down real fast. I am a demon and jump on his chest and start pounding him with the ball in the face. There's blood from his nose and everywhere.

The next thing I know the world was turning. I saw sky, then clouds, then the top of the palm trees, then a glimpse of a passing truck, then more sky, then the same clouds. I was hanging in the air and spinning round and round at the end of a huge black arm connected to an army first sergeant named Tino Escalera. He had been watching the game and said if I didn't stop hitting the fat boy I might kill him, and the Cuban army would lose a good man, meaning me, Jose Manuel Vigoa.

The army? Wait a fucking minute! I'm still a kid! Vigoa's not joining no army!

Three days later the giant sergeant came back to our field and told me to get home right away. My mother wanted me. "*Chico, no mas juegos hoy! Beta a la casa y madre, rapido!*" the sergeant said. "Boy, no more games today! Get going to your house, hurry up!"

I thought he meant my mother was sick or dying, and I ran like the devil to my house, which was almost two miles away. I raced frantically through a field, across a creek, and then down an old dirt path. When I got to the village, one end of the little street was blocked by a shiny army motorcycle. In front of my house sat an olive green staff car, right in the middle of the street. A slender Cuban army lieutenant sat inside smoking a cigarette. *"Chico, tu futuro está aquí—apúrate!"* "Boy, your future is here—hurry!"

I ran into the little three-room house and then stopped. Sitting in our living room on the old lawn furniture we used as furniture were two men. One was a colonel in the Soviet army in full uniform. The other was a civilian, a Cuban from the ministry of something; I don't remember. My beautiful mother was looking scared. My younger sister was in the back trying to listen. All the neighbors were outside whispering to each other. *What has Manolo done now? It must be something real bad.*

The two men stood up and smiled. The Cuban military and our bene-factors from Russia had been watching me for some time, the Soviet colonel said in very good Spanish. (I will always remember his uniform; although he was a barrel-chested man with surprisingly slender legs and delicate feet—like a dancer, almost—it was the most beautifully tailored suit I ever saw.) The Russians thought I had spirit, the colonel said. I was a fighter. I was a little tiger. I was a smart boy, though I had much to learn. I was a leader. During the hard years, I took care of my family, the colonel said, and now it was time for my bigger family to take care of me.

For all of these reasons, the Russian said, I had been selected to go to the Soviet Union for more schooling and some military training at a later time if I was good at school. And if I worked hard and did well, maybe I could earn a commission and serve the internationalist cause.

It was 1973. I would spend parts of the next seven years freezing my ass off in Mother Russia or burning under a tropical sun fighting in civil wars. The first two years, I was homesick and hated my life. In all, I made three trips to the Soviet Union on a military jet with other Cuban boys ages thirteen to sixteen. In 1978, after being informally adopted by a So-viet general who took an interest in me, I was commissioned a second lieutenant in a Cuban unit of the famous *Spetsnaz*[1] special forces. I would train in bases all over the great Soviet empire, from Moscow to Kiev, from the Suvorov Military School to the Frunze Academy and officer's basic school. I would spend six months in Angola, Africa, in 1979 and, after a quick leave, three more violent months in Afghanistan at the outset of 1980 in a special operations force.

---

[1] Literally, "troops of special purposes."

I would go to places where people I hardly knew wanted badly to kill me, and visit garden spots that gave me lice, a nearly fatal spider bite, sunburns, frostbite, and fevers. I would survive rockets, mortars, land mines, artillery barrages, air assaults, ambushes, snipers, road accidents, women with knives, children with hand grenades, what you Americans call "friendly fire," and much more. I would learn wonderful skills: How to assassinate an enemy agent. How to set an ambush. How to spot an ambush. How to rig a booby trap and how to deactivate one. I learned how to read a map, a blueprint, and a compass. How to field-strip an AK-47 during a firefight in the pouring rain and how to treat a gunshot wound in combat. I was promoted to first lieutenant at the age of twenty.

What was it all for? In Afghanistan I had a vague idea why we were there—and by "we," I mean the Soviets and their Cuban helpers—but in Angola there were so many factions, and armies and advisers and intelligence services, I lost count. I was never more scared than I was in Angola. Who was the enemy? Everybody was the enemy, and watch out for the lions—they'll get you too. In the field, I never had enough sleep, enough food, enough water, or even a weekly shower.

Somehow I even survived the generals, ministers, and bureaucrats who started this bullshit to begin with. What were we Cubans doing in Angola and in Afghanistan? Fidel and Raul Castro, his reclusive but tough younger brother, wanted to save the new government of Angola from the CIA, Henry Kissinger, and the South Africans. Although the Russians provided weapons and aircraft, Angola was our fight, and I think we did pretty good. Hell, I know we did well! You can look it up: Cuba saved the ruling government from the Western powers and corrupt warlords, and the MPLA is still in power today.

OPERATION CARLOTA, THE NAME of Cuba's military intervention in Angola, began on November 5, 1975, when Cuban battalions threw back South African forces sponsored by the CIA. I missed that nasty little fight. Angola was my first combat assignment, in the fall of 1979, just as the rainy season began, and this is where I began to *seriously* distrust all government. By the time I flew into the capital of Luanda from a staging area at Brazzaville in the Congo, Cubans had been in Angola for almost four years. To be honest, things were relatively calm during my stay in Angola—the big fight, the famous battle of Cuito Cuanavale in 1987 and 1988, when the Cubans defeated the South Africans, was still to come. By then, I was elsewhere.

Not that I didn't have some excitement during my little vacation in Africa. By the time I arrived, the MPLA was in power after driving out the Portuguese and declaring independence, but it was still under siege from rival guerrillas operating in the north and south and supported by outside powers. It took the MPLA fourteen years to liberate the country, and now the new government had to fend off Kissinger and the CIA, the South Africans with their modern army, and two rival Angola movements: Holden Roberto's FNLA (Front for the National Liberation of Angola) and Jonas Savimbi's UNITA (National Union for the Total Independence of Angola, or, in Portuguese, Uniño Nacional para a Independência Total de Angola).

The Angolan war would last for twenty-seven years. A half million people would die. Many would be displaced. Cuba would commit more than 30,000 troops and suffer between 4,000 and 5,000 men killed in action. When you compare the population of Cuba to that of the U.S., that KIA ratio would be like America suffering 150,000 battle deaths in a war—three times that of Vietnam.

Now comes the crazy part that I still don't understand, and I was there! The FNLA was based in the north and was supported by Zaire, the Bakongo people, various mercenaries—and the United States. UNITA was based in central Angola and was backed by South Africa, China, France, Great Britain, "the Ovimbundu of the Angola heartland"—*and the United States*.

Since FNLA and UNITA also were fighting each other, it looked like the Americans finally had done it: They were starting so many wars, they got confused and wound up fighting themselves.

One day in Angola, I was in the bush with two ten-man squads, one comprised of MPLA troops and the other consisting of my own Cuban special operations troops. I began to notice my MPLA men slowing down and walking in what I called the "creep" mode. My African tracker was now sniffing the air. I began to do the same, and I picked up the scent of many men somewhere ahead. Fortunately, we were downwind. One of the basics of guerrilla warfare, or even conventional infantry fighting, is not to practice normal hygiene in the bush. Soaps, deodorants, toothpaste, liquor, aftershave, tobacco, food, other drink—even the smell of your girlfriend from the night before—can give away your position as much as a loud bell. These strange scents differ from what local peasants know and can be carried for miles by a slight breeze, causing animals to become nervous and telling the enemy someone is coming.

We advanced over a small hill, broke into a clearing, and suddenly there they were: at least one hundred men, maybe a full company, resting alongside the trail. I unslung my rifle, but the Africans in my force said, "No, no, no *problema,*" and told me to relax. According to our Africans, the troops in the clearing also were from the Popular Movement for the Liberation of Angola, the faction we were supporting, and no threat. My own Africans began to talk with the other men like they knew each other.

We continued down the hill and walked alongside the encampment. Just as we were moving back into the bush, shots were fired from our rear. Our "allies" had opened fire on us. Those weren't MPLA troops, those were FNLA soldiers. This was the lead element of a regiment that had crossed into Angola to launch another FNLA offensive. The reason that my MPLA Africans misidentified the FNLA Africans was that some tribes fought for both sides.

Two of my MPLA men were dead. Two Cubans were wounded, not seriously, and they were still in the fight. We ran fast for the next hill under fire from a disorganized but pursuing enemy. There were already fighting holes [foxholes] and craters on the ridge from a previous battle, and we jumped in, set up our light machine gun and only mortar, and braced for the attack. We were outnumbered at least ten to one. I called for air support. Looking through my field glasses, I could see the FNLA troops regrouping, with a white man—a *very* white man, with reddish blond hair and a beard—giving orders. I got real nervous when I saw what he was doing: The officer, probably a South African, began talking on the radio, most likely to his air controller, since they were too far out from artillery. He was reading a map he held on the back of one of his men and talking real fast.

This was going to be a hard day. The big question was, who would get fighter support first?

The enemy launched one determined assault up the hill, took casualties, and retreated. Nearly an hour after I called for air cover, and with the FNLA gathering below for a new assault, I heard the shriek of a fighter overhead. I looked up, and my mouth went real dry. I watched a Mirage F-1CZ drop out of the sky on a bombing run. This was not good. The FNLA used the French-made Mirage aircraft with laser-based range finders. We had MIG-21s and MIG-23s but no Mirages in our squadrons. I guess the South African captain had more influence than I did, because his aircraft arrived first.

After making one pass, the Mirage flew over our position, thinking we were the friendly unit—and bombed the enemy FNLA rifle company by mistake. One pilot made one foolish mistake, and half the FNLA company was dead or wounded.

Our MIGs finally appeared, chased away the Mirage (whose pilot probably thought he'd won the battle all by himself) and then circled the battlefield wondering what to do next.

As our two MIGs argued over targets among themselves, I said, "Let's get the fuck out of here!" and moved my recon team off the hill. I gave up trying to direct the aircraft, and we ran like hell. I don't trust any pilots right now. I saw what the Mirage did to his own troops—I didn't want that to happen to me. The MIGs, our MIGs, could make the same mistake.

As we reached the woods, I heard a series of loud explosions. I looked back at the hill we'd just vacated. I was right.

The MIGs had made a perfect rocket attack on the ridge and unleashed a shit storm on our former position. I don't think any of us would have survived. The MIGs made a second pass. More big explosions like thunder from the devil, with fire and clouds of dust. The ground shook beneath me like an earthquake. The brush on the hill began to burn. Thanks to the Mirage and the MIGs, nobody would be assaulting the hill anymore, and our little battle was over.

The MIGs gained altitude and soared away like great eagles. When we made it back to our regiment and base camp, a sharp argument broke out: Should we find the MIG pilots and buy them a round of drinks? Or should we take them into an alley and cut their throats?

On December 25, 1979, the Soviet Union invaded Afghanistan, supporting the Marxist government against Muslim mujahideen insurgents. Thus began the bloody ten-year war between Soviet forces and the guerrillas that would result in an estimated one and a half million deaths, including ninety thousand killed in combat. Nearly five million refugees fled the country and five thousand villages were destroyed. Jose Vigoa's war journal gives January 4, 1980, as the date when Cuban special forces arrive to assist their Soviet brethren.

Chapter 6

AFGHANISTAN: HAVE A CUBAN

In the spring of 1980, three months after the invasion of Afghanistan, Major Sergei Kamenev, staff intelligence officer of the Fortieth Army, Union of Soviet Socialist Republics, sat on a wooden ammunition box behind a boulder on a rocky hillside and watched the troops dismount on the plain below. There were three boat-shaped BTR-60 armored personnel carriers and a pair of Ural four-ton trucks from a convoy that halted at a dirt road intersection ninety kilometers east of Jalalabad, a strategic military and trade city in eastern Afghanistan, on the way to the Khyber Pass. Unlike the fair-complexioned, sunburned Russian infantry lounging idly on the side of the road, the new arrivals were lean, deeply tanned, and energetic as they dug fighting holes, set up heavy machine guns and strung wire. These were elite troops, officially designated *Spetsialnoye Nazranie* by the Soviet Intelligence Directorate, though known to the world as Spetsnaz. Although the men wore desert camouflage and the uniform of Soviet airborne units, the arrivals were not Russian or even eastern European. Nor were they gypsies, as some of the Russian soldiers by the roadside speculated.

"My, my," the Soviet major said from his concealed hillside perch two hundred meters away, adjusting his binoculars as the men on the road unloaded their equipment. "Welcome to Afghanistan, my dear friends. So you've come to help Mother Russia."

It was the music from a Sharp cassette player on the tailgate of the sand-colored truck that gave away the newcomers, even before the major could focus his 7 × 30 field glasses at the scene below. Infectious music, lighthearted, with a blend of Caribbean and African rhythms. The major recognized the beat. He had served a year in Havana as a military intelligence officer for the Soviet Embassy, and—a guitar player himself—he knew good salsa when he heard it.

Abruptly, the music ended, a sergeant bawling that the men were now in a combat zone, telling them to maintain noise discipline. The wind shifted, and the major could hear the voices now, emotional, argumentative, a chorus of Spanish talking in the Cubans' famous rapid-fire cadence. Then one loud basso profundo above the others: "*Oye, Chico!*"

Even without the binoculars, the major could see what was happening. A huge dark-skinned noncommissioned officer, probably a first sergeant, snapped his wrist in the direction of a short, barrel-chested corporal standing by the remains of a tree. The corporal jumped. A gleaming silver blade from an NR-2 multipurpose combat knife had cut into the tree trunk barely two inches from his left ear.

The corporal stared at the knife, then at the big sergeant. "*Hijo de puta! Maricón!*"

On the hill above, a red-haired adjutant lieutenant assigned to the major, turned and asked, "What did the little guy just say?"

"He called the giant sergeant a son of a whore and a faggot."

The sergeant below chuckled at the corporal's insults, such vulgarities normally considered grave and deeply offensive in the machismo Cuban culture. The other Spetsnaz stopped their work and waited for the anticipated brawl.

The corporal carefully propped his Viper sniper rifle against the tree trunk, pulled the knife from the tree, and charged his tormentor. The sergeant roared with laughter again, thrust out his massive right arm and promptly clotheslined the corporal, who fell to the ground with a thud. The beaming sergeant retrieved his knife.

A sharp voice from outside the circle of Cubans: "*Basta!*"

With one word and the flick of his hand, a young officer ordered the men back to work. The soldiers, antagonists included, immediately complied.

The major, looking on from the hillside fort of stones, would remember the first appearance of the wiry Cuban first lieutenant; even from a distance, he stood apart. Jose Manuel Vigoa Perez, a platoon leader and Angola veteran, wore a Havana Industriales Blue Lions baseball cap to go with his starched custom-tailored field utility uniform. Four hand grenades hung from his web gear. He carried an officer's sidearm in a small, triangular tan leather holster polished to a nearly new sheen. An

AK-47 with a wire handle was slung behind the lieutenant's field march-
ing pack. He chewed on an unlit Cuban cigar much too large for his slender, deeply tanned twenty-year-old face. He had a long forehead, dark
eyes, pointy ears, a receding hairline, and closely cropped hair. Like many
Cubans of Spanish descent, Vigoa's face was dark with a heavy black stub-
ble, although he had shaved the night before. He was not a large man, but
his carriage was that of a leader accustomed to command and obedience.

In a combat zone, where enemy eyes might be watching at any moment, the men did not salute their officers. Even so, when Lieutenant
Vigoa approached, the men came to attention and nodded slightly in spite
of the regulations.

The major also noticed the Cuban's walk: a jaunty hop-and-skip motion that almost seemed an expression of merriment, a dance step without music, a gait he would later place as that of a prizefighter approaching
the ring.

"I THINK THE AMBUSHERS are going to ambush the ambushers of the ambushed," a voice behind the major said.

A strong aroma of vodka announced the presence of *Starshiy
Serdzhant*[1] Mikhail Molotov, a powerful, square-shouldered Russian
from Leningrad and a close friend of the major's from their days at the
Special Forces Faculty of the Ryazan Airborne School, and later at the
Reconnaissance Combined Arms School in Kiev.

The major chuckled in agreement. It was a complicated plan with too
many twists and turns, too many variables.

An elegant scheme on paper, relying as much on the known temperament and psychological makeup of the parties as the strength of the
enemy, its weaponry, or the terrain: Entice the enemy with a militia column that would be sacrificed at the outset of the operation to draw the
mujahideen south, deeper into Soviet-controlled territory. It was hoped
that the mujahideen, under attack on three sides and seeking cover from
the Spetsnaz fire, would jump into the gulley on the west side of the
road—and into the ditch laden with antipersonnel mines, antitank
charges, and the heavier improvised explosive devices, or IEDs.

The USSR had rumbled into Afghanistan on Christmas Day 1979,

[1] "Senior sergeant" in Russian.

seeking to rescue a secular Marxist regime under attack by Muslim fundamentalists. This was a war in which even the names and identities of the belligerents seemed upside down and deliberately misleading. (The mujahideen, the insurgents, were Islamic "revolutionaries" seeking to throw out the Soviet invaders and a Marxist government that called itself "revolutionary.") Ignoring the fact that tribal warlords changed sides like a soldier changed socks, the USSR dispatched more than one hundred thousand troops. Ten years and fifteen thousand battle deaths later, the Soviets would withdraw for good on February 2, 1989, leaving behind more than one million mujahideen and civilian dead, and five million refugees. The Soviet invasion of Afghanistan, opposed by the U.S., China, Pakistan, and other nations, was unpopular at home and wrecked an already floundering USSR economy. Many historians believe that the high cost and dismal failure of the invasion of Afghanistan was a major cause of the collapse of the Soviet Union.

The major, more than most, had no illusions about the war. Often he recited a poem by the Englishman Rudyard Kipling. Sometimes he played his guitar and improvised a tune:

> *When you're wounded an' left on Afghanistan's plains*
> *And the women come out to cut up your remains*
> *Just roll to your rifle an' blow out your brains*
> *An' go to your God like a soldier.*

In turn, Molotov liked to quote the contemporary Oxford historian Sir Michael Howard about the three rules governing great empires and whether they should intervene in distant civil wars (although the major thought it was John Stuart Mill, the nineteenth-century British philosopher and political theorist who offered the advice):[2]

1. Don't get involved in faraway civil conflicts. They are mean, dirty, brutal affairs, and everyone will hate you when it is over.
2. If you must enter the fray, pick a side.
3. If you do intervene, choose the side that will win—*and make sure that it does.*

---

[2] Although Mill did caution against the hazards of such intervention, as did George Washington a century earlier, Howard in fact outlined the three principles cited by the sergeant.

The Soviet Union managed to break all three rules. Still, the Cubans were happy to lend a hand to their revolutionary brothers. Trained in the Soviet Union, bloodied in the Angolan civil war, these *Tropas Especiales,* modeled after Spetsnaz brigades and trained by Soviet officers, were the best Fidel had to offer.

The major studied the new contingent with a practiced eye. While the Russian infantry languished by the road, the Cubans moved with urgency. There were four teams of ten men each, the major counted, and they seemed determined to outdo one another in vigor and efficiency. Some of the men carried Soviet RPGs; others, American M16s; still others, AK-47s or 5.45 mm AKS-74s. Each man packed a 5.45 mm PRI automatic pistol, and some had silencers. Most of all, there were the knives. The men would interrupt their work to thrust and parry with the knives and to swing their entrenching shovels, the favorite weapon of the Spetsnaz at close quarters.

The Russians watched as the Cubans carried crates of antipersonnel mines to the side of the road. Other men reached up from the ditch and manhandled the boxes into the ditch and out of sight. The seeding of mines in the gully continued for another hour, and the pace began to slacken when a noncom began to bark orders urgently, and the Spetsnaz troopers ran in every direction.

Gunfire erupted down the road, maybe two klicks distant.[3] Scrambling out of the gully, a dozen Cubans ran to the other side of the road. The road, so congested less than a minute earlier, was now clear.

Pop! Pop-pop-pop-pop!

Automatic gunfire from the village. The enemy was approaching. The radio was now eerily silent. There would be no frantic call for "bumblebees"[4] or artillery today.

The Cubans were now concealed in their positions. Only Lieutenant Vigoa could be seen, standing by the side of the road and watching serenely as a tall, skinny Cuban sprinted in a zigzag pattern down the road from the direction of the rebel-held village.

The sharp crackling of small arms and the rattling of automatic gunfire increased in volume. AK-47s. *Theirs or ours?* the major wondered.

Vigoa continued to stand by the gully, chewing on his cigar. Suddenly

[3] A *klick* is military jargon for a kilometer (1,000 meters), or about five-eighths of a mile. Two klicks would be roughly one and a quarter miles.

[4] Slang for gunships (ground attack aircraft).

the ground shook. A series of booms, perhaps one click away, pulsated down the road. Moments later the remnants of the militia column could be seen stumbling down the road, fleeing the onrushing enemy.

As the major adjusted his field glasses, a geyser of dirt erupted in the midst of three retreating militiamen. *Thump!* When the dust settled, no one stood or moved. Three bodies littered the ground. The other militiamen had disappeared. There were no visible survivors.

The major now could see mujahideen troops, leapfrogging in clusters of three and four, coming up the road. The muzzles of their rifles sparkled.

"Well, Sergeant, ready to join our Cuban friends and defend all peace-loving peoples?" the major said to Molotov.

"Fuck no."

"I admire your patriotic fervor," the major said. "Now let's see how our Cubans fight on their first day in sunny, beautiful Afghanistan."

THE CUBANS, LED by their fast-moving first lieutenant, fought with discipline and nerve. When a platoon of mujahideen reached the crossroads and launched a counterattack at the Russian rifle company dug in below the foothill, Jose ordered a counterattack by the Spetsnaz. The Cubans bolted from their holes to meet the attack screaming war cries, firing from the hip, and butt-stroking the mujahideen with their rifles in hand-to-hand combat. The rebel charge began to falter.

The major and senior sergeant exchanged glances when the Cuban lieutenant climbed atop a burning armored personnel carrier (APC) with a pistol in each hand.

Caught in the crossfire of the dug-in Soviet infantry and the forty-man Spetsnaz unit, the rebels did exactly what the Soviet planners had hoped for: They returned the gunfire, fell back to the gully without panic, slid into the large gully, and set up a wall of heavy fire. This was a well-equipped and professionally led rebel battalion.

The major held his breath and took a swig of vodka from his sergeant's leather-wrapped canteen. He had just taken his first drink when it happened.

Thump! Thump!

Two quick explosions in the gully. And then:

Boom!

A curtain of earth shot upward to hang in the air for a brief moment before dissipating. A cloud of gray-brown dust and smoke hung over the southern rim of the road. All firing stopped.

The shock wave knocked down the major and toppled his aide, who grabbed the canteen to ensure its safety.

Then came the screams.

The major and sergeant began to pick their way through rocks and brush to descend the hill. The major stared at the senior sergeant.

"Mother of God."

Crouching behind a burning APC, Kamenev and Molotov could see the road and the gully. The area reminded the major of a half-completed highway, the soil scraped and churned by large earthmoving equipment. The terrain was covered with pieces of clothing and decorated with red splotches, along with shattered equipment and what looked like a few soccer balls resting on the road waiting for the teams to begin play.

The major and the sergeant reached the road and paused. Even by Afghan standards, this was a hellish scene. There was a strong smell of human feces. The soccer balls, seven in all, were human heads. There were severed limbs and coils of viscera strung for at least two hundred yards down the road. There also were survivors, God help them.

They blew themselves up, the major thought.

In a sense, they had done just that. When the mujahideen moved into the ditch to redeploy after the ambush, they inadvertently set off mines even before the Cubans could detonate their larger IEDs and heavy mines. The initial percussions triggered one massive explosion and turned the gully into a river of fire. The engineers had done their job well.

The Cubans poured out of their positions, weapons on full automatic, and moved across the road toward the jagged crater left by the explosion. The amazed Russian infantry, largely intact, faces covered with dirt and dust, remained in place and watched in awe.

Lieutenant Vigoa advanced first across the road, stepping over and around the torn body parts like a man delicately avoiding puddles on a muddy street. A mujahideen lieutenant crawled out of the smoldering ditch and sat in the middle of the road. He was a terrible sight—in fact, it seemed a medical impossibility that he was still alive. One arm was missing, and his heavily gouged right cheek and cratered eye were little more than raw meat. The poor man was certain to die, the major thought, but perhaps was worth a brief interrogation.

"What do you think, Sergeant?"

"I'm fresh out of questions," Molotov said.

Jose Vigoa, unlit cigar still in his mouth, walked up to the rebel officer. He directed two teams to the edge of the gully to finish the day's
work. No further order was necessary; the killing already had begun. The
Spetsnaz stood alongside the ditch and commenced firing into the living
and dead. Gradually the screams stopped. A few of the bolder Cubans
jumped into the gully to search for survivors and cut off ears as trophies
of battle. The mangled rebel lieutenant sitting on the road asked for
water. Vigoa poured cool water into the man's open mouth, but the rebel
began to gag and vomited a ball of coagulating blood. Vigoa pulled the
lieutenant straight up and stuck his cigar into the man's bloody mouth.
He lit the cigar.

A nervous murmur of disapproval passed through the hardened
Cuban troops.

Vigoa stood beside the dying man and addressed the men. "Wanna
tip-top smoke?" he said in English, mimicking a TV commercial. "Have a
Cuban!"

Lieutenant Vigoa took back the blood-smeared cigar, drew his pistol,
and finished off the Afghan soldier with a three-shot burst to the head.
Then he put the cigar back in his own mouth.

All in all, the major would have rather been back in Moscow writing
his novel, or perhaps composing a few verses of poetry for the tall, leggy
blond violinist who lived up the stairs with her fat girlfriend. The senior
sergeant, by now rendered sober and pale, would have preferred a tour of
duty to Havana or Washington, DC, or even Damascus—anywhere but
to this useless, mean, barren place populated by wild people, religious
zealots, foul-smelling peasants, liars, swindlers, corrupt politicians, degenerate warlords—and now Fidel's Tropas Especiales, also called Spetsnaz, who seemed to enjoy their work a little too much.

Later, when the major and his senior sergeant got decidedly drunk,
Kamenev told his friend a secret. Lieutenant Vigoa, whose cruel comedy
sketch shocked and angered many Russians and disturbed some of the
Spetsnaz as well, may not be as crazy as we think, he said.

"Remember that song I used to sing about the young soldier calling
out to his father?"

"The sad song," the senior sergeant said.

The major sang a verse.

Don't call me, Father, don't disturb me . . .
We're drifting in fire and blood . . .
And we won't see each other again.

"Mikhail Molotov, did you see the expression on Lieutenant Vigoa's face after he walked away from the dead rebel, when his men could no longer see him?"

"No, I did not."

"He looked stricken, repulsed, ashamed. He went into the brush and vomited."

"Then why—?"

"I think the lieutenant wanted the men to know the truth about Afghanistan."

Chapter 7

DUEL IN THE SUN:
JOSE RETURNS TO CUBA

By 1980, as Cuban troops confronted American advisers and CIA agents in Angola, the U.S. chief of mission in Havana was a Texas-born ex-marine combat veteran named Wayne Smith, a genial, able State Department veteran and the Forrest Gump of U.S.-Cuba relations: He always seemed to be at his post during critical historic upheavals. Smith was posted to the U.S. Embassy in Cuba from 1958 to 1961, when Fidel Castro's rebels marched from one end of the island to the other. He witnessed the final days of Batista and the triumphant arrival of Castro in Havana to cheering throngs. Smith was in Havana when the U.S. broke off diplomatic relations and closed the embassy. By the time of Angola, Cuba and the U.S. maintained small "missions" in each other's capitals, though full diplomatic recognition had been canceled twenty years earlier and the economic boycott was entering its third decade.

Once more America's man in Havana, Smith again had a ringside seat to history. The savvy diplomat later returned to Cuba in 1979—just in time for another seismic upheaval that would reverberate for decades and send Jose on another journey.

MANY BELIEVE THAT the Mariel boatlift, also called the "freedom flotilla" by exiles and their conservative allies, was a spontaneous event brought about by a Cuban uprising, an incident at the Peruvian Embassy, and Fidel's short temper. In fact, according to Smith, the boatlift percolated for years and was the result of bureaucratic indifference by the State De-

partment, miscalculation by the Cubans, and the famous law of unintended consequences.

"It all started when we convinced Castro that we should allow Cuban-
Americans to come back to Cuba and visit," Smith later explained.

So far, so good. The returning Cubans were well behaved. The Castro
government saw an opportunity and charged the returning exiles considerable fees to reenter Cuba. Now the law of unintended consequences
began to take effect, affecting both parties. The returning Cubans, visiting their relatives, told about life in America, a land of plenty with Big
Macs and radial tires for even the lowliest worker. No doubt some of the
descriptions of the good life were exaggerated, but poor relations in Cuba
listened with great excitement.

"As the visitors talked about life in America, everybody had five cars
and sixteen TV sets," Smith said. "People living in Cuba said, 'Wow, we
want to get in on that great life too.' But at our interest section, we were
not set up to issue that many visas. We were overwhelmed."

Jose Vigoa recalls the excitement, confirming the diplomat's account:
"Many family members brought with them food, pictures, clothes, and
abundant gifts that were not seen in Cuba. Many were simple things, but
we were dazzled by the colors, smells, and shapes. It all was so different."

The law of unintended consequences, part II:

"The Cubans who wanted to leave became increasingly insistent,"
Smith said. "They began hijacking boats at pistol point and sailing up to
the U.S. They hijacked a garbage scow and forced it to sail to Key West."
As the hijackers arrived, the U.S. government processed them routinely, as
though they were ordinary refugees, and admitted them into the country.

The law of unintended consequences, part III:

The Cuban government was appalled that the hijackers were not arrested on the spot upon reaching U.S. shores. Wasn't the United States
talking about fighting terrorism in all forms?

Smith found himself face-to-face with an indignant official who
wanted to know what the Americans thought they were doing. "We have
noted, Mr. Smith, that when these *hijackers* come to the U.S., *you are ad-
mitting them!* You're not making any statement to the effect that at some
point you're going to start imposing maritime hijacking laws. At some
point, someone is going to get hurt. We insist that you take a position on
this terrorism."

At that time, the U.S. was the target of airplane and ship hijackings all over the world. Smith felt that the Cubans had a very good point: If we didn't jointly crack down, the terrorism would grow. He cabled the State Department and suggested the U.S. acknowledge the Cuban position—terrorism was terrorism. The cable was never answered.

The unintended law of consequences, part IV:

In February 1980, a high Cuban official summoned Smith. "People continue to hijack boats and are taking vessels under life-threatening conditions," the minister said. "If you don't do something, we may feel called upon to open up a new Camarioca [a smaller boatlift in 1965] and allow people to come down and pick up their relatives in small boats."

In March Fidel Castro himself warned the U.S. in a speech that the Cubans would take unusual and dramatic action if the hijackings continued. The U.S. remained silent. The hijackings continued.

The law of unintended consequences, part V:

On April 1, 1980, an unemployed man named Hector Sanyustiz seized a bus and crashed through the gates of the Peruvian Embassy. Within forty-eight hours, more than ten thousand Cubans broke through the gate and entered the lush gardens of the embassy, where they camped out and demanded visas.

The occupation of the Peruvian grounds made headlines around the world. Cubans and Americans were caught by surprise. Privy to classified information as chief of mission, Smith learned through his sources of an emergency high-level meeting among surprisingly sanguine Cuban officials.

"What are we going to do about this?" a senior official asked.

"Well, we can open Mariel Harbor. It is just down the island to the west, less than an hour from the Peruvian Embassy," a Cuban security official proposed. "Let's announce that people [from the U.S.] can come down and pick up their relatives from the Peruvian Embassy by boat."

Another voice: "Why just them? Why not let *anyone* who wants to go take off? If they don't want to be part of the revolution, fine, let them go. The majority will stay and be part of the revolution. Let's allow those who don't want to be here to leave."

In the end, the Cubans convinced themselves that a few thousand malcontents would take up Fidel's offer and depart on small boats from Mariel to South Florida. In fact, between the first week of April and October 31, 1980, 125,000 Cubans left the country, although this number included a significant number of prisoners and mental patients released from jails and asylums and offered their freedom if they would head north. Wayne Smith confirms that the Cubans also used the boatlift as a cover for scores of "sleeper" intelligence agents.

"The Cubans certainly did send in agents. Why not? What an opportunity!"

Smith watched in dismay from his Havana waterfront post as decades of mutual fear and loathing between the U.S. and Cuba produced an unexpected blowback against both nations, with the freedom flotilla turning into an ugly and dangerous debacle.[1]

Jose Vigoa, on leave from the Cuban army, lived less than thirty minutes from the small fishing village that was about to become world famous—and part of history.

---

[1] Smith would continue as chief of mission until 1982 and eventually leave the foreign service after sharply disagreeing with U.S. policy toward Cuba. In recent years, he has advocated normalized relations and the end to the U.S. trade embargo.

Chapter 8

JOSE: MY JOURNEY TO AMERICA

By April 1980 I am back in Cuba on leave to see my mother. I notice the airport is not that busy, and there are few cars on the road. There's very little fuel. The power is turned off most of the time because the generators can't run without oil. I take a bus to a town west of Havana, and it stops because the gas tank is empty. So I have to walk.

I see the new Cuba. Everything was slowed down. I ended up hitching a ride on a cart with some sugarcane workers, men with dark mahogany skin almost blackened from the sun, and their cowboy hats made of straw. The cart was pulled by an old horse so tired and farting so much I thought he would drop dead right on the road. There was nothing on the roads except for a few horses and mules like the one pulling us—and the Russians. Cuba was one big Soviet military base by the time I got home. There was a special forces training camp in Caimito. Russian frigates and nuclear submarines were at Mariel Harbor. Troops were everywhere, but no more Russian ICBMs pointed at Miami, thank God.

It was a strange sight: Old American cars were parked alongside the road, their hoods up, their gas caps open, sometimes nobody around— out of gas. The Russian convoys would rumble by—not many tanks, but many heavy trucks, APCs, staff vehicles, antiaircraft flatbeds bristling with guns. I wondered what they knew that I didn't; were the Americans getting ready to launch another war? Were the terrorist mobs from Miami (that's what Fidel called them) going to take another shot at invading Cuba?

I was still in uniform. I felt stupid riding in the cart and, after a while, humiliated. This was my country. What the hell was going on? Why am

I sitting with the sugarcane cutters in an old cart that must have been nailed together before Teddy Roosevelt and those cowboys rode up the hill in Santiago? And the Russians have the oil, and the machines drive down the road like it's their road and their country.

The more I thought about this, the more angry I got. I didn't have anything to eat at the airport. So now I am chewing on raw sugarcane like I used to do as a child, and the Russian soldiers—young like me, only blond and sunburned—started yelling, "Bad for your teeth!" and "Rinse after eating!" and "Your teeth are going to fall out, muchacho!" At one point, a convoy stopped alongside my cart. Just then my horse let out a loud you-know-what and did a number-two job right in front of me. The Russians were screaming with laughter. Assholes.

I was so embarrassed that I got off the cart a mile from home, even though he was going right by my mother's house. I did not want anyone to see me like this. No fucking way. I wound up walking home.

I told you that my mother, Hilda Perez, is one of the most beautiful women in Cuba. When I saw her, my heart melted. She was still lovely, but very thin. My homecoming was very emotional. My family didn't have much. The American embargo never did break our spirit, but it made us suffer.

In Cuba we have an expression that I will have to translate for you. Well, first, if you have women or young children reading this book, maybe they should skip ahead and bypass this chapter. I don't want to offend anybody or have President Bush throw you in jail for writing a dirty story.

Anyway, the Cuban expression I want to tell you about is *loco pinguo*. Literally, *loco pinguo* means a man who is fucking crazy with his big dick.[1] Someone with guts and courage to do something that is outrageous. For example, two American gangsters might sit around and say, "Oh, that motherfucker had balls to rob that bank." In Spanish, we would say that someone is *loco pinguo*. This term, however, is reserved for people who do *really* crazy things.

On the fourth day of my leave, a man hijacked a bus outside the Peruvian Embassy, took a bunch of people hostage, and then drove the bus

---

[1] Not to be confused with *loco de pinga,* an offensive term meant to seriously insult. Loosely translated into American profanity it means punk or asshole. In contrast, *loco pinguo* is a term of admiration.

into the iron gate while two Cuban guards opened fire. One of the guards was killed. Anyway, the hijacker gets inside the embassy, and even though he is a hijacker, and somebody is dead, he wants asylum. Now let me tell you, that is a real loco pinguo hombre.

Remember that the American boycott had been underway for twenty years. Cubans had little food, less oil, and no consumer goods. By 1980, the first rule of life in Cuba was *pay attention*. You see people running in one specific direction? Don't waste a single second trying to figure out why, just run toward the direction the others are running, and once you get there, *then* you ask what is going on. And that is what happened the day of the forced entry of the Peruvian Embassy in Havana.

After the bus rammed the gate, more than ten thousand Cubans climbed over the bus, the gate, the wall, and scrambled into the embassy. Fidel went on the air and in so many words said he was tired of people saying Cuba was "an island prison," he was tired of all the bullshit, that ours was a just and noble revolution, and anybody who don't like it, well, fuck you, get off the island. Fidel said we don't need any more *gusanos* (worms), or other losers, bums, perverts, homosexuals, imperialist lackeys, and counterrevolutionaries. Get the fuck out of here!

I no longer thought about sleeping for a month. This was exciting! I lived less than ten miles from Mariel. This was my country, my backyard. I said to my brother, Hey, let's go and see what's happening. By the time we got there, the place was like a big carnival. Hundreds of American boats, including cigarette speedboats worth millions, luxurious yachts, smaller cabin cruisers, little fishing boats—anything that could float. On my first day, I was surprised at the security—there wasn't any. I walked in, flashed my ID, looked around like I knew what I was doing, saw a couple other officers I recognized. We rolled our eyes, touched our dicks, and looked over at this big Hatteras yacht out of Palm Beach that had the most amazing women I had ever seen, wearing the most amazing bathing suits while shaking their incredible asses to what I called "noise music," or American rock and roll.

The women were wearing—this is what I called them—naked bikinis. I later learned they were called string bikinis. I couldn't believe it. Man, did I come to attention. Always did like those Yanquis. These women on the yachts were like models. Tall. They had legs that went on for days. And those naked bikinis. What the fuck is this? The other guys, including a captain I remembered from Angola, looked at each other. Fidel, you never told us about this! You been holding out on us!

I drank my first Coca-Cola, given to me by one of the women in the naked bikinis. As I drank it, I heard this tremendous noise. One of the high-performance boats, painted all black, was getting under way. The thunderous noise from the huge engines hit the mountains and echoed back.

I also was confused. Everybody was having a good time. Until that morning, I don't think I ever knew an American. Like I said, they always were portrayed in the Cuban media as monster faces. Everywhere. I hated the Americans. I always said that when I die, let me take a few with me. Now Mariel.

I went home in great excitement. I was twenty years old and had seen good men die in faraway places for reasons I did not entirely understand; I killed people I did not know or really care about, except they were trying to kill me. Suddenly all the doubts and suspicions I had about Cuba and its wild politics came to the front of my mind.

I then had one of my crazy ideas.

I would jump on one of the boats, go to the United States, and pay a little visit. Then, when I was tired, I would steal a boat or fly a plane and come home. I was trained to do this. It was only 90 to 120 miles. Coming back would be easy. I thought about my Spetsnaz friends.

"Hey Vigoa, where the fuck you been?"

"Oh, on vacation."

"Oh yeah, where did you go?"

"Oh, Miami Beach. Then Palm Beach. I spent a few days on Broadway. Nothing much."

At that precise instant, I was a changed man. I didn't realize it at the time, but I had changed my belief system, and I had changed sides in one instant. I told myself it was a joke, something temporary, that I would come back. Deep within me, that was not true. I argued with myself, but the argument was already over when I saw those women in the naked bikinis and drank the Coke. I told myself, Jose, if the Americans are our number one rival or nemesis, I want to know how they think, how they live, what are their beliefs, what kind of culture do they have, what was their country all about. I told myself that I could use this information in the future and create unique ways to defeat the enemy. Of course, all of this was bullshit. I had the fever to go to America like everyone else.

I returned to Mariel the next day. The road was filled with buses and trucks, with people hanging on from all sides. Everything was different, more intense, with more police, army, secret police, even Russian military. I knew some of these people. I had to be careful. I acted like I was there on official business. About two miles from the harbor there was a staging area where the buses were taking people. They had a family area, an area for street people, an area for educated people, and one compound of lean, hard-looking men with all kinds of fierce, wild tattoos. These were the criminals; I realized this right away. I knew some of these men, too. They were prisoners. Some were murderers and rapists.

I bluffed my way past the patrol and started talking to a man who stole cars for a living and had been sent to prison for ten years. I knew him from my neighborhood. He said that one day the prison officials said all the prisoners could leave on the boatlift. They would be treated badly in America, but if they wanted to go, they could go. The men were greatly excited, but some were afraid. They smelled a trap. I, too, thought it might be a trick. My old friend, who signed up to leave, looked worried.

"What if they say we're traitors and shoot us?" the car thief asked.

I made a little joke. "That could still happen. But at least you won't get seasick."

"This is only a fraction of what there is," the thief whispered, pointing to the overcrowded camp. "They're setting up compounds like this all over the area. Filled with people let out of the jails. Some crazy people, too."

Suddenly, I felt powerful arms grab me from behind. I found myself looking into the fat, ugly face of a secret police captain.

"What the fuck do you think you're doing here, Lieutenant?"

I started to curse him back—I don't let people talk to me like that—but then I saw there were six or seven cops behind him looking like they'd love to beat my ass. I started to say something about who I was and where I had been, and he just spit on the ground. "Fuck you, I don't care about that."

I started to talk, and the cops started to move forward. The ugly captain told me that if I said another word, he and his men would bust me up real good. I shut up. He wandered off to abuse someone else. I went down to the docks.

That night I boarded the *Lady Lee,* a big new shrimp boat out of

Florida, made of steel. I'm not a sailor, so I can't say how big it was, but it looked maybe 120 to 140 feet long and very wide, almost like a tugboat.

The American captain explained that we would have to wait for clearance to leave. What happened was, the Cuban government played a little trick on the Americans. You could enter Mariel Harbor, but you had to pay, and you had to take other people on board, and not just the ones that hired you.

As the boat filled up, I began to notice other young men about my age climbing aboard the *Lady Lee*. I counted about twenty-three of these men. I knew they were military like myself. I could tell by their physical condition and bearing. Some were from intelligence. One of the agents, who was very well dressed and cordial, became a good friend of mine, and we stayed together on the trip. He told me little about himself and asked me no personal questions. That was normal. He knew who I was. He saw my military boots, the belt buckle with the Spetsnaz symbol, my short haircut, and energetic movements. The agent taught me how to deal with the American authorities when I arrived, what to say, what to do, how to pass through customs and the FBI. I would say I was a student and anticommunist, and that if I went back, they would kill me and my whole family.

"My whole family? They'll believe that?" I asked.

"Sure," he said. "As soon as you say *communist,* they'll believe anything."

He asked me to open my mouth. I did. He looked inside. He said the Americans looked for tattoos even in your mouth. I had none, not even on my arms.

I became very hungry and went down with the intelligence agent to the dock to buy some food. It was there I met a beautiful girl in a yellow bandana. I was actually startled when I saw her, and I think I said something stupid, like "Whoa." It was like one of those movies where two people meet in a crowded place where there's all kinds of dangers and spies, and people are saying good-bye and nobody knows what will happen.

I can still see her. She was the granddaughter of one of Batista's favorite businessmen, one of the fat cats who gave the dictator big "commissions" that later were called bribes. He left with Batista on New Year's Eve 1958, and, being the gallant gentleman he was, he left his family behind. The girl, with long jet-black hair, was unlike any woman I had ever seen. Tall for a Cuban, with wonderful porcelain skin and the face of an angel. She was eighteen. I wanted to take her by the hand and walk off the dock into the famous sunset, as they say in the cinema. We were talking a little, and I could see she was shy but also sophisticated and mature. Like rich people can be. She didn't dress like a wealthy person, though. Very modest, with a long skirt and this canary-yellow scarf around her neck. "It's so I don't catch cold," she said. Her parents were not coming, and she was traveling with her grandmother.

You may not believe this, but I was a perfect gentleman. I became very concerned for her safety when she pointed out her boat. It was about twenty-eight feet long, with a ten- or eleven-foot beam. Like a toy yacht. It already was crowded with people, some of whom looked rich, some of whom looked like criminals. The boat was from Miami. Someone was making a real killing on this trip. I thought the boat was too small, and I said so. It was overloaded.

"Why don't you and your grandmother come on my boat?" I said, pointing to the *Lady Lee*.

The grandmother was standing nearby, and she did not like me. She thought I was trying to pick up her granddaughter and had evil soldier intentions. For no reason at all, she started screaming at me and telling me to get away from her granddaughter. She actually cursed me. People started staring. I could see my friend from the intelligence service looking at me with an alarmed expression. He motioned for me to come back to the boat. He began looking around for police.

I wanted to tell the nasty, wrinkled-face granny bitch to go fuck herself, but I did not. I felt sorry for the girl. The granny was one of these old-fashioned Spanish-type women with a very exaggerated sense of class and social standing. To her, I was trash. Unfit to be in the company of the lovely girl, much less to offer my assistance. No wonder they wanted out of Cuba. But what the hell, I wasn't that worried. If her little boat was seaworthy enough to make the trip from Miami to Mariel, it would make it back safely to Miami, especially in such fine weather.

I would see the beautiful girl and her yellow bandana again.

It was kind of a happy and sad time for all of us. Some of these people had to know they would never see their homeland, family, and friends again. I was okay. I was a single, twenty-year-old man who was ready to see the other side of the Florida Straits, to explore a country I did not know but had been taught to hate. All those years, I was told the Americans were behind every shortage, every war, every act of imperialism, every mean and wrong thing done to our little country and other countries too.

But now, somehow, I wanted to go there. I would look right into the monster faces and see what I could see.

Chapter 9

LITTLE SAUSAGES

From his perch atop the ship's pilothouse, Vigoa heard the shrieks of the refugees over the roar of the hurricane-force wind. He was reminded of an amusement park he once visited outside of Havana and the high-pitched cries of young people on the thrill rides, but what started out as a Sunday afternoon amusement was fast becoming a horror show. Vigoa had never seen such winds, or seas, or skies *that* red in the morning or *that* black in the afternoon. The ninety-mile journey to America on the shrimp boat *Lady Lee* was fast becoming a struggle for survival.

"The Cuban government told our captain and the other boats that the storm had passed," Vigoa said later. "But when we left, and the city behind us began to disappear in the mist, we could see the sky getting real black and hear the thunder ahead. I turned to the Cuban intelligence officer I met at the dock and asked one question: 'How could this happen?' He just looked at me and shrugged."

Within the hour, Vigoa knew his journey to America would be yet another unsolicited, unanticipated life-or-death experience.

A steel vessel out of South Carolina, the *Lady Lee* was 120 feet long, sturdily built, and captained by an able mariner of eighteen years' experience who had seen heavy weather before—but never at this time of the year or in these waters. A commercial boat, the ship was about to become part of the sad history between the two neighboring but hostile nations.

"Everybody knows how bad the weather can get between the Bahamas, Florida, and Cuba and how suddenly the weather can change," Vigoa said. "It was crazy. The waves were forty to fifty feet high. I mean, *real* high. When the boat went down, and the waves went up, I could see nothing but water. It was like being under the water, no sky, no nothing.

Then we went to the top of the wave like on a giant roller coaster, and we looked out and saw an even bigger mountain of water. The boat was here, the mountain was there, and we were about to climb that big hill and maybe fall off on the other side."

The Cuban intelligence officer, whose name was Roberto, and who Vigoa claimed to be a spy, took Vigoa to the pilothouse, and they climbed onto the roof. Roberto tied Vigoa tightly to the radio communications mast. Jose did the same for him.

"This is the safest place," Roberto said.

Vigoa laughed. He loved black humor. "You said 'safest,' not 'safe,'" he told the spy, who smiled.

It began to rain heavily. Lightning flashed across the sky, followed by thunderclaps. The ship began "to feel kind of funny, like it was slipping on ice," Vigoa said. The seas were becoming rough and steep. "It looked like the waves had waves," said Vigoa. "Some of the smaller boats were trying to turn back, and at least one overturned. We kept moving. It was too hard to turn around."

The *Lady Lee* began to pitch and roll, and large waves crashed over the bow, throwing up spectacular geysers of water. "I don't get seasick, thank God," Vigoa said. "But almost everybody else did get sick. It was bad. The boat was overcrowded. They pushed everybody they could into the boat like sardines. And the weather kept getting worse. After two hours, the sky was pitch black. It was the early afternoon. I don't think we're going to ever see Key West. Okay, Jose's time is up, too bad, I won't get to see no more women in naked bathing suits. But all these other people. So many women and children."

The irony was not lost on the Cuban defector. *I survive big guns and little guns,* he thought, *spears and clubs, machetes and mortars—and now I will sink beneath the waves and drink salt water because Mother Nature is playing a little joke.*

Roberto found fault with the vessel's passage. "We're heading for Key West, but this is a dangerous way to sail," the spy said. "It's safer to head into the waves. The captain is going to try to outrun the storm, but he can't steer the boat as well with the waves behind us, rolling under the ship and pushing it around. He will have to slow down."

Vigoa was no blue-water sailor, but he knew instinctively the trawler was in trouble. He watched as four crew members hurriedly strung life-lines about the boat and handed out life jackets, even though there weren't enough for even a fraction of the refugees. The orange preservers were handed out to women, children, and the elderly. There were no unseemly arguments. The Cuban male belonged to a machismo culture like few others; there would be no cowards today. The hard men among the passengers, with the tattoos of daggers dripping blood, the ones Vigoa knew to be convicts newly released from prison, could have taken all the life jackets, but they only scowled and told the deckhands that every orange vest would go to the families, or the crew would be swimming soon.

Suddenly the ocean was ascending rapidly. *Like an elevator climbing too fast,* Vigoa thought. The *Lady Lee,* a 140-ton vessel, shot upward. They were riding on a gigantic wave. Just before the wave broke, the boat stopped, hung on the breaking crest, and shuddered, then careened into the trough below.

Abruptly, the diesel engines stopped. Vigoa could hear a clanking sound—the shifting of gears—then there was the noise of the wind. The bow of the ship slammed into the back of the next great wave, creating a tremendous plume of black water that drenched Vigoa, the spy, and the other passengers huddled on the deck below.

Vigoa could feel—actually, he could see—the boat slide sideways into the trough, and that's when the American crew of the *Lady Lee* looked grim, and the captain began to shout orders. Vigoa was fascinated by the bridge crew's exertions. Going too fast in front of the storm and the heavy swells meant the boat might fly off the front of one wave, plow into the back of another, as had already happened once, and fall off to one side—an event sailors call "broaching." If thrown in the trough, the *Lady Lee* would have to maneuver quickly out of the trench or risk being rolled over by a large wave. But because the ship had lost forward motion, or "way," there was no longer water passing over the rudders, and it would take time to regain momentum and pick up speed.

How to get out of the trough? Vigoa watched with excitement as the engines roared to life, and the boat began to pivot to starboard, climbing back atop another giant wave and once again running ahead of the wind.[1] The captain was using his throttles and the pitch of his propellers to get in front of the seas and avoid "beam" waves.[2] The intelligence agent looked relieved. "That was close," he said. "But if we don't turn into the wind, we're going to roll over." The spy dragged his finger across his throat.

[1] *Starboard* is the naval directional term for right as one faces the bow; *port* means left.
[2] A beam sea, or beam wave, is from the side.

Caught by the fierce wind, the door of the pilothouse banged open. Vigoa could hear fragments of the voices on the bridge through the wail of the wind. Like a man who slips on a wet floor, his feet shooting out from under him, the vessel again began to fall off a huge wave. "Left engine full, swing 'er back," the captain commanded as the *Lady Lee* plowed into the backside of another wave. "Get her out!" the captain screamed. Its forward momentum stopped by a massive wall of water, the *Lady Lee* began to slide to the left and into the trough.

The engines roared again. The first officer rammed the left throttle forward while simultaneously reversing the right engine and giving it full power. The ship wallowed in the trough, took a heavy wave on its port beam, and began to roll to starboard. The ship tilted 5 degrees. Then 10. Then 20, 30, 40. The ship was almost on its side.

Tied to the mast over the pilothouse, Vigoa winced as the ropes tightened and cut into his chest and shoulders. He could now see nothing but water. *Time to start swimming,* he thought. *Time to get real wet.*

The trawler leaned hard on its starboard side as another huge wave gathered on the port beam for a renewed onslaught.

Fearful of this alien and dangerous world, Vigoa also was fascinated. So much happening. So many feelings mixed together. Anxiety. Terror. Hope. Despair. And for Vigoa, a feeling of absolute helplessness. In battle, a man could fight his way out of an ambush. Here, halfway from Mariel, Cuba, to Key West, Florida, he was at the mercy of the seas and dependent on others, something he did not like.

Vigoa would remember this moment of his journey to America: The engines whining at full RPM. The women screaming as they slid across the decks. The children crying as they slipped from their mothers' arms and rolled down a passageway and into a bulkhead before being retrieved by deckhands. The men and women praying to an assortment of gods: Catholic, Santeria, Regla de Ocha, Babalu Aye, Evangelical, voodoo. And Jose would not forget: The *Lady Lee* shuddering, straining, rocking to starboard, falling, falling, falling. The vessel's steel hull creaking and groaning. Roberto, dedicated communist, avowed atheist, making the sign of the cross.

Just when it seemed certain the *Lady Lee* would continue her roll to oblivion, the ship rose out of the water and turned to starboard, climbing out of the trough while balancing on its starboard side, almost like a windsurfer pushed over by a hard gust while still racing through the water. The trawler began to ascend the next wave. Once more, the wind was at the vessel's back.

For the moment, the *Lady Lee* was safe. Vigoa had just witnessed a textbook exercise in heavy-weather boat handling.

On Sunday, April 27, 1980, thirty miles north of Cuba, sixty miles south of Key West, Florida, the *Lady Lee*'s likelihood of broaching, capsizing, or pitchpoling increased exponentially as the storm grew in fury. Disaster had struck the Mariel boatlift. Beginning with two small boats seeking to transport dissidents from Cuba with Castro's approval, the so-called freedom flotilla exploded to more than one thousand craft three days later. Many of the boats were too small or not seaworthy for the trip across the Florida Straits even in calm seas.

Now the storm. Two freak tropical lows—one from the Gulf of Mexico west of Cuba, the other from the Bahamas northeast of the island—converged off the Florida Keys, creating what the United States Coast Guard would officially term "a mini-hurricane" in its after-action report. Captain Jim Decker, the commanding officer of the Cape York patrol boat out of Key West, described the big blow as "a furious storm of magnificent proportion, almost hurricane strength." Wind gusts were recorded at seventy knots, the strength of a young hurricane. Monstrous waves topped forty feet, enough to endanger even a naval warship or large commercial freighter.

The timing of the storm was catastrophic. Coast Guard Seventh District officers later computed there were at least one thousand boats shuttling between the U.S. and Cuba at the time of the Sunday storm, and even more boats in the Florida Straits by the time of a second series of gales, on Thursday, May 1. Many boats were without safety equipment, the operators lacking training in basic navigation and seamanship. Almost all the crafts, some designed for bays and sheltered inlets, some as small as eighteen and twenty feet, were unsuited for the blue-water navigation, much less severe weather. Some were without radios. Few had sufficient life jackets.

On April 29 there were seventeen hundred vessels at Mariel preparing to leave. Radar and aerial observation logged another nineteen boats heading to Florida from Cuba and sixty-seven heading to Cuba from Florida. There were four hundred more craft waiting at Key West. In all, there were more than two thousand boats somewhere in the Mariel pipeline despite heavy weather.

As for the *Lady Lee,* her credentials and seaworthiness were not in question, and the trawler would soon demonstrate its true character. It was a well-maintained ship crewed by professionals that could make the passage from Mariel to Key West without incident, even in what sailors call "dirty weather." Of course, this was no ordinary dirty weather, and on April 27 the very survival of the fishing vessel would hinge on a single decision that would be made almost too late. In the hours to come, the vessel nearly would founder, the crew almost would mutiny and refuse orders, and once again Jose Vigoa would be called upon to do the unthinkable.

THE FIRST CRISIS aboard the *Lady Lee* came three hours out of Mariel. The two weather fronts collided, and a sudden storm with the fury of a small typhoon barreled into the Florida Straits, directly in the path of the one thousand–boat exodus.

Vice Admiral Benedict L. Stabile later described the scene in the official Coast Guard history of that blackest of Sundays:

> On Sunday, 27 April, at about one o'clock in Key West, the weather went to hell—a "mini-hurricane" passed through. Winds shut down the Naval Air Station, which typically occurs when they go above 60 knots. The group had 22 maydays, serious cases involving danger to life, *in about five minutes.* It was instantaneous disaster.
>
> The large cutters also were inundated with SAR (search and rescue) calls. The volume of cases became so heavy that accurate records could not be kept. At one time, *Ingham* [a cutter] had five vessels in tow and an estimated 14 persons on board, taken from four or five swamped boats. These had to be left adrift.

With all of its rescue vessels committed, the Coast Guard did the unprecedented: Boats in distress that managed to get through on the overloaded guard channel were placed on a waiting list or told to radio other vessels for assistance. The *Lady Lee* was one of the vessels called into action to assist other vessels when the Coast Guard could do no more.

Just before two in the afternoon, the shrimp boat, its speed reduced to six knots, its spindly outriggers fully extended to provide stability, and its refugees on deck clinging to netting, hatches, lifelines, masts, booms, rafts, and each other, monitored a series of mayday broadcasts from small craft taking on water and sinking.[3]

The captain of the *Lady Lee* called for volunteers from the passenger ranks to assist the crew in search and rescue operations. Vigoa and the Cuban intelligence operative were among the six refugees who stepped forward. At least two of the volunteers, judging from their tattoos, were hard-core criminals dumped into the boatlift by Castro.

For the next hour, the heavily laden *Lady Lee* slowly circled the swamped and stricken craft, plucking survivors of sunken boats from the turbulent seas, rigging a bridle with towlines, pulling survivors out of boats that were beyond rescue, and setting the abandoned crafts adrift. Finally the *Lady Lee,* with five small boats in tow, was ready to resume its course. Only now the seas were huge and even more fearsome. Vigoa passed the captain on his way back to his perch on the roof of the pilot-house. The captain smiled wanly at Vigoa.

"First time at sea?" the captain said.

"No, just my last," Vigoa quipped.

"If this gets any worse, maybe my last too," the captain said, suddenly bear-hugging Vigoa as the boat fell off a huge wave, dived forward, and then slammed into another wall of water. The captain held both men steady, winked at Vigoa, and then hobbled back into the pilothouse.

Returning to his ledge atop the pilothouse, Vigoa looked past the stern of the *Lady Lee*. Five small boats crowded with refugees, strung together one by one, trailed the shrimp boat. The largest was twenty-eight feet; the smallest, eighteen feet. All were crowded. The *Lady Lee* had reduced its speed even further, but the small craft were barely afloat. Vigoa knew that the girl with the yellow scarf and her grandmother were in the first boat.

How long could they survive? Vigoa stood and gripped the signal mast, looking to the stern of the *Lady Lee*. The procession of small craft under tow would appear briefly at the top of the waves, then disappear completely for minutes at a time. Vigoa thought he saw the girl with the yellow scarf sitting near the front of the first boat, but he wasn't sure. *I should have forced her to come with me. That stupid old woman! Even if their boat doesn't sink, Grandma will die of fright before we reach Key West*. Vigoa began to curse

---

[3] Vigoa called them "arms." The outriggers hold the nets away from the ship as the vessel trawls for shrimp and fish.

so loudly and with such vehemence that some of the sobbing women on the boat stopped crying and stared. The intelligence agent looked at Vigoa curiously.

"I could see the people on my own boat," Vigoa said. "They were in bad shape, vomiting their lives out, very scared, very sick, lots of women, children, old people. On the little boats, it must have been hell. Nothing but terror and misery as we dragged the little boats through the giant waves."

Vigoa had a bitter thought. He later recalled, "What started out to be fun turned into a survival operation, like being on a battlefield again. Most of the time the rain was so heavy, the spray so thick, I couldn't see anything. But sometimes the boat would go way, way up on a wave, and I would look down and see what I did not want to see. There were bodies floating in the water as we passed by. Patches of debris, including red five-gallon fuel containers, empty life jackets, Styrofoam coolers, aluminum folding chairs, a suitcase, clothing, boards, a few tires. One boat was filled with water but still afloat. It was a rowboat. A rowboat! Nobody was in it. They were long gone. The little boats towed behind the *Lady Lee* were strung together one by one. They looked like Italian sausages or perhaps Spanish chorizos. The *Lady Lee* was a big strong boat, especially built for the harsh, mad seas, but even then we were like a little seagull on the ocean, and if that were so, how could the little sausages make it across the straits?"

A better question might have been: How could the overloaded *Lady Lee* make it to Florida while pounding through hurricane-force winds and dragging five smaller craft? The shrimp boat was too low in the water. The pumps were working full-time but not keeping up with the rising water from the huge waves coming over the bow. The boat was in constant danger of broaching.

In heavy seas, a vessel needs to maneuver swiftly and precisely—or, in the sailor's term, smartly. But because of the smaller boats trailing behind, the *Lady Lee* was now slow to respond to her helm. Steering was sluggish and unpredictable.

The captain knew something else: It would get worse. If the *Lady Lee* survived its journey through the Florida Straits, it would reach the area south of the Florida Keys and more shallow water. The waves, dragging across the bottom, would pile up and grow more steep and violent. *If you lose control in this weather,* the captain thought, *the next wave will get you.*

After all, big waves often come in sets of three. Sailors call them the three sisters.

As Vigoa worried about his chorizos, the bridge crew of the shrimp boat realized they were running out of options. Seamanship was seamanship. The *Lady Lee* had one chance: It could change course, turn into the wind, quarter the waves, hove to (stop), and ride out the storm. Because of the inherent danger of a beam sea, this maneuver into the head sea would have to be done gradually in a long, cautious loop, with the ship turning into the wind and waves, tacking like a sailboat to avoid capsizing.

It was obviously the right decision. So why delay the change in course? Because with the five small boats in tow, the *Lady Lee* could not turn at all.

"We have to turn into the seas and heave to, but we can't," the captain said aloud. All the men on the bridge stared. They knew what he meant. "The boats we're towing are serving as an anchor. We have to turn into the wind, or we'll roll over. But we can't maneuver with those boats."

There were an estimated 123 refugees and crew aboard the *Lady Lee;* there were 38 people on the smaller boats towed by the trawler. The smaller craft would have to be cut loose and it was clear that once they were on their own, the small boats would have virtually no chance of surviving.

"You know what we have to do," the captain said to his second officer.

"Yes sir."

"Then do it."

"I can't, sir. That would be murder."

The captain was stunned. In their six years together, no member of his crew had ever disobeyed an order during an emergency. Within seconds, another crew member refused to sever the towlines.

The captain explained that this was nothing new in the annals of the sea. They were like an animal caught in a steel trap: Sometimes the only way out is to chew off your own paw. A terrible choice, a horrible decision, but this was the way it was—and making such a decision had been a captain's prerogative through centuries of seafaring. The decision to release the small boats had to be made now, the captain urged. The *Lady Lee* was out of time.

"*We have to turn this fucking ship around now!*" the captain roared.

The men stared at the deck. No one moved.

The captain's face reddened. He seemed about to say something but stopped. A tall, powerfully built deckhand, a native of Nassau in the Bahamas, a seaman known for his great strength and friendly disposition, stood in the open hatch.

"I'll go, sir." He pulled a fire axe from its cradle.

"You'll need help," the captain said.

"I know someone."

The deckhand disappeared into the blackness and the roaring wind. He motioned Vigoa to come down from the pilothouse roof. They spoke briefly. With a machete and a fire axe, the two men worked their way to the stern of the *Lady Lee,* followed by Roberto, who held Vigoa by his belt buckle as Jose leaned over the stern to examine two towlines—made of heavy, one-inch-gauge rope—that were tied to cleats at the stern.

The three men could see people in the first boat, about twenty yards away. A handsome Spaniard from Santiago de Cuba, standing in the bow of the twenty-eight-foot, single-engine powerboat that was first in line, waved at Vigoa. The girl in the yellow scarf sat behind the Spaniard. Vigoa could not see her face.

The Spaniard, when he saw the machete and the axe, must have understood their meaning. On this day, he had worn his best suit, perhaps expecting to be greeted happily by his family and friends at the dock in Key West. He wore a starched white shirt and a red tie that was too long. He yelled something, but his words were drowned out by the wind and noise from the trawler's engines. He waved again, then sat down and bowed his head.

The girl took off the yellow scarf and waved it in the air. The wind caught the scarf. It spiraled upward and disappeared into the blackness.

Vigoa raised the machete. Swinging it high overhead, with both hands, he brought the blade down upon the towline. Once, twice, three times the machete came down. The heavy line still held by a slender thread. Furiously, Vigoa hacked at the rope. It broke loose and whipped into the sea.

By now, the deckhand from Nassau had begun to chop at his towline at the opposite corner of the stern. The others in the small boats saw what was happening. They began to scream and wave. Men shook their fists.

Jose could hear the words *cobarde* (coward) and *singao* (man without honor). To a Cuban male, these were fighting words, but Vigoa could only bow his head in despair.

One more towline remained.

An older woman in the second boat held up a small child as if to say, "You are killing the young ones too." The angry men continued to scream insults. Vigoa felt sick. *These are not soldiers in battle. These are innocent people. How could this happen?*

The lines finally were cut. The five small craft seemed to follow the *Lady Lee* for a few seconds, then drifted away in disorder. The end came quickly. The larger boat, with the girl who once wore the yellow scarf, was the first to founder. Vigoa could hear its small engine rev frantically as a large wave tossed the boat sideways. Another big wave thundered over the craft. The sound of the motor was stilled, and the people disappeared into the spray and waves.

Many years later, Vigoa recalled the image: "The small boats, they were like sausages strung together in a row. They floated apart, one after the other, the men begging for us to come back, the women crying and screaming and waving, waving, waving. There were five little sausages, and then four, and then three, and then two—and then no more. Some nights, I can still hear the screaming."

AFTER SEVERING THE TOWLINES, Vigoa, Roberto, and the Bahamian deckhand were returning to the pilothouse when a rogue wave slammed into the port beam of the *Lady Lee*. The ship rolled sharply to the right, but the helmsmen saw the wave coming and reacted swiftly. The *Lady Lee* recovered.

Vigoa, the deckhand, and the spy were thrown across the deck, Vigoa striking his head on a wire shrimp basket. "I felt like someone hit me on the head with a big hammer," he recalled. "I was out cold for a few minutes until another wave splashed onto the boat and woke me up. The deckhand from Nassau and the spy were kneeling over me, asking me if I was all right. I was about to answer when there was a tremendous boom and a flash of light. I thought, *Oh no, we've been torpedoed or hit a mine! The Cuban border patrol is shooting at us!* Or something bad like that. There were sparks coming from the pilothouse, like tracer bullets." In fact, the signal mast behind the *Lady Lee* had been hit by lightning, breaking a large radar and radio array into pieces and showering the roof of the pilothouse with shrapnel. A small fire erupted but soon died. The *Lady Lee* was now blind, without radar or radio communications.

At first, Vigoa and Roberto thought the lightning to be a sign from God, who surely was venting his anger at the crew and the vessel for cutting loose the five small boats and leaving the refugees to drown. But when the two men returned to the pilothouse and examined the roof, they realized that if this was divine intervention, it was more benevolent and forgiving than they first thought. The roof of the pilothouse was pockmarked from the shrapnel. A large, scorched radar screen sat on the spot where Jose had rested.

"Good thing you're so clumsy," the spy said to Vigoa, tracing a jagged hole on the roof with his fingers, "or we'd both be dead."

Free of its burden, the *Lady Lee* carefully maneuvered into the wind and rode out the storm before finally returning to its original course. The great waves began to diminish. The heavy rain became a light mist. The sun broke through. Steep seas turned into six-foot swells and breaking whitecaps.

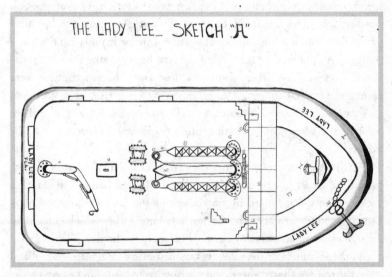

The vessel Lady Lee, as sketched by Jose Vigoa twenty-four years after its harrowing voyage from Mariel Harbor, Cuba, to Key West, Florida, during the Mariel boatlift. COURTESY JOSE VIGOA.

Twenty hours after leaving Mariel Harbor in what was scheduled to be a six-hour passage, a catnapping Vigoa heard a familiar sound, a heavy thumping. He jumped up and began shouting.

The dot in the sky grew closer. It was a United States Coast Guard helicopter from the Key West Naval Air Station.

Exhausted, thirsty, hungry, seemingly at the end of all human endurance, the refugees aboard the *Lady Lee*—the crew would call the ship *Lucky Lady* in the years to come—staggered to their feet. The orange and white colors of the U.S. Coast Guard flashed by as the helicopter circled the trawler. Then it hovered overhead, the pilot asking over his exterior speaker if the *Lady Lee* was without radio communications. The captain appeared on deck and signaled that his radio was inoperative. The pilot acknowledged the message and ordered the trawler to follow him to Key West. He pumped the fingers of his right hand twice, indicating the number ten. The *Lady Lee* was only ten miles from Florida.

They had made it. The *Lady Lee* was safe. The storm had passed, the Coast Guard was overhead, they were closer to Key West than they realized.

A rebel yell came from the pilothouse. The vessel's collision alarm began to sound in celebration of the *Lady Lee's* salvation. The refugees, all on their feet, began to cheer. Some of the younger passengers began to dance. The convicts hugged one another and shook hands with the other refugees. An old man by the bow of the boat began to sing the Cuban national anthem. The others joined in. Jose and Roberto the spy were among the loudest singers. The exodus was to America, to be sure, but these were still Cubans, and most hoped to return someday. The anthem was based on a heroic nineteenth-century battle, and the Cubans sang passionately.

As the *Lady Lee* entered the Key West channel, the battered boat passed the Coast Guard cutter *Dauntless* as the sleek American ship left for sea. The Coast Guard by now knew of the *Lady Lee's* ordeal. The *Dauntless* sounded its horn three times in tribute. Other vessels chimed in. Dozens of horns and sirens welcomed the *Lady Lee* home.

As the shrimp boat threaded its way past every imaginable vessel and craft, the refugees heard cheers and applause from land. They waved back. One man on the shore, with a powerful voice, grinned and yelled, "Keep the wet side down and the shiny side up!" The passengers laughed. But when they saw the American flag by the Coast Guard station, many of the

Cubans, and even the rough men from Castro's toughest prisons, began to weep.

The *Lady Lee* moved slowly now, preparing to dock, the first officer in control, carefully gauging wind and currents, moving the ship with short bursts of the throttle and gear shifting.

An object on the foremast attracted the captain's eye. He squinted. A brightly colored pennant flew from the rigging. It was a yellow scarf.

DRUG SLINGER

As thousands of dissidents, criminals, psychotics, and spies flooded Key West and its overloaded Immigration and Naturalization Service processing center, Jose Vigoa posed as a student fleeing political persecution and coolly talked his way past Immigration and FBI interrogators. After undergoing preliminary processing, Vigoa was flown on a military transport to Fort McCoy, Wisconsin, an army base and a former World War II prisoner of war camp. Vigoa later would describe the detention center as a place where detainees ran the camp and guards looked the other way. "There was no law," he said. "The guards were corrupt. Everything could be had if you had the money—guns, dope, prostitutes, and forged papers included. People were getting stabbed and killed all the time."

As the weeks became months, Vigoa grew worried. Some Marielitos were transferred abruptly to federal prisons, others were sent to mental hospitals. "I was beginning to think I had made a terrible mistake. I thought maybe they would keep me in this place forever, even though I was sponsored by one of my relatives living in the U.S. My mother's brother, my uncle Faustino Perez, had been living in Las Vegas for a long time and agreed to find me a job and give me a place to stay."

On July 22, 1980, the machinery of the INS finally spit out the case of Jose Vigoa. Over the phone, his uncle explained: "You're coming to Las Vegas, Manolo, I just got the call from Immigration. You're going to be released to me." The next day Vigoa was ordered to report to the camp office early in the morning. "You're out of here," the official said, handing Vigoa an airplane ticket for travel from Milwaukee to Chicago on a commuter airline, and from Chicago to Las Vegas on a TWA flight. Vigoa was given a Spanish-English dictionary, $20 in travel money, and a set of

INS papers—including what the detainees called a "parole" document, which would enable the Cuban refugee to acquire a driver's license in Nevada and obtain legal employment.

The trip to Chicago was fun, Vigoa remembered, with a friendly, wise-cracking pilot giving his passengers a guided tour over the beautiful Midwest countryside on a bright summer morning. Most of the thirty-plus passengers were from the camp, and they looked out the airplane windows silently. Some of the Cubans wept.

Searching for the TWA gate at Chicago's O'Hare International Airport, Vigoa became lost. "I started asking questions in Spanish, but nobody understood me. Then I found a Latin-looking police officer and asked for help. He smiled at my terrible English and noticed the English-Spanish dictionary in my hand. He started talking in Spanish." The officer checked Jose's ticket, was startled by the time of the flight, then ran with Vigoa to the gate.

Vigoa again felt panic when he reached Las Vegas, as his Uncle Faustino and half brother Juan Pedro Sanchez were delayed in traffic. He tried to make a collect call on a pay phone, but even when using a memorized English phrase ("Hello, I would like to make a collect call"), Vigoa could not be understood. He was about to give up, when he looked outside at the street. His uncle and brother had arrived. The three men rushed to greet one another.

In the past six months, Jose Manuel Vigoa had answered Fidel's call to arms, flown across the world to help safeguard a Marxist revolution, dodged rockets and mortar rounds, hopped a ride on the freedom flotilla, survived a teeming detention camp, and even made it through Chicago's O'Hare Airport on his first try. Now, the child of the revolution and the soldier of empire was cruising the Las Vegas Strip in the American town that proudly called itself Sin City. The fire of the capitalist enterprise seemed a physical force: It was 112 degrees when Vigoa arrived on the afternoon of July 23, 1980.

"I felt like I had walked through a time tunnel and was in another world and dimension," Vigoa said of his first days in Las Vegas. "It was a profound feeling, strange and new, good and bad, sad and happy. A tornado of thoughts raced through my mind. How could I adapt and live in this place? There was one surprise after the other. There were moments of melancholy and depression, and in the beginning I was very homesick, but also I was impressed—and I was free."

The boy who once stole chickens to help feed his family encountered his first American supermarket. On their way home, Uncle Faustino stopped at the Safeway on Charleston Boulevard and Boulder Highway. It was clean, fully stocked, brightly lit—and to Vigoa, huge! The employees, including many Latinos, were friendly and helpful. Vigoa never imagined such a place existed. "When I was a little boy, and I didn't like what my mother had for dinner on the table, I used to say, 'This *thing* again?' My mother always said in reply, 'If you want to eat better, you have to marry a rich girl.' She had another saying: 'If you want to eat ham, go to the U.S.' In our house, *ham* was the word that meant good things that you could find only in America."

Supermarkets were not the only discovery. One day Vigoa decided to visit another Cuban family living five blocks away from his uncle's house. When Vigoa walked through the front door of their home, he was overwhelmed by the stench; the Cuban couple had fifteen dogs running loose in the house and a half dozen cats of considerable ferocity and size. "The smell was terrible," Vigoa said. "You can't imagine how strong the dog stench was. And it got more weird when I looked in the bedrooms. There were several seven-foot-high marijuana plants growing."

"Do you smoke marijuana?" Vigoa asked the owners.

"No, it's for the dogs and cats," his host said. "The plants give us a good income so we can go to the market and buy meat, chicken, and fresh fish to feed the animals."

Vigoa later said, "I found this business with the smelly house, dogs, and plants a little crazy—and painful. In my country, people were struggling to put food on the table, and here people are growing marijuana to support the comfortable lives of their pets."

Then, too, there was a new career. In early October Vigoa rode on his uncle's bicycle to the Showboat Hotel & Casino to begin his first job in America: busboy in the coffee shop for $5 an hour and tips. Vigoa earned barely $1,000 a month, but it was a beginning, and his expenses were few. When he bought a 1979 Ford Mustang on credit at $181 a month, he discovered the city's Latino nightlife and began meeting pretty women.

Vigoa liked to dance, and he performed vigorously on the disco floor, to the delight and amusement of the buxom Latin girls who sought energetic partners for the music and the bedroom activities that often followed. Some Cuban men thought disco dancing less than manly, but no one ever said that to the muscular Marielito, who more often than not

Jose Vigoa as seen in 1983, three years after arriving in Las Vegas. With a new video camera and a Mustang hardtop, the twenty-three-year-old Cuban was enjoying the good life in a booming Las Vegas.

COURTESY VIGOA FAMILY.

took one woman or more home. One of Vigoa's partners described his dance moves: "Well, he was very different," she said, smiling at the thought of Vigoa's aggressive, even furious, gymnastics on the floor. "Let's just say he made up his own dances, whether the music was Donna Summer or Cuban merengue. Some people laughed, but some of us women found him very sexy. And in bed, he was a bull."

Luisa Farray was one of three Cuban sisters from Havana who came to the U.S. in the Mariel boatlift after breaking onto the grounds of the Peruvian Embassy with their father. The Farray sisters enjoyed a good party and could be found in the 1980s at all the Latino nightspots: El Jardine, El Matador, and El Bandito. Ten months after arriving in Las Vegas, Vigoa met Luisa, a compact and fiery-tempered young woman, at a club. They married in July. The same year, Anna, their first daughter, was born. To support the family and to make ends meet, Vigoa sold his beloved Mustang. He was promoted to the position of "runner" at the Showboat, a combination of room service attendant and supply clerk.

But soon Vigoa's newfound responsibilities began to weigh on him. "I really liked my job," he said. "I had lots of friends and got the chance to meet many famous athletes, including the Nicaraguan champion Alexis Arguello, many Puerto Rican fighters, wrestlers like Andre the Giant, and many more. My English language was improving daily. It was a fun job, but I didn't want to be a runner forever. Most of the people I knew were drug dealers making lots of money, and although I didn't want to go back to doing wrong things, I couldn't help my family with what I was earning. I began to have dark thoughts."

Doing wrong things. It is likely the adolescent Jose Vigoa was active in a Cuban black market, as were many street youths. Vigoa would admit to acts of brutality during combat in Afghanistan against the equally fierce mujahideen. But now he was contemplating something far different— graduating from delivering drugs to famous athletes and rock stars at up-scale Strip hotels to becoming an actual gangster himself.

Vigoa would remain on the right side of the law until April 1984, when a bitter hotel strike erupted. Thousands of men and women restaurant workers were out of work. The Culinary Workers Union sought a modest hourly wage increase, but the affected hotels refused to budge. Vigoa seethed. "I never understand how the owners of the casinos and hotels thought. For all the money they made, and all the contributions the workers made to that enormous profit, the workers had to fight hard every four years for a small increase, even when everything else was going up in price. The workers had to go on strike to get the 'wealthies' to pay a few more cents per hour. I am not saying dollars, I am saying cents! Many of the workers could not afford a strike—and I was one of them. A union strike meant an immediate disaster for the family. But to me, it was like a tiger or shark smelling blood. Now I had the excuse to do what I did best. If I couldn't make money honestly, I would make it at the end of a gun."

Luisa would have to go back to work. The baby would be placed in a day-care center on Twenty-eighth Street at $240 a month. A reluctant and ashamed Jose took Anna, now three years old, to the center. That night, he returned early to pick up the child. Outside, Jose paused to look through the front windows. The day-care workers sat at a table drinking beer and playing cards while the unattended children were locked behind a glass partition and left by themselves in dirty, unmade single beds without food or drink. The children were wailing. Frantically, Vigoa searched for Anna. He found her sitting on the floor.

"My child's eyes were swollen red; I realized she had been left there and had been crying all day," Vigoa said. "The children were hungry. They had not been fed. I charged into the center, went to my child, took off her diaper, and in my poor broken English demanded an explanation. Why was my baby's diaper filled with urine and number two? Her bottom was raw. The smell in the room was terrible. None of the children had been cared for, none of the babies had their diapers changed."

"I'm gonna turn this place into a fucking parking lot!" Vigoa roared in his broken English.

Much later, Vigoa remembered the incident with barely restrained anger: "Now I became dangerous. My demons were out. I went back to my car, put my baby in the child seat, and returned with a baseball bat. I decided to break legs, ribs, and heads."

Metro police cars arrived. Somehow Vigoa managed to avoid arrest—perhaps because the police had seen this sort of day-care child abuse before.

Two weeks later Vigoa sold his first rock of cocaine in the black ghetto known as the Naked City.[1] Vigoa "came heavy" to every street transaction. He had a .45 semiautomatic stuck in his belt and a partner with a Tec-9 submachine gun as backup hiding in a nearby truck. When Vigoa's second customer pulled a cheap handgun and tried to steal the drugs, Vigoa pushed aside the rusty Saturday night special, pulled the .45, and pistol-whipped the hapless addict across the mouth.

Vigoa concealed his new enterprise from the family as best he could, but in the end he expected Luisa to accept him for who and what he was. Drug dealing was against the law, but this was Las Vegas, a city dedicated to vice. In Vigoa's mind, he was as hardworking a businessman as any car dealer, banker, or casino owner. "I didn't want welfare, I didn't ask for food stamps, I didn't seek charity for my family, and I paid my fucking taxes. I didn't enjoy killing, or crime, but if that's how I could take my family out of poverty, then that's what I would do."

It was the summer of 1985, and Jose Vigoa was twenty-five years old. Like so many immigrants throughout U.S. history, he longed for acceptance and even respectability in his new country. Vigoa promised Luisa that he was using crime merely as a means of transition, because so many doors were closed to Cubans with heavy accents and odd customs. Vigoa vowed to make money fast and then turn to more legitimate enterprises.

[1] So named because in the 1950s and 1960s, showgirls and dancers lived in the smaller motels and sunbathed in the nude at poolside.

He vowed his child would never again live in squalor and that his wife would not be forced to clean the toilets of wealthy Americans. Although Vigoa's world view remained Marxist, and while he recoiled at the disparity between rich and poor in Las Vegas, one way or another Jose Manuel Vigoa intended to make a name for himself by tapping into the booming Las Vegas economy.

Indeed, in his new career as a fledgling Las Vegas dope slinger, Vigoa was about to succeed beyond his wildest dreams.

BOOK THREE

SOLDIER OF EMPIRE
IN LAS VEGAS

Chapter 11

LIVING THE LIFE

There were, in fact, two young men who came to Las Vegas at the out-set of the 1980s determined to make their mark in a tumultuous city un-dergoing rapid-fire change. The new arrival, too, was no stranger to violence and the culture of the street, with its brutish action and raw en-ergy. This newcomer also lived by the gun, although he would seek to en-force the laws and not flaunt them.

In June 1981, at about the time Jose Vigoa waited tables at the Show-boat Hotel, John Alamshaw, twenty-six, packed his worldly goods into his new blue 1981 Toyota Celica, pulled out of the driveway at 7201 Fos-ter Street in Morton Grove, Illinois, and headed west on Route 55, once known as Route 66—the famous cross-country route (1926–1984) where a man, according to the famous song, could get his kicks. Arriving in Las Vegas three days later, Alamshaw took the entrance examination for the Las Vegas Metropolitan Police Department, breezed through the test and finished nineteenth out of one thousand applicants.[1] On November 2, 1981, his official hire date with the department, Alamshaw began his sixteen-week training program at the police academy. He excelled there. In fact, Alamshaw was one of the most educated and prepared rookie cops Metro had ever seen.

Alamshaw's timing was auspicious. No longer just a sexy resort for Southern California gamblers and those wanting to catch the nightclub act of a faded movie star, Las Vegas was attracting big money, new own-ership, and what seemed to be every construction crane from Denver to Los Angeles. In spirit, Las Vegas continued to be brazen and defiant, a

---

[1] Alamshaw would have scored even higher but for the fact that he lacked military service. Metro gave added points to applicants for years served in the armed forces.

place of primary colors and neon glitz, only now it was a boom town with enough loose cash to float a European war, a $6 billion tourist gambling habit, and enough advertising for every form of sexual "escort" service imaginable to fill 120 pages of the local telephone book. The population of four hundred thousand would double in the next eight years, and by the time Jose Vigoa and John Alamshaw hit town, Vegas was the fastest-growing city in the nation.[2]

For nearly four decades, this had been a mob-owned town, but that era, too, was coming to an end. On Alamshaw's watch, the gangsters who operated Las Vegas cashed in and moved out. The Flamingo, Sands, Dunes, Tropicana, Desert Inn, Riviera, Aladdin, Frontier, and other mob-owned or teamster-financed resorts were sold to colorful tycoons like the eccentric recluse Howard Hughes or the brilliant Israeli Meshulam Riklis. A procession of Fortune 500 companies acquired properties and real estate, attracted by the stunning profits of the "gaming" industry (a public-relations term for gambling, booze, and hookers). The "boys" no longer called the shots.

Which also meant that a vacuum of power existed. The discipline and ruthlessness of men like Marshall Caifano, Anthony (The Ant) Spilotro, Moe Dalitz, Aladena (Jimmy the Weasel) Fratianno, Johnny Rosselli, Gus Greenbaum, Bugsy Siegel, and Raymond Patriarca no longer ensured order. As the lawyers and accountants took charge, thousands of casino security employees, long the backbone of Strip protection, were disarmed and ordered not to engage criminals with deadly force on hotel property, much less provide backroom retaliation. Old-timers scoffed. Was this any way to run a gambling resort? It would be up to the men and women of Metro to step up and take charge.

"The mob wasn't driven out of Las Vegas by law enforcement," Metro deputy chief Ray Flynn said. "It was the era of the IPOs that ended the boys' long run in this town. The initial public offering—the lucrative buyout."

It was time for reorganization, to brace for the storm, and there were plenty of new issues on the city's horizon: a cocaine epidemic, the franchising of black and Hispanic gangs from Los Angeles, a wave of illegal immigrants, a growing homeless population, and an increasing disparity between the haves and the have-nots.

[2] The population of Clark County would top 1 million by 1995, 1.3 million in 2000, and 1.7 million by 2006. The population was projected to surpass 2 million residents by 2008.

Unlike eastern cities that often employed a police chief appointed by the mayor or city council, Las Vegas's streamlined police department would be run by an elected sheriff who would serve for four years without term limits. Drawing from the ranks of able (or politically astute) captains and lieutenants, the sheriff was given the authority to appoint an under sheriff, an assistant sheriff, and nine deputy chiefs who eventually managed investigative services, detention services, two patrol commands, technical services, special operations, human resources, homeland security, and a division of professional standards.

From approximately 700 men in 1980, the department expanded to more than 2,400 officers by 2006. But even after that spurt, Metro remained well below the national per-capita average in sworn officers, as the city's growth continued. The average U.S. police department in 2006 employed 2.4 officers per 1,000 residents. In Las Vegas, which also attracts more than 38 million visitors a year, there were only 1.86 cops per 1,000 citizens. And every month 7,000 new arrivals poured into town to seek jobs and homes.

JOHN ALAMSHAW, FOR one, neither noticed nor cared about the statistical crisis. He was delighted to be in sunny Nevada ("The added sunshine per year makes you happier") and away from the corruption and cold of the Midwest. Las Vegas offered glamour, affordable housing, and good pay. And everywhere Alamshaw looked, there were beautiful women.

One morning, while driving through the old MGM Grand parking lot to gawk at the fire-ravaged hotel on his second day in town, Alamshaw noticed a tall, leggy redhead in a miniskirt and a tight sweater. The young woman smiled and walked up to John's Celica.

"You've got Illinois license plates," she said, leaning through the open window. Alamshaw caught a whiff of her perfume, and the woman's breasts brushed against his left arm. "I'll bet you're from *Chicago!*" she said, as though she too were from the big city on the lake.

"Yes, I am," Alamshaw beamed, marveling at what a friendly town Las Vegas was turning out to be.

Alamshaw recalls what happened next. "She then reached in, grabbed my crotch, squeezed my cock, and started to unzip my fly, asking me if I'd like to be her date for the next hour."

And what did the intrepid twenty-six-year-old policeman say to that?

"Stop it! What are you doing?"

Now the redhead was halfway in the car, groping with *both* hands. "Don't you want to party, sweetheart?"

"Get your hands off my dick! Let go of me! I'm a married man."

The young woman stepped back, pouted briefly, and then shook her head sadly. "You mean you're *not* from Chicago?"

Welcome to Las Vegas.

This introduction would become one of Alamshaw's favorite stories when, as a training officer, he showed the ropes to probationary policemen. But the existence of thousands of sex workers—some of them housewives from Los Angeles earning extra money on weekends; some of them tough streetwalkers carrying weapons—also was an issue with which Metro had to contend.

Sheriff John Moran, weary of complaints from businessmen and city officials about aggressive streetwalkers harassing tourists and local residents, announced he would launch one of the city's periodic crackdowns on prostitution in Las Vegas. There had been halfhearted efforts to clean up the Strip before, but this time the sheriff was determined. The ladies of the evening were growing bolder, not only propositioning potential customers directly but physically accosting them and blocking their way as they tried to pass on the sidewalk. Even worse, some of the young women were performing sex acts in bathrooms, alleys, and other public places along the Strip rather than pay for a hotel room. The worst spot for aggressive solicitation was at the corner of Flamingo and Las Vegas boulevards, where as many as forty to fifty women congregated on one block, yelling at cars, leering at male tourists, even exposing themselves.

"The next thing you know, there I am with my training officer, John Lipski, on the roof of the Dunes Hotel," Alamshaw said. "We were the spotters. One of us watched through binoculars, the other handled the radio. Otherwise, if we were on the street, the hookers would see us and keep walking without making contact with the men."

Alamshaw would serve as the "eyeball," a police term for the officer who actually maintains visual contact on the suspect, and Lipski would log the contact. When three contacts were made, Alamshaw or Lipski radioed a nearby police van, and the cops would peel out from their hiding place behind the Barbary Coast Hotel and Casino and scoop up the ladies. As many as twenty to thirty women would be arrested in a single night and then be transported to a parked bus for processing. Most would be released the same evening, with the suggestion they be more discreet in canvassing for clients. "We would sit on chairs about three feet from the edge of the roof, enjoy the sights and sounds of Las Vegas in the cool night air," said Alamshaw, "and the waiters would bring us coffee and cream on sterling silver trays. We had a little table and anything we wanted. If we were hungry, they'd bring us sandwiches or desserts."

The operation continued for weeks—until a streetwalker happened to look up and see the two policemen on the roof looking down with binoculars. "When they finally did spot us, we just moved over to the Flamingo." But by then the numbers of prostitutes had dwindled. In the months to come, continued pressure from the vice and patrol unit kept the Strip clear.

"What a job!" said Alamshaw. "I'm getting paid good money, I'm watching these hookers, they're getting snatched up."

One day the young policeman was on foot patrol on Las Vegas Boulevard. He chatted with pretty girls, later recognized a local hooker and asked about business. A veteran New York cop came up and introduced himself. They talked about their respective jobs, the usual shop talk, and then the NYPD officer shook his head and laughed.

"Who do you have to pay to get a job like this?"

Alamshaw understood what the New York cop meant. There was glamour and show business, but Vegas also was a friendly place where the local people, from mafioso to the mayor, knew one another. And in those days, Vegas was affordable. Cops could eat for free almost anywhere on the Strip—the unwritten rule being that you tipped your waitress generously, and you didn't go back to the same place more than once a week. Even the mobsters were approachable and mostly friendly.

ALAMSHAW CALLED IT "living the life." To be a Metro cop in the 1980s was like playing a character in a big-budget movie amid beautiful women and famous gangsters. Whether posing for photographs with tourists in a crisp khaki uniform, or rubbing elbows with famous movie stars who treated Alamshaw like a celebrity, or lounging at a sunshine-splashed pool with six-foot-tall showgirls in the middle of January, Vegas and the life of a Metro cop was a long, long way from the gritty, tough North Side of Chicago or the small, often dull Morton Grove Police Department.

And policing the storied Strip was even farther from the young officer's modest roots.

John Alamshaw, son of John and Elaine Alamshaw, grandson of immigrants from Iran who ran a roadside vegetable stand,[3] was born on July 22, 1955, in Evanston, Illinois, and shortly began to walk a fine line between that of a rambunctious youth and a delinquent.

Later in life he would say, "I was always on the razor's edge—when it came to being on the right side of the law, I could have gone either way. Some of the kids I grew up with went to jail. Others became gangsters."

There was, for example, an early childhood incident that took place on a late spring afternoon in 1959 on Broadway, a bustling main boulevard on the North Side of Chicago, not far from Wrigley Field. It was a pleasant day, temperatures were in the high sixties, kids were out playing, parents chatted on the front stoops of their three-flat apartments, and one of Chicago's more affluent citizens tooled down the street in his late-model convertible.

John, all of four years old and holding a metal pail, watched the shiny yellow car drive down the street. Then the boy flung the bucket as hard as he could into the air—and into the convertible's windshield. The driver took one look at his ruined windshield, slammed on the brakes, spotted the boy, and the foot chase was on.

"I took off running, and I ran and ran as fast as my little legs could go," Alamshaw recalled. "I found this stairway to this big building, and I hid under it."

Alamshaw had gone to ground. The victim, however, was familiar with the neighborhood and, having been a delinquent himself, knew exactly where little boys were likely to hide while lamming it. John was quickly found, taken into custody by the driver, and pulled by the ear to the front of his house, where his father and a small crowd of neighbors had gathered. When the boy saw his father, he broke loose from the convertible owner, ran to the stoop, and jumped into the elder Alamshaw's arms. The victim could not help but laugh at the boy's predicament, and a settlement to cover damages was quickly negotiated to the satisfaction of all.

Well, nearly all. His father took off his belt and gave young John an introduction to what would someday be the boy's life work: crime and punishment. *You are responsible for your actions.* In the decades to come, John Alamshaw will recite this mantra many times to criminals swept

[3] All of John's grandparents, on both sides of the family, were born in Iran of Assyrian descent and came to the U.S. at the turn of the twentieth century.

from the streets, the unremorseful confronted in interrogation rooms, youthful offenders, hardened wise guys, his own men—and his children.

There would be other lessons learned on the streets of Chicago: There are consequences when you do wrong. Take your punishment. Learn from your mistakes. Don't cry and apologize, just don't do it again. Right and wrong are more than abstract concepts. When you break the rules, you can hurt innocent people, and that's just not right.

Alamshaw would learn some lessons the hard way. In one incident, he was mistaken for a purse snatcher. In another, Alamshaw, then a junior at Nicholas Senn High School, "ditched" classes with a buddy on the pretext of selling tickets to a dance and went to rival Lake View High School on North Ashland Avenue. The two boys began wandering the campus. This was more serious than it might appear: The practice of "visiting" other high schools was strictly forbidden in Chicago, and the campus's full-time uniformed Chicago policeman spotted the two youths, determined they were truants, and placed them under arrest.

"We were handcuffed," Alamshaw said. "We faced multiple criminal charges. I knew right away we were in trouble." One possible outcome following the arrest: expulsion from Senn High in his junior year. This would mean no high-school diploma, no college, and to John's mind, no advancement in life beyond menial jobs.

The arrest paperwork was nearly complete, the handcuffs were on, and John Alamshaw was about to enter the criminal justice system, when he asked the veteran patrolman if he knew a Chicago policeman named Sam Joseph.

"Sam Joseph? Sure, I know Sam Joseph. Who doesn't?" The policeman eyed his young suspect more carefully.

"He's my dad's cousin. My second cousin," Alamshaw blurted out.

Sam Joseph was no ordinary cop. He was perhaps one of the toughest policemen in the history of the Chicago Police Department and one of the bravest. When attacks on homeless men began to rise in the city's skid row district in the mid-1960s, Sam went undercover, pretending to be drunk and vulnerable. But when a mugger flashed a knife or moved in with a club or even a firearm, Sam sprang into action and produced his shield and gun.

The policeman at Lake View High School looked John Alamshaw over one more time. "Okay, kid, you know Sam Joseph, I'm cutting you and your buddy loose. But I don't want to see you again."

Once again Alamshaw had fallen on the right side of the line.

Nicholas Senn High, on North Glenwood Avenue, was one of the oldest schools in the city. "We had some major riots at our school," Alamshaw remembered. "They were *racial* riots. They took place during my freshman and junior years. In some cases, the school was shut down for several days. Typically there were twenty-five or more squad cars surrounding my school. The black students would travel to our school on the train. They then walked from the train station to the high school. There were racial incidents during the walk—restaurant windows were busted out, and people thrown through the windows—and this expanded to the whole school. Whites would chase blacks, and blacks would chase whites. We were constantly fighting."

Like many boys in his neighborhood, Alamshaw joined a "club" loosely affiliated with Senn High School. The adolescent clubs of North Chicago in the early 1970s were more social organizations than criminal gangs, but members of Alamshaw's grandiose-sounding Sigma Phi Delta club were in fact street-hardened youths more than willing to fight for their turf.

Belonging to the club also meant safety in numbers. White or black, large or small, if you assaulted one member, you took on the entire pack. Many of the club initiations consisted of brutal beatings. Some organizations attacked applicants with two-by-four boards. "Mine wasn't that way," Alamshaw explained later. "When I went in, I had to take a series of kicks. Someone would hold you up against the wall. The others, wearing steel toe boots, would get a running start, come up, and kick you as hard as they could. The plan was to drive you into the wall. Make you go into that wall. Some guys got hurt real bad. Some cried. If you cried, that was bad, because there were thirty guys in the club, and then they would all try to break you. Some would get you from the back, and you would really get hurt. The point was to see if you could take it or not. And you had to get through two nights of that." Mostly, however, the clubs dedicated themselves to beer drinking, partying, and meeting young women who had clubs of their own.

Alamshaw is remembered by contemporaries as a slightly built youth with hair down to his shoulders and the beginnings of a dark, scraggly beard. Even tempered and possessed of a quick wit, Alamshaw asserted himself in class and argued with teachers. Like so many blue-collar kids who had already working, Alamshaw had a few dollars in his pockets, a car, and an emerging streak of stubborn independence. Restless, he wanted to break free. He thought that teachers were boring, school was a drag, and adults over thirty were not to be trusted, like leaders of the counterculture said. And although Alamshaw would attend at least one anti–Vietnam War rally—he enjoyed the spirit of rebellion but also wanted to see if hippie girls were really that promiscuous—in time he would reject the rhetoric of the counterculture and dismiss politics altogether. The boy was neither a radical nor a candidate for the Young Republicans. He wanted to be a cop. It was an idea that began when he watched with growing excitement the heroics of Efrem Zimbalist, Jr., who portrayed Inspector Lewis Erskine on the long-running Sunday night television series *The FBI*. "From the time I was a little boy, I watched the *FBI* series and other police shows; I knew what I wanted to do."

His timing was curious for someone who had no strong political ideology. Police, like the military, were not exactly popular in those revolutionary times. Riots occurred in the cities, entire neighborhoods were put to the torch, violent protests against the Vietnam War tore the nation in two. Alamshaw saw all of this and was undaunted. There were problems, to be sure, but America wasn't that bad. And anyway, *somebody* had to restore order.

At a glance, Alamshaw would have seemed an unlikely candidate for the rigid culture of police work. The scruffy look, the skirmishes with teachers, the increasing tendency to question authority. On the other hand, Alamshaw was supporting his family and filling Dad's shoes more and more each day. For $2 and $3 an hour, Alamshaw cleaned pots and pans at a frozen-food company, a dirty job that ended at midnight. During his senior year, he worked at a grocery store stocking shelves on the graveyard shift—he would work all night and go to school without sleeping. Alamshaw worked for a mannequin company, shaving the heads of the lifelike figures. He was so skilled and quick, he was given a raise after the first week. And if you walked the streets near the Cubs' ballpark, you couldn't miss Alamshaw. There he was, on his Schwinn bike, pedaling furiously around the North Side, delivering drug store prescriptions. Summers, Alamshaw worked inside Wrigley Field during baseball season, unloading trucks and handing out ice cream to the stadium vendors. And when he was old enough to drive—his first car was a used 1962 Buick convertible with one hundred thousand miles, a red Naugahyde interior, and bald tires—he delivered flowers. "It was a flashy punk's car,"

Alamshaw said later. "I was always getting stopped by the police and harassed, at least until they looked inside and saw all the flowers."

Beyond all of that, as Alamshaw's high-school years wound down, the boy underwent a profound change. In his senior year, the listless C student suddenly began racking up straight As. The fresh kid was gone; a more mature student buckled down and respected his teachers. It was as if someone had thrown a switch. And in a sense, someone had—the young man himself. Alamshaw knew exactly what he wanted: a college education. A wife and family. A career in law enforcement. He knew what he had to do.

CONTINUING THE ACADEMIC pace shown in his final year of high school, Alamshaw was a motivated scholar from the outset at Bradley University, a private school in Peoria, Illinois, halfway between Chicago and St. Louis. Bradley was a three-hour drive from the North Side, but to Alamshaw it might as well have been on the moon.

To pay for his education, Alamshaw worked as a steward at his Delta Epsilon fraternity house in exchange for free meals. He worked two more jobs while carrying a full load. On top of that, his mother took out a loan, and John received a grant.

Alamshaw graduated with honors in the spring of 1977, married his high-school sweetheart, Cindy Kawahara, and within weeks took the exam for the Morton Grove Police Department. Not surprisingly, after four years as a criminal justice major at Bradley, with classes in criminal law, patrol tactics, police administration, and crime scene investigations, the test proved as difficult as reading a stop sign. Alamshaw breezed through the examination and wound up with one of the highest scores of the year.

With his brooding brown eyes, a now stocky physique, and heavy beard, Alamshaw often was mistaken for a Hispanic. Although he spoke no Spanish, he frequently portrayed Latino criminals during police undercover operations (which led to several close calls when the real crooks addressed him in Spanish). Instead, the son of a carpenter and construction worker, he was one of approximately four hundred thousand full-blooded Assyrians living in the U.S., a proud member of a Semitic people whose roots in Mesopotamia (what is now Turkey, Syria, Iran, and Iraq)

TAXICAB AUTHORITY—STATE OF NEVAD

MARTINEZ, JUAN

11190

ACE CAB CO.   Expires 06-09-8

THE TAXICAB AUTHORITY OF
THE STATE OF NEVADA REGULATES AND SUPERVISES TH
TAXICAB INDUSTRY.
TELEPHONE 386-5393
This permit must be posted in space provided in each on-duty taxicab.

Administrator

T.A. R5-72 (Rev. 4-84)   PROPERTY OF NV. ST. TAXICAB AUTHORITY

John Alamshaw often assumed a Latino identity during his undercover work in drugs and frequently posed as a cab driver complete with license and a fake Hispanic name.
COURTESY JOHN ALAMSHAW.

date back to 2400 BC. The Assyrians were fierce warriors in a culture where battlefield success translated into wealth and power. "Just remember," Alamshaw liked to say, "the word *assassin* comes from the name *Assyrian*." He was right, too. In the time before Julius Caesar and imperial Rome, the Assyrians, famous for their iron swords, armor, battering rams, and the discovery of the 360-degree circle, built a civilization on conquest and battle.

Morton Grove recruiters knew talent when they saw it, and John Alamshaw was hired immediately.

THE YOUNG RECRUIT was put to the test almost at once. The urgent call came just after seven in the morning from the suburb of Niles, a small town next to Morton Grove. There had been an accident involving a train and its engineer. By the time Alamshaw arrived with his patrol sergeant, the snow had stopped abruptly. From a distance, as Alamshaw emerged from the patrol car, the scene in the yard alongside the railroad tracks was quite lovely. A blanket of white. A glistening patch of pure driven snow. Or maybe not so pure driven at all. As the two men approached the accident scene, the sergeant handed Alamshaw a large coal shovel.

"What's this for?" Alamshaw asked.

The sergeant offered a bleak smile but no answer. As the two men moved closer to the accident scene, John's stomach tightened. The sergeant pointed to a lump of flesh in the snow.

"This used to be a human being," the sergeant said. "Take a good look, son. Still want to be a policeman?"

Years later, Alamshaw recalled the incident in vivid detail. "I remember the snow at the train accident. There were body parts all over the snow, splotches of red. I remember seeing fingers at various locations. The gentleman's head was missing from the upper lip. One leg was off, one arm was off, and he was split down the center. Our job was to contain the major scene, look for the body parts, and bring them back to the major scene. That's what the coal shovel was for. We took the shovels, scooped up the flesh and debris, and put it all in a single body bag."

The sergeant watched his young recruit carefully, but Alamshaw neither flinched nor hesitated. "That was my first real experience with the human body, and how fragile life was, and how so sudden—and I mean *sudden*—a man's life can disappear whether he wanted it to or not, or whether he was ready or not, or responsible or not, or good or bad." Alamshaw would make two jarring discoveries that day. "The clean, attractive, orderly world we think we know is only a thin veneer," he said later. "Most people know only the glammed-up fantasy world of hype and packaging and don't understand what lies beneath the surface. Also, it isn't the triple murder that shocks the cop, or the vicious rape or the child abuse, it is the random, senseless nature of violence and death. People see only the surface and the fantasy because the horror—the evil—doesn't affect them personally. Once it affects them personally, they look at the world differently, and *then* they are terrified and *then* they want more police.

ALAMSHAW PATROLLED THE streets of Morton Grove for two years. The pay for a rookie cop in suburbia was barely $14,000 a year, and although there were gangs and the occasional drug-related murder, most of the time there was not enough action to suit the young patrolman. It was time to move on. The Chicago Police Department, the second largest in the nation at that time, might have seemed an obvious move for an ambitious young policeman, but Alamshaw knew better. Some applicants to the Chicago Police Department had jumped the waiting list by making payoffs, and promotions were bought and paid for with generous kickbacks to superior officers. The word among cops was to check out Las Vegas. The pay was good, the cost of living low—and how could you top the lifestyle?

Las Vegas it would be. Breezing through the Metro Academy, Alamshaw was a full-status officer by the summer of 1982. Metro cops worked hard in the middle of the latest Vegas expansion, and they partied even harder. "We would drink all night until five and six in the morning," Alamshaw remembered. "Then we would go home and get five or six hours sleep, work out for a few hours to stay in shape, and then go back to work. That was our day. What a life!"

In this way, Alamshaw was typical of Metro officers of that era. The city fathers may have changed the name of the department, but in the 1980s, these were still white, good-old-boy cops in the tradition of the Old

John Alamshaw and other uniformed Metro officers, including a future Clark County sheriff, during the late 1980s: (L-R) Alamshaw, Dennis Thompson, Doug Gillespie (elected sheriff in 2006), Debbie Dauthier.

COURTESY JOHN ALAMSHAW.

West—rowdy, high-spirited cowboys with a star. Metro cops had a reputation: Hard nosed. Physical. Politically incorrect.[4] There was, for example, the impromptu party at Love's Bar held at four in the morning in the
summer of 1985. The story is told by Alamshaw, who cautioned the writer
not to name all the names. "I can't tell you everything. Some of the participants are now high-ranking officers. Besides, I've got to live in this
town and work with these people."

It all started when ten policemen in civilian attire began drinking at a
cop bar at 1:00 a.m. after completing their swing shift tour from 3:00
p.m. to 1:00 a.m., a favorite of Metro officers to this day. Vegas is a
twenty-four-hour town. One can get drunk at any time of the day or
night. It is possible to gamble, enjoy a six-course meal, get laid, go grocery shopping, catch a show, go to church, or get married at midnight at
a drive-through chapel with an Elvis impersonator officiating.

It was a fiercely warm night, the temperature was still hovering at 100
degrees at midnight, and the drinking in the cop bar was heavy. By 2:30,
all of the revelers were, according to our witness, "getting thoroughly
stupid."

It is believed that at least one of the young policemen said he was getting bored listening to all the cop talk and drunken bullshit. Another said,
"Why don't we do something?" Still another cop suggested that the
group ride around in John Alamshaw's brand-new super-duper white
Dodge 4 × 4 short-bed truck.

"Okay by me," Alamshaw said. "Where you want to go?"

"Let's check out the five hundred block on Jackson Street—let's check
'em out," another cop said.

"Sounds like a plan," Alamshaw replied with a nod.

Jackson Street was in a black neighborhood known for its all-night
bars, tough characters, and heavy drug traffic near a shoe-shine stand.

The ten policemen left the bar, piled into Alamshaw's truck (with at
least four burly cops crammed into the back), and roared off at speeds not
entirely consistent with local traffic ordinances. Memories are hazy, but
there may have been a second vehicle of cops following Alamshaw's
pickup. After a somewhat erratic journey—the concept of designated
driver was not yet embraced in these parts—and with Alamshaw's stereo
system playing the theme song from *Miami Vice* at full volume, the off-

---

[4] In 1974 the police and sheriff's department combined to become the Las Vegas Metropolitan Police Department or in the local shorthand, Metro.

duty posse roared down Jackson Street and past the notorious Love's Bar and Grill,[5] a popular west side establishment tolerated by the authorities because it was a convenient place to serve a warrant, provided you brought SWAT with you.

Although it was four in the morning, the street and sidewalks were filled with late-night carousers, purveyors of street pharmaceuticals, and an assortment of young working girls accompanied by their business managers. With the arrival of the pickup truck, a few of the citizenry scattered into the shadows, but most stuck around. The denizens of 500 Jackson Street were not easily intimidated.

Years later one participant would claim the provocative appearance of ten white cops in a crime-infested black ghetto was about controlling the streets and sending a message: We are police; we come here because we can.

As the ten off-duty police piled out of the truck, various handguns could be seen dangling from their belt buckles. Despite the hour, the place was packed. When Alamshaw and his colleagues went noisily into the bar, the place fell silent. The customers could hear the ticking of the ceiling fan as it turned. Even the Metro officers may have had second thoughts, for they too were rendered momentarily mute as they sauntered up to the bar. Alamshaw's alcoholic buzz began to clear. *This may not be such a good idea. It wasn't hard to walk in; will it be so easy to walk out?*

A bar regular known as the Fat Man, sitting at a far corner table by the rear exit door, heaved to his feet, lumbered to the bar, and slowly looked over the visitors like a man checking out a new animal at the zoo.

"Either you motherfuckers are crazy—or you be cops."

"We be both," Alamshaw said, breaking into his familiar smile, an expression both pleasant and melancholy.

"We be 'The Man,' " said his burly fellow cop at the next stool.

"We be *Metro,*" said a third officer, who would someday achieve high rank in the Las Vegas Metropolitan Police Department.

"Well, shit," the Fat Man said and shuffled back to his table.

The cops ordered a round of drinks for themselves. The room remained sullen and tense until one of the policemen spun around on his stool, faced the room, and bellowed:

"Any serious drinkers here?"

---

[5] In later years, some of those on the expedition thought the bar was called the New Town.

"What's it to you, bitch?" a voice shot back.

"'Cause the next fucking round is on me. Metro's buying!"

The room burst into table-banging, glass-clanking, order-shouting bedlam, punctuated by a few salutes to the valor of the local police and a flurry of "motherfuckers" of undetermined meaning.

The cops bought the next round. And the round after that and the one after that. Pretty soon the sinewy and knife-scarred drug dealer at the other rear corner table, a silent partner in the bar and a local enforcer with a serious rap sheet, was buying the cops a drink, and the police moved to the tables to join the customers—where they bought even more alcohol for all hands. The lone waitress would later recall that she ran her skinny legs till they nearly fell off, and this would have been the worst night of her life except that the white boys were throwing dollars at her like she was one of the blonde bitches at the titty bars the white boys like so much.

"We bought everybody drinks," Alamshaw recalled many years later. "That night we ended up hanging out with people who generally didn't trust us and who never drank with police. I think we shocked the people in the bar, and maybe we shocked ourselves. There were a few tense moments. Something could have happened. Our entrance wasn't sedate. But it turned out all right in the end."

For a few hours at the notorious saloon, there was a rare and peaceful truce in the ghetto. The improvised party among whites and blacks, cops and citizens, lasted until dawn, when the ten policemen staggered out of the bar, climbed into Alamshaw's truck, and headed for home. Of the visit to the west side ghetto, Alamshaw later said, "Oh my God! If something like that happened today, we'd all be disciplined."

It was 1985. Las Vegas was not only growing but growing up. In the next decade, Las Vegas's two-fisted police, including the young cop from Chicago, would be modernized, professionalized, sanitized, computerized, rendered politically correct, and introduced to heavy and unwelcome jolts of affirmative action. On Alamshaw's watch Las Vegas became a famous city. An expensive, crowded, and decidedly more dangerous city. A city where cocaine, aka blow and nose candy, turned streets and alleys into war zones. It was snowing in the desert.

Chapter 12

TONY MONTANA

*m*idnight. September 1988.

The gray BMW sedan with dealer tags pulled in front of the low-income apartment building on the east side of Las Vegas. A heavyset Mexican accompanied by a muscular bodyguard stepped onto the street and climbed the stairs of the apartment to the third floor. The building was a former motel, with the front doors of the units opening onto a concrete walkway visible from the street.

As the two visitors knocked on the door of apartment 317, a black SUV with tinted windows pulled behind the parked BMW. The fat man looked down at the SUV and nodded. The driver flashed his lights in recognition.

Across the street, in another apartment complex on the third floor, Vigoa watched carefully through Russian-made night vision binoculars. The bulky Mexican and his bodyguard knocked again on the apartment door. There was no answer. The unit, leased by Vigoa in the name of one of his customers and used for drug transactions, was empty tonight. Jose swung the glasses to the street and the SUV. The night vision was good; Jose could see, inside the vehicle, the glow from a cigarette that was lit and quickly extinguished, provoking a profane rebuke from other occupants in the blacked-out vehicle. From their vantage point, Vigoa and his support team had a clear view and a clear field of fire. Just after midnight, Vigoa and three members of his drug crew, all heavily armed and positioned at open windows in a darkened apartment, counted their human targets. In the manner of a surgeon preparing for a major operation, Vigoa looked over tonight's instruments of choice: a Colt AR-15 assault rifle with six fully loaded magazines, a Heckler & Koch HK-91 assault rifle with scope and three more magazines, and a freshly cleaned and lubricated Colt Python handgun with boxes of ammunition.

Slowly, Vigoa pulled back the curtain of the window overlooking the street, the two vehicles, and the apartment building. The fat Mexican, still panting from the climb up the three flights of stairs, continued to rap impatiently on 317's door. But it was the SUV and its occupants that Vigoa watched carefully. A double cross was about to become a triple cross, Jose knew. The fat Mexican, posing as a buyer of Jose Vigoa's narcotics, had no intention of paying for the goods. He planned on taking them and killing anyone who resisted. "I will shoot the crazy Cuban in *both* eyes if he says a fucking word," the Mexican told his men, a threat relayed to Vigoa by an informant.

Vigoa was aware of the scheme. He also knew the Mexican's real name, his home address, the names of his wife and children, the number of assailants in the SUV, and the preferred weapons of his would-be killers. He knew the Mexican's credit rating and how many of his credit cards were in arrears. There would be no drug sale tonight—that was certain—but there would be violence.

Vigoa picked up the AR-15 and took aim. His three companions tensed at the window and lifted their weapons as well. Vigoa shook his head. "*No ahora,*" he said. Not now. He returned the rifle to the table.

What Vigoa called the Fiery Demon was stirring now; it would soon be awake. Vigoa could feel its raw power and white heat gathering strength throughout his body. Once he had feared the feeling and thought that it drew him into a life of crime and brutality, but Vigoa knew better now. The Fiery Demon was his shield and salvation, the primal force that kept him alive.

It was awake and growing stronger, and it would soon be free to do its work.

SINCE THE HOTEL workers' strike in April 1984, since becoming a full-fledged gangster, the time had passed quickly for Vigoa. He had survived nearly five violent and turbulent years, and by the fall of 1988, he was arguably the most successful Marielito criminal in the country. Vigoa, known on the street as Manolo, was a drug trafficker with cartel connections on both coasts.

Vigoa's rise was decidedly American, a kind of dark and violent Horatio Alger success story. Vigoa began in the trenches of the drug trade, selling freebase cocaine, or "rocks," in ghettos while learning the business from the ground up. In the beginning he also served as "muscle" for crack dealers on the west side of Las Vegas. At that time, the area was a drug-infested hellhole of crime and poverty mere blocks from the north end of the Strip and west of what is now the Stratosphere Hotel.

Vigoa earned $2,000 a day "covering the back" of Cuban crack dealers. When his Cuban employer suddenly dropped out of the drug business (the rare soul who made his money and retired peacefully), Vigoa took over the franchise. Supplying fifty addicts, Vigoa saw his cash flow double within six months. This was serious money, but Jose was learning. "The crack addicts would kill their own mother for a rock," Vigoa recalled. "There were better ways to make money. The crack business was dangerous because it was wildly unpredictable. Some of those people were crazier than *me!*"

Vigoa's sophistication was growing by the day. He understood not only that a drug lord's power flowed from the barrel of a gun but that money laundering was the real secret to longevity in the narcotics underworld. Vigoa was as comfortable with the white-collar criminals who processed his money into taxable revenue as he was with murderous collectors, enforcers, and street-level dealers. "I'm a good citizen, even though I'm not even a citizen," he liked to say. "I pay my taxes to the penny. I just don't say where the money really came from. Otherwise, I'm completely straight with the IRS, and they don't bother me, no way."

In 1986 Vigoa began to sell pure cocaine to more affluent customers. He was now making upward of $50,000 a month in profits, buying homes, "living like a king," but also facing new problems. The issue was always how to explain one's sudden wealth. In Vigoa's case, the dilemma was how to account for the sudden infusion of cash, not only to his wife and family, but to the government.

The answer was to move into more legitimate business to launder the cash. Vigoa bought a body and paint shop that on paper must have looked like the most successful body and paint shop in the history of car repair. "I was paying $20,000 to $30,000 to the IRS every quarter. The IRS didn't care where the money came from—all they wanted to know was how much I was making and were they getting their share." He began cultivating professionals to help manage the cash. American bankers and financial planners looking for quick cash under the table were eager to help. "White-collar criminals don't need guns to make money, they just help me and make a little too," Vigoa said. "My English wasn't that good, but I began to notice whenever there was an opportunity to make money, people understood me just fine."

Although the clientele had improved, the threat from drug thieves who preyed on dealers remained a constant problem. Here Jose differed from other dealers, some of whom paid protection money to the rip-off gangs. Jose welcomed the interference. There would be no tribute, only retaliation. "They want to harvest the apples," Vigoa was fond of saying, "but they don't want to plant the seeds or fertilize the ground or grow the orchard. I will bury these animals in the orchard."

From his beginnings as a crack dealer, to his days as a cocaine supplier to more affluent clients, and now as a high-level cocaine distributor to cities throughout the U.S., Vigoa was a student of the drug trade. He adapted new tactics as his business grew. Like any good CEO, he wondered: Can the risks be reduced and the cash flow increased? He thought he could do just that, not only by fending off rival gangsters and the police, but by stabilizing the business and controlling the anarchy and violence. He studied the business and analyzed all of its components, from the most critical to the mundane. He sought new ways to recognize and avoid police stings. He reviewed pricing, delivery systems, partnership issues, relations with cartels. He examined his intelligence gathering and communications. He began to train midlevel confederates and build layers of insulation between himself and the actual sale of drugs.

Between 1984 and 1990, Jose Vigoa developed what mainstream entrepreneurs would call a business plan and a corporate philosophy, complete with goals, assumptions, revenue projections, marketing strategies, alliances, and a code of conduct for himself and his employees.

For a child of communism, he was turning out to be one hell of a capitalist.

Many dealers were also addicts and used their profits to support their habit, but Vigoa did not. His abstinence was not about morality—it was about life and death. "You have to keep the brain clear," he warned his confederates. "You have to be alert at all times, even when you're sleeping or making love or with your family. You have to see farther than other men and around corners. You have to see into the hearts of men. You have to read the eyes of your enemy and know they are about to strike, or someday they will try to kill you."

One of the benefits of staying clean was that Vigoa never made the mistake of trusting anyone; he automatically assumed that any newcomer was a thief or an assassin. This was a basic rule: Never trust anyone you don't know and haven't done business with before. If the fat Mexican at the east side apartment complex, for example, were an honorable man seeking to acquire good product at a fair price, he could be expected to arrive with a bodyguard but not a small force of gunmen.

Another Jose Vigoa precept: Always control the meeting place. This was critical, similar to maneuvering your enemy into a disadvantageous position on the battlefield. He employed multiple apartments to conduct his business. They were always in "hot" neighborhoods—undesirable, crime-ridden environments where tenants came and went freely, and where proper ID was not required. The apartments were on side streets with multiple avenues of egress and ingress. This attention to what military strategies call terrain would become a Vigoa trademark.

The meeting places shared another characteristic: They could be easily placed under surveillance without fear of detection. This was of utter importance to Vigoa because he employed a private-investigation firm—a full-time, high-end, well-known PI company that worked energetically for Vigoa Enterprises around the clock. "This was my secret weapon," he reflected. "No one, even those close to me, knew that I used a well-known private investigator from a big PI company in town. I used him to check out new customers. I used him to investigate people I had known for years to see if anything had changed with them financially or with their credit rating. My man was very good. Federal agents use fake names, of course, and a good background check can uncover this. The federals and police never give up their real home address and always provide a phone number from a house rented by the FBI. When the investigator discovers this, the next step is to check the utility bill. It tells a lot. Sometimes, when things didn't add up, the PI would follow the subject 24-7 until we learned everything. We found many people were not who they said they were. Some had legitimate reasons, some were trying to set me up, some were robbers who moved from city to city, like the fat Mexican. This private-investigator service was full-time and very expensive. But it was worth every dollar."

The use of a well-connected PI also served another purpose, one familiar to many mainstream business managers: Collections was often an issue in the drug business. "The private investigator would help me find customers who took off with my money or drugs. In a matter of weeks, I would find my runaway clients. Some were living like kings. Oh, this was fun. I really enjoyed going after someone and seeing in their eyes the surprise of being found so fast. What they didn't realize was I knew all about them *before* they ran away. I knew where they were likely to go, where their family lived, the name of their girlfriend. That was always an unpleasant surprise, when we go to the girlfriend's house, call the client, and say, 'Guess where we are, you dumb-ass.' "

Determining that he was not yet ready for global trafficking, Vigoa analyzed the top two tiers of the drug trade and decided to focus on the smaller market sometimes neglected by the big players. As Vigoa saw it, there were two types of customers. There were the "little sharks," who purchased fewer than 50 kilos (125 pounds) of cocaine per month for street resale or to supply well-heeled customers. These were profitable deals but small enough for Vigoa to know the buyer intimately and to maintain control, security, and intelligence. There also were the "big sharks," who purchased between 100 and 500 kilos per month. Although Vigoa enjoyed the credit from the cartels to deal on this level, he may have found the $1.2 million wholesale price for 100 kilos sobering.

Also, supplying the big sharks required heavy security, greater man-power, and a larger nationwide organization. Vigoa realized the big sharks inevitably appear on law enforcement radar, especially that of the DEA (Drug Enforcement Administration, part of the U.S. Department of Justice) and FBI. Vigoa was satisfied to swim with the little sharks while slowly building his drug empire, which by 1988 had expanded well beyond Las Vegas.

In addition, Vigoa began to dream of building lower-income and middle-income custom homes for the masses. Like others, he realized that the unbridled growth of Las Vegas was not a passing stage. By the late 1980s, four thousand to six thousand new residents were pouring into Clark County each month, and they had to live somewhere. Vigoa had the cash flow to build those houses.

In 1988 Vigoa's reputation among the cartels and major drug players was that of a tough, smart, and honest dealer. A little mercurial and vio-lent, even for this business, but someone who could be counted on to live up to his word and pay the money on time. To the Miami wholesalers, Vigoa was a rising star in a hot town. Although a Marielito—not a positive credit on anyone's résumé in those days—Vigoa was considered a stand-up guy in the business, and in the coming years, he would prove this reputation to be well founded. In recognition of his reliability, the cartels sold cocaine to Vigoa for $12,000 a kilo—thousands below the usual price.

In the drug trade, as in all business, the one blindingly unassailable rule for success was to buy low and sell high, and that Vigoa did. In New York he sold cocaine for $25,000 to $27,000 a kilo; in Seattle he charged between $35,000 to $40,000 a kilo; in Alaska, $45,000 to $50,000. Delivery of a 100-kilo load could generate close to $2 million in profits. Better yet, the occasional well-publicized drug busts that took place in Miami, New York, and Los Angeles sharply reduced the supply of narcotics. Vigoa always maintained a cocaine reserve for dry spells, and as a result of the police crackdowns, his profits soared. For Jose Vigoa, the war on drugs was a net gain.

Vigoa and his crew spoke in a primitive code. "NY 25" meant that a New York customer wanted 25 kilos. If there was more than one customer in New York, the order might be "NY A 25, NY B 10, NY C 35."

In the beginning Vigoa made the deliveries and picked up the money himself, backed by gunmen. The meetings would take place either at locations owned by Vigoa or in midsize hotels. After the order was placed by phone prior to the meeting, Vigoa would have the option of determining when and where the delivery was to occur. "I would then call my customer back and set the meeting for as fast as I could, giving me just enough time to make my surveillance," he explained. "My requirements were simple: I wanted to be able to view the entrance doors, check out the perimeter, look for suspicious vehicles and people acting funny. If this was going to be a police setup or a hit by a rival gang, I would be able to detect the problem, and more than once I did. When I spotted trouble, I played stupid just long enough to set up my own trap."

Once assured that the meeting place was in order and the transaction legitimate, Vigoa would call his delivery crew that waited nearby. Messenger and guard would arrive and transfer the drugs to Jose, who would then make the delivery in person. Eventually Vigoa trained others to deliver the drugs and pick up the cash, but there was one exception: If the deal was perceived to be a setup, a hit, or a rip-off, Vigoa insisted on dealing with it personally.

—

AS FOR THE fat Mexican, Vigoa knew from his intelligence gathering that a purported $50,000 cocaine sale to a new Mexican street crew was in fact a drug rip-off. Vigoa was the intended victim. The declared buyer was from El Paso with a reputation for robbing and sometimes killing other drug dealers. There were three gunmen in the SUV with pistols and automatic weapons, and they were there to kill Vigoa on behalf of a rival drug dealer and steal his money as compensation.

At 12:24 a.m. the fat man gave up knocking on the apartment door, returned to the street, and dialed Vigoa's number on a pay phone. The bodyguard remained on the third floor, leaning over the railing and watching the street. The bodyguard whistled at the fat man, who looked up. Grinning, the bodyguard unzipped his fly and began urinating over the side. The fat man laughed too.

Vigoa's phone, on mute, began to blink. He picked it up.

"You late," the fat Mexican said.

"How many dead men you got in that nice SUV?" Vigoa said pleasantly.

"What?"

"I said, how many dead men? Maybe three, maybe four? But they can't be as fat as you, or the tires will blow out."

"Fuck you, man!" the fat man snarled before realizing what Vigoa had just said.

Vigoa put down the phone, swept up the AR-15, and leaned out the window. "Hey, *come pinga,* you tough enough to chew on this?"

There were three quick shots followed by a full automatic burst. Vigoa's crew opened fire from the other apartment windows.

The Mexican, his eyes wide open, his mouth agape, bounced up and down to the rhythm of the heavy gunfire, then dropped to the ground, his torso bending forward, his body folding like a pocket knife.

Vigoa concentrated his heavy fire on the SUV. The driver of the SUV managed to start his engine before a dozen rounds shredded the windshield. The car lurched forward, banged into the BMW, and then stalled. The left rear door started to open. More rounds poured into the car. The car alarm began to go off.

Vigoa looked up at the third floor. The bodyguard taking a piss was frozen in midstream.

"I'll get him, Jose!" one of Vigoa's gunmen yelled.

"No, he's a famous man, let him go," Vigoa commanded.

The gunmen turned.

"Who is he?" Ramon asked.

"Oh, you heard of him." Vigoa started to laugh. "He's the dude you always hear people talking about. He's the dude left holding his dick!"

Chapter 13

BONES

In 1987, when Jose Vigoa's reputation was that of a lethally volcanic drug lord, John Alamshaw's standing among other cops was generally favorable. In his fifth year at Metro, the Chicago native was known to be intelligent, honest, more mature than most, and well educated. He had a quick, puckish sense of humor. He was conservative like most of his fellow cops, steady, even-tempered, resistant to change, respectful of tradition, and "a stand-up guy"—cop code for a brother officer who will come to your aid if you seriously fuck up.

But in one crucial area, Alamshaw, for all his training, education, and experience, was an unknown, though this too was changing. Something was coming, hard and cold, and for Alamshaw it would bring about one more test—and a career-defining moment. On a steaming Las Vegas afternoon, John Alamshaw, surrounded by an angry mob and unable to summon help, found himself asking a policeman's most gut-wrenching question: How many people will I have to kill in the next few minutes to survive this day?

The young policeman never saw it coming. By now a Special Weapons and Tactics (SWAT) sergeant, Alamshaw drove an unmarked car into a drug-infested area known as Donna Street in North Las Vegas. This was routine. Immediately his black Thunderbird was surrounded by cocaine dealers. This was part of the drill as well. "Within seconds of being in the area, numerous sellers made contact with us," Alamshaw said. "When two subjects came up to our vehicle (one acted as a lookout, the other as a seller), one subject stuck his hand in the window of the passenger side and showed us approximately ten rocks of cocaine. At that point my sergeant and I agreed we would take these two dealers off the street."

Alamshaw and the sergeant jumped out of the undercover car.

"Cops!" one suspect yelled as he took off down the street.

"They're running," Alamshaw shouted to his partner.

"As I exited the driver's door, and the sergeant exited his door, the subjects got nervous and started running," Alamshaw said. "I took off after the guy holding the drugs, and the sergeant took off after the lookout."

After chasing separate suspects in opposite directions, Alamshaw and his sergeant found themselves six blocks apart. This was not a good tactical situation. Alamshaw had no radio, no handcuffs, and no backup. He carried a 9 mm Walter PPKS pistol that held seven rounds and no spare magazine or baton.

The drug dealer, a young man of ample size and some notoriety in his world, was now cornered in the projects and out of breath. The two men faced each other panting heavily. The dealer looked at Alamshaw, assessed the growing number of local residents gathering nearby, and began to smile.

Although he had never attended classes at the Metro Police Academy, the suspect understood the first rule of police work:

DO NOT ATTEMPT TO MAKE AN ARREST—
UNLESS YOU CAN *MAKE* THE ARREST.

The two men continued to confront each other, cop and dealer. Alamshaw could hear footsteps and a rustle behind him. The shuffling and scraping of a mass of people. The crowd grew larger—and closer. The drug dealer chuckled. This was the dealer's neighborhood, and the cop was about to find that out.

"Hey, little man," said the dealer, "you live here too?"

"No, I don't. *Metro.* You're under arrest."

The dealer grinned broadly, his gold-capped front tooth sparkling in the sun. "No shit."

"You're going to jail," Alamshaw said.

"I ain't going nowhere," the suspect said in a stage whisper audible to the approaching locals. "You best look behind you, officer."

Alamshaw turned just in time to see the crowd advancing across the street and a half-empty Bud Light beer can fly through the air. Alamshaw ducked. The can missed Alamshaw's head by inches and bounced off a low wall, splashing the drug dealer's leg with beer. The dealer whooped and laughed again, dancing to the side.

Alamshaw, in his report:

> A large crowd of about forty local residents soon gathered around me. To make it worse, the subject's family was in the crowd. The mob surrounded me by about 280 degrees. They were agitated and hostile. They kept walking toward me, telling me I wasn't going to be able to take him with me. I would point the gun at the crowd, then swing the weapon back at the subject while attempting to keep the subject under control. I kept going back and forth, but the crowd kept advancing.

It wasn't that the drug dealer was the most popular man in the neighborhood or that the local people approved of drugs—a poison that corrupted their children, ravaged entire families, sucked the local economy dry, and ignited savage gun battles in the impoverished district—or even that the black residents hated the police. This was something more fundamental.

A young woman carrying a toddler spoke for some of the crowd when she yelled, "Get the fuck out of our neighborhood, white boy!"

Alamshaw was now cut off, and the crowd was becoming an angry mob. Its younger members began throwing rocks, bottles, and even pieces of a broken cement block. The debris rained on both Alamshaw and the drug dealer. Another beer can skipped off the sidewalk and bounced into the drug dealer's knee. He cried out.

"You hit the *wrong* motherfucker!" the indignant suspect said.

By now it was apparent that both arrestor and arrestee were in harm's way.

The dealer began to negotiate with the cop.

"Yo, my man, you best lets me go. Somebody gonna get hurt here very soon."

Alamshaw moved his pistol from the crowd to the dealer's head. "You're going to jail," he said firmly. An unopened bottle of Heineken, suggesting a more sophisticated palate, flew through the air, bounced off a fence intact and crashed onto the sidewalk, showering them both with glass and more beer. The dealer began to panic.

"Just lemme go. Go about your business, I go about mine."

"The crowd was within ten feet of me while backing me into the driveway of a house," Alamshaw later wrote. "I kept my prisoner close by at gunpoint. I pounded on the door of the house trying to get somebody to call the police. I knew my sergeant was looking for me, and by this time I was really concerned. I pounded on the door, and no one answered. I knew I was in real trouble."

An ancient, heavily taped softball flew out of the crowd and bounced benignly at Alamshaw's feet.

The alarmed dealer offered Alamshaw a way out: If Alamshaw backed off and canceled the arrest, the dealer would wave his arm, and the angry mob would "part like the Red Sea."

"Shut up," Alamshaw snapped.

The dealer pleaded with the SWAT officer. "Ah, look here, Detective, we both gonna get got if you don't let me go."

Alamshaw dodged another beer can and shook his head. "I'm taking you to jail." The mob pressed forward.

Backed against a small house, Alamshaw was trapped. He knocked on the front door. "At this point," he recalled, "I realized I was going to have to shoot somebody or be killed myself. This was becoming a riot. Only it wasn't clear who the crowd was after—me, the suspect, or both of us. Now individuals were running up and swinging at me. Another tried to grab me by the arm and pull me into the throng. The mob pressed me against the fence by the driveway. My subject kept trying to get away from me while at the same time agitating the crowd. Several people said they were going to take him and then get me."

Alamshaw pounded on the front door again. He could hear the resident inside lock the door and draw the curtains. Alamshaw silently counted the number of rounds in his semiautomatic pistol—not nearly enough to deal with the angry mob. *How many will I have to kill to end this?*

Many policemen go their entire careers without ever discharging their firearm on the street. Now Alamshaw, literally backed against a cement block wall, was prepared to empty a fifteen-round magazine into a howling mob.

Two men, one huge, hopped over the fence and advanced forward. One swung a board torn from a picket fence. *This is it,* Alamshaw thought, slipping his finger from the trigger guard to the trigger. And then, a split second from catastrophe, the onrushing rioters stopped.

Their heads turned. As if on cue, almost the entire mob turned to look up the street.

They saw police cars hurtling around the corner. Flashing red and blue lights bathed Donna Street. Sirens wailed. Then the sound of many vehicle doors opening and closing. Police reinforcements.

"Within seconds of my having to make a life-altering decision, the cavalry appeared," Alamshaw said. "I didn't know how or why. The units poured into the area. Everybody you can imagine."

Squealing around the corner came patrol cars, gang units, SWAT cops, and even the fire department. Guns drawn, the police formed a battle line and approached the crowd. The mob began to disassemble, and the two hoodlums closest to Alamshaw melted into the night. The drug dealer, seeking to save face, took Alamshaw's left hand and raised it overhead with his own, like a boxing referee anointing the winner of a title fight. The mood of the mob changed from murderous to almost festive—and the crowd did indeed part as the policeman and his prisoner walked to Alamshaw's car.

As Alamshaw and his prisoner moved through the open corridor, the crowd began to applaud.

"That white boy, he's got heart!" somebody shouted.

"He's a shorty, but he's *baaad!*" a woman yelled.

The locals chuckled and then began to drift away. They were unimpressed with all the flashing lights and police firepower. After all, this was Donna Street, and they had seen it all before.

Alamshaw went back to work. "I borrowed a set of handcuffs and put the drug dealer in the back of a cruiser. He looked at me and seemed relieved. Alamshaw later met the woman who called the police. She worked in the records section of police headquarters. "Why didn't you open your door?" he asked her.

"They would have knocked it down anyway," she said. "I knew you were in trouble, and I called the police."

The Donna Street altercation answered more than a few questions about the character of John Alamshaw. Word got around among gangsters and lawmen alike. As Alamshaw cruised through the toughest of neighborhoods, the miscreants would recognize the policeman with the drooping mustache. They would catch his eye and nod.

One day Alamshaw walked down the corridor of his substation. "I'm taking you to jail," a voice from an unseen detective said from within a cubicle.

A few steps more, and there was another comment from another unseen cop working at his desk. "Hey, bro, I'm taking you to jail."

Alamshaw laughed. He had made his bones.

Chapter 14

THE FBI VERSUS JOSE VIGOA

*n*ever let it be said that FBI agents, those neat, courteous, well-spoken gentlemen in conservative gray suits and sensible black shoes, lack a sense of humor. The dour ghost of J. Edgar Hoover aside, these G-men can be *funny*. Consider:

It is four o'clock in the afternoon on April 4, 1990, in Las Vegas. Another pleasant and sunshine-filled Nevada day. Five FBI agents in a convoy of vehicles that includes a 1979 black Corvette used in undercover work pull up to the Sahara-Lamb mini storage facility at 4375 East Sahara Avenue, a half mile east of the I-15 freeway. Jose Vigoa may have limited his flourishing drug enterprise in terms of customers, but in the dope culture, little sharks have a way of attracting big sharks of another species: the FBI drug squad. After two years of distant courtship between America's premiere law enforcement agency and Las Vegas's most aggressive drug lord, the two factions are about to make each other's acquaintance.

Strangely, what is about to transpire will be an accidental encounter that neither Vigoa nor the FBI has sought or desired. Seeking to avoid a head-on confrontation and arrest is Supervising Agent George Lyford. "We identified the storage warehouse and had enough probable cause to get a search warrant," Lyford recalled of the storage yard raid. "Our intent, and we discussed this beforehand, was we didn't want to bust him because that would have caused us to have to take him to court right away—which means you have to file an affidavit, which means you have to give discovery and lay out your case. So we came out with the idea to get a search warrant, search the storage shed, take the drugs, and leave the search warrant inside."

By FBI standards—by any agency's rules—this was a highly unorthodox operation. The agents would seize whatever dope they found, plaster the warehouse with copies of the search warrant—and then leave. If Vigoa appeared in the middle of the raid, and the agents found dope, they would merely write Jose a ticket. "It would be *just* like a parking ticket," Lyford said. "We decided we were just going to take the drugs and leave the search warrant, which you are required to do by law, and then he's not charged. He can't go to court, we don't have to give any discovery [including the identity of an informant or undercover agent], and our investigation can continue."

Irregular but creative. "If you do something like this, it creates a whole series of problems for him," Lyford said. "Where's my drugs? Who has got my drugs? What's going on? And if he owes somebody for those drugs, yeah, that's a problem. What's he going to do when the cartel asks for their money? Come knock on *our* door and ask where his drugs are? We would smile and reply, Okay, what, Jose? Do you want to admit this is your property?"

Lyford shook his head. "It didn't quite happen that way, of course."

AT 4:03 P.M., MORE OR LESS on schedule, the FBI raiding party, which included Lyford and special agents Dan Storey, Brett Shields, Rick Baken, and John Wilson, pulled into the exterior parking lot of the Sahara-Lamb mini storage area, entered the office, and identified themselves to the manager, Louise Grudier. The agents dressed informally, without the usual FBI jackets and ball caps. The FBI men were directed to storage locker 436—the unit had been rented by Jose Manuel Vigoa on February 20—and Murphy's Law immediately kicked in. The lock on the shed door was massive; an ordinary bolt cutter would not work. After grunting and straining, banging and shoving, the agents went to work with a crowbar. "We had to derail the storage shed entry door and force it into an open position," Baken said. By 5:09 p.m. the storage shed was finally open.

The Vigoa unit appeared normal at first glance. Fairly new and in good condition, the shed measured twenty feet deep, twelve feet wide and twelve feet high. Baken entered the rectangular room to find chest-high boxes to the right and left and a narrow aisle down the middle leading to a work space in the rear. The unit was otherwise packed to the high ceiling with furniture, clothing, appliances, a toy box, sporting equipment, and other junk. Baken was dismayed. *We're never going to get through this,* he thought. *It'll take four or five men an entire week to open every box*. But the veteran agent, who joined the bureau in 1969, always believed that if you worked smart, you didn't have to work as hard. "The shed was just too big and too full," Baken said. "So I took a folding chair, opened it up in the alley in front of the shed, and just sat looking at all this stuff. This is what I remember most about that day. It was just too big of a project, and I guess because I was lazy and didn't want to go through that tedious process, I just put a chair in front and thought about it. If I were a dealer, how would I be able to get to the dope but also have it well hidden? So I thought about it some more. It actually was a very nice day to bask in the sun."

By then the other agents were rooting through the piles while muttering under their breath about the dickhead slacker lounging on the chair in front of the shed. Baken got off the chair, walked down the narrow pathway in the middle of the shed, and noticed a blue rollaway bed. He moved in closer. The experience gained from twenty years of FBI work, including tours on the drug squad and the organized-crime squad, told Baken this was the place to search. He reached between the folds of the mattress and pulled out a large sandwich bag filled with more than 230 grams of cocaine. Next to the mattress, in a maroon cloth bag, was a loaded Colt Python .357 Magnum revolver and two boxes of ammunition. Then Baken observed a wooden table with a black bag underneath it. They emptied the bag's contents. A dinner plate covered with a white, powdery residue, a weighing scale, two bottles of boric acid, plastic baggies, grain alcohol, and duct tape. Drug paraphernalia. Under a wooden desk in the rear of the storage unit, about five feet from the mattress, the agents also found, neatly stowed in their respective cases, a well oiled Colt AR-15 rifle modified for full automatic fire and a high-end Heckler & Koch HK-91 rifle that also had been "altered to permit select fire capability with both fully automatic and semiautomatic firing," as Special Agent Richard A. Crum, a firearms expert, would later testify.

The agents had found what they wanted: dope, gear, and firearms. Before leaving, they taped the search warrant on the interior walls and front door. "Too bad we didn't do this three days ago," one of the agents quipped. "This would have been a great April Fools' joke for Mr. Vigoa."

—

JOKE OR NOT, the raid on the storage shed had been years in the making. Since 1988 the FBI considered Jose a rising star in the world of drug distribution. A special operation called CuCoke was set into motion, and Vigoa himself was given the code name Tony Montana.

As many as thirty agents and technical experts eventually worked the Vigoa case in one way or another, but it was a frustrating investigation. The bureau was familiar with the hide-and-seek techniques of high-level distributors, but this Cuban seemed more wily and insulated than most. Vigoa still was in business, and he wasn't slowing down. His construction company was booming, he was investing in Florida real estate, and—to finance his capitalist endeavors—Vigoa was moving Lady Snow all over creation.

Then Ariel Gonzalez, a Cuban immigrant, walked off the street and into the FBI's fortified regional office at 700 East Charleston Boulevard in central Las Vegas. His appearance was the law enforcement equivalent of finding a winning lottery ticket in the trash. Gonzalez announced to the receptionist that he had important information about drug traffic in Las Vegas. After a short wait, he was taken to the office of Special Agent Dan Storey. When Gonzalez dropped the name of Jose Manuel Vigoa, Storey realized this was an important moment in his own career.

Storey summoned agent Larry Brito, who spoke Spanish fluently. When Gonzalez casually mentioned that he knew a midlevel drug pusher named Jose Diaz, Storey asked the name of Diaz's supplier. "He's an old friend of Jose Vigoa," the informant replied. "Vigoa is his supplier." Storey and Brito exchanged glances. When Gonzalez mentioned that Jose Vigoa had just received a major new drug shipment, Storey and Brito were excited.

Brito agreed to go undercover and make the buys. Ariel Gonzalez was promptly engaged by the FBI as a paid confidential informant, a status that placed the Cuban several echelons above the everyday snitch. The agents conferred with their supervisors. "This may be an opening," they said. At the moment there wasn't enough evidence to prosecute Vigoa, there had been no "hand to hand" buys (meaning directly from his hands to those of the FBI undercover agent), and there were legal and tactical reasons not to move just yet. Other cases could be compromised, Lyford warned. "We don't have a case just yet." So what to do?

The FBI could continue the investigation in the hopes of gathering useful evidence while allowing Jose's crew to sell or farm out the coke to lower-echelon networks. In the realpolitik world of narcs versus drug dealers, this theory made sense. The only thing worse than *not* making a bust was making one that prematurely revealed what evidence had been gathered and exposed FBI sources.

A decision was made: Don't arrest Vigoa. Continue to build a case. Find a way to penetrate the layers of insulation that shield him. But also, somehow, keep the new shipment of cocaine off the street.

Storey was appointed case agent. His team included Brito, a bilingual former Texas cowboy and part Apache who had spent his first ten years at the bureau as an undercover agent. Brito would pose as a combination dealer and pimp named Antonio (Tony) Villarreal who supplied cocaine to prostitutes. Also on the team were Rick Baken, the son of an FBI man, a twenty-year veteran, and a former Mafia undercover agent; Brett Shields, a tall, athletic, sandy-haired rookie working his first case, who could pass for a graduate student; and George Lyford, the supervising agent of the Vegas drug squad, an ex-marine and former Buffalo deputy sheriff, who would serve as senior special agent, overseeing Storey. Lyford's addition to the CuCoke team suggests the operation was at this point a high-priority undertaking: A veteran agent with seventeen years on the job, including tours at FBI headquarters in Washington, Lyford is tough, hard nosed and decidedly old school.

Brito's assignment was to use Ariel Gonzalez as a go-between, make contact with Jose Diaz, befriend the older man, and arrange to meet Vigoa, the main target. Brito would pose as a buyer who has come to Las Vegas to "cool off" after legal problems back in Texas. He wanted to buy cocaine to sell in Chicago. On November 3, 1989, at eleven-thirty at night, Brito arrived at the home of Gonzalez, who then called Diaz and introduced Brito on the telephone. Brito, in his undercover role as Tony, said he wanted to buy four ounces of coke for his prostitutes. They agreed on price. Diaz said he could deliver the powder within two hours.

Brito alerted his surveillance team by radio. The first meeting between Brito and Diaz was set for 5:00 p.m. at the 7-Eleven store at the corner of Missouri Avenue and Boulder Highway. The FBI moved into position. At 5:10 p.m. Diaz rolled up in a maroon Oldsmobile sedan. The two men met at the front door of the 7-Eleven. "Let's do this in my car," said Diaz, who grinned self-consciously but otherwise appeared calm and cordial. They both got into the Olds. There was no small talk.

"Do you have the stuff?" Brito asked.

"Yep."

Diaz offered a plastic bag that contained "a white crystalline substance said to be cocaine," Brito later reported. Brito handed the dope dealer $3,600. "Would you mind counting the money, make sure it's okay?" the agent said. Diaz was happy to comply. They shook hands. Brito and Diaz agreed to do more business in the future.

At the FBI office, Brito and Storey removed a portion of the powder and tested the sample for cocaine. There was a sigh of relief: The preliminary field test was positive. The agents tagged it and shipped the bag to the DEA laboratory in San Francisco for further analysis. The report came back as high-grade cocaine, as good as the lab had seen in years. "My supplier has lots more in a large stash," Diaz told Brito, giving the undercover agent his home phone number. By giving Brito his number, the dealer was encouraging Brito to bypass Ariel Gonzalez and call Diaz directly.

From this point forward, the FBI recorded phone calls between the agent and his dealer. An electronic monitoring system known as a pen register also was connected to Diaz's phone, with court approval. This device recorded the time and phone number of every incoming and outgoing call from Diaz's telephone number.

On November 15, 1989, the two men talked again. Brito was getting bolder as he cultivated Diaz, and the pair developed a friendly rapport. They also talked in code. A "fish" meant an ounce. A "whale" was a kilo. Such a quantity is normally sold by a cartel to a major supplier or from a regional supplier to a street dealer. The cost of a kilo in 1989 ranged between $16,000 and $18,000 wholesale. The two men haggled over price. "You know the person that catches it—if you buy more than five fishes, he will give you a better price," Diaz said.

The FBI agents reviewed the data produced by the pen register. A pattern was emerging. Diaz would take a call, then immediately make a call. They recognized the number dialed: It was Jose Vigoa's home telephone.

For the next few months, this pattern repeated itself again and again. By December the surveillance teams were tracking Vigoa, and they noticed that he went either to the Allstate U-Lok Storage facility on Boulder Highway or, later, to the Sahara-Lamb storage facility. On April 3, 1990, Brito drove to the Ariel Gonzalez residence. He intended to call Diaz and place an order for more cocaine. Brito called, but there was no answer. He dispatched Gonzalez to the Diaz house. At 10:18 in the morning Gonzalez's phone rang. Brito hesitated but decided to answer the informant's line. It was Gonzalez, now at the Diaz house, who put Diaz on. The drug dealer sheepishly explained that his telephone cord had been accidentally disconnected, and he couldn't hear the rings. Brito placed another order.

At 10:36 Diaz called Brito—"Your fish have arrived; come on over." An FBI surveillance agent radioed an urgent call to Brito: Vigoa was still at the Diaz house. Brito quickly drove to the Diaz apartment, hoping to meet Jose Vigoa, but he missed the drug dealer by less than a minute. After buying 140 grams of coke, Brito asked Diaz about purchasing "flake," a cocaine of very high quality that is shaved straight off the actual brick, uncut, and is 80% to 90% pure.

Diaz said that wouldn't be a problem. He could acquire large quantities of flake cocaine from his usual supplier, who had the cocaine stashed about an hour's drive away. The same supplier as before, he said.

As the two men talked, Diaz blurted out more information. His supplier had an abundance of new dope, an estimated eighty kilos or more with a street value of more than $1.6 million. The high-quality cocaine will hit the street in a matter of days. A big shipment. Many kilos. Many buyers. Place your order now. First come, first served. "Quantities may be limited," Diaz joked.

For the CuCoke agents, the moment to strike was at hand. A search warrant was obtained, the raid scheduled at the storage shed, a portion of the dope and weapons found.

AS THE AGENTS celebrated their small victory, the ultimate target of the FBI also was thinking about the storage shed as he turned east on East Sahara Avenue and headed for the facility. It was 5:44 p.m. Vigoa sat behind the customized wheel of his silver-blue 1987 full-size Ford pickup, a jacked-up vehicle he called "Big Foot" from the smash-'em, crash-'em television shows and arena spectacles. He was in a strange mood. Not worried, necessarily, but restless. Something was in the air, but he couldn't say what. It wasn't financial concerns, certainly, as business was booming. He was building four custom homes in northwest Las Vegas; he had broken ground for a 5,000-square-foot custom home on a half acre at 8972 Hickam Avenue west of Butler Street; he owned another upscale house in Miami, held in the name of an associate; and his own home, at 1708 Weeping Willow Lane in southeast Las Vegas, had doubled in value. Vigoa had upward of $1 million in cash spread about Las Vegas and the U.S. in banks.

And right now Vigoa had more than $4,000 in fifty- and hundred-dollar bills in his pockets as he drove his favorite truck. So why was he so irritable and anxious? It turns out the electricians had failed to show up on schedule at one of his custom homes under construction, and this created a chain reaction. Until the electrical work was done, the drywall crew couldn't do its job, and the painting and detail work would be delayed as well. Jose wanted to go to the job site and kick some ass, but instead he had to make a pit stop at the storage facility to pick up a small amount of coke for Diaz.

Vigoa saw the storage area ahead. He passed a police car and slowed down.

Jose Diaz had been a friend for many years. But when the dishwasher came to Jose Vigoa for cocaine to be resold, Vigoa begged off. "No," he told Diaz, "I'm out of the drug business." Vigoa had met the older man through his uncle, Faustino Perez. Diaz, fifty-nine years old, was still a server and dishwasher in the employees restaurant of the Showboat Hotel. Diaz also had a comely, high-spirited mistress on the side, a twenty-two-year-old illegal alien from Colombia with a little girl. From time to time, Vigoa would see them at one of the many Cuban nightclubs in Las Vegas. The Colombian woman was beautiful, with long black hair, sculpted legs, and dark eyes. Vigoa was amazed. How did the old man wind up with her? But for a big man, and at his age, Diaz managed to keep up with the willowy girl. Like many Cuban males, Diaz was reborn on the dance floor.

One night at the Matador, while Vigoa watched Diaz and his girl-friend, he had a change of heart.

"There was no way I could turn my back on him," Vigoa said. "Jose Diaz was a Cuban, and that counted for something. The look on his face told me everything. 'Manolo,' he said, 'I need your help.' I said, 'Jose, how many times do I have to tell you, I don't have any drugs.' His face fell. Finally I felt bad, and I said, 'Okay, Jose Diaz, that's not a problem, I have a friend in that business, just give me some time.' "

Jose Vigoa had just made one of the most fateful decisions of his life.

AT 5:50 P.M. Vigoa reached the storage facility on East Sahara Avenue. He began to punch in his code number, then he heard the voice of a woman from the office who was trying to get his attention. "Sir, I'm sorry, you can't go in; the gate is broken."

Vigoa finished punching in the code, and the gate opened normally. He figured he misunderstood the manager. He heard male voices from around the corner and thought it was somebody moving in or out. Then he saw the men. They were thirty to forty feet away. One was sitting on a folding chair looking bored, two others were standing in the little street talking, and another man, tall, sandy haired, and young, had just come out of the storage shed. The door looked bent.

The men stared at Vigoa. The Cuban realized that two of them were standing in front of his storage shed, and at least two others were *inside*—and now two of them began walking toward him. One of the men, big and powerful, was yelling at Jose. Both were waving wallets in the air with small gold objects pinned to the front. Jose could not see the gold badges, but he knew what they were. FBI. If these were Metro cops, they'd be waving pistols, cursing, and threatening to blow you away. Except for the undercover agents, you could tell the FBI by their haircuts, their manner of speech, and their businesslike demeanor.

Vigoa slammed the gearshift into reverse and stomped on the accelerator pedal. The big truck surged backward and swerved from side to side as Vigoa drove toward the main fairway of the storage area. Vigoa wheeled around the corner to the right, chased by agents Lyford and Baken, who managed to catch up and block Vigoa's path to the front gate. Vigoa shifted into first gear and gunned the truck forward. Lyford was directly in his path. To save his partner, Baken dove headfirst into the truck's front cabin through the passenger window and tried to stop Vigoa from running down Lyford. There was a brief scuffle—Vigoa later said there was a fistfight, Baken says there was not—and then Baken was thrown off the vehicle as Vigoa whipped the steering wheel back and forth.

Vigoa headed for the front gate. Agent Lyford was again in front of the truck. Lyford recalled, "He shot past Rick, and he's heading for me. I've got a gun in my ankle holster. Do I go for my gun or get out of the way?" In the end there was no time to go for the firearm. The veteran agent jumped up and forward. He landed on the hood of the truck, pushed off the left front fender, and rolled onto the pavement. Baken and Lyford heard the truck engine whine at maximum RPM, and they looked up. Vigoa, still accelerating, rammed the locked steel gate at more than forty miles an hour. The gate burst open as though made of cardboard. Hardware flew through the air. The truck roared off.

Baken jumped into the black Corvette and followed Vigoa. Three more carloads of agents joined the chase. "Now he's assaulted agents, and *now* he is going to be arrested," Baken said. Baken took a guess at which way Vigoa would head. "I thought to myself, *He's heading in that direction, east, but there is no place to go.* I mean, you get to Lake Mead and the mountains, and then what? I figure he had to come out the other way, so I went into the subdivision north of the search site."

His hunch turned out to be right. Vigoa, who knew the area well, had circled back and darted into one of the hundreds of new home-building sites in Clark County where the streets remained unpaved. "I saw this big dust cloud coming my way," said Baken, "so I blocked the road with the Corvette and got behind it with the weapon I had. Sure enough, here he comes, barreling down on my vehicle at a high rate of speed. A Corvette is made of fiberglass, so my car was no match for that big truck with its big cow grill."[1]

Then the agent realized that Vigoa was not going to stop. He jumped back in the Corvette. "He was going to ram me, and that was definitely life threatening, so I pulled out of the way. He never even slowed down. In fact, he sped up." The sports car shuddered as the Ford truck roared by, missing the Corvette by inches. Baken gave chase—but not for long. "There was so much dirt and gravel that I realized that without any visibility, and at these speeds, the danger to the community was too great. Innocent people could have been hurt. That would have been the ultimate tragedy, and we have to avoid that at all costs."

Vigoa had gotten away, but only for the moment. Within two weeks,

[1] A cow grill, also known as a grill guard or bullbar, is a large aluminum bumper subframe attached to the front of a truck. It is designed to fortify the front end in the event of an impact or a collision with road obstacles.

Jose Vigoa, represented by a criminal attorney named Kevin Kelly, contacted the FBI and agreed to surrender voluntarily.

ON AUGUST 9, 1990, one year after Jose Diaz first sold cocaine to Larry Brito, a federal grand jury returned a nine-count indictment charging Vigoa and Diaz with multiple counts of possession, conspiracy to sell, and the actual sale of cocaine. Vigoa was also accused of the unlawful use of a firearm during a drug transaction and two counts of assault on a federal officer. He blamed himself. "I try to help a family friend, I change my routine, and now I am fucked very big," Vigoa told a friend.

If convicted of all nine counts, Vigoa could have wound up serving twenty or more years in federal prison. And when Jose learned that an FBI agent had infiltrated his organization by setting up Jose Diaz with four undercover sales, he was furious. The Justice Department was trying to link him to the well-documented Diaz cocaine sales. At the very least, there would be conspiracy charges, Kelly warned his client. Jose knew what that meant. The asset forfeiture laws could enable the government to confiscate everything and every dollar Jose had.

The trial, titled *United States of America v. Jose Manuel Vigoa and Jose Diaz,* took place in the U.S. District Court the fourth week of November 1990, seven months after the storage facility rumble and escape. The prosecutors, led by Howard J. Zlotnick, outlined their case with supreme confidence:

> This case involves an undercover investigation wherein Special Agent Laurencio C. Brito infiltrated a narcotics organization and uncovered a cocaine distribution conspiracy between Jose Vigoa and Jose Diaz. Agent Brito met Diaz through confidential informant Ariel Gonzalez on August 29, 1989. On April 4, 1990, a search warrant was issued based on tape recorded phone calls between Diaz and Brito where the undercover agent would inform Diaz he wanted to purchase cocaine, followed immediately by a call printed on a pen register to Vigoa's residence, surveillance of Vigoa to storage lockers and back to Diaz, culminating in deliveries of cocaine by Diaz to Brito. During the execution of this warrant, Vigoa attempted to assault agents Lyford and Baken with his 1987 blue Ford pickup, Nevada registration 064CGR. Agents uncovered cocaine and firearms during the search.

Zlotnick and his team of federal prosecutors would prove to be well organized, creative, and bold. The government argued that one or two links between Diaz and Vigoa might be explained, but five, ten, fifteen? Too many coincidences. Kelly, the defense lawyer, appeared overwhelmed by the government's confidence and seemed to lose heart as the trial unfolded. Kelly's counterattack was disjointed. He bounced from one theme to another, tried to impugn the integrity of the FBI agents, and mocked the government's impressive charts and graphics as "glorious." Kelly tried to argue that the FBI had been less than forthcoming.

In fact, to a degree the government was bluffing. Yes, the prosecution had Diaz cold, but Vigoa was still a difficult conviction. At no time had the FBI or Brito ever come into contact with Jose Vigoa. There were no hand-to-hand sales between the Cuban drug trafficker and any FBI agent. And at no time did any agent discover Vigoa with drugs on his person, in his vehicle, or in his home. There were no informants, nobody who turned against the drug lord. The storage area was used by multiple persons.

But what about those coincidences? Four times the federal prosecutors walked undercover agent Brito through the moment he negotiated on the telephone the purchase of cocaine from Diaz. The pattern never varied: The agent and dealer agreed on quantity and price, then the dealer would say he needed to call his supplier; moments later, sometimes immediately, Jose Diaz would dial Jose Vigoa's home telephone and speak to someone at the Weeping Willow address.

The pen register. It was both the strength and the weakness of the government's otherwise tidy case. It showed which number was called, whether the phone was answered, and how long the call took place. It did *not* identify who answered the phone or record the actual conversation. This was significant. There was another alleged drug dealer living at the Weeping Willow Lane residence: Juan Sanchez, Jose's half brother.

Sanchez was intended to be the star defense witness. He was a more likely suspect than Vigoa but was not charged. Why not? Because the bureau was out to get Vigoa after the incident at the storage yard, the defense asserted. The prosecution braced for his appearance. Sanchez could blow the government case sky high. But on the third and climactic day of the trial, when the witness was due to appear, Sanchez arrived with a lawyer who said his client would plead the Fifth Amendment against self-incrimination if asked whether he was a drug dealer or whether he stored drugs in Vigoa's storage shed or whether he took calls from other drug dealers at the Vigoa home where he lived.

Judge Howard B. Turrentine then launched a judicial missile right into the heart of the defense. The witness would either testify without restriction, or he would not testify at all. "You can't blow hot and cold," the judge said. Kelly's chance to confuse the jurors by creating an alternative suspect and a large dosage of reasonable doubt had evaporated.

In his closing, Zlotnick poked fun at the defense. "Juan Sanchez, he's lived over at Weeping Willow. He was on one of the rental contract forms. As I recollect the evidence, I think it was on the Allstate U-Lok rental contract. So he must have done all of this. That's the way the argument is going. And what the argument is, ladies and gentlemen, it's what I'm going to refer to as the 'octopus argument.' What an octopus does— and what a squid does, for that matter—it will squirt out a whole bunch of ink, and when it squirts that out, it will escape into that ink cloud from whatever predator is chasing it. And that's pretty much what this Juan Sanchez argument is. It's a smoke screen. It's an ink screen to take your focus off of the testimony that you heard.

"The dope belonged to Vigoa, the calls were made to Vigoa, and it's time to put Mr. Vigoa in jail for a long time," Zlotnick concluded with a flourish.

Now it was Kelly's turn to make his final closing argument. Riveting it was not. In a courtroom awash with government charts and graphs, pen register tapes, and tape recording transcripts, Kelly had virtually nothing. He began by reciting the obvious, that one was presumed innocent until proven guilty. He went on to briefly explain reasonable doubt. Themes were introduced and then quickly discarded. The judge checked his watch. The one-hour time limit for closing arguments was running out.

The jurors deliberated for barely two hours. When they returned to the courtroom, they found Jose Vigoa guilty on all nine counts. Vigoa was sentenced to a total of nineteen years and one month in federal prison and stripped of all remaining assets.

Why the harsh sentence when so little dope was found to begin with?

"Vigoa tried to run down two FBI agents," Brito said after the trial. "That's when he upped the ante."

BOOK FOUR

COLLISION

Chapter 15

VIGOA MAKES A CAREER CHANGE

After serving seven years and two months in a series of federal prisons in Texas, California, and Oklahoma following his conviction on drug and assault charges, Jose Vigoa was released on November 8, 1996, and immediately rearrested by agents of the Immigration and Naturalization Service. Vigoa was outraged.

"When is this bullshit going to end?" he said. "I have served my time."

"Don't you want to see Cuba again?" the guard snickered. "I'm sure Fidel will meet you on your arrival."

Transported to the Arizona State Penitentiary in Florence, Arizona, Vigoa represented himself in a deportation hearing. He lost the case. Although the court ordered Vigoa's return to his homeland, the sentence was moot: There was no treaty between Cuba and the U.S. and therefore no place to go. Vigoa was released on $2,000 bail and allowed to remain in the country. The INS gave him a bus ticket for Las Vegas. He tore it up and flew back to Las Vegas on America West Airlines on December 13, 1996.

"While in federal prison," Vigoa recalled, "I began to prepare myself for my eventual release. I took college courses and earned straight As. I studied business. I learned how to read blueprints. I took business law and finance and many other courses. I wanted to be a different person. I was determined *not* to go back into the drug world. I had three children now. I knew what drugs did to people and the crimes they committed to afford their habits. I was preparing myself to be responsible, able, and to choose the right way, according to society's laws and customs."

Returning to Las Vegas, Vigoa worked at a drywall company that paid $15 an hour. It was tough, messy work, but it paid the bills and gave Jose a new set of skills that would be useful when he began to build new homes. Then the owner became gravely ill and committed suicide, and the company folded. Vigoa resumed his job search, showing employers his college transcripts and certificates, along with references that praised Vigoa's organizational and leadership talents.

In a story he will tell many times in the coming years, Vigoa claims he was hired as a foreman at a construction site and was doing well until Pedro Durazo, his federal probation supervisor, arrived at the workplace. Durazo called Jose into the mobile office. The head of the company was sitting at his desk and looked uncomfortable.

"Did you tell him, Jose?" Durazo asked Vigoa.

Vigoa shrugged. "Tell him what?"

"Did you tell him you're a convicted felon who tried to run over two FBI agents? Did you inform your employer you were a drug dealer?"

Vigoa said nothing.

The manager sighed. "Jose, I'm going to have to let you go."

Years later, Vigoa spoke of the night he decided to abandon the construction dream and go to war against the system.

"It didn't take me too long to realize I was a fool for believing I could start over. I applied to many jobs that I was qualified for. But my prior convictions always showed up like ghosts, along with my probation officer. All that education, all those plans, all those dreams, were fantasies and gave me false hope." By the spring of 1998, scarcely a year after his release from prison, Vigoa considered the system rigged and malicious. He was bitter and angry. In truth, Vigoa was an ex-con with a history of violence and drug dealing, no prospects, and a relentless probation officer. It was time for a career change.

Vigoa recalled the turning point: Working at a construction site in Henderson, Vigoa and a fellow laborer named Oscar Cisneros, who had just arrived in town from a small village in Mexico, watched a Brink's armored car pull in front of the elegant, upscale Sunset Station Hotel & Casino. The guard and messenger seemed bored. The driver of the truck appeared to be reading in the cab "and was not paying attention." The Brink's men went into the hotel pushing a small two-wheel cart and within ten minutes emerged from the casino. The dolly was piled high with see-through plastic bags stuffed with currency.

Vigoa looked at Oscar, a pleasant twenty-one-year-old with broad shoulders and a heavy accent. "I think we got a new job," Vigoa said.

"But they got guns," Cisneros said.

"What you want to do, Oscar, shovel shit for the rest of your life?"

On May 25, 1998, Jose Vigoa, employed as a painter by Briscoe Drywall and declaring $10,041 in taxable income on his 1997 federal return—in a town where parking valets earn upward of $60,000 a year—returned to the Sunset Station Hotel & Casino, this time with a Glock 9 mm pistol, Oscar Cisneros and his .45, and, possibly, a third man. Vigoa was back in the game.

There would be no turning back after the Sunset Station incident. The attempted robbery would prove to be both a dress rehearsal, a final examination, and a sharp reminder that only fools and drunks launched ambitious ventures without well-trained personnel, good planning, and proper tools. Jose would laugh about it later, but in truth the Sunset Station job nearly was the gang's last.

There are two versions of the robbery attempt at the Sunset Station Hotel & Casino.

According to police, a Brink's armored truck arrives at the south entrance of the Sunset Station at about 11:08 a.m. Chuck Fichter is the driver. Randy Easton and Steven Keeney are the guards. Easton and Keeney go inside the casino to pick up money while Fichter stays with the truck. In keeping with company policy, the engine continues to run. The police report continues: "There was more money than they could carry, so Easton went back out to the truck, retrieved a cart, and went back inside. Easton and Keeney exited Sunset Station with the money on the cart. They walked to the rear of the truck and opened the rear doors so they could load the money."

A speeding red Oldsmobile Toronado sedan pulls up to the left side of the Brink's truck. Three gunmen wearing black ski masks are in the vehicle. One of the passengers points a pistol at the guards and orders the men to freeze. Easton is the first to see the firearm and realize what is happening.

"Gun!" he yells.

The guards at the rear scramble for cover by running to the right side of the truck, putting the armored vehicle between them and the gunmen. The passenger with the gun gets out of the Olds, but when the guards draw their pistols, he jumps back inside the car and speeds off, crashing through a construction fence. No shots are fired. The getaway car is later found in the Galleria Mall parking lot, across the street from the casino, wiped clean of prints. It is a stolen vehicle.

Vigoa gives a different version of the failed robbery.

The Sunset Station Hotel & Casino is chosen because it is one of Jose's favorite hangouts and is located in a familiar neighborhood. The casino also fits Vigoa's strategic criteria: The hotel is near the I-15 freeway and a major shopping center where a getaway car can be safely positioned; there are many smaller streets and avenues of escape by the hotel; and the year-old casino is booming.

Vigoa anticipates a major score. "The whole plan was to intercept the guards while they were pulling the cart out of the casino," he explained. "I had seen it before, stacked with bags of cash! Oscar was driving the day of the robbery, while I was hiding in the backseat of our stolen Oldsmobile Toronado. We saw the two Brink's guards walking out of the casino pushing the cart with a huge load of clear plastic bags filled with cash. There was no question about it; you could see right through the bags."

In Vigoa's version, the first stage of the robbery goes perfectly. The guards return from the hotel with sacks of currency stacked atop the overloaded cart.

"Don't fucking move!" Vigoa yells.

Vigoa and Cisneros approach the Brink's men with guns drawn. The guards freeze. The driver does not appear to notice there's a holdup in progress.

"The guards obeyed my order instantly without any problem," Vigoa said. "I now had the two guards under my control and all the money. All of this happened in full view of the casino customers coming and going. They watched like it was some kind of a movie or something. Oscar's job was not only to drive but, after stopping the car, he was supposed to load all the money bags into the Oldsmobile. And then everything went to shit."

Vigoa is leaning forward to grab the money when Cisneros screams, "The car! The car!" Vigoa looks to his left. The Oldsmobile is moving. Cisneros not only has forgotten to set the parking brake, he has left the car in drive.

The Toronado is on an incline and starts to roll down the grade. Its trajectory will take it in front of the big armored car. Vigoa realizes what this means. He looks at the guards, who appear puzzled.

"There I stood. Holding the guards at gunpoint while my unoccupied getaway car drives off. I made a very quick decision, and I made it fast. It was either our lives or the money. I knew at once the car was moving out of the safe zone and into the danger zone, where it could be crushed by the Brink's truck."

Vigoa has studied armored car operations, probably with the help of an inside source, and he recognizes the imminent crisis. The safe position for the getaway car is the parking lot, where it cannot be rammed by the heavier armored truck. Armored truck crews are trained to use the truck as a weapon, a battering ram, when under attack. That's why the truck's engine remains running. The driver is at his post, with his foot near the accelerator.

Vigoa thinks quickly. The armored car driver is now keenly aware he is being robbed and probably has seen the car in motion. At any moment, the big truck might roar forward and crush the smaller sedan, turning the getaway car into a mangled wreck.

Vigoa knows what must be done. Leaving the bags behind, he and Cisneros sprint toward the car, pile inside, and speed off. The Oldsmobile crashes through a construction fence before Vigoa can regain control. The two men drive to another location, switch cars, and make their escape, leaving three baffled guards behind holding at least $1 million in currency on the cart.

Vigoa is humiliated. He squeezes the grip of his Glock handgun and considers dispatching Oscar Cisneros on the spot. It won't be the last time Vigoa thinks seriously of killing a crew member after a job.

"We were so close but for one stupid, childish, amateur mistake! I was so mad at Oscar I thought seriously of shooting him in the head as soon as we reached my trailer on Boulder Highway. I really wanted to kill him when I got there. It was a tremendous, ridiculous mistake, and it forced me to abort the entire operation with the money at my feet and the guards under my control. Eventually I cooled down. Oscar was Oscar. What could I expect? This wasn't Angola or Afghanistan, he was a common laborer, someone who knew how to use a shovel and not much more."

But to the crew's surprise, Vigoa is calm in the days following the failed heist. He sees the bigger picture. Except for this one absurd blunder, Vigoa and Cisneros would be wealthy men. Ambushing the guards was not difficult. Next time there would be no schoolboy mistakes. And there *would* be a next time.

"This was our first robbery attempt. I was frustrated, but having seen all the money in front of me, there was no quitting now. More than ever, I wanted to plan the next job and move forward. I wanted to create turmoil and fuck the casinos and drive the police and federals crazy."

Four months later, Vigoa, Cisneros, and Pedro Duarte would do that and more. The next target would be the largest hotel in the world.

Chapter 16

STORMING LAS VEGAS

It is September 20, 1998, 11:26 a.m.

The MGM Grand, at the corner of Las Vegas Boulevard and Tropicana Avenue, is not only the grandest complex in Las Vegas with its 170,000-square-foot casino, 6.6-acre pool complex, four thirty-story towers, nine signature restaurants, and 5,044 guest rooms. It is also the biggest hotel in the world.

Certainly it has been a lively weekend at the MGM for the Texas high rollers, Beverly Hills swells, Columbus car dealers, and Pittsburgh gynecologists. The celebrated Mexican boxer Julio Cesar Chavez is in town for a championship fight. The famous crooner Juan Gabriel is drawing large crowds. Sexy new nude revues push the envelope between teasingly erotic and soft porn. Money is pouring onto the Strip, and Wall Street loves Vegas. The city is growing at a phenomenal rate. The long, blistering Vegas summer finally is over. What could possibly go wrong?

Two Brink's guards, having collected cash and checks from the MGM casino's main cashier, enter a passageway and appear in the hotel's surveillance video for the first time. They are escorted by a hotel security employee. The three men enter the frame of the video on the bottom left, at about the eight o'clock position, and can be seen walking through the corridor heading toward the exterior doors. Their backs are to the surveillance camera. They have just left what is called the Hollywood Casino and have entered a passageway that's about seventy feet long and thirty feet wide and leads to the exterior doors. The exit doors leading to the street are easy to recognize in the video frame: They are at the top of the picture and identifiable because of the bright Nevada sunlight visible through the cracks of the doors. This illumination creates a hot spot at the top of the picture as the camera's automatic lens tries to adjust to the differing light levels.

The Brink's truck is on the other side of the doors. The driver, sixty-five-year-old Ronald Wachlin, a 270-pound veteran employee, is filling out paperwork that documents the previous pickup at the Tropicana. Fifty-two-year-old Werner Boehnke is the Brink's messenger who physically handles the money and signs the receipts in the ninety-second exchange in the cashier's cage. He is the first figure to appear in the video. Boehnke pushes a two-wheel metal dolly in front of him. Although difficult to see in the video, the cart holds a large gray canvas sack that measures about two feet by two feet. It is filled to the brim with more than $1.5 million in currency and checks from the main cashier's cage.

Walking about seven paces directly behind Boehnke is Brian Lane, twenty-four, a new employee who has been with Brink's for four months. In armored car parlance, Lane is the guard. Both Lane and Boehnke carry .38 revolvers, which remain in their holsters, secured by a leather strap to discourage accidental discharge.

This is a routine that's repeated at least three times a week. The Brink's crew, consisting of the messenger, the guard, and the driver, pull into the hotel valet-parking driveway. They back down a small driveway to the Hollywood doors, where they are met by a hotel security guard, who opens the doors and leads the crew through the passageway to the casino. Once the three men reach the casino, the hotel employee props open the passageway door to facilitate their return. The Brink's men walk through the casino, enter the main cashier cage, pick up cash and other receipts, sign for the money, and then return to the truck through the same breezeway.

Of the $1.5 million in the canvas bag on the dolly, $349,829 is in cash.

At 11:26:08, Boehnke, Lane, and Leland Jimenez, a casino guard, are back in the passageway, having picked up the cash and checks from the main cashier's office. On the videotape, the three men can be seen moving in a single file from the casino toward the outside doors and the waiting Brink's truck. One second later, the robbery begins.

"Put your hands in the air!" Vigoa yells at the three men, appearing suddenly from the left rear quadrant of the guards. Oscar pops into the frame from the opposite side and repeats the command. The order is given at least five times, the guards later tell detectives and the FBI. Police and agents will play and replay the tape for months to come after realizing this was a carefully planned heist executed with precision timing.

Vigoa is moving quickly. He wears a dark jacket, light trousers, and a baseball cap. Both arms are stretched out. Vigoa has a semiautomatic pistol in each hand, and, although the weapons are barely five feet from the unarmed casino employee's head, Jose actually is pointing the weapons at the two Brink's guards, who continue to move toward the outside doors. Oscar Cisneros is on the right of the video picture. He covers the opposite flank of Boehnke and Lane.

It is a perfectly choreographed robbery. Vigoa and Cisneros have overtaken the guards from the rear and have achieved complete surprise.

"We don't want to hurt you," Cisneros says. "We're after the money. Give us your guns and go back to the casino."

"But get your fucking hands up now!" Vigoa says sharply.

Lane is startled but thinks it's a joke. He actually smiles at Cisneros. *These guys are really crazy,* he thinks. The young guard is in a casino, he's armed, he's transporting more than $1.5 million, and he knows that armored car guards are sometimes bushwhacked. But until this moment, Lane never has been robbed, and the thought of being robbed at the MGM Grand on a Sunday morning does not immediately compute. At 11:26:11, the three men are within twenty feet of the exit doors. But now Vigoa moves up, his semiautomatic pistols even closer to the messenger and guard.

"Don't even think it," Vigoa snaps, gesturing at the door. "Nobody is going through those doors."

To Lane, Vigoa appears massive, at least the size of a National Football League defensive tackle, and Lane later will tell detectives that Vigoa is between six foot two and six foot five in height. Vigoa is actually five foot nine and weighs 170 pounds. This is not uncommon with victims of an armed robbery or assault. When one looks down the barrel of a gun, everything is magnified. Vigoa, a compact, wiry man, becomes a giant.

The skipped-frame surveillance footage, though lacking resolution and color, is nonetheless revealing. Cisneros has closed on Boehnke and is within a few feet of the money bag. Although the robbery is only three seconds old, the dolly already is swinging to the right side of the messenger and is in front of Cisneros. The messenger is not resisting.

At 11:26:13 Cisneros lifts the canvas money bag off the cart. Vigoa and Cisneros are less than fifteen feet from the outside doors. Now he begins the more awkward task of collecting the firearms from the Brink's employees. The video is paused again. Later the same day, Lieutenant John Alamshaw will freeze the video and notice that the leader of the gang is at the eight o'clock position and is covering Boehnke and Lane at point-blank range.

Lane no longer thinks this is a joke and has stopped in his tracks. There is nothing cowardly about his actions—his pistol is not only holstered,[1] it is held in the holster tightly by a safety strap. To reach for the pistol would be an act of suicide.

At 11:26:14 the messenger, Boehnke, raises his hands, but Lane does not comply. He either is contemplating his next move, or he's stunned. It will take Lane another five seconds to comply with the orders to raise his arms. *That little hesitation could have gotten him killed,* Alamshaw thinks when he later views the tape.

There is a brief delay: Cisneros is having trouble relieving Boehnke and Lane of their revolvers. He doesn't notice the leather straps and tries to tug the pistols out of their holsters.

"Goddamn it, these fuckers are stuck!" Cisneros curses.

"Come on—just pull the goddamn pistols and throw them into the bag!" Vigoa barks.

"I can't, I can't, they're stuck!" Cisneros says, shaking the messenger's holster. Finally the Brink's men, fearful of an accidental discharge, show Cisneros how to release the leather strap. The young Mexican collects the pistols.

"Go back to the casino," Vigoa orders the three men. "And don't look back."

Vigoa pushes open the exit door.

At 11:26:32 the white light at the top of the video frame suddenly explodes into a sunlike burst that envelops Vigoa and Cisneros. Then they are gone.

At 11:26:36 the Brink's men, relieved of the money and still raising their hands, walk out of the picture frame—and into the casino, led by the MGM security guard.

Vigoa's crew has taken barely twenty-four seconds. Now for the escape. It will not be nearly as effortless. In some respects, this is the most

---

[1] Armored car guards may not brandish their weapons on casino property no matter how much money they're transporting, according to hotel policy.

**As captured by a hotel surveillance camera, the MGM ambush is sprung
during the September 20, 1998, robbery. Vigoa is the figure on the left
with a gun in each hand coming up behind the unsuspecting guards.**
COURTESY MGM HOTEL.

telling stage of the crime—and a good test of Vigoa's leadership skills.
For if the actual robbery is committed in record time and proves to be a
masterpiece of crisp execution, what happens next almost ends the Vigoa
crime spree.

With Vigoa leading the way and Cisneros carrying the Brink's bag, the
two men bolt from the south wall doors. Pedro Duarte is the getaway
driver assigned to pick up Vigoa and Cisneros in the valet parking area,
less than twenty yards from the doors.

"We did good, Oscar," Vigoa says as the two men stride into the valet
parking area, ready to jump aboard the pickup truck.

But he stops in the driveway. "What the fuck?"

There's no white pickup truck. Duarte is nowhere to be found.

"Keep moving, keep moving," Vigoa says to Cisneros.

"Should we get a cab?" Cisneros asks.

"Oscar, let's go, we gotta get the fuck out of here!"

The armored car is still in the driveway, its driver waiting patiently for
the return of his crew, when Wachlin looks up and sees the two men,
oddly dressed for this time of year, running in front of the truck. Wach-

lin notices that the larger of the two men is carrying something bulky in his arms. Wachlin looks closely, then gasps. It's a Brink's bag. It is a *full* Brink's bag and Wachlin knows where he's seen it before. "That's ours!"

Wachlin throws two emergency switches in the truck. The first activates a police-style siren on the truck. It begins to scream loudly. Cars pulling into the driveway slow down. Parking lot attendants turn and stare. An MGM security guard standing in the driveway, yet unaware of the robbery, reaches for his radio but doesn't call his supervisor because he doesn't know what to say—the driver is in the truck, and there's no sign of trouble.

The second switch activates an emergency signal that's broadcast to Brink's headquarters. Even if Wachlin is killed or disabled in the next few minutes, the company will know the truck is under attack or that something is seriously wrong.

Wachlin wonders if he should dial 911. *Maybe that WASN'T our canvas bag.* Then his radio crackles. The decision is made for him. It's Boehnke.

"We've been robbed, we've been robbed!"

"What?"

"We have been *robbed!* Call 911. Alert the company. *And stay in the truck!* They're coming your way."

The Brink's driver pulls his truck forward ten yards, stops, then calls 911 to report the robbery.

Vigoa is startled. The truck's siren is on, and the vehicle is moving. *It's only a matter of time,* Vigoa thinks. But there's still no sign of armed guards or police. *We can still get out of here. Where is that fucking Pedro?!*

Vigoa and Cisneros break for the Hotel San Remo across the street, a predesignated rallying point. And finally the two gunmen catch a break. The normally busy East Tropicana Avenue, the street that feeds traffic into the MGM, and a main artery that connects to Las Vegas Boulevard and the Mandalay Bay, Excalibur, New York–New York, Monte Carlo, and Boardwalk hotels, is without traffic.

Vigoa and Cisneros sprint across the wide street. Vigoa races ahead, reminding one witness of a nimble football halfback breaking into the clear. Cisneros is like the lumbering tackle who can't quite keep up but doggedly runs down the field anyway. Vigoa connects with Duarte on the cell phone. Duarte is back in the MGM driveway, frantically looking for his confederates.

"San Remo! San Remo! Meet us on the first floor," Vigoa pants.

"I see you, I'm coming!" Duarte yells into his cell phone. He tries to explain his disappearance: "I try to wait for you, but the man in valet parking, he make me go. I parked too close to the armored truck. I was in the red zone."

Vigoa, incredulous, cuts him off. "Get over here now! And when you get here, get in the back. I'm driving!"

Tony Kazmierczak, a fifty-four-year-old blackjack dealer at the San Remo, is taking a break in a small garden off the hotel's casino with other employees. He is startled to witness "two young Hispanic males run up the parking ramp, through the garage, and down the ramp toward me," he later tells the FBI.

Kazmierczak watches the two men carefully. One throws a white object into the back of a white pickup truck. Both men get in the truck. The pickup pulls out, speeds down the ramp, its gears grinding as the driver hurriedly shifts. Believing the two men were breaking into cars in the garage, Kazmierczak notifies hotel security. The dealer does not see Duarte, who lies flat on the bed of the truck as ordered. Vigoa remains calm as police cars roar into the hotel driveway. He pulls out of the garage, takes an access road behind the hotel, and works his way back to Las Vegas Boulevard. Then he switches cars at the Boardwalk Hotel & Casino, unloads Duarte (who has his own car in the garage), forces Cisneros to hide in the trunk of his 1977 Chevrolet Caprice, and drives away. As Vigoa heads to the I-15 exit ramp, a Metro black-and-white sector car pulls alongside. The young officer stares at Vigoa, who is alone and driving normally. The police are looking for three suspects in a white pickup truck. The patrol car moves on.

"As I headed west to the freeway, I made a right turn onto Tropicana," Vigoa said. "At this time I looked back at the MGM, my old friend, and what a scene it was! Police were everywhere. A police helicopter was overhead, buzzing around like a mad hornet. The entire property reminded me of a circus. I got the hell out of there and headed up the I-15."

Police and the FBI will painstakingly review surveillance video from the MGM Grand, San Remo, and Tropicana hotels, reconstructing the crime second by second. They will discover that Duarte, despite his initial mistake in parking next to the armored truck and getting chased away, remained in the area searching for his mates.

"In a way, Pedro's vanishing act was a good thing," Vigoa says later. "We were tested. After Pedro got chased off from valet parking, we didn't fall apart or panic or act stupid. This is the way it is in real combat. There always are surprises. Nothing ever goes the way it is supposed to go, and a plan is only a first step. There always will be an ebb and flow in the fight. It's how you react to surprises that matters. We did well."

Vigoa's new enterprise had generated its first revenue stream. There would be no more drug business for Jose Vigoa. He would go straight to the casinos, the armored cars, and the cash.

THE POLICE RESPONSE to the MGM heist is considerable. John Alamshaw arrives to supervise the scene, which is swarmed by police and the FBI. The robbery section uses a rotation system in assigning manpower. Gordon Martines, a prickly, temperamental detective active in politics and known to be difficult to manage, is next in line on the day of the MGM robbery and is appointed primary detective. Martines will be responsible for filing reports, determining the direction of the investigation, and briefing Alamshaw and his sergeants.

Almost immediately there is controversy. Without consulting Alamshaw, Martines reaches out to two colleagues, Luis Araujo and Kevin Skehan of the problem-solving unit[2] in the Southwest Area Command substation (the division responsible for the Strip and the west side), and assigns them to the case. The PSU officers will trace the stolen license plates of the getaway pickup truck to a storage yard on Boulder Highway, where they discover that Jose Vigoa is the on-site watchman responsible for security. When the PSU officers try to talk to Jose, he walks away. Araujo and Skehan do not pursue the suspicious security man but report the incident to Martines, who takes no action to locate Vigoa on that day—even when it is discovered that Vigoa is a convicted felon with a significant criminal history. Even worse, the incident at the storage yard is poorly documented, leading to a serious lapse in communication later in the case.

"This is about tactics," Alamshaw says aloud as the police enter the cavernous lobby of the MGM Grand through one set of twenty double doors. To the right are the hotel rooms. To the left is the biggest casino in

[2] Problem-solving unit: a tactical team within a Metro substation. PSU officers work for the area command's captain and focus on particular problems in that district. PSU members are not full-fledged detectives but rank a notch above patrol officers.

Las Vegas. The detectives turn left and walk past row upon row of slot machines, blackjack tables, and roulette wheels. The detectives come to the emergency doors that lead to the passageway and eventually the outside valet parking driveway. The emergency exit consists of four sets of doors located near the Hollywood Theatre, a 740-seat venue for headliner acts such as Tom Jones and David Copperfield. The cashier cages are to the right.

An anomaly becomes apparent. It is seventy-five to one hundred yards from the front door of the hotel to the passageway. The suspects are believed to have loitered in what the casino bosses call pit 6, an area replete with card tables and roulette wheels, or they may have hung around blackjack machines. In fact, the videotape will confirm this. Vigoa and Cisneros are seen striding through the vast room looking decidedly out of place with their bulky attire, caps, and sunglasses.

"It's a long way to go with nobody spotting them," Alamshaw says. "Long sleeves and body armor. A *long* way to go."

Alamshaw looks around the casino. Blackjack tables are fifty feet from the emergency doors. Most are occupied. *There were a lot of people around. A lot of people to interview. But what would they have seen?* Still, they have to be questioned. "You want to make sure your witnesses have been secured and secluded to some extent because you never know—a witness might be a suspect too," Alamshaw says. "You want to bring in as many officers as you can, whether patrol, detectives, or motorcycle, and you might bring in traffic officers to work the scene outside or block off a street. You want to get your witnesses interviewed as quickly as possible before they cross-contaminate each other by exchanging information and opinions."

By midafternoon Alamshaw and his team have viewed the video and talked to the Brink's men. The investigators now have a clear and complete understanding of the crime and even know the second-by-second whereabouts of the getaway car and why it was not in place when the gunmen bolted through the side doors.

Alamshaw also suspects the robbery represents something new, something robbery detectives have not seen before. "They weren't your typical robbers," he reflected. "Clearly this was not a spur-of-the-moment thing. It wasn't a crime of opportunity. The crew had done their homework. It was obvious they had body armor and probably were heavily armed. That wasn't your average robber who lived in Las Vegas at the time."

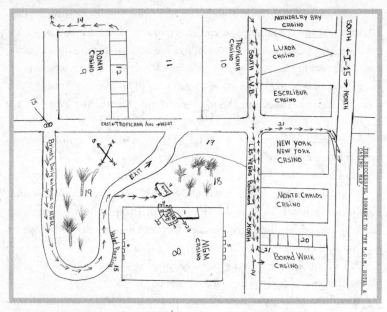

A 2004 Jose Vigoa hand-drawn blueprint of the MGM heist.
COURTESY JOSE VIGOA.

A hotel security guard comes up and hands John a .38-caliber Smith & Wesson revolver, neatly sealed in a plastic bag for evidence purposes. "We found this in the driveway, sir. They just tossed it as they ran out."

"Did you get the other revolver?" Alamshaw asks.

"No sir. The Brink's men say they put the other piece from the second guard into the money bag."

It is a warm day, but the robbery supervisor feels a chill. He turns to an FBI man, who agrees with Alamshaw that the bad guys understood *tactics*. "I hope these guys aren't from Las Vegas," Alamshaw says. "I'd hate to think they're sticking around. This was more than professional. This was a tactically sound, well-planned operation. They made some serious money today."

THAT THEY DID. As the police study the surveillance tape, interview witnesses, and search for forensic evidence, Vigoa begins a strange ritual, half superstitious and half scientific, designed to keep the police and federal agents at bay. That night he wraps the stolen money in aluminum foil, buries the package in a secret location, and then places the money under surveillance to ensure there are no hidden transponders broadcasting the location of the currency. Vigoa learned a great deal in federal prison, including techniques used by banks and casinos to track stolen money.

"A tracer can be as small as a grain of rice," Vigoa tells Cisneros and Duarte. "Like a drop of paint. It's almost impossible to find when you're in a hurry. Tracers are received by satellite. They use GPS technology that enables police and FBI agents to home in on the stolen money within an hour of the crime." Vigoa develops what he calls his "tracer killer" technique. Using a roll of commercial aluminum foil three feet wide and one hundred feet long, Vigoa wraps the money bags. "You go back and forth many times with the foil, left to right, right to left, over and under, shaping it like a Mexican tamale until it is covered with foil that's an inch thick."

Vigoa believes the aluminum foil will defeat all GPS or other tracking signals unless the electronic unit is especially large and powerful. He is essentially right. This kind of shielding, however crude, is likely to block most GPS-based tracking transmissions. However, banks are more likely to use GPS locator technology than are casinos.

A week later the money is retrieved, and the split is made: half to Vigoa, the remainder to Cisneros and Duarte. With deep satisfaction, Vigoa neatly arranges stacks of $20s, $50s and $100s on the dining room table. Not bad for twenty-eight seconds of work. A good beginning, Vigoa concludes, despite Duarte's tardy arrival.

In the hours shortly before the MGM Grand robbery, the family of Jose Manuel Vigoa Perez was not unlike hundreds of thousands of working-class households in Clark County, crammed into a small $800-a-month three-bedroom rental unit, burdened by debt, earning a combined declared income of $28,858. But by nightfall on Sunday, September 20, 1998, the Vigoas financially have vaulted back into the ranks of the American middle class. They are not only flush, they are about to finally become American consumers for the first time since Vigoa went to prison in 1990. First there will be a modest celebration for all: Vigoa takes his wife, three daughters, and other family members to Disneyland, the first trip to the amusement park by any member of the Vigoa family. There is a photograph of the Vigoa family at Disneyland from that magical week in Anaheim, California, taken with the Magic Castle in the background. The younger girls, Belladonna, twelve, and thirteen-year-old Maria, are wearing Mickey Mouse ears and clearly are having the vacation of a life-time. The seventeen-year-old, Anna,[3] wears a red Disneyland sweatshirt and a face full of cotton candy as her mother laughs heartily. Vigoa is in the middle, holding Maria's and Belladonna's hands. He neither smiles nor frowns. With the spiraling towers of Cinderella's castle behind him, Vigoa seems to be looking off in the distance, perhaps straining to see what lies ahead and wondering how long these gloriously happy days between the sharp and dangerous excursions can possibly last.

Returning home, Vigoa buys his daughters Hewlett-Packard, Everex, and CompUSA computers. "Now you will earn straight As, write letter-perfect papers for your teachers, and prepare for college," he tells them. "Everyone will go to the university. I want you to be doctors and lawyers and work in air-conditioned offices." Vigoa and Luisa talk about buying a new home. They begin studying the classified ads in the local newspaper, the *Review-Journal,* carefully. They whisper together late at night.

Two weeks after the MGM robbery, Robert Kay Sarozek, a sixty-one-year-old businessman, receives a telephone call from Vigoa in response to a real estate ad Sarozek is running in the newspaper. A meeting is arranged at the house that's for sale on Sandy Slate Way. Vigoa arrives with Cisneros. Sarozek gives the two men a tour of the neat, attractive three-bedroom, two-bath tract home in a quiet middle-class neighborhood. Vigoa says he wants to buy the house and peels off ten hundred-dollar bills that he gives to the seller as good-faith money to hold the residence.

Vigoa returns that night with Luisa and the girls. The children run through the house, peek into bedrooms, talk excitedly about who will be assigned what room, and shyly whisper that they will have two bathrooms, like the wealthy people. Sarozek is struck by the closeness of the Cuban family, the devotion of the man the girls call *Papi.* Vigoa pays him another $5,000 in cash.

On Wednesday, it is decided the sale price will be $169,000, less a $19,000 down payment. Sarozek will carry the mortgage note. After a brief meeting inside the house, Vigoa takes out $13,000 in hundred-dollar bills to complete the down payment. Then there is an awkward moment. Jose tells Sarozek he can't be the owner of record because of problems with the IRS and INS. The house will have to be in the name of his friend

---

[3] To protect the innocent, the first names of the Vigoa daughters have been changed.

Oscar Sanchez Cisneros. Sarozek agrees, and the deal is closed—seventeen days after the MGM robbery.

There will be other purchases, large and small, during the months to come, but nothing resembling a wild spending spree. Vigoa buys a 1999 Nissan Pathfinder from Towbin Nissan for $31,673, and, once again, Cisneros steps forward at the last minute to front the deal. The SUV becomes Luisa's full-time vehicle, even though the title is in Cisneros's name. For himself, Vigoa buys a 1992 cherry red Chevrolet Silverado pickup truck for $12,000 and pays for the used truck with $100 bills. A new house should warrant decent furnishings, Vigoa agrees, and on March 13 Luisa will buy a new living room set from the Furniture Expo in Henderson. The $888 bill is paid in cash.

In keeping with Vigoa's policy of maintaining a low profile, there will be few luxury items purchased after the MGM robbery. On March 27, six weeks after Luisa's thirty-eighth birthday, Vigoa buys his wife a 1.2 carat diamond; he pays $1,251 in cash. On April 24 Vigoa purchases two heart bracelets and a black Pierre Cardin watch from the same store for $544. On November 20 the Vigoas pay $535 cash for diamond hoop earrings bought at Lundstrom Jewelers.

Otherwise, the spending spree will wind down after new wardrobes are purchased for the children and Luisa. Still seething from the government's seizure of his construction company, Vigoa vows to come back as a builder on an even bigger scale, defying his critics and enemies. "I want to be building good, affordable homes for people who work hard, have a family, and pay their bills on time," he tells Luisa and Oscar. And maybe later, once established as the Cuban builder with style and class and real good prices, Vigoa Construction will create the Villages of Vigoa near Henderson, south of Las Vegas, with estate homes starting at $1 million, smaller houses for hotel workers and limo drivers, and even townhomes and apartments.

All of this, of course, will take lots and lots of capital.

And Jose Vigoa, future builder extraordinaire, knows exactly where to find that start-up cash.

MANDALAY BAY AND
THE GREAT CAR HEIST

Nine months after the MGM Grand heist, the Desert Inn robbery turns into a pitched battle when two tough Brink's guards unexpectedly fight back. This definitely is something new, a twist the police haven't seen before: a furious firefight off Las Vegas Boulevard that sprays the Sports Book parking lot, the Desert Inn itself, and the Thunderbird Hotel across the street with gunfire.

When John Alamshaw reaches the scene, he is convinced this is the same gang that struck the MGM. The precision planning, the gunmen's willingness to wait for hours in the rosemary plants, their having selected the most lucrative of all the armored car routes, and the sheer boldness of the robbery—an armed confrontation in broad daylight—surpass anything the robbery lieutenant has seen before in Las Vegas.

There's something else that disturbs the veteran detective: The gangsters are becoming more violent, as if they want to trigger an all-out gunfight.

"They were lying in wait," Alamshaw tells one of his robbery detectives. "They did their research, they maintained surveillance, they hit the right truck. But what makes this special once more is the use of tactics and the willingness, almost eagerness, to have an armed confrontation with people who have weapons. That's unusual. Most criminals lack that kind of nerve. Of course, the people we normally see don't use AK-47s and body armor, either."

As for Vigoa, the gangster is surprisingly upbeat after the failed robbery. Vigoa views the DI heist as an instructive lesson in tactics and timing. The Desert Inn also teaches Vigoa that no detail is too small—

engaging guard Donald Bowman too soon may have cost the crew $7 million left behind in the truck. Still, Vigoa has $130,000 from the MGM job stashed away in a secret bedroom compartment in his new home. He is in no hurry and intends to make his next play a good one. Vigoa personally will surveil six hotels on the Strip, one bank, one car rental agency, and two armored car companies between late June and October in 1999.

The Mirage is scheduled to be the next target in August, but Vigoa changes his mind after scouting the site. The escape routes are too few, the gang could wind up trapped inside the hotel. Vigoa decides to hit the Mandalay Bay.

Vigoa will spend two weeks playing the slots at the Mandalay, having the occasional drink at the casino bar, analyzing internal security, counting the footsteps from the cashier's cage to the emergency exit doors on the north side of the casino—the distance is two hundred feet from cashier to exits—and timing the Brink's messenger and guard as they pick up cash from the hotel's cashier.

This time Vigoa decides to assemble a veritable fleet of late-model cars to be used in multivehicle getaway operations. Las Vegas is a city of rental cars driven by thousands of tourists each day, and that gives Vigoa an idea that will become a linchpin of future robberies. Instead of acquiring getaway cars through repeated carjackings, which add to the risk of every operation, or buying stolen cars from other criminals, which exposes the Vigoa team to informants, the crew will take advantage of a poorly managed, largely unsecured Thrifty Car Rental franchise on 376 East Warm Springs Road.

During the next six months, during two nighttime raids, the audacious gang will steal seventeen vehicles from the rental lot. Thrifty's will become Vigoa's personal transportation depot for future heists. "There was an ordinary chain-link fence on the east side of the lot," Vigoa said. "All I had to do was cut off the chain around the gate with my heavy-duty bolt cutter. It was so easy, even with several Thrifty employees working in the front of the lot vacuuming and washing cars."

The first car theft will occur in late September when Vigoa, Cisneros, and a third confederate slip through the fence and take away a dark maroon 1999 Jeep Grand Cherokee, a dark green Jeep Cherokee, and a new light blue Plymouth Voyager minivan. "We drove them in the streets for many special purposes, just like they were our cars, changing the license plates with out-of-state tags every week," Vigoa recalled. "Sometimes I felt like these were my cars, I drove them so often and openly. Well, for all practical purposes, they *were* my cars. Nice vehicles, too. I'll have to buy one someday."

ON THE NIGHT of October 10, 1999, Jose Vigoa's men park the stolen minivan at the Parkway Inn, a small motel at 5201 Industrial Road, about a two-minute drive from the Mandalay Bay. Vigoa then goes to the hotel, sits in the lounge, has two drinks, and looks around the casino one more time. His eyes focus on the cashier's cage and the carpeted walkway to the exit doors. *What have I missed? Are there any loose ends?* Satisfied that the crew is ready, Vigoa goes home for a few hours of sleep.

By eight o'clock the next morning, the gang is in place, standing beside a flight of cement stairs that leads to a bank of emergency doors on the northeast side of the hotel. When the Brink's truck is spotted pulling into the hotel driveway, Vigoa and Cisneros enter the casino through the side doors. The getaway car, the maroon Jeep Grand Cherokee, is parked at the foot of the stairs, but not illegally or too close to the armored truck.

Kyle Carney and Kenneth Huderski step out of the Brink's truck. They unload a dolly, enter the hotel, visit the cashier's cage, collect receipts, and sign for $88,868 in currency.

The Mandalay Bay robbery, beginning at 9:10 a.m. on October 11, later will be described by the chief deputy district attorney as having "the exact modus operandi of the MGM/Brink's robbery." There will be one minor variation: Instead of surprising the Brink's men in a closed passageway off the casino, Vigoa and Cisneros spring out from behind a row of slot machines in the open casino as the guards push their dolly toward a set of emergency doors.

The moment is captured on surveillance video. The Brink's employees, pushing their cart through the casino as they have done hundreds of times before, are halfway to the exit doors.

"Don't move!" Vigoa orders. "I want to see your hands in the air!"

The startled guards are shoved against a wall and have no time to draw their weapons. Once again, Vigoa brandishes two semiautomatic pistols: a Ruger 9 mm in one hand and a heavier .45-caliber Glock 21 model in the other. In accordance with Brink's and casino rules, the Brink's employees have their .38 Smith & Wesson revolvers holstered and secured. Cisneros moves in, unbuttons the safety strap of each holster, and quickly collects the guards' firearms. He dumps the weapons into the money bag, grabs the canvas sack, and steps back.

"Don't do anything crazy," Vigoa orders.

The disarmed guards stare at the retreating gunmen but do not move. The surveillance footage shows the entire robbery from a camera mounted high on the ceiling. It is not possible to make out the faces of the gunmen. In a series of videos taken by different cameras and later assembled by the hotel security staff for police, Vigoa and Cisneros are seen running down the center of a carpet when they encounter a man and a woman coming from the other direction. Politely, Cisneros moves to the left while Vigoa peels off to the right and zigzags through a cluster of slot machines. The couple continue their stroll without even turning around.

When Vigoa and Cisneros burst through the exit doors and clamber down the concrete stairs, they encounter Jay Kanner, a hotel employee. Kanner stares at the two gunmen and looks Vigoa directly in the eye. Vigoa barks a warning. "If you talk or say anything, we'll come back for you later!"

Caught on surveillance tape: After disarming guards and scooping up bags of cash off the money cart on the morning of October 11, 1999, Jose Vigoa and Oscar Cisneros sprinted through the Mandalay Bay casino past hotel guests and employees who barely noticed.

COURTESY MANDALAY BAY HOTEL.

The maroon Jeep Grand Cherokee is waiting on the street at the foot of the stairs. For the first time in four operations, the flight from the crime scene will go smoothly; Vigoa and Cisneros jump into the SUV and drive off. The crew heads north toward the motel, where the second layoff vehicle has been positioned. The Jeep passes under the I-15 freeway and pulls into the Parkway Inn, where the gunmen abandon the vehicle, split up, and leave the area in separate cars. By now, sirens can be heard approaching the Mandalay Bay.

Although not the most lucrative robbery, the Mandalay Bay heist will be the gang's model heist—blazingly fast, without resistance, and exactly according to plan. The actual robbery of the two Brink's guards takes less than one minute, and the getaway even less time. By the time police arrive, the gunmen are long gone. No one can agree in which direction the suspects fled, descriptions of the getaway vehicle vary, some witnesses describe the bandits as black men, and there's no ballistic evidence or fingerprints.

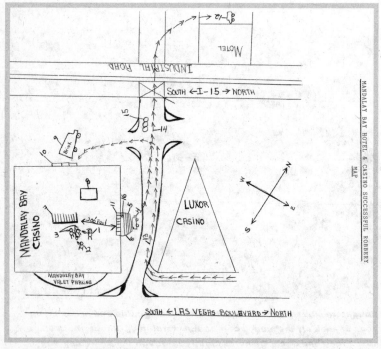

Jose Vigoa's drawing of the Mandalay Bay heist, a "lick" that was executed flawlessly. COURTESY JOSE VIGOA.

Vigoa is so confident after the robbery that thirty minutes after leaving the Strip, he returns there to study the police response. To Vigoa, seeing the police racing around the Strip is wonderful entertainment. "I was back on the I-15 in another vehicle, without the money or any firearms, and I found myself passing by the motel where we abandoned the first getaway car, the maroon Cherokee. I looked down from the freeway and into the parking lot of the motel we used, and I saw a real madhouse. Hordes of cops. A dozen police and detective cars surrounded the motel. Men with guns everywhere. There were Metro and news helicopters thumping overhead. It was so exciting and so damn funny, I wanted to pull over and watch the circus. I almost honked my horn, I was laughing so much."

The source of Vigoa's mirth? "The police had discovered our getaway Jeep at the motel, and they were going door to door with their guns drawn, maybe even kicking in a few doors, thinking we were there."

On January 3, 2000, the gang makes Las Vegas history by stealing eleven cars from the Thrifty lot. Vigoa's men arrive in a car carrier, play salsa music on a tape deck, drink Corona beer, and act as though it's a normal shipping job by a regular carrier crew moving cars from one Thrifty lot to another. Thrifty employees later tell a grand jury nighttime car shipments are a common occurrence, and they thought the shipment was authorized. Based on the descriptions of the thieves, Alamshaw realizes this is the stickup gang—and believes the crew is stockpiling equipment for a new assault on the armored cars and casinos.

The lieutenant is right. Vigoa has big plans for the year 2000. With new assault rifles, night-vision binoculars, bugging equipment, a cache of C-4 explosives, a fleet of shiny new rental cars, and funds to spare, the gang is finding its rhythm. Vigoa believes the gang has little to fear from either the police or the FBI. The "stupids," as he calls them, are inept, disorganized, and no closer to catching the gang than when the robbery spree started, he tells his crew.

But this was not true.

On October 21, 1999, the front desk receptionist at the U.S. Probation Office informed Pedro Durazo, Jose Vigoa's probation officer for four years, that there were two visitors in the lobby. "It's the FBI," said the secretary. In walked special agents Brett Shields and Rich Beasley of the bureau. "Pete, sorry to bust in on you," Shields said, "but we've got to talk."

"What about?"

Shields leaned over the desk. "What can you tell us about Jose Vigoa? And have you ever heard of two knuckleheads named Oscar Cisneros and Pedro Duarte? Your client Vigoa and his buddies are spending a lot of money these days."

TO BE SURE, Vigoa and crew were spending freely—and making up for lost time. Vigoa had spent seven dismal years in a succession of federal prisons dreaming of this moment. Now Vigoa would dress like a Miami playboy and buy his family new homes and cars. Luisa and the children, who lived below the poverty line during their father's absence, would have nothing but the best.

Vigoa felt invincible. He ridiculed the police as "doughnut eaters" who were lazy and made most of their cases through informants, not real police work. As he cased Strip hotels, scouted banks, and followed armored cars, imagining that he could harvest this wealthy city for years, Vigoa thought of his periodic trips to Florida to buy kilos of cocaine for his Vegas clientele. After taking care of business, Vigoa and friends would charter a boat and go deep-sea fishing. The fishing and bait would attract schools of sharks. Sometimes the sleek gray predators would tear at the bait or wait until the fishermen caught their fish and then viciously attack the catch just before it was pulled from the water. The water splashed and boiled and turned a dark red. *I am like the shark,* Vigoa thought. *Fearless— and feared.*

Like the shark, Vigoa thought he was driven by a primal urge, even addiction, beyond his control. Perhaps his robberies were not about good or evil, money, revenge for past injustices, or even family. They were about power, violence, danger, and the thrill of the hunt. The sharks did what they did without remorse, and so did Vigoa. The police could not possibly comprehend this, Vigoa thought. *They have no idea who or what they are dealing with.*

Chapter 18

EVE OF BATTLE

The police and FBI may not have understood the psychosocial forces that drove Vigoa, but by the time of the Mandalay Bay robbery, Jose Vigoa was now officially a person of serious interest in a major investigation that was rapidly gaining ground after months of lost opportunities and stagnation. Gordon Martines had been relieved as primary detective, and in the future would take assignments from John Alamshaw and other supervisors. When Alamshaw and a new team of detectives and FBI men began to review the case, they realized that the prime suspects had been there from the beginning of the investigation:

Vigoa, who controlled the lot from where the license plate used in the MGM robbery was stolen, was related to Pedro Duarte, who left behind his red truck with another stolen license plate at the Desert Inn. Pedro was Jose's brother-in-law. Oscar Cisneros, who fit the description of the second gunman at all four heists, was the front man for Vigoa in a series of financial transactions, including the purchase of a house and a new car. The purchases were made within weeks of the MGM robbery. Luis Suarez, another Cuban with a felony record, appeared on the police radar as a fourth suspect. Another stunning link is revealed: Suarez was the boyfriend of Vigoa's sister-in-law Caridad Farray, a former Marielito.

Martines's independent action in farming out robbery duties to cronies on the problem-solving unit—assignments not approved by Alamshaw—also would reverberate. Small errors would become major blunders as the serial robberies unfolded.

And then there were the three Farray sisters, married or linked to three gang members. "What is this, Ma Barker and kin?" Alamshaw said in a reference to the violent Depression-era crime family. "We may have our first crime family here. The question is, Are the women involved, or are they innocent victims?"

Alamshaw was beginning to feel the heat himself. He was an experienced cop and the former commander of internal affairs knew where many secrets were kept. He understood the first law of police management: accountability. Somebody will have to take the fall if the gang isn't stopped soon. There were no overt threats, Alamshaw recalled, but no shortage of barbed comments and innuendo.

"There were briefings and crime management meetings, and the robberies came up, and I could feel the pressure. You got looks. It wasn't what was being said, it was what was not being said. I knew we had to get this solved. I knew the gang was getting ready to hit us again, and I expected the worst. My gut told me it was going to get a lot worse before it got better. I knew they were stealing all these cars, but why so many? And what were they doing between robberies?"

WHAT THEY WERE doing was regrouping, shifting tactics, and getting ready for another assault on the city.

After the audacious Thrifty Car Rental heist in January 2000, officially recorded by Metro police as the largest single car theft in Las Vegas history, Vigoa and his men retired to the desert for more training, a review of the first five robberies, and an unveiling of future targets. While the media and public exulted over the new millennium, Vigoa maintained a tight focus. During the next twelve months, the gang would launch an all-out assault on Las Vegas casinos and armored cars. There would be no more Desert Inn fiascos. Vigoa vowed to "shoot like deer" anyone who resisted.

Yet for all the excitement and rolls of $100 bills now stashed within hidden compartments in bedrooms at Vigoa's and Oscar Cisneros's homes, Vigoa was restless and uneasy as he buttoned his Windbreaker against the raw desert wind on a brisk February morning in 2000. Since the first robbery attempt on May 5, 1998, at the Sunset Station, the Vigoa casino and armored car raids had been stopped cold at some locations while proceeding with clockwork precision at others. The gang seemed snakebit in some robberies and fantastically lucky in others.

The crew had amassed more than $600,000 in cash and stolen property in eighteen months, along with $330,000 more in usable casino chips and negotiable checks. But the robberies had been dogged by foolish mistakes and serious lapses in discipline. To complicate matters, Pedro Duarte had been forced out after the debacle with the getaway car at the Desert Inn and after personal conflict with Luis Suarez.

On the other hand, Oscar Cisneros, the easygoing Mexican laborer with no criminal history, was useful as a front man in transactions funded by stolen casino money. He was steady and reliable, and the irony was not lost on Vigoa. Duarte and Luis Suarez were family and fellow Cubans, but it was Cisneros who emerged as Vigoa's closest confederate, the heavyset second shooter often mentioned in police reports and witness statements.

Vigoa liked Oscar. The Mexican never complained, he had few vices, and he followed orders. Cisneros could even be trusted to serve as the owner-of-record for Vigoa's various acquisitions. Weapons, body armor, and some of the loot were stashed at Cisneros's other home at Cordelle Drive in northeast Las Vegas. Vigoa's three daughters called the Mexican "Uncle Oscar."

All in all, maybe the Vigoa crew could never function with the precision of Spetsnaz commandos, but they could be taught to obey simple orders and execute Vigoa's well-drawn plans. Later he would write: "One of my special skills, in war and in crime, was to drill my men hard by simulating the mission again and again, sometimes twenty or thirty times. There was no room for error. The police and military find this out all the time. Even when you train well, there will be mistakes. In my business, I can commit five successful robberies, but if I make one small mistake or allow my men to become careless and undisciplined, then we will all die or go to prison with long elephant sentences."

Whatever faults the team had, no one questioned Vigoa's authority. He continued the training between crimes and over the course of the crime spree formulated a set of tactical rules that will be studied by police and professional criminals for years to come.

IN A DESOLATE part of southeast Nevada five miles from the Las Vegas water and sewage treatment plant, in an area marked by sagebrush and the occasional burned-out car, Vigoa mustered his men on a Saturday morning in mid-February. He had picked his training site well: five miles up a dirt road off Vegas Valley Road East. No major highways nearby. Difficult to access. No police patrols. No aircraft flight paths overhead. Actually, the location was a good place to dump and burn a body, Vigoa reminded his men. Vigoa liked to spook his charges. "Valentine's Day is coming up," he needled, "and you know what can happen if you piss me off." Even Cubans and Mexicans had heard of the grisly 1929 St. Valentine's Day Massacre in Chicago. Those Italians were tough.

"You will have the ferocity of a tiger and the heart of a great warrior," Vigoa told Cisneros, Suarez, and a third crew member who has never been identified or prosecuted. At times Vigoa spoke English. Other times he abruptly broke into Spanish or Spanglish, the mixing of the two languages, popular among young Latinos. "It's important that you shoot fast without looking or aiming," Vigoa said on what would become a typical day of simulated robberies and firearms practice. "Trust your ability, train your mind. You become your weapon, and your weapon becomes you."

In midmorning that same Saturday, Vigoa interrupted target practice. The cutting winter wind that everyone complained about during the nippy February morning abruptly fell off, as if to herald Vigoa's announcement.

He held up four fingers and stood silently. No one spoke. Everyone knew Vigoa liked a little drama.

"*Quatro más,*" he said. Four more. "We gonna be busy now. Three more robberies and, after that, a big surprise for everybody. You're going to have more money than you can spend in a hundred lifetimes. Then we get the fuck out of here."

First the gang would strike an armored car as it made a pickup at a prosperous bank in Henderson, Nevada, a tony suburb twenty minutes southeast of the Strip along I-215. Las Vegas is often cited as the fastest-growing American city, but that is not true, Jose told his men. Henderson is the real boomtown. Not a place for the rich and famous, perhaps—certainly not for the working people, people like themselves—but a shiny new city of 240,000 built for the middle and upper middle class—casino bosses, lawyers, doctors, and accountants raking in six-figure incomes amid this economic explosion. There are fat bank accounts, and miles and miles of glitzy new shopping malls along Stephanie Street, with payrolls and cash receipts transported daily by armored cars that make stops at local banks.

"Henderson is fat and ripe, like the big mango back home ready to fall," Vigoa said. Vigoa explained that after the armored car job in Henderson, the team would return to the Las Vegas Strip for two more casino strikes. This crime spree would be followed by a job so brazen and so outrageous that people would write songs and make movies about them all.

Cisneros and Suarez remained silent. Vigoa studied his men carefully. Cisneros, the quiet one, stared at the sand and appeared to be counting expended shell casings. Suarez, frowning, seemed stricken, like a man suffering from severe indigestion.

Vigoa's dark mood returned. *Look at them! No enthusiasm, no high fives, no celebration, no fire. At least Pedro would have whooped and danced a few steps of the salsa in the sand.*

But he knew what it meant. *They are afraid.*

"The casinos we rob will be famous casinos. The biggest."

Cisneros looked up. Suarez scowled.

In what he called the Spetsnaz tradition of fierce leadership, absolute discipline, and reckless courage, Vigoa sought to challenge his men, to stiffen their backbones, to drill them to a sharp point, and, somehow, under the bright Nevada sky, to rally the men. But could Vigoa make warriors out of construction workers, plumbers, and painters? *I call them my team, but they are no team at all.* For all the rules and the drills and the rehearsals and the fiery Marxist talks about the wealthies and the fat cats and speeches about the Anglos' long history of brutal exploitation and how Americans themselves ruled by the gun during the frontier days—for all of that, Vigoa had dwindling confidence in his team. Vigoa lay awake at night thinking of the blunders by his crew, as when Duarte defied orders and took his own car to the Vagabond Motel after the DI robbery and wound up in a police interrogation room explaining what his car was doing there with stolen license plates attached to the original tag with rubber bands. *Rubber bands!* thought Vigoa. *With his own license plate underneath!*

Finally, Cisneros broke the spell. "Are we going to hit Caesars?" the Mexican asked.

"No."

"The Mirage?" Suarez asked. "I know you been there a lot."

"No. I checked out the Mirage real close. Not good for us. Only one way out. We could get trapped and shot to pieces."

The black moment having passed, Vigoa turned. "First we take the New York–New York."

A pause. Another theatrical moment.

"And then we hit the Bellagio!"

The Bellagio! "Where beauty meets luxury," as the billboards promised on the road from the airport. Perhaps the most elegant of all Las Vegas hotels, it featured seven upscale restaurants, seven bars, six cafes, 3,933 rooms, and thirty-six floors. Plus $5 million worth of ultra-high-tech cameras and security electronics.

Cisneros grinned, although Vigoa thought Oscar would have been happy if the target were the Easy Sleep Motel in Pahrump. An uneducated Mexican youth, Cisneros was now the nominal owner of two Las Vegas homes, a new Pathfinder, and a pickup truck. Cisneros was a true believer.

Suarez was not. On hearing the news, the big Cuban gasped. "You fucking crazy? The *Bellagio?* They got three million cameras there, chico. What you wanna do that for? We get killed."

For a moment, Vigoa thought seriously of taking his Russian-made sniper's rifle with the long wooden stock and butt stroking Luis's face into a bloody pulp for his insolence, as a lieutenant might have done in Afghanistan, but he remained calm.

"I told you this before," Vigoa said patiently. "Cameras don't shoot nothing. Cameras don't catch nobody. Cameras don't show shit if we wear our disguises, get in, and get out quickly. Don't worry about no cameras. They won't hurt you."

Cisneros chimed in: "We could shoot them out!"

Vigoa sighed. "That might take a little time, Oscar. They got two thousand cameras there, and some you can't even see."[1]

After the big announcement, Vigoa put his team back to work. The curriculum included target practice, with each gunman switching back and forth from handguns to rifles and automatic weapons. They practiced fire and maneuvering, leapfrogging from one position to another, or running in short, choppy steps before falling on one knee and then into the prone position, firing their weapons throughout the exercise. The men learned about "suppressing fire"—maintaining a stream of rounds to keep the opponents' heads down.

Vigoa taught the technique of advancing or falling back by echelon. He explained the terms *base of fire* and *line of fire*. Base of fire: a steady stream of rifle fire to keep the enemy's heads pinned down. Line of fire: a

---

[1] Jose was close. Bellagio security head Stephen G. Koenig confirms there are more than 1,600 surveillance cameras on line at the hotel, and, indeed, many are concealed pin cameras that blend into the walls, facades, and countertops.

wall of men in line blazing away in one direction. The men learned arm and hand signals because they weren't supposed to talk. Vigoa explained the basics of cover and concealment, made famous by the Japanese in World War II. He instructed the men on obfuscation (smoke), boundary overmatch, firing from a moving vehicle, penetrating armor, the use of grenades. Vigoa told the gunmen how to avoid muzzle creep—don't get careless and allow your weapon to wander during a skirmish, bringing your comrades under fire. He pointed out the risks of funneling (bunching up) and other common small-unit errors. The weapons used by the gang at that time included: one Smith & Wesson .38, one Smith & Wesson .40 semiautomatic, one Ruger 9 mm P-85, one Glock .45, one Ruger .357 revolver, one AK-47 assault rifle, two Norinco MAK 90s (a Chinese version of the AK-47), and two Russian-made VEPR .308-caliber sniper rifles. And by now the team could recite the Vigoa's Rules almost word for word:

1. No talking during a job, except when "freezing" the victim (ordering him to stop and drop his weapon). Absolute silence among unit members.

2. Plan A: Disarm guards. Plan B: Kill them without hesitation if they resist.

3. Vigoa, and Vigoa alone, gives the orders when to retire to the getaway car.

4. The second getaway vehicle (technically known as the first lay-off car) will be within running distance of the job because the armored car driver has been taught to use the truck as a battering ram and could damage the first car at the crime scene.

5. A minimum of three lay-off cars per job. These vehicles, plus the first getaway car—the one whose license plate number everybody writes down with great excitement—make a total of four cars per job.

6. Speed is essential—one minute and out. (When Suarez starts to protest that it will take that much time just to gather up the loot, Vigoa cuts him off: "This is not the movies, chico, people have cell phones, they call 911, and the stupids will race out of their doughnut shops for a little action.")

7. No lay-off cars to be stored in casino lots, because security has been writing down plate numbers. Use apartment lots.

8. Chaos is key. (Vigoa to crew: "Who knows what *modus operandi* means?" Silence. "Good, because we don't have one. Be unpredictable. This is war. Predictability gets you killed.")

9. Leave nothing behind.

10. Ski masks and dark clothing. Always wear gloves. Leave the masks on until we reach the third getaway car.

At the end of that Saturday training session, with the smell of cordite heavy in the air, Vigoa gathered his men in a semicircle. They squatted on the ground.

"Now we get real serious," Vigoa said.

Cisneros and Suarez exchanged glances. *Serious?* Another armored car, the New York–New York, and the Bellagio are *not* serious?

"You said the armored car in Henderson and two casinos. What's the other target?" Suarez asked. "What's the big surprise?"

For the first time that day, Vigoa smiled broadly.

"Brother Luis, when we count the money from the Bellagio, I will tell you what you need to know. Until then, do what I say, and you will make your family, and my sister, and your brother-in-law very happy."

Suarez persisted. "I gotta know, what's the surprise? I gotta think about this. I have a family."

Vigoa walked to within inches of the bigger Suarez while maintaining the broad grin. For a moment it appeared the two men might fight. Suarez stood his ground, although his eyes widened.

"You're right, Luis. You have a right to know. I keep nothing from you. You are family."

"So what are we doing after the Bellagio?" Suarez mumbled, not as aggressively as before.

Vigoa stepped back and addressed all three gunmen. Within days after the Bellagio job, the team would rob a three-axle armored car the size of a tractor trailer on its route from the Bank of America vault to a downtown Los Angeles bank. High explosives would be used. From casinos on the Strip and downtown, the ten-wheeler carried an estimated $100 million.

JOSE VIGOA, WHOSE personal and professional foundations ran more along a military and criminal plane, fired off one last round into the

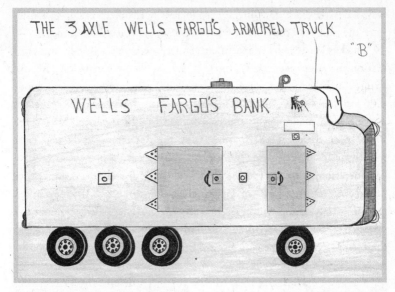

The final job of the Vigoa crime spree, planned for early June 2000, was to be a violent attack with explosives on an oversized "super" armored car that made a weekly run from Las Vegas to Los Angeles. This is Jose Vigoa's drawing of the truck.

COURTESY JOSE VIGOA.

rusted car, which by late afternoon was now less metal and more jagged holes. The remains of a front fender promptly fell into the dust. Vigoa fired again, emptying the drum magazine of the stumpy Chinese-made AK-47 assault rifle, originally designed by Mikhail Kalashnikov in 1947 and today the most popular automatic weapon in the world.

Whump!

Clackety-clack!

Whump!

Clackety-clack!

The shots echoed across the valley floor.

TO THE NORTH, those charged with defending their city from Vigoa's attacks knew nothing of the desert training, but they expected further robberies and braced for more violence. The question was not whether but when. The irony was inescapable. No longer protected by ruthless organized crime figures who kept crime out of the city in their own brutal way, Las Vegas became vulnerable to increasingly brazen casino robberies once the mob sold out. Vigoa was the first to exploit this opening.

The Las Vegas police department, confronted with an exploding population and a cop-per-citizen ratio that was well below the national norm,[2] struggled to keep up with more than 3,300 robberies a year and about 6,000 violent crimes. In 2000 Lieutenant Alamshaw had three sergeants and eighteen detectives in the robbery unit to be deployed over three shifts seven days a week. It often took the detectives weeks and even months to investigate some holdups and burglaries.

The crime rate reflected the arrival of six thousand new residents per month, the "franchising" of Los Angeles gangs in Clark County, and a booming tourist population that on any given day equaled the citizenry of Salt Lake City, as more than thirty-seven million visitors a year clogged the casinos, showrooms, and hotels. Before the Vigoa gang launched its raids, fewer than 1 percent of all armed robberies involved casinos.

Yet Las Vegas did survive. Maybe the city's defenses were breaking down because of cautious new liability policies handed down by lawyers designed to avoid $10 million lawsuits in the event of a firefight and civilian casualties. There were many changes: Casino guards, armed to the teeth in the days of the mob, were mostly without firearms. The newer hotels had open cashier cages without bars or even bulletproof glass. The city was in the midst of runaway growth, and as a result, the police department was seriously undermanned. But Vegas wasn't helpless.

If the system was broke, or in transition as the Fortune 500 owners learned the ropes, the community had another resource: its own modern-day version of a tough sheriff and his hard-riding posse. Las Vegas may have been a soft target when it came to the loose cash moving up and down the Strip, but the men and women who pursued the Vigoa gang were anything but soft.

The defenders of Las Vegas included Metro detectives, suburban policemen, the FBI, the CSI forensic unit (made famous by the hit television series), federal parole officers, and a team of aggressive prosecutors from the district attorney's office. Hotel security staff, although mostly unarmed and under highly restrictive rules of engagement, manned an estimated sixteen thousand surveillance cameras. One supervisor in the video

---

[2] Significantly below. Las Vegas in 2000 deployed 1.7 sworn policemen per 1,000 citizens, a ratio that increased to 1.86 by 2005. The national norm in big cities is 2.4 per 1,000.

"eye in the sky" casino surveillance unit, a former U.S. Army scout, would play an important role in the defense of Las Vegas against the Cuban commercial terrorists.

Deputy Chief Ray Flynn, the boss of all Metro detectives, summed it up for many when he said in an interview that Las Vegas no longer had an inferiority complex: "Las Vegas is the tough little town that became the tough big city. And we apologize for nothing. I think for the longest time, Las Vegas thought about apologizing because we have gambling here, because we have twenty-four-hour drinking here. And then we realized America wants to come here."

The lawmen, generally proud of their modern-day boomtown, were a varied lot. There were former recon marines, army rangers, navy corpsmen, Vietnam combat veterans, Gulf war reservists, and future Iraq war combatants among the police, CSI, firefighters, SWAT team, and problem-solving unit.

There were FBI men with impressive résumés who at first blanched at the thought of assignment to Sin City but grew to like the town. There was a future district attorney on the case, Dave Roger, a man of impeccable manners who was in fact a tiger beneath his immaculate white shirts and well-cut suits. Roger worked alongside Pamela Weckerly, a pretty, auburn-haired violent-crimes prosecutor who was no slouch herself— the young woman had her first baby while prosecuting a gangster for attempted murder.

There were strict button-down Mormons, at least one hard-drinking detective whose doctors gave him one year to live, another detective who moonlighted as a high-school football coach, a paramedic studying for his doctorate, and a detective boss from the streets of Chicago with a tough reputation. One supervising lieutenant at the Henderson Police Department was not only the first woman in her department but the first female supervisor; later she would vault to the rank of deputy chief.

And there was John Alamshaw, juggling resources, borrowing manpower, clamoring for overtime funds, maintaining peace with the FBI, and keeping Gordon Martines, who seemed to be conducting his own investigation, under control. Alamshaw knew when to push his cynical detectives and when to back off. Although the lieutenant was a former commander of the dreaded internal-affairs unit, the men considered him above all a street cop, fair and good hearted, and not the typical "suit." In matters of ethics and personal conduct, Alamshaw led by example: He wrote a check each month to the department to cover personal calls he might make on his office phone. A sign on his wall read: I Work for God.

By the year 2000, Alamshaw had made more than a thousand arrests personally in his career; his units (robbery, major crime, and violent crime) had solved more than five thousand crimes, including the capture of eighteen serial robbers who accounted for three hundred noncasino stickups. This case of serial robbery and attempted murder was different. The casino bandits were unlike anything the police had ever seen, shifting their targets back and forth between armored cars serving casinos *and* the casinos themselves. *I would not want to be a messenger for Brink's, Armored Transport, or Wells Fargo,* Alamshaw thought. The detective lieutenant sensed the worst was yet to come. He would need to marshal all his resources and deploy his best men to stop this one-crew crime wave. The defenders of Las Vegas would be put to the test.

ONE UNLIKELY FOOT soldier in this brewing conflict was at this very moment standing in front of a full-length mirror in northeast Clark County, resplendent in his freshly pressed dark blue trousers, crisply starched sky blue uniform shirt, polished black leather gun belt, and two semiautomatic pistols, one on each hip. He was an unlikely warrior and not even a sworn peace officer. The young man wore a large Armored Transport company patch on his right sleeve. A million dollars, let alone $100 million dollars, was not on his mind. He had six dollar bills in his tattered wallet. He made barely $20,000 a year before taxes.

The young man frowned, cocked his head, and squinted menacingly. A gunfighter's hard face. The boy tugged on his wispy, barely visible mustache, scowled once more, and then—he laughed. A big toothy grin with lots of upper gum on view and an ungainly if deliberate boyish yelp. Looking more and more like Jim Carrey and less and less like Clint Eastwood, the young man turned around.

We have a record of this moment in a color photograph taken by his mother, Shala Premack, who chuckled at her son's mugging before the mirror. In the snapshot, which today occupies a place of honor in at least three homes in Las Vegas, the twenty-three-year-old is wearing a dark blue baseball cap that seems a little too big for his head, and his right hand rests on his right hip, just above the gun belt. The kid wears black cowboy

Gary Dean Prestidge in his Armored Transport uniform in 1999.

COURTESY SHALA PREMACK
AND THE PRESTIDGE FAMILY.

boots with the Armored Transport uniform. All in all, a friendly and open face.

Shala took another picture. "Oh, look at you now, Little Gary! Just look at you now." Shala looked down at the floor. "I like the cowboy boots. Are they new?"

They were. When you earn $20,000 a year before taxes, you don't do your shopping at the marble-lined Forum Shops at Caesars Palace, but these were first-class goods made of expensive snakeskin. The boots were the pride of Gary Dean Prestidge II, known to close friends and family as Little Gary. Dad, nicknamed Big Gary, was a former jockey. People loved the joke: Big Gary was five foot five; Little Gary was six foot tall, filling out and still growing. In his fancy boots, Little Gary stood at least six foot two.

Check him out. Gary was wiry, but not skinny, putting on weight and muscle, weighing 160-plus pounds, still maturing physically. Gary Dean had bushy eyebrows that once provoked endless teasing, accenting a long, slender face. The boy in Gary Dean was fading rapidly, the man was coming on fast. Gary Dean, once he filled out, was going to be a good-looking young adult.

Little Gary. Gary Dean. Gary Dean *the Second*. Professionally known as Security Officer Prestidge of the Armored Transport company, a sometime driver, sometime hopper, a guardian of the tens of millions of dollars that moved up and down the boulevards of Las Vegas. One of the few security guards in Las Vegas who wears two pistols. A firearm aficionado. A crack pistol shot. And a lad who takes his job seriously.

Youth. Skill. Courage. Duty. All of these virtues will influence the order of battle as the Cubans prepare to storm Las Vegas once more. Actually, Little Gary was safe at the time of the picture taking. He worked in the vault at the Armored Transport company office in east Las Vegas, shuffling paperwork, logging money, and preparing the next day's packages for delivery. Prestidge was in his third year at the company. By all accounts, he enjoyed the work, and, in a company marked by labor strife and a budding union movement, remained below the office politics radar. Despite his age, Prestidge was liked and respected in a workforce populated largely by older men. Fellow drivers and messengers came to Gary for advice on firearms, holsters, and other accessories. To be sure, Gary Dean was an eccentric, with his cowboy attire, country music, and what the men called his enthusiastic, gung ho attitude. But he also knew guns, could shoot, and was a real nice, respectful kid who gave nobody any grief.

Gary Dean did have one concern that he expressed earnestly one night to his parents. He said that other guards on at least one truck route told of being followed by suspicious men for several days in a row. Hispanic men. Otherwise, during his time at Armored Transport, Gary Dean had drawn his gun once only, to keep an angry motorist from climbing into the truck to beat up his driver after a road rage incident. It was something that everybody laughed about later, but Gary Dean was beginning to realize that Las Vegas was becoming a big and violent city.

In that winter of 2000, Prestidge talked about leaving the Armored Transport company and armored car work. He wanted to work for another year and move on. Maybe even join the fire department or military and complete his education, gaining financial aid for college and eventually majoring in forestry. He loved the outdoors.

Thrilled at the news, his parents urged Little Gary to quit right away. They never liked his job. Around the country, armored car guards were being shot at like second lieutenants in battle. It could happen here. Just read the *Review-Journal* or watch TV. Why, it's happening even now, his father said.

"Did you read about that gang knocking off casinos?" his father asked. "They seem to be bushwhacking armored cars!" Dad noted that at the Desert Inn, the guards came under fire from automatic rifles. Two of the Brink's men were shot. They could have been killed. "Every day I told Gary that it's not worth dying for another man's money," the father recalled. Gary knew all about the robberies. He even knew one of the wounded guards.

There was something else the son said from time to time that deeply disturbed his parents and others who loved the free-spirited young man. Gary Dean's remark would trigger polite but urgent conversations between father and son.

He didn't want to hurt anybody and loathed violence. For all of his hiking and shooting, he neither hunted nor fished. Life was precious. But if somebody tried to rob one of his trucks, well, Gary Dean knew what he had to do:

"I'll go down fighting," he said. "I will do my job."

Gary's father was shaken. The boy didn't understand the real world where high-velocity bullets maim and kill. Did Little Gary know what he was saying? It sounded like a line from one of those country and western tunes Gary liked to sing in his used pickup truck.

In fact, Gary Dean did find such a song. A fan of George Strait, Garth Brooks, and Alabama, Gary also liked the lean rock of Tom Petty and the Heartbreakers with its 1950s and 1960s influences. One of Petty's songs stuck in his mind:

> You could stand me up at the gates of hell,
> but I won't back down.

Some of the older men, who definitely would not stand their ground for the wages paid by the Armored Transport company, laughed at Gary Dean. "That's what you say now! Wait'll some homey points a sawed-off in yer face," they said.

GARY DEAN WAS born on February 5, 1977, in Needles, California, raised in the Mojave Valley in northwest Arizona along the Colorado River and brought to Las Vegas by Shala and Gary Prestidge, Sr., at age eight. He is a character out of a Norman Rockwell painting. Growing up in Arizona and Nevada, Gary Dean pitches a one-hitter in a Little League game and plays in the desert with his sister Julie building forts.

By junior high school, the thin, friendly, slightly zany Prestidge boy discovers superheroes, from Wyatt Earp to Indiana Jones. Action figures, cartoon characters, war heroes, cinema tough guys—they all are part of the fantasy world that takes hold and never lets go. The child's imagination runs wild. He draws sketches of cowboys and gunfighters in class and later on the job.

More so than most boys, Gary Dean becomes seduced by a popular culture awash in larger-than-life characters. To Gary Dean these are not fictional or exaggerated versions of real life, they are role models, men to admire and emulate.

Looking back, Gary's obsession must have seemed harmless at the time, even when he lost interest in baseball, and his previously excellent grades began to fall off as early as the eighth grade. Gary admired the virtuous and the brave; how could that be a problem? Why worry if the kid seemed to be drawn more and more to the dreamlike and fantastic with each passing year?

His parents saw no reason to call in a child psychologist. Little Gary was going through a stage. Little Gary may have been immature, but he knew the difference between reality and fiction. Besides, the boy didn't do drugs; he barely drank, for God's sake.

In fact, there is some evidence to suggest that Gary Dean's fixation grew stronger as he passed through adolescence and into adulthood. Although distressed by Gary Dean's declining grades in school, over time the family got used to the boy's runaway imagination, and friends didn't seem to mind, although they poked fun at him from time to time, nicknaming him "Tex." They howled when Gary showed up at his prom wearing a tuxedo jacket and blue jeans. Chuckled when Gary went out and bought a leather jacket, riding boots, and a hat just like the one Indiana Jones wore. Gary practiced for hours with a bullwhip and became quite skilled, able to snap branches off a tree.

In February of his senior year, Gary Dean abruptly quit school, three months before graduation. Without a high-school diploma or GED, Gary Dean was not qualified to join the police or fire department, as he once hoped. At eighteen years old, immature and unfocused, he was not a candidate for the military, with its structure and discipline.

In 1997, at the age of twenty, Gary Dean Prestidge II became a guard

Gary Dean Prestidge in his Western cowboy attire.

COURTESY SHALA PREMACK
AND THE PRESTIDGE FAMILY.

for the Armored Transport company. "He liked it," Shala recalled. "He was finally a protector, a guardian. He could carry a gun. He was proud of that." His father was not happy. "Every day I'd say to him, 'Why don't you let me get you a good job and a safe job?' He'd laugh and say, 'I love what I'm doing, Dad.' I had to respect that."

IN CONTRAST TO Gary Dean, Ricardo Sosa rarely talked about the risks of an armored car job. As long as his paychecks cleared the bank, Ricardo was happy.

Richard (Ricardo) Sosa, born on July 31, 1952, migrated to the U.S. in 1981 from San Salvador, El Salvador—the same year that Jose Vigoa and John Alamshaw arrived in Las Vegas. After originally settling in East Los Angeles, the Sosa family moved to Nevada after a homeboy put a pistol to Mr. Sosa's head during a Bank of America holdup. Settling in Las Vegas, Ricardo became the patriarch of a family that included wife Norma, a petite dark-haired beauty from Santa Tecla, El Salvador, and five children, two from a previous marriage.

A dependable colleague who stands up to company bosses more so than most, Sosa is known among the guards for his fast and daredevil driving while trying to service all those stores and casinos on run number five. His partner, Kevin Prokopich, likes Sosa for his good humor. "A great smile all the time," he recalled. "So friendly. Very positive, protective of his family, and a hard worker."

The Sosas live in a small, neat home on Willard Street off Boulder Highway northeast of Henderson in an area called Whitney. The Willard Street section of Whitney is home to the workers of Las Vegas: the maids, busboys, servers, and laborers. This is the area where Jose Vigoa kept his "roach coach" trailer and pretended to live. If Henderson is affluent, modern, and marked by runaway growth, Whitney is cluttered and aging in places—a neighborhood where the money plays out.

By the spring of 2000, Ricardo Sosa tells everyone that he intends to escape that marginal existence and obscurity. At five foot eight and 185 pounds, Sosa is a vigorous, barrel-chested man who worked long hours in a succession of security jobs in California and Nevada. He decrees that his children—Michael and Jacqueline Lopez, from a previous marriage; and Richard, Edwin, and Sabrina by Norma—must break away from the underclass. Under their father's no-nonsense direction, the kids study hard, go to church, stay out of gangs, avoid drugs, respect their elders, and plan for college. Ricardo holds a family barbeque every Sunday. He plays soccer in the morning on weekends or watches his muscular sons play.

Norma is the love of Sosa's life. They marry in 1994 after a five-year courtship and come to Las Vegas in 1997. Ricardo wants his wife to quit her job as a maid at a Strip hotel. Son Edwin, twenty-three in 2004, recalls that his father even decided what Norma would wear. "He took her to stores to buy her clothes. He would say, 'Why don't you wear this, why don't you wear that?' "

At the outset of 2000, Prestidge and Sosa follow news reports concerning a heavily armed holdup crew knocking off casinos and armored cars on the Strip. Gary Dean talks about bringing his thirty-round Ruger Mini-14 rifle to work should he be assigned to an armored truck servicing the Strip hotels. A semiautomatic rifle based on the M14, the Mini-14 could make a difference in a prolonged firefight. Even so, the route from Henderson to Boulder City, Nevada, is not considered dangerous. Besides, Prestidge now works inside the company vault at 1685 South Palm Street on the east side of Las Vegas. He is no longer assigned to the armored cars.

The following week Sosa and his regular partner, Kevin Prokopich, are scheduled to man the long Henderson route on truck 3280. Prokopich is one of the fastest hoppers in the company, a rawboned, energetic young man who bolts from the truck and charges into stores, sometimes running into customers and shoving them aside. Only now Prokopich is coming down with the flu. "I'll try to ride out the week," Prokopich tells Sosa before breaking into a heavy, wracking chest cough. "But I don't know if I'll make it." Unless Kevin improves, manager John Zamora will have to find another hopper to ride the new ten-ton Ford truck as it barrels through southeast Clark County.

By Wednesday, March 1, Prokopich's temperature is 103 degrees, and he tells his wife he is having difficulty breathing. Candice Prokopich is a nurse. Candice takes her husband to a hospital, where X-rays are taken. The diagnosis is unmistakable: pneumonia. Prokopich would be off for at least a week. Manager Zamora considers riding the truck himself but then thinks of the perfect replacement: Gary Dean. The kid knew all the routes and liked working outdoors.

On Friday, March 3, Prestidge is up by six. He brushes his teeth in the shower, runs in his Hanes underwear to the dryer to grab a fresh sky blue shirt, and eats a bowl of Cap'n Crunch cereal on the run.

Prestidge checks his weapons at the kitchen table. First priority: his primary weapon, the Smith & Wesson 9 mm semiautomatic with an eleven-round magazine.

He operates the slide, jerks a live round into the chamber. Then turns to his backup piece, a Kel-Tec P-11 semiautomatic handgun billed by the maker as the smallest and lightest 9 mm pistol made. Almost palm size, the Kel-Tec has a ten-round magazine and weighs only fourteen ounces— a popular choice among police and military as a secondary weapon. Little gun. Lots of firepower. Plenty of recoil. Prestidge sights the pistol, blows off a few specks of dust, and polishes away the first hint of rust with a soft gray rag that is damp with gun oil.

At 7:10 in the morning, Gary Dean "Tex" Prestidge II, badge number 1325, looks sharp in his crisp blue Armored Transport company uniform. Prestidge carries a pen, matchbook, vitamin pack, Craftsman utility tool, micro tape recorder, triangular knife, Uncle Mike's gun belt, and a Sprint cellular phone. He wears the Smith & Wesson on his right hip and the five-inch Kel-Tec on his left.

Gary Dean Prestidge then steps into his prize 1999 Ford pickup truck and goes to work.

Chapter 19

A PICTURE-PERFECT DAY

On the morning of March 3, 2000, in Henderson, Nevada, the weather is clearing, the sun is finally out after several days of rain. The merchants in the Target Shopping Center stock their shelves for a big weekend while packaging the previous day's receipts for pickup by the armored truck that arrives every morning just before noon.

A picture-perfect day in southern Nevada.

Melody Rogers, forty-six, a registered nurse at the Monte Vista Behavioral Health Care Hospital, is doing her week's grocery shopping, trying to beat the Friday afternoon rush. Melody has one of the most challenging jobs in Clark County: She evaluates emergency room patients who have suffered severe emotional breakdowns or drug overdoses.

Also pulling into the parking lot is Susan Berry, thirty-five, a teacher at the J. C. Fremont Middle School.

Tonya Keith, twenty-nine, is inside the Ross Dress for Less store, browsing through a dress rack. Gary Housley, sixty, has just withdrawn cash for the weekend and, against doctor's orders, is heading for a pizza parlor a block away. *A slice of pizza with a little pepperoni never killed anybody,* the civil engineer thinks. Housley walks to the restaurant and notices there are people everywhere on this gorgeous day in Henderson, Nevada.

Taking an early lunch break is Sergeant Joe Molinaro, forty-six. He is a six-foot-one, 220-pound cop and former marine from New Jersey who's built like an NFL linebacker. But when the fierce-looking officer suddenly smiles, a mischievous and boyish grin gives away Molinaro's secret—he is a friendly and good-natured man. At the moment, Molinaro studies the menu at Carmine's Little Italy sports bar, a cop hangout that looks like a gigantic peach-colored cash register with baseballs and basketballs fixed to its front. Molinaro is joined by Sergeant Jackie Miller. In police jargon, the two uniformed sergeants are on a code 7 break for lunch. They talk about personnel evaluations, training—and what a quiet week it has been.

Detective Eddie Newman is starting to feel hungry while enjoying the promise of an early spring. Considered by some to be the toughest cop in the city, and possibly the most irascible, Newman does heating and air-conditioning work on his off-days with the department's approval. Today he's ten miles away, standing on the roof of a two-story house in Boulder City, repairing a fan motor. Newman ponders a doctor's recent opinion that after years of hard drinking, his liver is shot. *They say I have one year to live. We'll see about that.*

Newman's boss, Lieutenant Jutta Chambers, is at headquarters, reviewing a case with two other detectives. Blond, athletic, and known to be a fair and able boss, Jutta is a symbol of change at 223 Lead Street, the ironically named address of police headquarters. An army brat and former air force K-9 officer, Jutta is the first female police officer to be employed by the Henderson Police Department and the first female supervisor. Chambers likes her job. She's weathered the sexism and chauvinism with dignity and grace and looks forward to a long career in Henderson. The city, even more so than its giant neighbor to the north, is booming. Unlike Las Vegas, however, Henderson can be very quiet, even a little dull. This appears to be one of those days. Chambers prepares to break for lunch.

FOR SHOPPERS AND POLICE ALIKE, the tranquility is about to be shattered, and, like Vegas, Henderson's smug sense of safety and security will pass into history. Jose Vigoa and his crew are about to launch their spring offensive.

Now huddled inside a silver-gray Plymouth Voyager minivan, Vigoa intends to surprise the lone guard and driver on Armored Transport truck number 3280. And by all appearances, it is a *superb* plan. The hopper carrying the money to and from the store, a distance of about seventy feet in each direction, is scheduled to walk between two nearly identical minivans positioned by Vigoa in front of the Ross store. On the left, facing Ross, is a stolen white 2000 Plymouth Voyager minivan, formerly in the possession of the Thrifty Car Rental company. Oscar Cisneros and Luis

Suarez are even now waiting inside the white van, which has no rear seats. Cisneros's job is to freeze the messenger. Vigoa will disarm the driver. Suarez's sole task is to remove currency from the armored truck once the guards are neutralized.

A second minivan is parked to the right of the Ross entranceway, as is seen from the vantage point of the armored truck. The side and rear windows of both Voyagers are blacked out by construction paper neatly taped on the inside of the glass. There are large cardboard boxes stacked behind the front seats, blocking an outside view of the cabin.[1] This silver-gray 2000 Plymouth Voyager, also taken in the Thrifty Car Rental heist, is backed into the parking space, "nose out." Vigoa is inside the silver van with his AK-47 copy, a Chinese-made MAK 90 with a seventy-round drum.

The objective, Vigoa reminds his crew repeatedly, is not the bag of money held by the hopper at this point. "We don't care about the store receipts. We want what's in the truck—that's where the big money will be found."

Vigoa checks his watch. For four weeks he's been stalking this particular armored car, its number 3280 painted all over the big truck. Vigoa has carefully timed the armored truck stops: He knows the messengers are in a hurry and pay little attention to their surroundings. Typically the messenger will spend between four and five minutes per store delivering coins and small bills to be used as change in the morning, although Jose knows that if the store manager is elsewhere in the store, or in the restroom, there could be another five-minute delay. Once the manager is at his desk, the messenger will pick up cash and checks from the previous day's business to be deposited in the bank at the end of the day.

Originally conducting surveillance at long range with binoculars, Jose in recent weeks has stood on the sidewalk in front of the Ross store watching the messengers scurry back and forth, even making eye contact. The harried, rushing men never seem to notice the Cuban with the cell phone who watches them so intently.

Vigoa is pleased to learn that the guards never change their procedure, which he considers "very stupid" but very helpful. When the messenger

---

[1] Jose Vigoa recalls parking the two vans at about 7:30 a.m. in front of Ross. However, Guynella Bosher, a teller at the credit union, is waiting for her boss to open the building when she notices the two vans arrive at 8:40 a.m. She thought the men were construction workers from a nearby job site. The Bosher time is probably more accurate.

returns to the truck, the driver will open the side door, the one the armored car guards call the "hopper door." And because the bulkhead barrier door behind the driver will be open due to a malfunction, the driver and the messenger will be exposed simultaneously.

They will strike at this precise moment. Everything must happen within one minute. Speed. Surprise. Daring. In and out.

A picture-perfect day in Henderson. A great day for a robbery.

Chapter 20

KILLING ZONE

Armored truck 3280 is on the move.

It is 11:25 a.m. on Friday, March 3, 2000, and halfway through its more than one hundred–mile route, the white diesel leaves the Galleria Mall, turns right on Stephanie Street, and heads north.

Ricardo Sosa guns the big Ford engine. The driver is determined "to make bank" before closing time, but it won't be easy. This is the notorious number-five route, and according to the guards who make the run, 3280 is possibly the most overbooked armored truck route in the region. Today Sosa wants to finish his work on time—March 3 marks his six-year wedding anniversary. Sosa has planned a celebration dinner tonight with Norma and the five kids at a Chinese restaurant.

Sosa has another concern: Kevin Prokopich, his everyday partner on the truck, has been out sick since Tuesday. Gary Dean Prestidge II, the replacement hopper, is more deliberate. Gary Dean refuses to run in and out of stores. He often smiles and jokes with shoppers and employees. While Prokopich never draws his gun during his wild sprints to and from the truck, Prestidge cradles the blue money bag in his left arm and holds his primary pistol, a Smith & Wesson 9 mm semiautomatic, in his right hand, concealed within the folds of the canvas bag.

Sosa urges Prestidge to pick up his pace. "I want to get out of here today on time." No gossiping with pretty girls or talkative store owners. It's anniversary night, and the Sosas love a good party. Prestidge laughs and teases Ricardo, calling him "Anniversary Boy." Sosa invites Prestidge to the party.

The truck makes a left-hand turn into the Target Shopping Center (formally known as the Whitney Ranch Center, though few locals call it that) and passes a Subway restaurant, a Vista Optical store, the Prestige Travel Agency, and the La Salsa Fresh Mexican Grill. It stops directly in front of the Ross Dress for Less store, about seventy feet from the front door. Sosa parks parallel to the clothing store, facing south, then punches a button to open the hopper door. At this time the driver's bulletproof interior bulkhead door is supposed to close, protecting Sosa from threats outside the truck while the guard makes his delivery. However, the electronic system is not working.

The hopper door opens. A pleasant breeze passes through the cabin for a few seconds. The truck interior is stuffy, and the brief burst of cool air refreshing.

At 11:28:55 a.m. Gary Prestidge steps out into the sunshine. The morning clouds are gone. As Prestidge walks briskly to the front door of Ross, the hopper door closes behind him while the bulkhead door behind Sosa remains open. A few pedestrians glance at the armored truck and the slender young man who walks briskly into the store.

Other eyes are watching too.

11:34:12. The front door of the Ross store swings open and out walks Gary Dean Prestidge, carrying the money bag in his left arm. There is $69,338.48 in the canvas bag, including checks, credit card receipts, and $4,930 in currency and coins. When Prestidge is within thirty feet of the armored truck, Ricardo Sosa places his metal clipboard in his lap and opens the hopper door by remote control.

This is the moment Vigoa has been waiting for.

11:34:29. The door to Cisneros's white Voyager minivan slides open.

Go, go, go, Oscar! Vigoa chants to himself. Every cell in the Cuban's body is electrified by anticipation. *We gonna have a good paycheck today.*

Cisneros, armed with a .38 revolver[1], and Suarez, holding a large duffel bag, step out of the minivan.

"Don't move!" Cisneros yells, advancing to within twenty feet of Prestidge. "Turn around slowly with your hands in the air!"

Prestidge is caught by surprise. All reason suggests that he must surrender at once or face violent retaliation, perhaps even summary execution. His weapon is hidden and pointed 90 degrees away from his assailant. Prestidge is moving in the wrong direction, toward the truck,

---

[1] Oscar Cisneros will later claim he was carrying a .40 semiautomatic Smith & Wesson. However, Jose Vigoa insists it was a .38 revolver and says that the two men argued over this choice of weapon because of its limited firepower.

with the gunman on his right side. The money bag is now heavy with cash and awkward to handle, a hindrance to any sudden counter movement. Cisneros has Prestidge cold.

But Cisneros does not know that the replacement courier is Gary Dean Prestidge II, that his nickname is "Tex," that Prestidge is a crack shot, that Prestidge has vowed never to give up the money, and that Prestidge has been fighting gun battles and looking death in the face for two decades, at least in his own imagination.

On hearing the sharp command from Cisneros, Prestidge halts his advance to the open hopper door and begins to rotate clockwise toward the Mexican. It is as though this maneuver had been rehearsed a thousand times.

For Cisneros and the Vigoa crew, this is about one quick score.

For Prestidge, this is about his very being and all that he believes.

What Prestidge does next will later be called heroic, reckless, valiant, brave, crazy, suicidal, and just plain foolish. But, in fact, there is no decision to be made, and what Gary does is—well, simply Gary. He is neurologically hardwired to fight, to resist, to protect the truck and the money with his life. Right now Prestidge's synapses are firing at speeds beyond comprehension.

Behind Prestidge, Vigoa realizes what is happening. He angrily jerks open his side door, the rifle's flash suppressor striking the door frame with a metallic clang. Vigoa is frantic. *Oscar! Pay attention! Shoot the motherfucker!*

By now, even Cisneros knows something is not quite right. He looks down at Prestidge's right hip. The holster is empty. Prestidge has pivoted a full 90 degrees and now faces Cisneros directly.

Looking on, Vigoa knows what's about to happen, but he can't fire. Not yet. Cisneros and Suarez are in the line of fire.

A plume of red and orange flame erupts from Prestidge's Smith & Wesson.

Crack!

The 9 mm round from Prestidge's semiautomatic hits the pavement, ricochets, and whistles past Cisneros's ear. For two, perhaps three seconds, the Mexican cannot move, like a man trapped in a bad nightmare. *He's shooting at me!*

Prestidge fires again, repeatedly. In local law enforcement circles they call it the "Metro walk"—a firing pattern in which the shooter squeezes off rounds a split second after his pistol clears the holster, "walking" the bullets up to the target. Prestidge now performs the Metro walk, the bullets advancing up the sidewalk to Oscar Cisneros.

Crack!

A second round from Prestidge digs into the sidewalk and careens into the truck before splintering into metal fragments.

Crack!

A third round tears through Cisneros's right calf, a through-and-through wound. The young Mexican yells, grabs his leg, and starts to hop backward. If not for the terrible life-and-death stakes of this encounter, the sight of bulky Cisneros dancing a jig in front of Ross while bullets fly would be comical.

Crack!

Prestidge's aim is now on target. A fourth round hits Cisneros in the chest, just below the heart. The gunman is knocked backward and nearly falls over. But he is wearing body armor, and the round is stopped. Now Cisneros's leg is spurting blood. "I'm hit! I'm hit!" the Mexican yells. He continues limping away, firing wildly, emptying his six-shot .38 revolver at the guard. One bullet hits Prestidge, possibly in the leg. The remaining bullets go high.

A woman with two children screams and runs into the store. Another mother throws herself on her two small children and begins to pray.

11:34:48.

Jose Vigoa is astounded. *Are these fucking Americans out of their minds?* The punk guard, the goddamn punk guard, he is not obeying, and now Oscar is bleeding and in trouble. Vigoa has had enough of what he calls hero bullshit. His mind is racing. Plan A is gone. Now for plan B. The lethal scenario.

Cisneros is not an excitable person, but he is excited now. Vigoa originally wanted Cisneros to use a semiautomatic handgun with a high-capacity magazine of at least twelve rounds, but Cisneros doesn't trust automatics because of their tendency to jam. Cisneros squeezes the trigger. *Click.* A dry hit. The pistol's cylinder is empty. Vigoa counted correctly: Cisneros has fired all six rounds of the revolver, and reloading in a firefight while hopping and bleeding and fully exposed to your opponent—who is *not* out of bullets—generally is unwise.

"Freeze!" Vigoa yells at Prestidge. The Cuban moves sideways, toward the truck, looking for the right angle. He is now behind the guard.

Gary Prestidge has one live round in the chamber and three in his magazine when he hears the command. If the young guard's tactical position was unfavorable when Cisneros first appeared, it is now murderously bad. Prestidge turns slightly to look over his shoulder and sees Vigoa holding what looks like an AK-47 assault rifle. Incredibly, Prestidge starts to move toward Vigoa to continue the gunfight.

Cisneros has retreated out of the field of fire, Suarez is out of sight, and Vigoa has a clear shot. The Cuban gangster fires twice. Compared to the sharp crack made by the 9 mm pistol, the assault rifle produces a series of loud thumping retorts, like small explosions. The first round hits the trigger guard of Prestidge's pistol. The deformed handgun spins in his hands. The guard staggers from the impact. The second shot hits Prestidge in the right knee, exiting in his calf. His legs buckle.

Vigoa fires again, pumping out two more rounds. Prestidge is hit in the right arm, resulting in another through-and-through injury that creates a large shoulder exit wound. The young man still grips the damaged Smith & Wesson with his right hand and clings tightly to the blue-trimmed money bag.

Prestidge reaches around for the Kel-Tec P-11 pistol on his left hip. Even Vigoa is amazed. Vigoa goes to automatic and fires two-shot bursts. The 7.62 shell casings fly through the air, landing as far as five parking stalls away.

Prestidge is hit in the chest and twice in the neck. He collapses on the sidewalk, a few feet from the right rear bumper of the truck. Prestidge rests on his right side, partially sitting, almost in a fetal position. His arms are outstretched, his right hand still clutching the pistol that has been spun around and now points directly at the young man's blood-specked face. Prestidge's wounds are catastrophic: one high-velocity 7.62 mm round cuts an artery in the neck; another punctures his heart.

It is 11:35.

The fierce gun battle between Gary Prestidge and the gang is over. It has lasted barely a minute. Vigoa thinks briefly of firing another burst into the prostrate body of the fallen guard but instead transverses his rifle to the left and takes aim at the driver. Ricardo Sosa can be seen through the open bulkhead door. The driver reaches for his shotgun.

"Let me see your fucking hands in the air!" Vigoa shouts. "Don't make me kill you, man!"

Sosa, having just seen his partner cut down, is in no mood to negotiate. He reaches for the shotgun on his left.

Vigoa fires a single shot into the cabin.

Boom!

The first shot rips through the barrel of the .12 gauge. Sosa reaches for his .357 Magnum handgun on his right hip.

Vigoa fires a two-shot burst. The first round hits Sosa in his right shoulder and is lodged in his body. As Sosa turns toward Vigoa, a second high-velocity round strikes Sosa in the right temple. The shot, which creates a pinpoint entrance hole below the right ear, leaves a gaping exit wound and obliterates most of the frontal bone, the orbit, and the left eye. Sosa slumps forward, his hands resting on his clipboard. From the rear, he looks like a man doing paperwork while waiting for his partner, head tipped forward only slightly. Despite the terrible wound, Sosa is still breathing, and his strong heart continues to beat.

It is 11:35:12.

Vigoa is incredulous and incensed. He glowers at Prestidge, now half sitting, half resting on the sidewalk. *Go ahead, kid, move again so I can fire another dozen 7.62 rounds into your body.*

Cisneros tries to climb into the truck to scoop out boxes of cash from the main cabin, but the first step into the truck is a killer. The pain from the gunshot wound is overwhelming, and now the Mexican is bleeding heavily.

"Go to the car!" Vigoa yells at Cisneros, who quickly limps away.

The malicious fates that assign Gary Prestidge this violent end and select Ricardo Sosa's wedding anniversary for the day of his death have not overlooked Jose Vigoa. The 3280 robbery, so carefully planned, is unraveling. The tight deadline for withdrawal has passed, and Vigoa realizes that once again he has badly underestimated the fiber of the men who guard armored trucks.

Another fucking circus, just like the Desert Inn! What a mess, what insanity! Vigoa's rage spirals into black despair as he surveys the scene: The young guard is down by the right rear bumper of the truck, dark red blood spilling beneath his right shoulder. The driver is not moving and probably dead. Vigoa looks around—a trail of bloody footprints leads away from the truck to a getaway car parked five parking spaces to the north. *Will Oscar make it?* Vigoa wonders. *And what the hell is wrong with Luis? Where the fuck is he?*

In fact, nothing is *physically* wrong with Luis Suarez, who even now is standing in front of the white Voyager minivan gawking at the scene like a motorist gaping at an accident. Suarez has survived the fusillade of bullets unscathed. Emotionally, however, Vigoa's brother-in-law acts like a man who just took a .12 gauge blast in the stomach. He stares at Vigoa, eyes wide open, body rigid and frozen.[2]

"What the fuck are you doing?" Vigoa screams at Suarez. "Why are you not in that motherfucker truck scooping out the motherfucker money! Get inside that motherfucker truck and get that motherfucker money *now*!"

Suarez doesn't move and is speechless.

Vigoa has seen that look before in Afghanistan, in Africa. Luis is beyond fear. He is in shock. The big man could keel over at any second in full cardiac arrest. Not that Vigoa cares. *I ought to shoot him in the head right now.* Vigoa orders Suarez to the Dodge Intrepid four-door sedan.

Suarez has voluntarily retired from the business of robbing armored cars. He is appalled and distraught. *Those poor guards are blown up, and Oscar, man, he's not lookin' too cool, either.* Still clutching the empty duffel bag, the hulking Cuban makes it to the maroon Intrepid that will serve as the first getaway car in the gang's three-stage escape. Money or no money, Suarez wants out of this place *now*.

Vigoa starts to pump his fist to signal withdrawal and then catches himself. A bitter laugh. There's no one to signal. Vigoa is alone. Though not for long. Inside the Ross store, there is panic and chaos. Women scream, children cry. In another tragicomic moment, one group of shoppers rushes excitedly to the front door to see what's happening, only to run into a second crowd stampeding to the rear seeking cover. Two mobs going in opposite directions.

Tonya Keith, looking for a new dress near the front of the store, hears a loud noise. "It sounded like kids banging on the glass," she later tells police. Keith looks outside. She sees a gunman firing by the armored truck. Keith runs to the back of the store, hides inside a clothes rack, and calls 911. As confused shoppers mill around, Keith screams, "Get back! Get down! Go to the rear of the store! Those are gunshots!" She recalls, "I was plunging through three racks of clothes trying to hide." She will later describe the gunman as a black man, one of three witnesses to do so, which briefly hampers the investigation.

Gary Housley, the engineer with a yen for pizza, also confuses the dark clothing with race. Housley runs into Villa Pizza on the south side

---

[2] Vigoa insists that Suarez did not fire his weapon. Police believe it was Suarez who fired a single nonfatal shot at Prestidge, and not Cisneros.

of the Ross but not before counting twenty shots. "Call 911!" he yells to a counterman. This is not Housley's first brush with disaster: He was at the MGM Grand on a construction job on November 21, 1980, when a fireball tore through a hotel floor, starting a blaze that killed 84 people and injured 679 in one of the worst high-rise fires in U.S. history. Housley missed certain incineration by a matter of seconds.

Melody Rogers sees Cisneros and Vigoa, realizes that the armored car is being robbed, and correctly notes that the men are wearing black ski masks and are not African-Americans, as other witnesses claim. One of the gunmen "is holding a large bag in his left arm." The nurse calls 911. The line is busy. Eventually she gets through and tells police, "One person is running and limping, holding onto his right leg." Rogers walks toward the fallen guard, ignoring the gunmen who are still present.

Through it all the 911 operators remain calm and attempt to cull timely information from hysterical gossip.

911 Dispatcher: "Henderson 911. What's the location of your emergency?"

Caller: "Hello. It's Stephanie Street and Sunset in the Vons shopping center in front of Ross. It looks like they shot an armed truck guard, and they're getting in a car. [*To other eyewitnesses gathered around the phone*]: What kind of a car?"

911: "What color is it?"

Caller: "What color is the car?"

Unknown Speaker [*a second witness, grabbing the phone*]: "Red, burgundy."

911: "Which direction is it going?"

Caller: "Oh, no, no, *it's still here* . . ."

The ninth call of the morning delivers grim news: The robbery may in fact be a homicide.

911: "Okay, so there's a man shot in front of the armored truck?"

Caller: "Yeah, right behind where they took the money [by the hopper door]."

911: "Okay, stay on the line with me."

New Caller: "Looks like there's an armored car robbery in progress."

911: "Okay, we've heard that there's shots fired."

Caller: "There's a man down."

In one call, the manager of Ross tries to brief the operator while directing customers to safety.

Caller: [*To the store customers*]: "Get in here! Get in here! Get in the back and sit down, please. Get in the back. Come here. Sit down. Come. Okay. Come. Sit down. But we don't *know* if they're coming back. Just sit down."

Some customers ignore the manager.

Caller: [*To customer*]: "Would you *please* get back in the store!"

911: "Did anyone get an idea of what kind of car it was? It was red?"

Caller: "You want me to go outside and *ask?*"

911: "No. I want you to—I want everybody that's in the store with you now to stay in the store with you. *I don't want anybody going outside.* Okay?"

It is a sound decision. While two of the gangsters have retreated to the maroon Dodge Intrepid, Vigoa is still at the truck.

It is 11:36:01.

Sergeant Joe Molinaro is about to bite into his steak sandwich at the Carmine's Little Italy sports bar when the radio comes alive.

"Attention all units, code 413 at Stephanie and Sunset.

"George 1, Edward 1, Edward 2, be en route.

"Code 3.

"It's possibly an armed vehicle—armored car that 407'd where shots fired . . .

"Sam 338, do you copy?"

Sam 338 is Molinaro's radio call sign. The George and Edward units are patrol officers under Molinaro's command. Code 3 directs the unit to respond with red lights and siren.

Code 413 means person with a gun. A 407 is a robbery.

Sergeant Molinaro bolts from the restaurant, climbs into his marked police SUV, and begins to question the police dispatcher, sometimes called "control" by officers.

"Control, Sam 338. Where are the victims?"

Dispatcher: "We possibly have a man down in the front of the store. We're trying to get further information now."

Seconds later another 911 call confirms the worst: One of the guards is on the sidewalk in a pool of blood.

Nurse Rogers, on her way to the supermarket, finds herself close by as the gunfight erupts. She fearlessly goes to the fallen Gary Dean Prestidge to render aid. Rogers checks Prestidge for vital signs. There are none. She finds a bystander with a cell phone who is already talking to 911 and passes on the information.

Caller: "There's a lady here—a nurse or something. She says there's nothing there; it's no pulse, no nothing."

The 911 operator clatters away on her computer, forwarding the news to the police controller, who provides a series of bulletins for police and fire units moving to the scene: "Stand by. We have approximately six to eight shots heard in the Vons parking lot. Break. We have further that the suspect vehicle is an older model Camaro or Firebird. This PR [person reporting] is advising a black vehicle. We also have one man down in front of the armored truck. We have rescue en route. We'll be staging. All units . . . code 3."

Molinaro: "Can we red this channel?"[3]

Dispatcher: "That's affirmative . . . Attention all units—code red channel one. Code red channel one reference a 434, 413, 407[4] at Vons. Code red channel one."

Molinaro: "Control, Sam 338. See if the air unit is up."

Dispatcher: "Affirm, it is up."

By now cell phones and pagers are going off all over Clark County. Lieutenant Jutta Chambers runs to the parking lot. She will be designated King 1 on the air.

Fire Station "tones" sound at stations 94 and 92, alerting paramedics and firefighters that rescue units are needed.

What Vigoa calls "shock time," the four-to-five-minute period when the authorities receive 911 calls, sort out conflicting reports, and mobilize their assets, is well underway. Vigoa knows this. He also understands that the gang is out of time. The one-minute schedule has been breached. True, the guard and driver have been eliminated, but how to divest the armored truck of its small fortune?

A siren can be heard in the distance. Vigoa climbs awkwardly into the armored truck. He thinks dark thoughts about Suarez. *I should leave him with the other dead.* The Cuban gangster is literally standing among boxes of cash but knows he must leave. He lifts up one box of money. It is

---

[3] To "red channel" a frequency is to dedicate the channel to a single ongoing crime. Until the scene is cleared, only calls relating to the armored car robbery may be broadcast on this frequency. Going red means the police believe this is a major crime. Summoning air units underscores this urgency.

[4] A 434 is an illegal shooting; 413, person with a gun; 407, robbery. Code 3 is lights and siren.

heavy. He tries to carry others, but he still has the rifle in his right hand. Dragging his rifle and a solitary money sack, Vigoa sees an old lady sitting in a Saturn next to the Dodge staring directly at him with wide, frightened eyes. Vigoa squints, looks again, and the woman has disappeared.

The three men tear out of the mall in the Dodge Intrepid, yet another souvenir from the Thrifty car theft. For the rest of the ride, Vigoa ignores Suarez and rebukes Cisneros. "What were you waiting for! Didn't you see what he was doing? You shoot him in the head when he pulls that bullshit!"

The gangsters encounter a traffic jam as they try to leave the shopping center: Shoppers have emerged from stores to gawk at the robbery scene. Vigoa has to honk the horn to avoid running over the onlookers. The gunmen head south back to the Galleria Mall and a second lay-off car, a 1999 black Jeep Cherokee,[5] that's parked in the north lot of the JCPenney store. Unlike the robbery, Vigoa's escape plan, using multiple vehicles as lay-off cars, works perfectly. By the time the gang gets to the Galleria and swaps cars, Henderson and Las Vegas police are looking for the red Dodge.

It is 11:37:40.

Sergeant Molinaro is now flying up Stephanie, weaving furiously in and out of traffic while yelling at obstinate drivers to get the hell out of the way. The sergeant vows that some day he will follow a fire truck on an emergency run and ticket every knucklehead who doesn't pull over. After a near collision, Molinaro reminds himself: *Make your best speed, but get to the scene safely. Don't wreck. Don't hurt anyone. Stay off the radio as much as you can, don't add to the confusion.*

The radio traffic is unclear. Are the gunmen still on the scene? Did they leave one shooter behind? How many are there? The police radio continues to update:

"All units en route. Suspects left in a red or maroon vehicle. They were on Stephanie toward Russell. Will contact Metro and advise when we get further information."

Molinaro approaches the shopping center now on his left. At first, everything looks normal.

There's the Target store, getting close. Gotta make a left. So much traffic, why don't they stop?! Okay, there's Vons, come on, come on, buddy, get out of the way.

---

[5] Police and prosecutor varyingly describe the Jeep as both green and black. Vigoa says it was black.

No, don't stop, move, goddamn it! Go, go, go, make a hole . . . Okay, okay, no time for a fender bender; hell, no time for a head-on crash, let's get to the scene in one piece . . ."

The sergeant scans the sprawling parking lot for a suspicious red car. He later recalls: "I'm trying to get there as fast as I can, but at the same time you gotta be focused on the suspects. They've got to be leaving at some point, and I've got to look for the suspects."

There's one other person acutely aware of the suspects in the red getaway car. Louise Hodges, a seventy-two-year-old retiree who works part-time at the Ross, drives directly into the middle of the robbery and gun battle. The Henderson woman pulls her Saturn into a parking space four stalls from the armored truck at precisely the moment the shooting begins. "I parked and everything, and I opened the door on the driver's side to get out, and just as I did, I heard *pop, pop, pop, pop, pop!*" she recalls. "I said, 'Oh, it's a robbery, it must be a robbery.' So I got back into the car and locked my door. Then I heard a man say, 'We got to get out of here. Let's go, man! Let's go!' And then he started running toward me, and I thought he had seen me." Parked next to the Dodge Intrepid getaway car, Hodges finds herself in the thick of the action. "So I lay down on the front seat, just all the way as far as I could get down, and just lay there. [The man] comes up on the other side of me and gets into a maroon car. He has a knit cap on. That's all I see, the back, because I didn't want to raise my head at all because I didn't want to get killed."

Terrified, Hodges begins to pray. She has chest pains and wonders if she will die. Hodges remains sprawled on the seat until a passerby raps on her window. "Miss, they're gone," Judy Steenhook says. Hodges sits up and begins to weep. "If he saw me, he would have shot me," Louise Hodges says over and over. She becomes hysterical and will be treated by paramedics later in the day.

Susan Berry, the schoolteacher, has an unforgettable moment of her own. Because of heavy traffic and pedestrians, the Dodge Intrepid with Jose, Oscar, and Luis pulls alongside Berry's car before it departs the shopping center parking lot. The teacher looks over and is startled to see three men in ski masks and black shirts. The schoolteacher and the gangsters are six feet apart. They make eye-to-eye contact. Then the gunman believed to be Vigoa turns away, and the Dodge speeds off.

It is 11:39:20.

Sergeant Molinaro notices all the civilians. *Watch out for those pedestri-*

ans, what are they doing, where are they going! For the first time, he sees the armored truck off to the right. The patrol sergeant is heading north in the parking lot. Now Molinaro makes a tactical decision: Instead of parking blocks from the crime scene and approaching cautiously on foot while using parked cars as cover, he pulls close to the armored truck.

"You become a cop because you have a protective instinct, and that came out big-time in this thing," Molinaro says later. "I was not going to let these guys hurt any more citizens if I could help it. I mean I drove right into the middle of the scene. I was tactical about it. I didn't just drive recklessly in. I looked around, but you know I had to get there. I could not just go behind the building and say, 'Okay, control, let's have a few more units staged here.' "

This decision to charge into the combat zone by himself will be widely discussed in the months to come.

Molinaro steps out of the car, his right hand gripping a 9 mm Glock sidearm. There's no sign of the suspects. Molinaro sees Gary Dean Prestidge on the ground. A male civilian is leaning over the body on the sidewalk, checking for life signs. "Mr. Prestidge was slumped down—not all the way down, but in a sitting position, and he was gray already," recalls the sergeant. "It looked like he had bled out. I knew he was dead. I was no more than five minutes out."

Molinaro presses his microphone button: "338," the policeman says, identifying himself to the radio dispatcher.

"Sam 338, go ahead."

"It looks like a 419," Molinaro says, using the code for dead body.

Joe Molinaro is now the sole cop at a crime scene where an armed robbery, a gunfight, a double homicide, and the shooting of a suspect have just occurred. But if Jose Vigoa is combat hardened, Joe Molinaro also has a military discipline. From the marine corp's storied Parris Island boot camp, through infantry training at Camp Lejeune, North Carolina, to the rigors of SWAT, the sergeant has prepared for this day throughout his adult life.

"I'm a former SWAT guy, and what SWAT does is condition you to this kind of experience," Molinaro says. "You are the authority figure. You are the calming force. Everybody else is going nuts. I know this is the big one. I'm trained for this. This is what you sign the paper for. This is your job."

The sight of the big cop in his crisp blue uniform, jumping out of the sector car to take command, bawling orders, weapon drawn and ready for action, inspires the crowd. This time there is a cop around when you need one. Molinaro seems to be everywhere, looking for suspects, giving aid, communicating with police dispatchers, talking to incoming patrol officers, pushing back the crowd, running through his own crisis inventory. "I wanted to make sure the suspects were not a danger to me or anybody else and that they were not still at the scene. My job is to preserve life and preserve evidence. I set up an inner perimeter about thirty to forty feet past the truck on each side, a big square. I wanted everybody out of the inner zone. I could see bloody footprints over there. I could see shell casings all over the parking lot. I also wanted to identify the witnesses and keep them here. Can't let anybody wander off because they don't want to get involved."

Molinaro is engulfed by witnesses. Everyone talking at once. Repeatedly the besieged sergeant orders people back from the truck and crime scene, and while some obey, newcomers arrive. No sign of the suspects but no sign of reinforcements, either. He remembers thinking, *I'm waiting for the cavalry. I've got to get these people out of here. It's like trying to push away water,*

Sergeant Joe Molinaro of the Henderson Police Department was the first officer to reach the murder scene, where already a large crowd had gathered.

PHOTOGRAPH BY JOHN HUDDY.

it just rolls back! I move them out, I turn my head, they come back. A sea of people. The patrol sergeant estimates there are at least twenty spectators encroaching upon the murder scene, and more are running to the armored truck from nearby restaurants, dental offices, credit unions, and travel agencies. "Everybody get back into the store. Move, people, get into the store!"

Molinaro hears sirens. The cavalry *is* coming. The airwaves crackle with traffic from incoming sector cars.[6]

The fire department gets there next. Captain Brian Tilton arrives in an ambulance designated EMS-2. A paramedic supervisor responsible for training other medics, Tilton is a nine-year veteran and future doctorate candidate in emergency medicine. He is barely a mile from the shooting site when he hears the call. He comes in slowly, watching for any sign of trouble. He passes the Target store and the armored car. Tilton parks his ambulance at the end of the parking lot to give other units room to maneuver. Although Tilton is the ranking supervisor, the incoming ambulance and engine companies have priority. They are fully staffed. There are two paramedics in the ambulance, four firemen in the big hook and ladder unit known simply as "the truck," and four more men in the vehicle the men call "the engine."

Mentally, Tilton runs through his own protocols: *Look past the obvious. Make sure you find all the victims. When you arrive, don't be like a moth to the flame; take some time to assess the surroundings, make sure that no one's going to get hurt, and then see if there are additional victims who may not be in plain sight.* Right now, however, everything is a blur. Tilton watches a harried police sergeant yelling at people to get back into the store. "Anybody else?" the paramedic says to Molinaro, gesturing at the body on the sidewalk and the driver in the truck.

"No one else right now," Molinaro says, his answer nearly drowned out by the wail of sirens and the raspy blast of a fire truck horn. Rescue 92 and Engine 94[7] have arrived. Unit TT-92, the big ladder truck, is close

---

[6] In Henderson and Las Vegas, police cars are identified by a number-name-number system. For example, 2 David 1. The first number gives the work shift of the unit. Number one is graveyard (10:00 p.m. to 8:00 a.m.), number two is dayshift (6:00 a.m. to 4:00 p.m.), number three is swing shift (3:00 p.m. to 1:00 a.m.). The middle name identifies the sector, or general area, patrolled by the officer. The final number gives the beat, a smaller area covered by the unit within the sector. In our example, 2 David 1 would be a day-shift patrolman working in the David sector and covering beat number one.

[7] There are two paramedics in the ambulance, four firemen in the long hook and ladder unit known simply as "the truck," and four more men in "the engine." The shorter vehicle that serves as the water pumper is, accordingly, sometimes called the water truck. The second digit of the unit's number represents the fire station. For example, 92 would mean fire station number two.

behind. The ambulance, to Tilton's surprise, pulls alongside the armored truck and stops. Usually fire vehicles stage outside the crime scene until given approval to enter the outer perimeter. Not today.

Michael Weissman, a former navy corpsman who has served with elite recon marine battalions, jumps out of the ambulance along with Mike Hargett. Marty Nelson is the engine captain. Tilton tries to open the armored truck's front driver door but it is locked. He sees Weissman and points to Prestidge on the sidewalk. "Check out the victim."

"We already have," Weissman replies. "Mike just took a look. He's dead."

Suddenly there's a shout from the cabin of the armored car. Marty Nelson is with the driver. "I've got a pulse! He's breathing!" Nelson will treat Ricardo Sosa. "I got off the engine," Nelson recalls. "I asked the police officer at the scene, 'Do we have any other patients?' Because seeing these armored cars, I know that there's two and sometimes three guards on these trucks. And we only saw the one guard on the ground. And he said, 'I haven't looked inside the truck yet.' So at that point, I walked around, and the side door to the armored car was open. And I could see a Hispanic gentleman sitting in the driver's seat."

Nelson notices that the driver's compartment and the main cabin of the truck are wide open. "There isn't a bulkhead with a door or anything in there. I remember before I made entry, I stood at the side door, and I can see in and see this gentleman sitting there. He is sitting upright. Just his head is down. And when I get in there, of course, the first thing I do is reach and check for a pulse. The metal clipboard is in his lap, and his head is down. So I reach and feel for a pulse. Yeah, he's got a pulse. So I move the clipboard out of the way. Tip his head back, open his airway, and he starts breathing. And that's when I holler at the paramedic captain that he's got a pulse and he's still breathing."

Nelson is an experienced firefighter. He has seen many dead people in the line of duty. What happens next, however, is profoundly disturbing. "This gentleman is sitting there in the driver's seat like he's waiting for his partner. He's ready to drive off. As I tip his head back and open his airway, I am looking at the back of his head for injury. I can't see one. And, of course, he has short, cropped hair, but I can't see a wound on the back of his head. And I can't understand. I think, well, maybe when the shooting starts, he looks over his shoulder and is looking out the door and maybe catches a glancing shot across the eye, but I don't see one."

Nelson leans forward, peers around the right shoulder of the driver and into the face of Ricardo Sosa. There's a terrible gaping wound where Ricardo's left eye socket used to be. Clinically, Ricardo Sosa is still alive. "He had what we call 'agonal respirations,' which are slow, deep breaths," Nelson says. Sosa's heartbeat is still strong. His pulse is regular. But in any meaningful sense, Ricardo Sosa has joined in death his partner, Gary Prestidge.

The driver's front door is opened from the inside by Nelson. What is called a C collar is placed on Sosa by Nelson and fireman Garren Fulmer to help support and stabilize his neck. As Bill Algeyer hurriedly sets up life-support equipment in the ambulance, firemen Gary Desh, John Dyer, and Hargett help move Sosa to the ambulance on a gurney.

"We got him turned, laid on the board, and got him out of the truck," Nelson recalls. Sosa is placed in the back of the ambulance, where he begins to bleed heavily. Sosa dies less than five minutes after his friend and partner Gary Prestidge.

Gary Prestidge is left undisturbed on the sidewalk. "You could tell there was nothing we could do for him," Nelson says.

Struck by Vigoa AK-47 rounds, the mangled handgun of Gary Dean Prestidge found by his body.

COURTESY CLARK COUNTY DISTRICT ATTORNEY.

Within a minute of Sosa's death, police reinforcements enter at both ends of the shopping center. Others are closing in.

King 1: "I already have my [detective] units en route."

2 Edward 2: "338, 2 Edward 2. I'm going to be arriving, where do you want me?"

Sam 338 (Molinaro): "North end."

Officer: "If you go up to the north end and block off the parking lot that side, we'll shut it down here at this end. Control, 2 Edward 1 and 2 Edward 2 have arrived."

What Vigoa calls shock time has expired. Police and fire units are mobilized and pouring into the shopping center, setting up road blocks and creating a preliminary perimeter. Yellow crime-barrier tape is quickly strung. Witnesses are gathered together. In newsrooms across the county, the media goes on full alert; within fifteen minutes the shopping center will be a madhouse with microwave trucks, squads of reporters, and television station helicopters thumping away overhead.

IT IS HIGH noon. Lieutenant Jutta Chambers and Detective Gerry Collins are among the first to reach the outdoor mall, followed by Henderson Police Chief Michael Mayberry and Captain Richard Perkins. As the lieutenant walks past the yellow tape, she learns Henderson has its first double homicide, its first armored truck murders, and first large-scale shoot-out at a shopping center. "Holy shit," Chambers says, stepping over shell casings.

Chambers takes charge. Henderson, in 2000, has only a small CSI unit. A call is made to Las Vegas Sheriff Jerry Keller, who has a more sophisticated crime lab. A five-member Metro CSI team is hastily assembled and dispatched to the scene.

Standing by Rescue 92 and Sosa's body, Brian Tilton is approached by a Henderson detective. The detective points to the body of Ricardo Sosa, now in the rear of the ambulance.

"Are you transporting?"

"No, we're not."

"Well, then, everything's got to be left right where it is because this is now a crime scene—everything stays, including your ambulance."

Tilton protests. "We need the ambulance in service; we're making runs all day!"

Lieutenant Jutta Chambers was the ranking detective at the double homicide who took charge of the crime scene.

COURTESY HENDERSON POLICE DEPARTMENT.

"Not in that unit. And leave the victim where he is, in the ambulance. Everything has to be locked down in the exact same spot it was when we got here."

There is something else, other than the loss of a valuable ambulance, that eats away at Tilton. "We asked the police if we could throw a blanket over the guard who was on the ground. And they wouldn't let us cover him, not at first. The whole day, from where I was standing, I watched a pool of blood drain all the way down to the end of the parking lot until almost fifteen feet in front of me. All day long, that's all I could see."

At 12:55 Eddie Newman shows up. Known for his independence, the detective finishes the roof air-conditioning job after being paged. He then goes home, showers, and changes clothes.

"Where have you been?" the normally tranquil Chambers barks on seeing Newman.

"Those folks are dead," Newman shrugs, looking at the body of Gary Prestidge. "They're not going anywhere."

But Newman realizes Chambers is pissed, and he's relieved that Gerry Collins is made lead detective. "I had only two words when I heard Gerry was lead: 'Thank God.' "

At 1:10 a five-person CSI delegation makes its way past the yellow tape. Al Cabrales is the supervising crime analyst, a veteran of twenty years with Metro whose father served for twenty-seven years as a Las Vegas policeman. Assignments are made: Jessie Sams will gather the evidence, and Joe Szukiewicz will photograph the scene. David LeMaster will write the CSI report. Terry Martin will prepare the diagram. There are so many police and firemen inside the yellow tape, Szukiewicz has to search through a crowd of more than fifty officers and firefighters to find his supervisor. Terry Martin is also struck by the bedlam. "It was very chaotic, a lot of noise. People are everywhere. Yet once you actually get inside the tape, into the inner perimeter, it is really quiet and calm."

Chambers confers with Cabrales, who tells her that the Las Vegas Metropolitan Police Department is happy to assist its smaller neighbor, but there has to be an understanding. "Such as?" Chambers asks with an eyebrow raised.

Detectives and crime scene technicians called the Ross crime scene the
biggest and most complex they had ever seen. The ambulance can be
seen next to the armored car, the top of which bears the letters AT.

"It's my understanding that you have requested our services," Cabrales says. Chambers nods. "I want to make it clear that if we come in, we will take over the whole scene process. We will not have you do part of it and then we do part of it. It's either all or nothing."

A pragmatic woman, Chambers smiles. "It's yours." Metro will do the crime scene work—but Chambers and the Henderson police will remain in charge of the overall investigation. This point will be made clear almost at once.

One of the new arrivals, invoking the FBI's jurisdiction under the Hobbs Act,[8] ducks under the tape and walks up to Chambers. "Since this is an armored car robbery, the FBI will be taking over the investigation," the agent announces.

"I don't think so," Chambers says politely but firmly.

Later Brett Shields arrives and settles the dispute over jurisdiction. The Henderson police will run the investigation, Shields says, and the FBI will assist in any way possible. Newman witnesses the initial confrontation between Chambers and the FBI man. He snickers, "Federal Bureau of Idiots."

The Metro CSI team goes to work. Although there's been an explosion in forensic technology in recent years, the successful crime analyst understands that it is the process and the protocols developed over decades that matter the most. Cabrales joins Chambers, Collins, and Newman in an initial walk-through of the scene. Joe Molinaro, crime analyst Rich Little, and the small Henderson staff have done good work; the area appears to be well preserved.

It is Cabrales who insists the detectives hold the ambulance in place. "Let's make sure that we have everything photographed, measured, and diagrammed before anything is moved or disturbed," the CSI supervisor reminds his analysts. Cabrales circulates within the yellow tape, assisting his crew on technical matters while keeping a close eye on their psychological response to the murders. This will not be an easy crime to forget.

"It was an emotional scene," Jessie Sams agrees. "Seeing Sosa in the van and knowing what we knew was disturbing. Obviously he was having labored breathing when they first got him into the rescue unit, and he

---

[8] The Hobbs Act gives the federal government jurisdiction when robberies and murders interfere with interstate commerce.

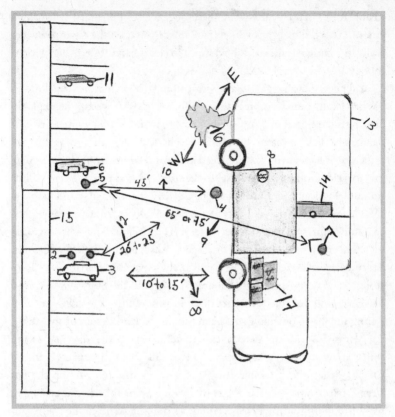

Jose Vigoa's blueprint of the March 3, 2000, armored car robbery and killings In Henderson, Nevada, sketched in 2004.

was in there with this huge hole and one-quarter of his head gone. It was vicious."

Police and fire personnel see dead bodies and blood on a regular basis but rarely show emotion at a crime scene. The Ross double homicide will be different. Rumors spread quickly through the ranks of police and paramedics, and, later, Metro CSI analysts, about divots in the pavement around and under the young guard. The men and women talk angrily about the murders as ruthless and brutal. Some believe the killer fired into Gary Prestidge after the young guard fell wounded to the ground. Some call the killings cold-blooded executions and doubt if the guards ever heard a warning. "These guys were ambushed," Nelson tells a fellow fireman. "And later I heard what these degenerates got away with didn't amount to a hill of beans." Next to Ricardo Sosa, on the right passenger seat, sits a large bundle of cash wrapped in cellophane. "A real big brick of money," Nelson remembers. "They didn't get it."

Cabrales guards against analysts coming to premature conclusions. "What I call tunnel vision is something we have to avoid," he explains. "Analysts see things only one way. They go in and see a few items of evidence, and they prematurely develop a scenario or thought process that *this* is the way it happened. They proceed in that direction, and in doing so they may overlook other, more accurate theories and evidence." There will be no tunnel vision in this investigation. CSI will spend the day and night on the scene. Szukiewicz will take more than 1,100 color crime scene photographs. Sams will find thirteen bullet fragments, four 9 mm cartridge casings, and eight 7.62 × 39 Tula Cartridge Works Russian-made shell casings. Terry Martin's sketches will be detailed and cover an area from the Ross store to a parking space four hundred feet behind the Subway restaurant. LeMaster will document the fact that the armored truck was hit six times during the shoot-out and that several rounds struck the front of the store.

Alamshaw's Metro detectives, including the entire day and swing shifts, arrive in force by 1:00 p.m. There's talk that the suspects could be the gang that's been taking down casinos and armored cars on the Las Vegas Strip. Some theorize the crew is made up of former military men, maybe high military, with Special Forces training. One of the Metro detectives called to the scene is Gordon Martines, the original lead investigator who has been relieved of his supervisory role and assigned to other cases. Now he will take assignments from Alamshaw, his sergeants, and others. Martines has a troubled history on this case. Considered conspiratorial and a loose cannon by some detectives, and a creative, resourceful cop by others, Martines is dispatched to the Ross crime scene but defiantly ignores the order. Instead he drives to Jose Vigoa's home on Sandy Slate Way and begins a self-assigned stakeout. He notices that Oscar Cisneros's red 1990 GMC pickup is parked in front of the Vigoa home, but Vigoa's pickup is missing. When Martines is ordered by Sergeant Robert DuVall to report to the Ross crime scene and forgo the stakeout, he protests but is overruled. Martines leaves the Sandy Slate home and misses the return of Vigoa and the wounded Oscar Cisneros. At the Ross scene, Martines is assigned to interview witnesses. Martines sharply criticizes the decision to pull him from the Sandy Slate stakeout. He later asserts it would have ended the case then and there. Although Martines refused to be interviewed at length for this book, he did observe that he thought the investigation was a failure.

Vigoa was asked what might have happened if Martines was waiting at the Vigoa home when the crew returned on March 3, 2000, from the Ross gunfight. "Tell Gordon Martines I would have lit him up like a Christmas tree," Vigoa said.

AT TWILIGHT A coroner van arrives. When the time comes to remove Sosa's body, the firefighters do their best to shield his face from onlookers; eventually a team of medical examiner investigators zips Sosa into a body bag for the ride to the morgue at 1704 Pinto Lane and the probing hands of Deputy Medical Examiner Gary D. Telgenhoff, who will conduct autopsies on both victims the following morning.

Gary Prestidge remains on the sidewalk under a white sheet throughout the day and night. Shields is standing near the body when he is startled by a familiar sound coming from beneath the sheet that covers the dead guard.

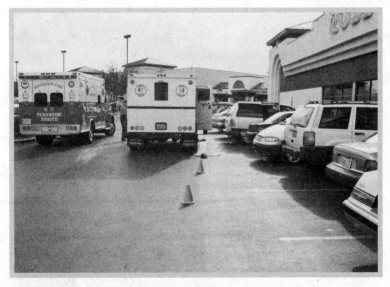

Gary Prestidge on pavement under sheet.

Shields remembers, "When we get to the robbery scene, the dead Armored Transport guard was down by the truck, covered by a sheet. It was late morning. But he remains out there under the sheet in the sun because of the crime scene and all the work we have to do in a double homicide. He was just a kid, and he loved his job as an armored car guard. But he's dead now, sprawled on the sidewalk. Five o'clock in the afternoon comes, his cell phone starts ringing. Everybody there just cringed. We saw ourselves lying there, our families calling us. 'Why aren't you home? When are you going to be home?' I don't know who was on the phone. Nobody answered it. The phone just kept ringing and ringing, and then it stopped."

Chapter 21

AFTERSHOCKS

Gary Prestidge, Sr., who repeatedly called his son's cell phone on Friday evening, learned of young Gary's death not from authorities or the transport company but by watching the local news. In an unfortunate breach of protocol, the anchorman reported the ages of the victims and said the slain messenger was twenty-three years old. At that moment Mr. Prestidge knew his son was gone.

As the horror unfolded in the coming days, Mr. Prestidge tried desperately to retrieve Gary's cell phone, wallet, and other personal belongings. The family wanted to hear Gary's funny voice-mail message one last time. You would call Gary, and the familiar voice would say, "This is Gary, and I might call you back if I want to, but maybe I will and maybe I won't 'cause you know how it is." And the young man would chuckle, and you knew for sure he'd call you back as soon as he could.

Gary's father never got back the cell phone or anything else, and all the people who called in those awful days after the tragedy and said they would stay in touch and follow up and pay a later visit, well, they never did, and after the trials and other legal mumbo jumbo, the memory of Gary just faded away. To this day Gary Prestidge, Sr., remains bitter at the authorities for this and other matters.

IN BILOXI, MISSISSIPPI, Gary Dean's twenty-four-year-old sister, Julie Prestidge, and mother, Shala Premack, fifty-two, told how Gary's murder devastated their lives as well. The worst part, his mother remembered, was how people would never even bring up Gary's name for fear of being rude. Because of this misplaced courtesy, their sweet, innocent boy just kind of disappeared, his name never spoken.

A petite young woman with a cherubic face and severe blond bangs, Julie wore a large green tattoo on her left leg from the knee to the foot that depicted a tree of life with a book and a mandolin at the base of the main trunk. At the bottom was Gary's date of birth, 2-5-77, and the day he died, 3-3-00.

Gary's mother, who has her son's long face and deep-set eyes, said that while Gary wanted to be someone who stood up for right and virtue, and while he was a crack shot, he wasn't a soldier of fortune or one of those white supremacists who were gun nuts. "His first Halloween costume was Superman," Shala said. Shala Premack (she divorced Big Gary in 1985, married Joe Premack, and moved to Mississippi) talked about her son's vivid imagination and his fascination with men of action.

Shala held a stack of photographs. One was of Gary Dean in his guard uniform and another showed the boy in his Indiana Jones outfit. With Little Gary, the fantasy and the reality, the popular culture and everyday life, overlapped and sometimes intersected, his mother mused. "Gary loved heroes," Shala continued, rummaging through the photographs. "And while I don't think that's so unusual for little boys, I do remember that when other children were getting out of the heroes stage, Gary did not. At about that time, he began to enjoy real weapons. At the age of twelve or thirteen, he saved up his money, bought a bullwhip, and taught himself to use it. At about age fourteen, he began to read gun magazines. He later became a very good archer."

At first Gary liked the armored company job because it fit his notion of being a protector, his mother said. But over time Gary Dean grew tired of the armored car job and dreamed of becoming a forest ranger or maybe a fireman. He could be the protector that way. "And he always loved the solitude and beauty of the forest," Shala said.

Then Gary's dad called and said somebody killed Shala's happy-go-lucky son in a robbery at the Ross clothing store.

After the funeral, Shala and Mr. Prestidge agreed to have Gary cremated. They scattered his ashes over his beloved mountains in southern Utah, and that is where Gary is to this day.

—

ON THE DAY of the shooting, Norma Sosa, Ricardo's wife, was happily running around the east side of Las Vegas preparing for her anniversary party. She got off early that day from her job as a maid at a Strip hotel, skipped lunch, and looked forward to a big Chinese dinner with her husband, children, and a few friends. That morning Norma dropped Ricardo off at the Armored Transport hub at six-thirty. They kissed, wished each other a happy anniversary, and then Ricardo told his wife that he loved her.

Mrs. Sosa came home to find sons Michael and Richard, and a friend named Cathy, gathered in the small yard by the front door. All three were crying.

"Cathy was saying that Ricardo was a good person," she recalled, "and I stopped her and said, 'What do you mean *was*?'"

Since the death of Ricardo, the Sosas have struggled to make ends meet. Norma is having trouble paying the bills. To help out Mother and the youngest children, two of the Sosa sons quit school to work in a toilet paper factory making the cardboard tubes that fit within the rolls. Daughter Sabrina abandoned her plans to go to college and ran away to Los Angeles. One of the sons joined a gang—something Ricardo never would have permitted—and the eighteen-year-old has been arrested for gang activity. The once flourishing Sosa family has slowly scattered like autumn leaves in the first cold winds of November.

Norma was still working at the hotel when we spoke, and she told a bizarre and disturbing story about an encounter there. Norma was walking down a hotel hallway when she saw another maid staring at her. The woman made "a weird face at me," she said. Norma was more puzzled than annoyed until she recognized the other maid from the trials and television coverage of Ricardo's death. It was Luisa Vigoa, wife of Jose Manuel Vigoa, the gangster who murdered her husband.

There are more than 1.4 million people living in Greater Las Vegas. There are 338 hotels and motels with 148,000 rooms for rent. Norma Sosa, widow of Ricardo Sosa, and Luisa Vigoa, wife of her husband's killer, work at the same job on the same floor in the same hotel on the same Las Vegas Strip.

THE AFTERSHOCKS FROM the failed robbery would extend even to the reputation of the dead guards, whose competency and integrity would be called into question by company officials. The evening of the murders, Prestidge's coworkers gathered at the killing scene. Manager John Zamora arrived and identified the bodies. Kevin Prokopich staggered out of his sickbed and rushed to the Ross Dress for Less store with fellow guard John Brogley. Kevin's appearance that evening at the Ross would be, as one cynical colleague later observed, a one-way trip to the intersection of Foolish and Brave: "Kevin should have stayed in bed. Career-wise, what he did that night was like jumping in front of a speeding freight train."

At the Ross, the furious Kevin angrily confronted Zamora, his boss, and there was an ugly scene. Zamora pointed to the long, meandering blood stain on the sidewalk where Gary Prestidge had fallen and allegedly said to Prokopich, "That could have been you." (Zamora later said he could not recall making such a remark.)

Prokopich erupted. "We warned you about that truck! We told you it wasn't safe!" the guard shouted. "We told you about the broken bulkhead door, we told you about those overbooked routes, and you did nothing! We talked to you about this shit, and you said we could find another job if we didn't like it! You said the company could always find someone to ride the truck if we didn't like it. You want to tell that to Gary and Ricardo now? 'Cause right now I am standing in their blood."

Fellow guards cringed when Prokopich began talking of "double hopping," a practice in which the driver leaves the truck with the guard to help make deliveries to stores on a busy route. "Kevin really got into Zamora's face," one witness said. "Started yelling at him. He said we talked to you about this shit and how the workload was so heavy they had to double hop, which wasn't allowed."

Even though double hopping saved time because two men make the deliveries instead of one, it was considered unsafe and was forbidden by company rules. According to Prokopich and other employees of Armored Transport, double hopping usually occurred during peak holiday periods and from time to time on overbooked routes. A more serious allegation made by employees was that Zamora and other managers were supposed to periodically conduct in-the-field surveillance of armored crews to ensure regulations were being followed. This clandestine monitoring, in which the managers were supposed to follow the trucks on their runs and maintain logs of transgressions, rarely took place, and reports were falsified, several guards charged. Multiple guards have said that managers tolerated double hopping despite its dangers, allegations that Zamora has denied.

Although there is overwhelming evidence that on March 3, 2000, Ricardo and Gary were *not* double hopping, and although there is further testimony there was no double hopping on truck 3280 in the weeks before the robbery by Ricardo, Kevin, Gary Dean, or John Brogley, the company would make a shocking announcement the next day to assembled workers. Carl Logrecco, a regional vice president of Armored Transport, blamed the murders on the purported misconduct of Gary, Ricardo, and Kevin. The men were double hopping on 3280 and other trucks, Logrecco told the employees, which is why they were hit. They were easy targets due to their own mistakes. Anybody else caught double hopping will be fired on the spot, the executive warned.

Some of the guards wondered if this could possibly be true. Didn't the reporter on TV say Ricardo was shot inside the truck? Wasn't that what the story in the *Review-Journal* said as well? Others quickly realized that the suits wanted scapegoats, and who better than the dead guards, who couldn't talk, and Prokopich, who was by now a nervous wreck? Kevin was suspended immediately and in a matter of weeks was fired.

The manner in which Gary Prestidge and Richard Sosa were blamed for their own deaths incensed many employees. Frank Severino, a stocky Chicagoan and former housing projects cop who worked at Armored Transport from 1997 to 2001, described the company's attempt to discredit the three as a malicious campaign of disinformation. "They did a hatchet job on Kevin—they consciously wanted to use Kevin, to use him as a scapegoat to cover their own butts," Severino said. "[They claimed] Kevin and Richard were double hopping, and it was their fault, and it was only luck that Kevin wasn't there and poor Gary got killed—that was the propaganda line that was being fed to the troops."

Severino contends that the trucks were unsafe at the time of the murders. The schedules were crazy, he says, and employees were mistreated. "They were always short handed. So a lot of times they would double runs up so that a route that was normally thirty-four stops would become fifty stops. I can remember personally at least two or three days when I was on a truck with a broken air-conditioner in the middle of the summer for twelve and thirteen hours. We had a thermometer on that truck. It read 136 degrees for twelve hours." Personal cell phones were forbidden, according to Severino, and handheld radios for use by the hoppers outside the truck were not provided until after the double homicide in Henderson.

Frank Severino was in a position to know about the machinations of Armored Transport in March 2000. "I was the weekend supervisor. I was privy to a lot of things that were going on in management," he said. "Before the murders, there was a meeting between Zamora and Kevin and Richard about some problems that they were having. I think that it came up at that time that the door was broken. I can also assure you that the reason it was taped was that, since the door wouldn't lock, when they'd be going around corners driving in traffic, that thing would be slamming back and forth all day long, okay? I know that for a fact, and I remember somebody specifically telling me that."

John Brogley, a large man at six feet and 260 pounds, is another former guard who thought the company's damage control to be sorely lacking. Brogley still works in security and does repossessions on the side. He confirmed the charges of Prokopich and Frank Severino, and he was close to the action: Brogley drove truck 3280 on Tuesday, three days before the robbery and gun battle, replacing Sosa, who took the day off. Brogley would have been on the truck had Prestidge been unavailable when Kevin was sick. Brogley was the employee who witnessed Kevin's outburst against John Zamora and Brogley was at the meeting when the company blamed the killings on the victims and Prokopich. "The first thing out of the district manager's mouth was the guards got killed because they double hopped. Which was a bunch of crap. They used Kevin as a scapegoat. They put the blame on Sosa and Gary. They said they made themselves a target by double hopping. Those were their exact words."

Brogley, in fact, knew all about the broken barrier door and the futile meetings with Zamora to remedy the problem. "Before the incident happened," he recalled, "it was routine that the sensors on that door didn't work, and they were fixed on a when-we-have-time basis. Brakes and stuff like that were a lot more important than anything else. Of course, afterward, whenever a door malfunctioned, it was fixed, but before then, no, they didn't care too much about it." There were multiple problems with the doors, Brogley explained, but the unreliable sensors were a major headache. Sometimes they worked, preventing the hopper door from opening when the barrier door was ajar, and other times they didn't, and both doors would remain open at the same time.

Armored Transport had approximately thirty-five guards and drivers operating a fleet of fifteen trucks, Brogley said. For all of this activity, there was only one mechanic. But were these problems reported by the drivers and guards? This important question is hotly disputed. Some guards at the time of the shooting say the broken door on 3280 was reported but not repaired. "Oh, yes, the branch manager knew about it," Brogley said. "Everybody knew about it. Everybody complained about it. Zamora's common phrase was, 'If you can't do the job, I'll find somebody else that can.'"

Brogley maintains the company knew exactly what happened at the Ross. The company's own actions after the homicides proves this, he said. "If anybody was seen with the bulkhead door open, they were history. That's one thing they jumped on." Brogley went on to say that for the next five or six days he observed the company's lone mechanic working solely on bulkhead doors and nothing else. In his view the company knew something was wrong.

John Zamora confirms some of the allegations made by AT employees. He recalls Prokopich "freaking out" at the crime scene and railing against the company for overbooked routes, and he agrees that some routes were too hectic, especially with only two men on the truck. Many of the AT routes required a driver, a guard, and a messenger, Zamora said. He admitted the armored cars were unguarded at night, as Vigoa said. But double hopping as the cause of the murders? Zamora said he was dumbfounded when company officials blamed the murders on the prohibited practice. "I'd never even *heard* of double hopping!" Zamora insisted.

Zamora sharply disputes the allegations of former guards who say the company, including him, knew of the problem but failed to remedy the defective door. The guards themselves rigged the doors open, Zamora said. The former manager said that no one ever asked him to repair an inoperative sensor. "I told the men to close the bulkhead door; I pleaded with them until I was blue in the face." Before the murders, a crew would be given a warning if caught driving with a broken bulkhead door; afterward, it meant automatic dismissal. Zamora conceded that the issue of malfunctioning or disabled barrier doors was not a company priority until after the Ross slayings.

Zamora would be demoted to assistant manager the week after the killings and eventually transferred to El Centro, California. After fifteen years with AT, Zamora left the company in 2003, disillusioned. "A suit from the home office met with me and said I had screwed up. I got the shit end of the stick."

But if the crew of 3280 were not double hopping, and even the branch manager says they were not, then why did Vigoa select 3280 instead of a Brink's truck on Las Vegas Boulevard carrying far more money? After all, run number five was a meager target for someone with the ambition of Jose Vigoa.

WHEN VIGOA PLANNED a robbery he looked for a weak point in the defenses. Neutralizing the driver was the key to the heist. Typically the driver was isolated in a locked steel cocoon, shielded by a bulletproof interior door that would slam shut whenever the side hopper door popped open. The driver sat next to a short-barreled shotgun, carried his own sidearm and had a radio to summon help. Except for the roof, the truck could withstand most small arms fire.

But during the final weeks of February 2000, Vigoa probed for weaknesses by breaking into the trucks at night at the unguarded Armored Transport parking lot at 1685 South Palm Street in Las Vegas. Vigoa carried a small notebook, made sketches under the beam of a small flashlight, examined the bulkhead door, and tested the interior controls.

From his daytime observations, Vigoa knew the barrier door was supposed to be closed when the side hopper door was open, and on most runs it was. This protected the driver from—well, people like Jose Vigoa. But when the Cuban picked the lock of 3280 and slipped inside the Ford diesel, he found duct tape over one side of the barrier door, possibly covering a sensor. Vigoa became excited.

"Armored car 3280 was inspected by me personally, on the inside and outside, including the main construction of the truck," Vigoa said. "I even tied a red plastic ribbon below the front bumper to identify the truck. Originally I was going to use explosives and blow the back door off the truck I picked. But then I found 3280. I would not have to stage my own Fourth of July after all. I realized what the tape meant. I knew from the duct tape the driver was not protected—and suddenly I realized I can get him. *I can get him!*"

When the hopper returned from the store, and the side door opened, there would be a window of opportunity of possibly twenty seconds enabling Jose to disarm or disable the driver. Vigoa was elated: "This was one good mistake that gave me the power to control and to shoot the driver if it were necessary, once the outside door was opened. The malfunctioning door located inside was *crucial* to my plans; it was perfect! I plotted that if I strategically positioned myself in the middle of a ninety-degree arc, with the side door forty-five degrees to the left, and the guard forty-five degrees to the right, I could control both men by gunfire if necessary."

IN LATE 1999 and at the outset of 2000, Prokopich and Sosa complained of being followed by teams of Hispanic men. Prokopich warned Zamora that one of the men boldly made eye contact with Kevin as he entered the

**The interior of AT truck
3280 with the open
driver bulkhead door.**
COURTESY LAS VEGAS
METROPOLITAN POLICE
DEPARTMENT.

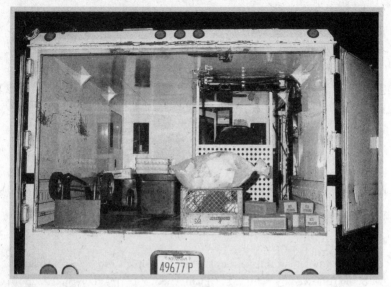

49677 P

Bullet-ridden but with most of the money left in the truck because of Oscar Cisneros's wound and Luis Suarez's flight, AT truck 3280 provided a flood of forensic evidence for investigators.

COURTESY LAS VEGAS METROPOLITAN POLICE DEPARTMENT.

Ross store and seemed to be taking notes. Prokopich says that he and Sosa, sensing trouble, asked Zamora and other managers to see to it that the broken bulkhead door be repaired before truck 3280 was dispatched on any further runs.

"The truck was not safe. We told them that," Prokopich said.

Zamora allegedly gave the familiar reply: If Prokopich and Sosa didn't want to ride the truck, he would find someone who would. The bulkhead door was malfunctioning for about a month, Prokopich said. And now Prestidge and Sosa were dead. When he told his story in the presence of his wife, Candice, Kevin's eyes filled with tears. "I went there, and I stood on Tex's blood." The lean young man closed his eyes and clenched his fists, and then let loose a scream:

"I told them the truck wasn't safe!"

INDEED, IT SEEMS he wasn't the only one who knew it. From the March 10, 2000, Armored Transport internal report by James O'Riley and George Reister relating to the deaths of Gary Prestidge and Ricardo Sosa:

Mr. Prestidge exited Ross holding the deposits inside the coal bag in his weak hand, and his weapon was drawn and in his strong hand. The hopper door opened. Prestidge apparently heard the van doors open and turned to engage suspects. Prestidge fired five rounds, striking one suspect in the leg. Suspects fired thirteen rounds, striking Prestidge once in the right hand and approximately four times in the chest area. Mr. Sosa received two gunshot wounds to the back of the head and died instantly.[1] The bulkhead door was in an open position.

And in the company's own report, never released to media or the victims' families, there is no mention of double hopping or the culpability of any Armored Transport employee. From the crime scene report prepared by David LeMaster, senior analyst for the crime scene investigation (CSI) unit of the Las Vegas Metropolitan Police Department:

Numerous bags of cash in apparent deposit bags were on the front floorboard area in bins. The partition door, which can separate the front driver from the rear storage compartment was "open." Duct tape had been placed at the upper driver side border of the door.

THE ROSS KILLINGS changed everything. Now the story was out. Las Vegas's dirty little secret was that a dangerous gang of gunmen had been raiding up and down the Strip like nineteenth-century freebooters from a Cormac McCarthy novel. A crime spree that began on May 25, 1998— *1998!*—was now a big dirty secret. To date the local media had covered the crimes in a workmanlike fashion. The national media, so accustomed to relying on press handouts from the powerful publicity organs controlled by the major hotels, was nowhere to be found. After Ross, the gangsters and their exploits became a front-page story locally, and the assignment editors at local television stations paid attention as well. The casino and armored car raids remained largely ignored outside of Las Vegas. Somehow, the powerful interests who ruled Sin City had their way in keeping this exciting story under wraps.

[1] The company's description of the wounds is not accurate. Gary Dean was hit seven times; Ricardo was shot in the head and back.

And a menacing story it was: The gunmen at large were brazen, brutal, ruthless, highly organized, heavily armed, unpredictable, and decidedly unimpressed with the vaunted security and firepower of Las Vegas. The city may have had more high-tech security cameras per square mile than any city in the world, but what good were they when the crew wore disguises, appeared out of nowhere, and disappeared like puffs of smoke?

The mayor, who knew a thing or two about gangsters from his days as a mob lawyer, politely asked when the fuck these crazies were going to be brought in. Lieutenant Jutta Chambers of Henderson, a polite woman new to the ways of the press, told a reporter something to the effect that "arrests are imminent" (they weren't) and got an earful from an irate John Alamshaw at Metro.

The police timed out the robbery second by second and soon realized that it nearly was what authorities call a "mass casualty" event. Had Suarez not bolted, and had he carried out his assignment to loot the truck after the gun battle, a fierce firefight between Molinaro, with his assault rifle, and Vigoa, with his AK-47, would have erupted. Arriving firemen and curious shoppers flocking to the scene would have been caught in the middle.

Vigoa later agreed with this grim scenario: "If my other partner does his job, if he cleans up the truck, it may happen that way; I kill the cop and anyone else who challenges me," Jose said. "To get the money, I would have stayed another minute, maybe two. If the police showed up, I would not give them doughnuts and coffee. After the guard shot Oscar, I was hot, and I wanted to fight."

Vigoa admits his crew fled the Ross parking lot with seconds to spare. "I could hear the sirens coming stronger and stronger. The police missed us by less than a minute. If Mr. X[2] does his job, lots of people get fucked up real bad."

The decision to pull Martines from the Sandy Slate stakeout becomes grist for still more head shaking among detectives. "If [Detective Martines] had been there another half hour, maybe forty-five minutes later, the gang would have showed up, and they would have dragged Cisneros into the house," Lieutenant Chambers said. "As violent as the gang was,

---

[2] As noted earlier, Jose Vigoa refuses to implicate either Pedro Duarte or Luis Suarez, both family members, in the crime spree. He refers to them as "Mr. X" and "Mr. Y." However, Oscar Cisneros identified both men in his confessions. Duarte is serving a lengthy sentence for his role in the Desert Inn shoot-out, and Suarez is in prison serving time for the Bellagio robbery. Police and prosecutors are convinced Suarez was at the Ross.

and with the firepower they had, could Martines have protected himself? Even if he didn't try to do anything and just sat there waiting for the cavalry, there is a good possibility something bad could have happened."

STILL, THOUGH THE killings were a horrific tragedy, it was because of them that the case finally came together. There was blood evidence at the scene that would tie Oscar Cisneros to the robbery. CSI analyst Jessie Sams's meticulous search for spent bullets and shell casings produced a stunning ballistics breakthrough. The same assault rifle used in the Desert Inn shoot-out of June 28, 1999, was used to kill Gary and Ricardo. And some of the evidence, discovered in a sad ritual on Saturday, March 4, 2000, came directly from the torn bodies of Gary Dean Prestidge and Richard Sosa.

In movies and on television, gunshot wounds are often depicted as neat, pinprick injuries, producing a small trickle of blood or perhaps a tidy through-and-through-the-body trajectory. In fact, the modern-day firearm, and especially the high-velocity assault rifle designed to stop the most determined enemy on the battlefield, is a vicious instrument capable of inflicting terrible destruction within the human body. From the March 4, 2000, report of the Clark County medical examiner, autopsy case number 00-01327:

The body is that of a well-developed, well-nourished adult Caucasian male, 180 pounds, 72 inches. Rigor mortis is full. X-Rays: Numerous deformed metallic fragments are within the right shoulder girdle with fracture of the clavicle and acromion process. Fragments are seen in the vicinity of the right axilla. Fragments of various sizes are within the right arm surrounding a comminuted fracture of the mid shaft of the humerus. Multiple fragments are in the right lower aspect of the abdominal cavity. A near pristine metallic projectile is in the soft tissue of the right hip/buttock. Right ribs two, three, four, and five are multiply fractured. There are seven wounds including: Perforating gunshot wound of neck. Path: Skin, subcutaneous tissue, muscle, left jugular vein, trapezius muscle, and skin. Exit: Situated on the top of the left shoulder 10.5 inches from the top of the head and four inches left of the midline is a gunshot wound of exit measuring one-quarter inch with no appreciable marginal abrasion. [Also:] Perforating gunshot wound of chest. Path: Skin, four intercostal space on the left edge of the sternum, pericardium, heart, right pulmonary artery, upper lobe of the right lung . . .

March 4, 2000: Autopsy of Ricardo Samoya Sosa: The victim suffered two gunshot wounds. One that entered the right temple and traveled from right to left, and slightly back to front, with no significant upward or downward deviation. The bullet exited through Sosa's left eye. Sosa also suffered a gunshot wound that entered his right shoulder and traveled right to left, with no significant frontward, backward, upward, or downward deviation.

The autopsy reports disturbed even the tough murder police. But the torn bodies of Gary and Richard had much to reveal. At last—there would be hard proof that this was the same gang.

AND THEN THERE were the funerals. They were crowded, jostling media events with live microwave trucks surrounding the funeral homes, swarms of reporters, and emotional and sometimes angry friends.

At the service for Prestidge, most of the Armored Transport staff appeared in work uniforms. Members of Prestidge's old Las Vegas El Dorado High School ROTC unit stood in full uniform. A large floral display was placed by the coffin and featured a banner that said, "Ride the Sky Tex." Some of the men, and many of Prestidge's friends, talked about the young man's love of heroes and his vibrant imagination. Kevin Prokopich, the sick guard replaced by Prestidge, said, "Gary was a gunfighter who would go down fighting." Some suggested that Prestidge was seduced by the popular culture and sent into harm's way by all those phony Hollywood tough guys. But one former colleague disagreed.

"Based on Gary's values and what he believed, there is no way Gary could *not* fight back," Frank Severino said. "He did a brave thing. Gary's resistance was so inherent in his character and so consistent with his American heritage. As a people, we are self-sufficient and stand up for what is right. Sometimes when you stand up against long odds, you don't always win."

Five days later Ricardo Sosa was buried. At the ceremony, his namesake Richard Sosa spoke for the family. "My father does not belong in this world filled with cruelty, hate, and crime," the young man said. "He is in a better place now, a better place than we are. It is messed up, it is wrong that it happened like this, but it did happen, and now we have to deal with it."

After the services, the sons of Ricardo Sosa talked among themselves about revenge. "We want to meet that dude," the brothers said to one another of their father's killer, while Gary Prestidge, Sr., wondered if the killer understood the enormity of his actions.

"Does he realize that he didn't just kill two people? He killed a lot of people, including me. He doesn't know how many lives he destroyed."

Chapter 22

JOSE: THAT WASN'T ME

What happened at the Ross was not me. *It was not me!* I didn't want to shoot no guards. I didn't do all that planning to have a gun battle in broad daylight. Think: I spent all that time following the armored trucks, watching and making plans. I broke into armored cars, planted bugs in the trucks. I timed the comings and goings of the guards, measured the exact distances they walked as they went in and out of the stores. I selected just the right vans to steal and where to steal them and how to store them and what license plates to use. I then, like some little kid, cut out black paper like they do in school to fit on the windows of the cars so no motherfucker can look in and see me. And then I went into the desert and mountains and rehearsed all of this, step by step, with my team. Okay, not a very good team, but my team. You Americans have a saying, good help is hard to find. You don't know how right you are. Ask me.

No, I didn't go through all the trouble of scouting and planning just so we could walk up to the guard and shoot him in the fucking head. All over the country—no, what I am saying? All over the *world,* bad men are robbing armored cars and hijacking trucks filled with valuable goods, and they don't plan *nothing.* They just use heavy force and shoot everybody and blow things up. They don't say nothing, either; no warnings, no drop your guns. They jump out of a car, fire an RPG, launch a little missile here, a little missile there, dial a cell phone number, activate a hidden bomb, throw a hand grenade and squeeze the trigger of a machine pistol until nobody's moving no more. Or maybe they "take" the truck, tie up the poor men inside, torture them for the combinations to locks or something, drive off to some empty lot or woods and shoot the guards.

I don't want to kill nobody in my robberies. I *didn't* want to kill the guards at the shopping center. But after the Desert Inn, I realize that every American has to be a cowboy. I call this the hero bullshit. You gotta be John Wayne and Mel Gibson and Bruce Willis, and you do stupid things and force me to do what I do, which is not stupid at all because to survive I will blow your fucking brains out. I will send you on the train to hell on a whim. My whim.

Now do you understand me?

After the Desert Inn circus, I decided to plan an attack so overwhelming, so powerful, so perfect, that even some stupid punk guard who watches too much television isn't going to disobey. When we did the simulations and rehearsals of the robbery, we used words like *freeze, control,* and *stop* the guards. We didn't say *kill* or *shoot* or *murder.* With truck number 3280, I improved the odds. There were only two guards in the armored truck this time, and not three like at the Desert Inn. One of the guards was in the truck busy writing reports, with a broken barrier door that was wide open. That left the kid outside by himself to face three of us, all with our guns drawn. A good plan. Who would be crazy enough to resist this perfect ambush? The gang had the training to take fifty armored cars and one hundred casinos if necessary. The training and skills were there, but, of course, you know the big truth: The most perfect plan is never so perfect because there is no such thing as a perfect plan. There are too many *ingobernobles*.[1] Some people can function perfectly fine when blood and dead bodies are spread over the ground. Some people can't function well *until* they see blood and dead bodies spread over the ground. Others can't take no trauma at all.

There were two things that happened at the Ross that I could not anticipate. There was a new guard, the kid who wore two guns, who filled in for the regular guard who was sick. The original guard, the skinny guy with glasses I watched for weeks, he never pulled his weapon when he jumped out of the armored car. He looked real nervous and ran like someone was chasing him. That gave us a big advantage from the start. The regular guard kept his gun in his holster, and he never looked around. But his replacement, Gary Dean Prestidge, did not run. He walked. And he had this little trick of holding his gun in the bag. Okay, that wasn't a

---

[1] *Unmanageables,* as in unpredictable intangibles.

big problem, we still had our guns pointed at the guard, and he's outnumbered three to one.

At first everything is working good. The truck arrives on schedule. The kid walks into the store and never notices my two vans. He comes out in about five minutes. Right on time. He isn't looking at nothing, like the driver. Then everything turns to shit. Real fast. That is the problem with the unmanageables—the things you can't imagine, the actions by fools and cowards and heroes that make no sense—they come at you real fast, like a bullet.

The other surprise is Oscar. My partner should never have allowed Gary Dean to move toward him with one of his hands hidden in his belt area after Oscar said freeze. This single hesitation by Oscar jeopardizes the entire operation. Mr. X, my other associate, never even uses his weapon and runs off. All of these mistakes force me to intervene to save Oscar and Mr. X by dealing with both guards. Oscar and Mr. X jeopardize my life, their lives, the guards' lives, and the entire operation. I am left with no other choice at the end.

You know what happened. Oscar finally becomes aware of Gary Dean's trick, and they both start firing face to face. I want to fry Gary Dean, but Oscar is too close, and his angle to me is very dangerous. When I hear Oscar's gun go empty, I yell at Gary very strong and angry, "Freeze, motherfucker!" Oscar is hit, bleeding and out of ammunition. He is dead meat if I don't do something.

I see the young guard is about to spend the remainder of his bullets and finish Oscar. Then Gary Dean tries to turn toward me like he did with Oscar, but I am ready for his game. I am full of rage and hate for this punk. All of this happens in fractions of seconds. I yell at the young guard outside the truck to *drop his fucking weapon,* or I will cut him in two. "Drop the gun, man!" He didn't listen. I get very mad. I'm trying to give this guard the opportunity to live; his life is in my hands. Actually, I don't want anything to do with his life, I just want him to drop the fucking gun! From my training in Spetsnaz, I have the ability to shoot with either hand, to use either handgun or assault rifle, to hit my target without aiming. During combat with Spetsnaz, this skill not only has saved my life but also sent many to their graves. I am pissed, the young guard is still not obeying, the precious seconds have passed, and I give the guard what he wants, I give him his wishes. I shoot him from the hip down, see the gun that he is carrying coming off his hand, see him going down. Maybe I leave him alone then—I am not here to kill people—but the kid tries to reach the ankle holster gun[2] that by now was plainly visible.

I fire more rounds into the body, all of them hit hard and true, and the guard bows before me, crumbles up, and sees his last seconds of daylight in this world. I had no more words for the punk. I wanted him dead, fast. He was not going to move again or try any more tricks. His ass was mine. It took me almost two seconds from my first warning to finish him. I decided at that precise moment the punk would die, no more wasting time, no more words, except for maybe the words "dead silent." Now you know what dead silent means and where it came from, don't you?

Before Gary Dean even touches the sidewalk, I turn to the driver inside the truck. "Don't fucking move, let me see your hands in the air!" He looks startled. He reaches for his shotgun. "Don't make me kill you, man!" This stupid man still didn't obey my order; he desperately wanted to pick up the shotgun. I fired a single shot and blew it right out of his hands; it flew out of his hands in pieces. He reached for his pistol. *Then* I shot him in the head.

I only wanted to clean up and to take the "feds' " money, as they took my money in the early 1990s [after his drug conviction]. I didn't get all the money in the truck, but I took two lives with me as my priceless trophies. I don't have their heads stuffed by a taxidermist and hanging in my cell wall, but I do have them in public records and their names in my paperwork.

You asked me if the Ross robbery could have been worse if Mr. X doesn't run away and he does his job, sticks around, and "cleans up" the truck for another minute or two. The answer is yes, there definitely would have been a *big* gun battle because the first police car entered the shopping center as we were leaving. But that is only part of the story. You don't know everything. In the event the police arrived too soon, I had special plans. From inside the van, I maintained contact on cell phones with Oscar, Mr. X, and two other men that I had positioned not too far away. The other two gunmen were assigned to Operation Break Out, an emergency plan to be activated in the event we were blocked, surrounded, or otherwise trapped by the police. This heavy response was basically a surprise counterattack, not a fighting retreat.

We left the money behind because I did not want to ambush the po-

---

[2] It was actually a standard hip holster slung low on the left leg.

lice. Even though I am a criminal, I do understand that police are there to defend good people and to protect the innocent. The mind of a criminal is evil. We think of creating destruction. It's as though evil spirits get inside the criminal's mind and control him. There are many kinds of spirits. For some, it's about money. For others, it's about sex, rape, killing, cheating others. It's not that I'm suddenly changing my views on life, but it is wrong to plot destruction against people just to harm others. That was never my intention. I believed if my plan was good enough, no person in their right mind would resist.

Had Luis performed his assigned task, Mr. X and I would have remained at the truck for one or two more minutes, and Oscar would have been waiting at the Dodge Intrepid getaway car with his own AK-47. With all those shoppers running outside to see the shooting, some pulling their children up to the truck to see the dead bodies, the police are correct: A gun battle with automatic weapons on both sides would have turned the shopping mall into a war zone; women, children, and everybody would die. I would estimate thirty or forty casualties, at least.

I still can't believe what happened with Mr. X. After he failed to scoop out the money from the armored truck, I remember yelling at him, but he was in shock and not functioning properly. I don't think he heard a word I said. I wanted to shoot him in the head and thought about leaving him with the other bodies, but I had reasons not to kill him.

The minute I saw Oscar's wound, I knew it was not too serious. I took Oscar to a secret apartment I had rented in southwest Las Vegas.[3] I started immediately to work on his wounds. I say "wounds," because the bullet from Gary Prestidge went through Oscar's legs, leaving two holes. I have a good friend in Los Angeles who is a doctor. I called him, told him how the wounds were, and—at his direction while still on the phone—inspected the damage and checked out vital signs and the condition of Oscar's muscles and nerves. The doctor thought this was a clean gunshot wound but said I need drugs. I couldn't get them in Las Vegas. I knew the FBI and police already had alerted all hospitals, clinics, and drugstores. I inspected the wound as I was told. I bought one bottle of 150-proof Bacardi Puerto Rican rum and made Oscar drink it. Oscar did not drink or

---

[3] While Jose may have had such an apartment, police believe that Vigoa and Oscar Cisneros went from the Las Vegas Athletic Club parking lot to the Sandy Slate home. This apartment safe house story, contradicted by Oscar, may be part of Jose's ongoing effort to protect his wife and children.

do drugs in his entire twenty-three years, so he got real drunk and passed out. While he was asleep, I checked out the wound more carefully and made sure there was no major damage. I probed inside the wound for any metal fragments. There were none, luckily, and I stopped the bleeding. Within a month we were ready to launch the final stage of our raids on the great Las Vegas Strip.

Chapter 23

THE NEW YORK–NEW YORK HEIST
(PLEASE DON'T SHOOT THE HIPPIE)

The bloodbath at the Ross in Henderson might have caused other gang-sters to pause and reconsider their line of work, but not Jose Vigoa. The Cuban and his crew stuck with their plans and launched new raids on the Strip to further confuse the police. "Las Vegas is a twenty-four-hour town where you can eat, drink, and fuck any time you want, even at four-thirty in the morning," Vigoa said.

On April 22, 2000, shortly before dawn, the crew struck the New York–New York Hotel & Casino in perhaps their most audacious crime to date. This time the crew would not only rob the money directly from the casino itself, they would loot the funds after they were collected from the gaming tables by armed guards.

Vigoa lingered in the New York–New York casino for about a week, drinking at the bar, playing slot machines, and watching casino opera-tions. "I began to notice how the hotel moved the money around, taking steel boxes from under the gaming tables filled with money and replacing them with empty boxes, and then putting the filled boxes inside an alu-minum pull cart," he explained. "They do the same with the slot ma-chines and then pull the cart, sometimes two carts, to a counting room. The money is later redistributed to the casino or held for a Brink's pickup. I learned this routine by heart. At first I thought we would do another Brink's robbery, but then the idea hit me to change tactics again and hit the hotel directly."

One night, while sitting at the bar nursing a beer, Vigoa noticed hotel employees pushing two carts toward the main cashier office. Progress was slow. The carts appeared heavy. Heavy with what? Heavy with cash, Vigoa realized, growing excited.

There was one problem. In every Vigoa robbery, speed was essential. And it was apparent that Vigoa could not break open the two carts and remove the cash in under two minutes or less—and in front of all the security cameras and guards.

Vigoa's solution was simple. "We wouldn't unload the carts. We would pull them through the casino at four-thirty in the morning after disarming the guards (if they even had guns) and roll into valet parking to our favorite Plymouth Voyager minivan."

Which is exactly what the crew did. After two hotel guards placed a pair of steel money boxes onto two separate carts, the gangsters sprung into action.

"I jumped out of my seat in front of the slot machine and pulled out my .357 chrome revolver," said Vigoa. "Don't move!" I yelled at the one cashier [later identified as Richard Rehm.] "Get out of here!" I said to a woman guard [Linda Tucker]. I guess the guards knew who I was. They froze. Oscar appeared from the other side with his gun drawn, picked up the smaller cart, and placed it on top of the main dolly. We then started pushing the cart through the casino. That was funny enough. But when we got outside and started to roll down a slight incline, the cart on top fell off and spilled money and chips all over the driveway."

A minor annoyance. Vigoa turned toward the open rear door of the Voyager and began to load the carts with Cisneros's help. Then he heard footsteps rapidly approaching from his rear. *Another idiot guard trying to play hero,* Vigoa thought, spinning around, thumbing back the hammer of the revolver and preparing to open fire on the intruder. "I am ready to shoot down like a dog whatever fool is trying to stop me. Before I even see the man coming up behind me fast, I *smell* him. A heavy marijuana odor. I see a man in a green cap and white pants reaching down at my feet and scooping up the spilt money. Right in front of me!"

The passerby, a man Vigoa later would call "the hippie," waved happily at Vigoa and his crew. "Hey, man, this is awesome, dude, this is radical," the gambler said, grabbing the spilled money and chips from the driveway and stuffing them into his pocket. "Man, good job, good job, man."

Vigoa was not amused. "I'm pretty sure he was stoned on lots of weed, but I don't care, this guy was pissing me off, and I thought maybe he's a cop pretending to be high or some bullshit hero from the hotel who doesn't know who I am. He was real close, grabbing money from under my feet! I still don't know why or how I don't shoot him in the fucking head. Somehow my instincts told me he wasn't a threat. I told him to get out of our way." The hippie just grinned and kept scooping up the money.

"Man, this is a robbery!" Vigoa barked. "Take your chips and disappear out of here before the police arrive and you're in trouble." The hippie still tried to scoop up more money. By now Vigoa was incensed. "You stupid fuck, get out of here, or I'm going to shoot you!"

The man giggled and continued scooping up cash and chips. Vigoa and Oscar Cisneros finished loading the carts and climbed into the van. They looked back. The hippie was still on the street collecting casino chips. "The last I saw of him, he was scuffling with security guards, who knocked him down. I guess they thought he was in the gang," Vigoa recalled.

In fact, the hippie's good fortune continued. After a brief scuffle with a hotel guard, the gambler scrambled to his feet and ran away. He was never found. Another visitor early that morning to the New York–New York casino was James J. O'Hara of Chicago, a police lieutenant attending a cop convention in town. Unarmed and aware of the robbery, the lieutenant could only watch as the Plymouth and its cargo of more than $100,000 in currency, coins, and chips sped away into the night.

Chapter 24

TASK FORCE

Lafayette Holmes was in a world of trouble. With a history of minor run-ins with the law, he sat opposite Special Agent Brett Shields and Henderson detective Ed Newman in a cramped interrogation room at 700 East Charleston Boulevard.

Too many white men in blue suits, Lafayette said to himself. The agents weren't cutting any slack at all, everybody shouting and talking bad like they were ready to pound Lafayette into the wall.

"Did you kill those guards?"

"What did you do with the money?"

"Why did you tell your girlfriend you did the crime?"

Lafayette could only stammer as he tried to explain away allegations by two of his girlfriends that he was involved in the brutal Ross murders. Agent Shields thought of the old *Honeymooners* episodes on TV when Ralph Kramden would be caught in one of his lame-brained schemes and start to babble foolishly, *"Ahumahumahumahumahum."*

"When are you going to stop lying to us?" Shields snapped.

"Ahumahumahumahum."

Lafayette was lying, and Shields was not amused. Neither was Newman. For hours the FBI had been working Mr. Holmes hard in connection with the double homicide after his girlfriend called Henderson police to say she thought her dippy-ass boyfriend, fool though he was, and a shiftless character to boot, had something to do with it. "Why, Lafayette just about said so, talking trash about doin' wrong."

It took Agent Shields quite awhile just to sort out the lovers in Lafayette's colorful life—young women who came and went like schools of fish. If there was a moral to Lafayette's current dilemma, it was that sometimes a man can have too much of a good thing. The women were the reason Lafayette wound up in the interrogation "box," and this time he actually was stone-cold innocent. Thirty-five-year-old Cindy Ann Johnson, also known as Cindy Matthews, approached the police and suggested that her boyfriend Lafayette Holmes might be involved in the Ross killings because of something Lafayette had said after the crime. From Shields's official report:

> Johnson stated she had paged Holmes because he had borrowed her sister Patricia's vehicle to go to work at the Total Warehouse, located at Lamb and Marion, three days prior, and then disappeared. Johnson stated that Holmes had returned her call after "this thing" had happened because she was watching it on the television. Johnson was then asked what she meant by "this thing." Johnson replied, "the armored car thing." Johnson stated that Holmes told her that he could not pick up Patricia's vehicle and deliver it to her because he had done something really bad.
>
> Johnson asked if anyone had shot someone. Holmes replied, "I'm not going to speak about that." Johnson was crying throughout this interview and became very agitated when confronted by other sisters that were present during this interview.

The interrogation of the hapless Lafayette lasted five and a half hours, and at the beginning the agents and detectives had thought they had their man. For one thing, Lafayette's story was changing every minute; obviously the suspect was lying, and his twitching eyelid seemed to confirm it. And that was true—only Lafayette was lying not because he was guilty of murder but because he was guilty of stepping out on his multitude of present and former and future girlfriends. When asked by Cindy Ann and another girlfriend where in the hell he had been all this time, Lafayette concocted a mysterious story about a robbery gone awry. To placate the ladies, Lafayette had come up with a whopper—and now he was in deep with the FBI.

Meanwhile, inside the FBI office, the word was spreading rapidly that Shields was interrogating the killer, and the suspect was about to confess everything. Case solved! One of the supervisors sat down at his computer and wrote a congratulatory e-mail to Shields. Without waiting to confirm the outcome of the interrogation, he pushed the "Send" button.

As the e-mail tripped its way through cyberspace, Lafayette Holmes, tired, hungry, and needing a drink, looked at Shields and sighed. Okay, it was time to face the music.

"I have to tell you somethin'," Lafayette said.

Shields leaned forward.

"Well, the real reason I didn't take back the car is because I was smoking crack again, and I was with this white girl up in her apartment, and I didn't want to tell my other girlfriend that's where the car was parked."

What about the armed robbery gone wrong and the shooting?

Lafayette broke into his bad-boy smile. The whole story was a fabrication designed to cover his drug-laced affair with the other woman and keep the ladies off his ass. "They be gals, but they can hit hard too."

In the interrogation room, Shields gave Lafayette a look so hard it might have stopped an onrushing freight train cold. "*You knucklehead!*" he thundered, instinctively believing Lafayette because he was starting to think the crackhead was too much of a mope to plan an armored car heist. Shields sat down, defeated.

Lafayette's story checked out. He was cut loose and left to his fate with Cindy Ann and the other irate women. The next morning, while Shields was on the FBI firing range honing his marksmanship, other agents came up and patted him on the back and offered their congratulations. "You broke the case! Way to go, Shields! You the man!" The premature congratulatory e-mail from the FBI supervisor had been sent to all the agents and their bosses too, and Brett Shields was mortified.

THE LAFAYETTE HOLMES story will come to symbolize the frustrations of the police and FBI during the two-year investigation. Indeed, the typical major felony investigation is an exercise in disappointment and mundanity. It is about logistics, budgets, politics, difficult personalities, rotating personnel, vacations, retirements, overtime limitations, false trails, paperwork, turf fights, goofballs like Lafayette Holmes, confused witnesses who call white black and black white, strokes of good fortune, and runs of horrible luck. This case was to be no exception. At one point in the investigation, Special Agent Rich Beasley looked hard at a transvestite dancer from a gay nightclub who said she was carjacked by a Hispanic man while taking her dress from the club to her car. She was so flustered during the interview, Beasley wondered if she was robbed or sold the car to the gang. Another carjacking victim was so surly and uncooperative early in the case, detectives followed him to California to check out his story. It was another dead end. He was just your everyday industrial-strength jerk.

Then there was the controversial near encounter with Vigoa himself on March 2, 1999, five months after the MGM Grand robbery. It took place at the storage yard at 5690 South Boulder Highway when PSU officers Louie Araujo and Kevin Skehan, brought into the case by Gordon Martines without John Alamshaw's approval, discovered that the license plate on the getaway car in the MGM heist had been stolen from an old car in storage. Vigoa not only lived on-site in a trailer, he was in charge of lot security.

The license plate on the getaway car, Nevada TGM 685, was found to be "cold plated," in police terminology—meaning it had been taken off a similar car, a common tactic by car thieves and other criminals. The PSU officers traced the tag to James Barron of Las Vegas, who was interviewed by Skehan on February 1, 1999. Barron said the plate, as far as he knew, was on his junked 1992 Mazda in storage at 5690 South Boulder Highway in a unit owned by Kathy Gianaclis. Later, Barron called Skehan back. He had checked, and the plate was missing from the car.

The next passage in the report has come under fire from other police and FBI agents. The April 2000 report states that after learning Vigoa controlled the site, the police ran a records check on him and found a SCOPE match with an ID number of 697364.[1] They allegedly learned, at the time of the first sighting or shortly afterward, that Vigoa was a registered ex-felon with a history of weapons, drugs, and violence. On March 2, 1999, detectives went to the lot to meet with another renter who claimed he had been burglarized. While at the Boulder storage yard, the police ran into a man named Bern Saucy. They asked what he was doing on the lot. Saucy said he was visiting Jose Vigoa, who lived there in a small trailer.

Skehan writes in his police report: "At this time, I asked Saucy if he would go and get Jose Vigoa and ask him to talk to us, since he was in charge of looking after the storages. I observed Saucy walk back up to the area where Jose Vigoa lives, enter the storage area, and go into the trailer. I observed the subject later identified as Vigoa, in and around that trailer, talking to Saucy. Both men disappeared into the trailer and did not come

---

[1] SCOPE is a national law enforcement database. The acronym stands for Shared Computer Operations for Protection and Enforcement.

back out. I walked up there and found that the gate going to their storage was locked. This activity was very suspicious to officers as to why Vigoa would not want to talk to officers about a possible theft. Detective G. Martines also responded to this scene."

At best, the discovery that Vigoa controlled the yard, ran from police, and was never declared a prime suspect early in the case (or interviewed by the PSU officers or the primary detective) was a lost opportunity; at worst, there had been sloppy police work when it came to accurately documenting the encounter and alerting future detectives about the site watchman's strange behavior. Some investigators would even suggest the report had been rewritten and embellished to cover this negligence. Martines, who was the lead investigator at the time of the storage yard incident, came to the lot and made no attempt to interview Vigoa, according to police records and other sources.

When members of the PSU unit initially prepared a flowchart tracking key events in the case from their perspective, the storage yard flight by Vigoa is not mentioned. Even a cursory investigation would have discovered that an ex-felon who claimed to be a part-time worker making minimum wage was in fact buying new houses, furniture, and vehicles with rolls of hundred-dollar bills, lying about his true residence and lifestyle, all of which were flagrant violations of his federal probation.

A year after the curious events at the Boulder Highway storage yard, FBI Special Agent Shields, newly assigned to the case, scrutinized the initial reports and found no reference to the incident with Vigoa. In a subsequent interview, Shields was asked why the police failed to further investigate after learning Vigoa had an extensive criminal history. Wasn't this an obvious red flag?

"I know the report says all that. *We* didn't know that," Shields said of Vigoa's criminal history. "Nobody in that team knew that. Whenever we were being briefed on their flowchart—the one we called the *anti*-flowchart—that was never brought up. Or I would have recognized Vigoa's name back then. So they didn't know that back then. Their portion [of the investigation] was simply to go follow up on a tag that was recovered, and it came back to that lot and whenever they apparently saw him and wanted to talk to him—the next minute he was gone. No way at that time did they know his history with us or anything else, because, otherwise, all kinds of bells and whistles would have gone off."

The bells and whistles remained silent. Martines continued as lead detective, and, despite the accumulating forensic material, the obvious involvement of Pedro Duarte, and the fact that Pedro was Vigoa's brother-in-law, the case continued to drift.

There were other complications in the early months, and self-inflicted wounds. Large police departments are not unlike other organizations when it comes to the care, feeding, and deployment of staff. People come and go. At the robbery section, detectives took vacations, were pulled from the small unit to handle special assignments, were transferred, promoted, or demoted. Personalities clashed. There were team players and detectives who were supervisory nightmares.

There was an incident with a veteran detective who refused to work with other investigators. He was sacked from the robbery section by Alamshaw. There was Martines, whose erratic behavior toward detectives and supervisors alike mirrored his investigative style. While he seemed to have periodic bursts of insight, the investigation never advanced. After the Mandalay Bay heist, Martines was relieved as primary investigator. He later ran for sheriff, was soundly defeated, and called the department inefficient and poorly led and "a good old boy network."

Sergeant Bobby DuVall, thirty-four, became Alamshaw's ramrod after the Ross murders. A devout Christian, DuVall was the perfect choice to help reorganize the investigation and tame the savage beasts. He wasn't a hard drinker, and he wasn't from the hard-bitten, profane school of men. Alamshaw met with DuVall behind closed doors. It was time to clean house, set a steady course, and catch the bad guys, the lieutenant said. Alamshaw had one other bit of advice for his young sergeant: Respect your opponent.

"We've never encountered anything remotely like this crew before on any level of Metro," Alamshaw told DuVall. Of the 3,500 robberies that took place each year in Las Vegas, almost all were amateur affairs by gang members, drug addicts, or lowlifes with the IQ of an ashtray. Not this crew. The gang would strike hard and then disappear. They were professionals, probably ex-military or police, and Metro would have to rise to the occasion and quickly.

"It had been buzzed to me before I got there that this case was basically unsolvable," DuVall remembered. "Certainly it had cooled off. Everybody seemed to be pulling in different directions. My first thought was, *We need to get everybody on the same page and with the same train of thought*." DuVall's initial action was to assign the case to Bob Rogers, a well-regarded self-effacing detective, and Tony Plew, who would shortly leave the case.

A LESSER MAN might have been discouraged by the borderline insubordination of Martines, the feuding among detective partners, the prickly nature of the PSU officers who felt neglected by the detective bureau and wanted more recognition, but John Alamshaw was undaunted. He had seen it all before. Detectives, and this was doubly so with the good ones, tended to be egotistical and occasionally contemptuous of authority—and that was on their better days. A good sleuth, John knew, was an artist best given free rein to do as instinct demanded. And any artist has to believe in his inherent superiority and his ultimate vision.

The problem was, there were so many robberies and muggings being committed each day in Las Vegas—and the police had to deal with them all. One couldn't tell the pistol-whipped victim at the mom-and-pop gro-

Lieutenant John Alamshaw, head of the Metro robbery section that investigated the Vigoa raids. The detective is a motorcycle and vintage "muscle car" buff.

COURTESY JOHN ALAMSHAW.

cery store, "Sorry, there will be no police response to your attack because all the detectives are out chasing a high-profile crew of crazy Hispanics who have upset the powers that rule Las Vegas."

A week after the Ross homicides, it was proposed during a meeting at Lieutenant Chambers's office that an ad hoc multiagency task force might be formed without a high-ranking person in charge. Alamshaw approved the idea because it fit his image of the good investigator working independently and with little interference. "I'm for the task force," Alamshaw said. "You don't have to preach to the choir. Let's get this investigation moving and catch the bad guys."

The working group represented the cream of Clark County investigators. From Metro came George Sherwood—a onetime college football star, big, handsome, ebullient, a hard charger—and his steady, thorough, thoughtful, detail-oriented partner, Bob Rogers. The Henderson Police Department would contribute Gerald Collins, an able detective and one of those who organized the group; and Ed Newman, the salty detective who had words with Jutta Chambers. Shields and Beasley would come from the FBI. Alamshaw knew these men to be professionals, and after the armored car shoot-out in Henderson, the detectives were motivated.

The task force met at an FBI undercover satellite office near Charleston and Pecos. The total space was less than 1,500 square feet. The furniture was so old, Shields worried that "if you pulled the drawer out, it was going to fall apart, and if the door slammed shut, you had to kick it." But, he said, nobody cared. "There were three phones, with a total of two lines. We shared."

The task force had juice. No longer would Alamshaw face manpower or overtime constraints. His entire robbery team rushed to Stephanie Street shortly after noon on Friday, March 3, 2000, and Alamshaw was prepared to throw every warm body into the investigation when necessary. "Just tell me what you need, and you'll get it," he told his men. This was an emergency, and the heat was on from all quarters: politicians, the media, and from the police department itself. Although he was vindicated in one respect—Alamshaw had warned captains Greg Jolley and Dennis Cobb that the gang would grow more violent with each crime—he knew that another casino gunfight like the one at the Desert Inn, or, even worse, an execution-style robbery on the Strip itself, would prove disastrous to the city's image as a sexy and boisterous but ultimately safe destination. Sheriff Jerry Keller could fend off the city's power brokers for only so long, and Alamshaw knew police politics all too well: "Shit rolls downhill. Entire units had been shaken up for a lot less."

The first Tuesday after the Ross killings, Alamshaw looked up to find Captain Greg Jolley, his immediate supervisor, standing in the doorway. Alamshaw respected Jolley, a former robbery lieutenant and a onetime homicide detective with an excellent reputation even among the smart, cynical murder police. Jolley, with only a slight smile, told Alamshaw that he should shine his shoes and wear his best Sunday-go-to-meeting tie: It was time to pay the sheriff a visit. Keller and the entire high command of Metro gathered every Tuesday morning at the weekly crime management system (CMS) meeting, based on the famous New York Police Department model.

"When?" Alamshaw said.

"Right now."

Alamshaw's mouth went dry. He knew what was coming from his days as commander of the internal-affairs unit. CMS could be an intimidating process. Sitting at a large square table would be the sheriff, under sheriff, and the deputy chiefs, including the head of investigative services, sometimes called the COD, or chief of detectives, in other departments. The sheriff and his men would question the captains one by one about the more notorious crimes in their jurisdictions, alarming statistics, or new trends in mayhem. The scrutiny could be intense and the questioning sharp, with the captains made to feel like suspects in the famous interrogation box. And woe to the captain who was not prepared—careers could be demolished in these meetings.

This week there would be a change of plans, Jolley told Alamshaw as they drove to the meeting. When it was Jolley's time to field the questions—and the armored car and casino crime spree would be the day's hot topic—the captain would pass the baton to his robbery lieutenant.

An hour later, Alamshaw faced the top brass of the Las Vegas Metropolitan Police, an experience he recalled as "very intense and uncomfortable." The sheriff wanted results. The deputy chiefs wanted a timetable. "When are you going to nail these lunatics? Now they're killing guards; soon some tourist will catch a round. Can you imagine the press if that happens, Lieutenant?"

Alamshaw was not resentful. He accepted the fact that sooner or later, especially in a high-profile case with multiple homicides, you could be summoned before the CMS panel and made to run the command gauntlet. All you could do was lay out the facts, avoid rash predictions, and do your best. Jolley was within his rights to defer to his lieutenant, and the case had been Alamshaw's from the outset. The real pressure, Alamshaw later understood, was from within. "I knew how serious this was. These were major casinos that were being shot up and robbed. I was hearing from deputy chiefs, captains, the media, hotel security people—but in the end, the most severe pressure was the pressure I put on myself."

Alamshaw finished his report and waited for the onslaught.

"So, Lieutenant, when are we going to catch these guys?" the sheriff asked. "Bullets are flying all over the place. Now we've got bodies."

Alamshaw paused and shuffled his papers. "We're getting close, sir. We're gonna catch these guys."

The sheriff, whose political skills within the department were second to none, leaned forward. If there was to be an outburst or reprimand—or, in the extreme, a headline-making summary removal of the lieutenant in charge of the case—it would come now. The CMS meetings were about accountability. Someone had to take the heat. And the Vigoa crime spree had been under way for nearly two years.

Instead Keller nodded. "Thank you, John. And good luck. We'll be talking again. We'll see you next week."

THEY *WERE* GETTING CLOSE, closer than they knew. This time Alamshaw's men were not groping in the dark. The Ross crime scene produced blood DNA, spent cartridges, footprints, and more than one hundred witnesses. The investigators read a report by Al Cabrales, the CSI chief, who said the planning of the Ross heist was intelligent and even elaborate. The gunmen appeared to understand the importance of forensics, and Cabrales was impressed with their tactics. "What was quite intriguing were the minivans that were involved, where they were set up, and how well planned that aspect was," he said later. "That clued us right away that this was not your average robbery gone bad. We spent a lot of time processing those vans, and we came up with nothing. Whoever did it was pretty sharp."

Terry Martin examined the vehicles at the scene and, later, at a police garage. Cabrales was right: There were no prints whatsoever. And Martin noticed something else. "They parked the vans early in the morning so that they could get the front spot, and they had the vans pulled in so the doors were facing each other," he said. "When we went inside the vans, they had black construction paper so no one could see in. From the windshield, they had piled boxes just behind the front driver and passenger seats to block out the rear cargo area where they were hiding inside, waiting for the armored car." *Surely there would be fingerprints on the construction paper,* Martin thought.

There were none.

The bulletproof barrier door designed to protect the driver did not go unnoticed. It was open at the same time the hopper door was ajar. Police were puzzled. They knew the barrier door is supposed to close whenever the side door is open, a basic safety feature of modern armored cars.

"We are dealing with professionals," analyst Joe Szukiewicz echoed. "They are ruthless. They are after the money, but killing someone doesn't seem to bother them whatsoever. They also were brutal, and it still affects me. I shop in the shopping center. I was there recently, and every time I go into that Ross or near the Ross, I look at the pavement, and I can still find the divots from the rounds coming out."

BY NOW THE NAMES Jose Vigoa and Oscar Cisneros were burning through the police radar. Pedro Duarte remained a suspect. Slowly the noose tightened. Surveillance on the Sandy Slate Way house, the hub of gang activity, proved fruitful. Vigoa was living beyond his means. One day FBI agents noticed another pickup truck in the driveway. It was registered to Oscar Cisneros, who lived in northeast Las Vegas on Cordelle. This would be the first appearance of Cisneros on the FBI scope and the emergence of a clear-cut link between Vigoa and his favorite henchman. In police jargon, detectives looked hard at Cisneros, "and we tore his life apart." They didn't like what they found. Cisneros, too, was living high.

"From the get-go, the task force had Vigoa and Cisneros on the board," Shields said. "We were putting every investigation up on the board and reinvestigating every robbery to try and find a common lead, something we had missed. We would task every lead to one of us in the group. We showed pictures from the MGM to Vigoa's probation officer, but we couldn't get a 100 percent ID."

There were investigations within investigations, and one of them, a financial study, convinced police and the FBI men they were on track in targeting the Vigoa crew. The problem with stealing a million or so dollars is that sooner or later a thief must account for his sudden affluence and luxurious purchases. The Vigoa, Duarte, Cisneros, and Suarez families, with pre-1999 household incomes of between $20,000 and $30,000 a year, were now buying homes, new furniture, SUVs, electronics, clothing, jewelry, and computers.

Richard Beasley, special agent of the Federal Bureau of Investigation, and, later, Bob Rogers and financial analyst Amber Wilson of the Metro Technical and Analytical Section, would document virtually every purchase the suspects made after the outset of the crime spree, and the forensic accounting would speak loudly. Beasley's idea to follow the money was sound police work. He discovered that one month after the MGM Grand robbery, Vigoa purchased the Sandy Slate Way home with a thick wad of hundred-dollar bills. He made a down payment of $19,000 in cash and had Oscar Cisneros hold the title. A 1992 Chevrolet pickup truck was purchased by Vigoa for $11,500 in cash, also in hundred-dollar bills. The vehicle was driven by Vigoa. Oscar, the front man for the gang because he had no criminal record, was the registered owner. Cisneros also purchased a 1999 Nissan Pathfinder from the Towbin Nissan dealer for $34,929, with a $9,000 cash down payment. The Nissan was parked in the driveway of the Sandy Slate home.

After the MGM robbery, Pedro Duarte's wife, Vilma Farray, spent $17,000 on their house at Carlos Julio Avenue in north Las Vegas. In March 2000 the Duartes bought a second home for $145,650 on Square Knot Avenue. In August 1999 Caridad Farray, Luis Suarez's girlfriend, purchased a $114,000 home on Buffalo Bill Avenue with a $10,000 cash down payment.

The financial data not only told the story of the criminal enterprise and tracked the disbursement of the loot, but it provided incontrovertible evidence for the district attorney later on. "All of a sudden, this mass of what you're looking at comes into focus," Beasley said of the financial shock waves. "There's an excitement. You know at some point the case is going to break."

In March and April, Beasley requested full-time surveillance be established on both Luisa and Jose Vigoa. The FBI deployed a crack surveillance team consisting of as many as six agents in six different cars. "On the day they started surveillance, I figured out where Vigoa's wife was living, and that was at the Sandy Slate address," Beasley said. "We found a vehicle registered to her at the Sandy Slate address. About that same day, surveillance picked up Vigoa getting into a red pickup truck. That red pickup truck was registered to the wife at the Sandy Slate address also. And he was on federal probation, and I don't believe his PO [probation officer] knew he had a vehicle."

The FBI went to see Pedro Durazo, Vigoa's probation supervisor. "Vigoa was supposed to be doing odd construction-type jobs," Beasley recalled, "and he was doing fine with his probation. I think Durazo had the impression that Vigoa was telling him what he wanted to hear for the most part. But there was nothing, really, to think he was doing anything wrong. We continued surveillance on Vigoa, and we discovered fairly early on that Vigoa was going to be hard to surveil. He would come out, and he would drive fast, and he would do a lot of U-turns. He was doing countersurveillance-type maneuvers. It's not unusual for a drug dealer to drive that way.

"I found the original owner of the Sandy Slate house," Agent Beasley continued. "He described how Vigoa had come to the house, looked around, liked it, gave him one thousand dollars cash, and later that night brought over his family, his wife and his two or three daughters, and told him that they wanted to buy the house. He gave the seller another five thousand in cash and then the next day, he came back with Cisneros and gave him thirteen thousand in cash and put the buyer's name as Oscar Cisneros."

Beasley's financial sleuthing represented a major breakthrough in the case. But even as he connected the dots, fellow agent Brett Shields was making another discovery that would turn his stomach. At the heavily guarded FBI office on Charleston Boulevard, in early March 2000, Shields studied a controversial chart prepared by Metro's problem-solving unit. The PSU officers, although not actual robbery detectives, had been asked to join the investigation by Martines without Alamshaw's authorization.

The document, officially known as the flowchart, attempted to connect a recent string of car thefts to the worrisome casino robberies on the Strip. The PSU chart was considered confusing and chaotic by FBI agents. The dates were out of order, the arrows pointed in every direction, and the boxes contained a bewildering range of disparate data. This was the infamous "anti-flowchart." As Shields reexamined the chart, the agent noticed a name in small type in the upper right quadrant of the flowchart. A stolen license plate used in the MGM robbery had been traced to a storage lot on Boulder Highway. Living in a trailer and controlling the site was a security guard with a Hispanic name. According to the flow-chart, the name of the guard was Vioga.

Vioga.

The name was maddeningly familiar to Shields, whose FBI career had begun nine years ago in Las Vegas with a major cocaine bust. *I know that name from somewhere,* he thought. In what would prove to be a pivotal if dismaying moment in the investigation, Shields blinked his eyes and looked again. His vision was momentarily blurry. Then, like a person un-scrambling the tile letters of a Scrabble board game, the FBI agent saw the name as it should have been written:

Vigoa.

Shields sprang to his feet. "I know that name!" Shields told Beasley. "It's not spelled right. I'll bet anything that's Jose Vigoa. We took him down nine years ago. A Marielito. Hard core. Heavy weapons. That's gotta be the same guy!"

Remembering that moment, Shields pounded his desk. "I was kicking myself that I didn't recognize the name early on and that the name wasn't documented on the early Metro reports when the PSU officers first en-countered Vigoa. But the name clicked for me when I took another look at the chart after the Mandalay robbery. I told [the other agents], 'If that name is misspelled, and it's really Jose Vigoa, then we have a good suspect. I arrested him back in 1991 on drug and weapon charges.' "

The misspelled name on the anti-flowchart. As events during the next few days would prove, a calamitous mistake. *We could have grabbed Vigoa and his whole crew before the Ross murders,* Shields thought, shuddering. The primary suspect in the casino crime spree had been in front of the police all along, from the MGM robbery on September 20, 1998, through the preliminary investigation in early 1999 when PSU police visited the site and spotted Vigoa lurking on the grounds. Almost from the outset of the case, the police had learned Jose Vigoa was in charge of site security and in effect "controlled the lot," according to detectives. The PSU cops also claimed they learned Vigoa was an ex-felon with a history of violence who was on supervised release from federal prison; a criminal who liked assault rifles and automatic weapons.

Despite his extensive criminal history and seven-year federal prison term, Vigoa was never interviewed by PSU officers, Metro detectives, or the FBI after being sighted at the storage lot on Boulder Highway. When summoned by a PSU officer during a visit on March 2, 1999, the Cuban slipped away from the site.

"This is our guy," Shields said aloud. The FBI agent reached for the phone and speed dialed Alamshaw. By chance, the lieutenant was skipping lunch to review transcripts from the grand jury investigation of the Thrifty Car Rental heist. So many stolen cars. Alamshaw wondered if the Thrifty theft was a prelude to something big. In serial crimes the bad guys usually became more violent as they went along. Maybe the rental cars were a key to the case.

Then the detective's phone rang. It was Agent Shields, a secretary said. "He says it's urgent."

ALAMSHAW WINCED AT the news of the bungled spelling, but he also saw the larger meaning of the discovery. After so many years of frustration and false leads, the clouds had parted to reveal a logical and symmetrical case. Everything fit: The Farray sisters married to individual crew members. A Mexican day laborer who becomes a real-estate mogul overnight. The newfound affluence of the Vigoa family. The Vigoa-Cisneros connection. The anti-flowchart. Jose Vigoa's reputation as a tough, smart, and violent offender with a yen for AK-47 assault rifles. The same model rifle used in the double homicide. And all that physical and ballistic evidence from the Ross murder scene.

Even so, the task force would move carefully and at deliberate speed.

According to Shields, "We had more tasks, more work to do. The last thing we intended to do was go out and interview Jose Vigoa and Oscar Cisneros. And that's when the Bellagio happened."

Chapter 25

JOSE: IF YOU'RE GOING TO STEAL, STEAL FROM THE BEST

The Bellagio was the hotel that scared Oscar so much. But we *had* to hit the Bellagio; it was the most prestigious hotel in Las Vegas, maybe even in the world. I used to dress up real nice during my surveillance and walk through the hotel pretending I was one of the wealthies who lived in a six-room suite, tipped with hundred-dollar bills, and ate in the restaurants where dinner for my family would cost eight hundred dollars. Instead I was the one who was going to *steal* all their money. They have slot machines where you can push a button for one thousand dollars a play. And they call *me* a degenerate!

Oscar and Luis still worried about all the cameras and security. Well, that's how they scare away thieves, I said. The cameras don't mean nothing if you wear disguises. They don't come out of the walls firing live bullets. The cameras don't grab your feet as you run by and pull you down. The cameras take pictures. If you're wearing disguises, who gives a shit about the cameras? Of course, if you're *not* wearing disguises, or if the disguises are no good, then you are one dumb-ass fuckup, and you are going to have a problem.

I had with me one cool special type of hat, mostly used for outdoor activities, like a fisherman's hat, and this would have protected my face from the cameras. But as we drove to the hotel on the morning of the robbery I switched hats, and put on the baseball hat I wore at the other casinos. I don't know why. I just did.

Maybe it was the birthday party the night of the robbery that took off the "edge," the feelings of excitement, danger, and intensity that I had before and during an action. In these moments my mind works at an unbelievable speed, faster and faster, and I feel strong enough to lift a house, and nothing can hurt me, and I live in the moment like a wild animal chasing and attacking its prey. This time I was too confident, too mellow, too sure of myself, and the party may have been the reason. It was held at the home of Luis Suarez, began the evening of June 2, 2000, and continued well into the early morning hours of June 3.

Cubans love to party. And since my release from federal prison, every gathering like this, with family and close friends but no outsiders, was like a farewell party for me. I learned long ago, in Angola, Afghanistan, in other places I cannot talk about, aboard the shrimp boat in the storm when I left Cuba, every day may be my last. There is no mañana, only now.

I was released from federal prison on December 12, 1996. From that time on, I slept two to three hours a night. I was always busy, enjoying every second—dancing, eating great food, wearing the best clothing, enjoying life—but always accepting the fact the world might end tomorrow. I have beautiful women, money in my pocket, a good family, and two Glock .45-caliber pistols—that is happiness.

It was a nice birthday party. The feeling was very personal and familiar with a family-type atmosphere. The truth is, I don't trust anyone outside the family. I don't believe in compassion or friendship, except as it exists within the family. The family is the only true love; the rest is pure momentarily mutual convenience.

Our food is always the best. That's why I work so hard: My family deserves the best. Cuban food looks wonderful, and it tastes even better. There are lots of spices, seafood, chicken, and pork, cooked in a very special way with rich, original flavors, never the same, so that every dish is a surprise and delight and very succulent. Our family dinners have elaborate salads, lots of fresh fruit and other vegetables, famous custard desserts, and ice cream. You can forget about any diet, if you are thinking of one; there are plenty of calories to last you a week, but it's good food and not cheap, either. (Oh, yes, if you are invited by a Cuban to dinner at his home, never refuse; that would be a great insult.)

I sat in a big chair half watching the television but mostly the people around me. I was satisfied. A few more jobs, and we would be done with this line of work. My federal "supervised release" was nearly over. The children were playing their games, running around and laughing. The adults were eating, drinking, telling stories, and dancing. The music was salsa and merengue from Cuba or the Dominican Republic. Happy music, sensuous music. The women were moving very sexy, shaking their great bodies. I drank a little but not too much. I was not drunk. The party was still going strong around midnight, and the dancing was getting real good when I took Oscar and Mr. X outside. I closed the door behind us. Nobody would listen. I never discussed business in front of my wife and kids.

"We're going to go this morning," I said.

Oscar, who drank a little but not too much, looked at me confused. "Go where?"

"The Bellagio," I said. "Go get the guns."

Oscar didn't say a word and left immediately. Mr. X and I began positioning the getaway cars; by five in the morning, three cars were in place.

I want to make it very clear, and anyone who says differently is a fucking liar, that I was not drunk or on drugs that night or later in the morning when Jose's little show began. I did not tolerate drugs on my team, anywhere near my house, and certainly not around my children. Drugs make people paranoid and stupid, and you can't be either when you're robbing armed guards or one of the most famous hotels in the world.

I wasn't high or drunk, but I was confident. Too confident. It was the mood of the party. I felt good and mellow, almost in a trance. I felt invin-

The Bellagio hotel, one of the elite Strip resorts and a target Jose Vigoa could not resist.

COURTESY MGM MIRAGE GROUP AND BELLAGIO HOTEL.

cible and it was then that I let my guard down. Just like the hotels did when the soft wealthies, lawyers, and accountants took over from the tough Italian gangsters.

So we went to the Bellagio, and we did our business. Little did I know the Bellagio robbery would be a turning point in my effort to make Las Vegas Jose Vigoa's personal ATM machine.

Soon enough, because of the Bellagio robbery and that one goddamn decision to wear the wrong hat, one of my team members would be dead.

My Fourth of July surprise for the $100 million armored truck from the central bank would be postponed.

My face now would appear on every television station in the city as the pigs launched the biggest dragnet in Las Vegas history.

My phone would be ringing off the hook. "Jose! I just saw you on television!" "Jose, how much did you get? Can I borrow some money?"

Every cop and federal agent was looking for me. But I wasn't going anywhere. I would be ready to send them all to hell, even if I had to make the trip with them.

All because of that stupid, goddamn, fucking hat.

Chapter 26

LAST CALL AT THE BELLAGIO

On Saturday, June 3, 2000, at 6:26 a.m., Vikrum Rajpal, a twenty-seven-year-old sales executive from San Jose, California, was up early on his last day of vacation in Las Vegas at the Bellagio hotel. Tomorrow it would be back to San Jose and another week of hotly competitive marketing. For the moment, the native of India intended to party nonstop.

After winning a few hands at blackjack and deciding to break for a deluxe Vegas-style breakfast with his brother, Sameer, Vikrum went to the main cashier's cage, an attractive station with its shiny brass, purple, and beige awning, and elegant marble counters, to convert $200 worth of chips into cash. There he encountered an annoying delay. A curiously dressed man in a white Florida State University baseball cap, oversized sporting jersey, bulky undergarments, and sunglasses was blocking the cashier window. Not the kind of clientele one expected to find at the Bellagio, Vikrum sniffed. The man in front of Vikrum was standing at the only open window and appeared to be taking up space instead of conducting business. "Holding up the program," Vikrum liked to say.

Oddly, the main cashier's desk of arguably the most elegant hotel in Las Vegas appeared open but unattended. Moments earlier, the San Jose tourist thought he saw at least four cashiers behind the counter.

Vikrum loudly cleared his throat. *Come on, dude,* he thought. *I didn't get up at five in the morning just to stand in front of the cashier's desk scratching my ass.*

The man at the counter did not move. Then the salesman's empty stomach rumbled. *Enough sweetness and light. Sometimes you gotta lead, follow, or get out of the way, and this jerk is going to get out of the way.*

"He didn't seem like he was doing anything or was going to leave,"

Vikrum Rajpal told Detective George G. Sherwood of the Metro robbery detail. "So I stepped to the side of him and kind of tried to shove him, shove him away a little bit, to get him out of the way so I could get my change."

The salesman found himself looking straight into the eyes of Jose Manuel Vigoa. Vigoa looked Vikrum up and down, then leaned forward and said, "This is a robbery. Move on. Get out of here."

Vikrum Rajpal uttered a polite thank-you, decided he could always cash in the chips at a later time, and began hurriedly walking backward as though he had done so all his life. "He was very calm and—well, articulate," Rajpal said. "Didn't stutter. Very clear. He kind of made it sound like he was doing me a favor. Like, 'Get outta here, this is a robbery,' you know?"

VIGOA'S NINTH ROBBERY was under way. Thus far in his Las Vegas crime spree, there had been "licks"—either actual or attempted—at the Sunset Station, MGM Grand, Desert Inn, Mandalay Bay, and New York–New York. There had been an aborted heist at the Venetian. There had been the record setter at Thrifty Car Rental and the murderous armored car robbery in Henderson.

The Bellagio was the crown jewel in the legendary MGM Mirage group.[1] Some people considered the Bellagio not only the most beautiful hotel in Las Vegas but possibly in the world. It was built on the site of the old Dunes Hotel, Frank Sinatra's famous hangout and one of the original mob operations. The hotel features 3,005 suites, fifteen restaurants, an eight-acre artificial lake, 2,000 hand-blown glass flowers on the ceiling, and a 120,000-square-foot casino. A person easily could wander the hotel's 4.8 million square feet for days and never see the same room, person, or decor twice.

Vigoa knew of this history, and he savored the idea of strolling into the Bellagio, flanked by two gunmen, and stealing money from the fat cats and the wealthies. What would Frank Sinatra and the old Italians think of that! Yet in a way, the old Marxist spirit from his Cuba days still lingered: The Mafia gangsters who founded the resort were long gone. Rich people owned these hotels now through large multinational corpo-

[1] Other hotels in the chain include the MGM Grand, Mandalay Bay, Mirage, Luxor, Excalibur, New York–New York, Monte Carlo, Treasure Island, and Circus Circus.

rations. These were not your everyday admirable entrepreneurs who invented a new kind of computer chip in their garage or a vaccine to prevent cancer, the Cuban believed. The way Vigoa saw them, these were the obscenely rich gaming operators who sent their corporate jets to pick up pizzas in Chicago, whose pets lived better than most people in the world, and whose losses would be covered by rapacious insurance companies. Besides, the casinos preyed on the middle class and took away their wages and college funds for their children. They were, in Jose's mind, fair game.

To Oscar Cisneros and Luis Suarez, the Bellagio was the province of the über-rich, protected by the most elaborate and complex security in the world. Who could not be impressed, or intimidated, by all those surveillance cameras! But Vigoa laughed at this apprehension. The police were expecting another armored car hit, so this time the crew would change tactics, penetrate deep into the lobby of the hotel, and boldly rob the main cashier cage. The location of the main cashier cage was the plan's weakness, Jose realized—it was in the middle of the hotel and not close to the front entrance. If the gang was spotted, and if the guards had their blood up, there could be a nasty firefight as the crew retired to their getaway car. Once more there would be three alternate getaway routes and multiple escape vehicles parked within a three-mile ring around the hotel.

"I said the Bellagio would be real easy, to give my team confidence, but let me add that this was not easy at all," Vigoa said. "The robbery would take men with heart and courage with so many guards and so much equipment, not all known to me despite my reconnaissance. I know from many gun battles and actual war that not too many men have the courage to execute this type of operation and to perform coherently and accurately."

The cameras at the Bellagio were many, and they were the best, Vigoa told his men, but when the robbery went down, the operators in the monitoring rooms, mostly old ladies, would be so flustered and scared, they'd be lucky to get the back of our heads. And they might even miss "Oscar's big fat ass."

Oscar laughed. "Maybe they love my ass so much they forget what they doing."

AS VIGOA ENTERS the hotel shortly after six in the morning Saturday, June 3, 2000, and slips into the men's room to put on gloves and adjust his clothing, Brian Zinke, thirty-three, a former U.S. Army scout from Pico Rivera, California, is nearing the end of his 11:30 p.m. to 7:45 a.m. graveyard shift. In the upstairs surveillance room, there is a lead operator, three other operators, and Zinke all hovering over an array of monitors. Twenty-one video screens are in the middle of each station, flanked by eight smaller monitors on each side. There are five hundred VCRs nearby connected to sixteen hundred cameras.

In the world of Las Vegas casino surveillance, Zinke is a rising star. After working as a security monitor operator at the Mirage hotel, spotting shoplifters in stores and drunks in parking lots, Zinke realized that the nongaming end of surveillance work was going to be a career dead end. "I started looking at the gaming end of it." Surveillance operators, as opposed to their security counterparts who watched nongaming public areas, monitor the action in the casino and scrutinize gamblers and the gambling. The gaming surveillance operator must know the games themselves almost as well as a dealer or pit boss.

Zinke was not a gambler. Undaunted, the young man set out to learn. He attended a local college that offered courses on casino operations. "I took table game classes," Zinke said. "I also took a dealing course for craps, and I wanted to prove to our director of surveillance that I could deal."

Now qualified to observe casino games from craps to blackjack, Zinke was hired as the lead surveillance operator in September 1998 when the Bellagio opened. By the morning of June 3, 2000, Zinke had been promoted to night supervisor on the graveyard shift. Zinke liked the high stakes and constant action. Even during the early morning hours, there were always blackjack games under way.

THE VIGOA TEAM enters the hotel lobby in single file, with Vigoa in the lead.

Zinke is in the surveillance room talking on the radio with Suzanne, a former California police officer, who is helping to adjust camera angles in the high-limit slot room where Arab princes and dot-com billionaires play the slots for $1,000 a pull. Next to Brian is an operator named Jason, who starts to chuckle. "Check out Joe Cool," says Jason at station B. The main color monitor shows a man in a beige baseball cap and large sunglasses walking up to the main cashier cage. He wears a blue sports shirt with the brand name Wilson on the front.

Jason pauses. There is something wrong with the customer, Jason begins to realize, other than the sunglasses worn so early in the morning. The man is wearing black leather gloves. Who wears leather gloves in June in Las Vegas? Jason blinks. Who wears leather gloves in a casino?

Jason is no longer smiling. He spots something in the visitor's hand, something held against his chest, now clearly visible and pointing into the cage.

"Hey, Brian, *this guy has a gun!*"

Brian looks. "Yeah, that's a gun," Brian confirms sharply. He turns to Vance at station A on his far left. "Get this out on the radio. The main cage is being robbed. Man with a gun. Armed robbery."

When Vance continues to stare at the monitor, Zinke grabs the radio: "Surveillance to security, we have an armed robbery in progress at the main cage; all units stay back. I say again, an armed robbery is in progress at the main cage."

Jeff Bonner, the security shift manager, acknowledges the alert. "Copy, armed robbery in progress. All security, stay back, I repeat, *stay back,* do not approach the suspects. Stay a safe distance back. Observe and report."

"This is a robbery," Vigoa tells cashier attendants at the counter. "Get out of the way. Move back." The employees scatter. Some go into the back room behind a door. Barely twenty yards away, a slot machine begins to clang, and there's the clatter of coins. Vigoa hears a blackjack player shout after a winning hand. Everything is as it should be. Vigoa moves up and down the counter, counting the seconds on his oversize watch. *This is good. Everybody's having fun. The casino is doing its business. Now I will do mine.*

In the surveillance room, Zinke puts down the radio and addresses his operators. "Vance on station A will be primary. Jason and John are to bring up the best camera angles of the event and call them out to Vance so that the best unlimited coverage will be mainly confined to one monitor. I will transmit descriptions to security. I want everything in front of me so I can call out suspect descriptions as they appear."

Zinke is not only taking control of all the cameras and tape machines on the Bellagio property, he is tracking the action as it moves from one part of the hotel to another—selecting the appropriate cameras as the gunmen enter the zone of coverage and then punching in the perfect shot for the main monitor and final edit. In TV this is called "cutting cameras." Zinke finds himself directing his own high-velocity crime drama with real participants and lives at stake.

Zinke detects movement on one of the smaller side monitors that cover the cashier cage. Two men appear in the frame and vault over the counter and into the cage. Using a black crowbar, the thieves begin cracking open drawers, scooping up cash, and stuffing the money into a black bag. Cisneros and Suarez have arrived to commit the actual "cleanup," or robbery.

Huey Roth, thirty-six, a cashier near the front of the cage, is among the first to encounter the gunmen. "I saw one gentleman walk up, put a bag on the counter," Roth said. "He told us, 'This is a robbery. Don't move.' At the same time, I saw a second individual jump the counter, come toward me with a bag under his arm. He stopped about three feet from me, pulled a weapon—it's a chrome gun—told me, 'Move to the back.' He waved the gun toward my direction. At that time, we moved to the back, no questions asked. I wasn't gonna—you know, didn't wanna upset him or have anything else happen."

Terry Potter, fifty-one, another cashier, is preparing to complete her shift when she is startled. "All of a sudden I heard this noise, looked over to the right of me, and somebody jumped over the counter. We were afraid that they were gonna come back where I was, in the rear."

The robbers are looting windows four, five, and six and stuffing the cash into a black plastic bag and what looks like a smaller gym satchel. The money is neatly packaged. It is standard procedure in the cage for hundred-dollar bills to be bundled into $50,000, $10,000, and $2,500 wads. The fifty-dollar bills are clipped in packs of $25,000, $5,000, and $1,000. The twenty-dollar bills are assembled into rolls of $10,000, $2,000, and $500.

Jayshree Patel, forty-one, is a booth cashier and gives one of the best eyewitness accounts of the heist. When Cisneros and Suarez leap over the counter, Jayshree ducks behind a pillar, too afraid to run. Then she dials security and makes the first call for help despite her fear. Her body is trembling. "Help, help, a robbery in the cage! There's a robbery in the cage! Help us!" Jayshree remains hidden but watches. She will recall that the gunmen were crisp and professional, like men who had done this before many times, and who brushed off the cashiers and their supervisors as if they were so many gnats. "It was quick, and they were very calm. There was no violence or nothing. It was cool, very cool."

The robbery begins at 6:27 a.m. At 6:29:43,[2] the crew half jogs and half walks toward the emergency doors that lead to the driveway and the getaway van. Unexpectedly, Cisneros stops at change booth 8. Even Vigoa is surprised, and he turns to glare at his comrade. Then he shrugs and nods approval. The robbery is now almost a minute over schedule.

Lawanda Taylor is the attendant in change booth 8 and she is about to become the first and perhaps only armored car or casino employee to actually exchange words with a gang member during the two-year crime spree. She is counting her money and preparing for a shift change when Oscar bursts into the booth waving his .45 pistol. Taylor had served in the military and knew firearms, especially the heavy-caliber .45. With all due respect to the Bellagio, this was not where she wanted to be, trapped in a change booth with an armed man.

"Can I get out, can I get out of your way? Please let me out of here!" Taylor says to Cisneros in the small, cramped booth. "Go, go, get out," Cisneros says. Taylor then runs head on into Vigoa, who sends her on her way with a wave.

As for Brian Zinke's video surveillance team, the electronic posse remains hot on the heels of Vigoa, Cisneros, and Suarez. Cameras have captured the robbery of change booth 8. There's an overhead shot that's so good it could have been plotted by a Hollywood director. Police have been alerted; by now Metro patrol units are charging down Las Vegas Boulevard from the north and across Flamingo from the east.

Zinke continues his play-by-play on the security channel. "Security, armed robbery suspects are now at change booth for another hit," Brian reports via radio.

"Copy, we're moving into position," responds Harry W. Czerniak, a security guard patrolling the outside of the hotel. "We'll be waiting for them."

Meanwhile, in the surveillance booth, John, a new employee transferred from another security unit at the Bellagio, is manning station D. John is a fast learner. His cameras pick up the Vigoa crew as they burst through the casino's emergency doors leading to the hotel driveway and the parked getaway van. The rookie operator alertly zooms in on the license plates. This time the escape vehicle is where it's supposed to be. "Our getaway car, a 1999 Dodge van, was parked in front of the Bellagio

---

[2] The digital readout on the security video provides a second-by-second chronology of the robbery.

A freeze-frame taken from a copy of the original Bellagio surveillance tape of the June 3, 2000, Bellagio robbery. The footage ran for four days on Las Vegas television stations.

COURTESY KVVU-TV, CHANNEL 5, LAS VEGAS.

in the valet parking area, as if it were a VIP car waiting for us," Vigoa said. "Inside that van was a real arsenal of weapons and ammunition, including thousands of rounds and several Russian-made hand grenades. We were prepared for a war if the police arrived in time and cut us off."

Vigoa was impressed by the quick response and tactics of the hotel security. "As we left the Bellagio, heading south to the big parking lot," he recalled, "I spotted several police cruisers approaching the Bellagio in silence. I could hear police sirens in the far distance, but the ones that I could see were without siren or red lights. When there's a robbery in progress, police don't get too close until they have proper backup and all their units in place. Police were very close that day."

So were the hotel security men, who were armed and in pursuit. Vigoa identified them almost immediately. "From the emergency doors at the front of the Bellagio, facing Las Vegas Boulevard, was about two hundred fifty feet," Vigoa said. "We ran that distance to our first getaway car. By now the Bellagio's security guards were all over us like mad African bees."

The Bellagio guards pull ahead of the gangsters and park along the curb. When the Dodge passes with the three gunmen, the hotel vehicle follows. The two vans travel south into what is called the oversized parking lot south of the hotel. Inside the Dodge getaway van, Vigoa warns Cisneros not to speed.

"Keep it normal, keep it cool," he cautions.

"They're still following us," Cisneros says.

Trailing the gang are three armed hotel guards in a dark green 2000 Plymouth Voyager clearly marked as a Bellagio Hotel & Casino security van. "Three wanna-be stupid superheroes," Vigoa recalled later. "They followed us at a distance of between one hundred fifty and two hundred fifty feet on a parallel track. I knew what they were doing. The police call this maintaining the 'eyeball,' or the eye, which means keeping the target under observation like one of those light airplanes that fly over the battlefield radioing the position of the enemy and spotting for the artillery. Unless I did something right then, sooner or later I would have to blow them all to hell."

Vigoa leans out the window and sees that the two vans are now in the parking lot. He pulls his .45 from his belt buckle. Cautiously, the hotel security van continues to pace his vehicle. "If the guards knew what I had on board our van, I think maybe they would have taken their meal break real quick. We had two large duffel bags filled with ordinance, including two thousand rounds of 7.62 mm ammunition for the Norinco MAK 90 assault rifles, five hundred rounds for the two Russian sniper rifles, six hand grenades, and hundreds of rounds for our semiautomatic handguns."

The gang's second getaway SUV is only a quarter-mile away, on the second floor of the Holiday Inn Boardwalk parking garage south of the Bellagio, across the boulevard from the Aladdin Hotel & Casino. "We were heading for the Boardwalk Hotel," Vigoa said. "We could wait and ambush them there and take all three out, or maybe send a little message and end this stupid chase right now."

Harry Czerniak was in the security van trailing the Vigoa crew. "We continued to follow the van," he remembered. "When we got about halfway through the oversized parking lot, we were parallel to the van and a little bit farther back. Then the passenger stuck his hand out the window, and we saw a weapon in his hand."

Vigoa opens fire: two shots in rapid succession. The first round hits and flattens the right rear tire, a remarkable shot. Vigoa has just fired from one moving vehicle at another moving vehicle seventy yards away, and with his first shot has disabled his pursuer. The second bullet bounces off the tire's metal rim and skips harmlessly through the parking lot. As the security van wobbles to a stop, the Vigoa crew darts into the Holiday Inn Boardwalk parking garage and switches to a green 1999 Jeep Grand Cherokee SUV. With Cisneros still driving, the SUV pulls out of the garage, sideswipes a parked white pickup truck, pulls onto Las Vegas Boulevard, and then heads to the I-15 south entrance ramp.

"Good shooting," Cisneros chortles as the crew works its way into the slow lane of the heavy freeway traffic. "I thought them hotel fuckers were going to follow us all the way home."

Vigoa shrugs. "Instead of hitting the tires, I could have put a round into the head of each of the superhero guards if I want to. But I don't want to hurt nobody. I just want to send a message, and I think I did. Finally they got it real good."

By now Zinke is on the line with his immediate boss, Director of Surveillance Pat Fischer, to report the robbery. "I think we've got good cov-

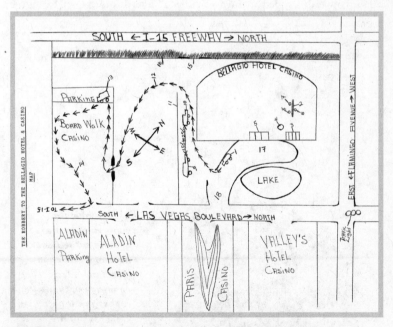

Jose Vigoa's sketch of the Bellagio robbery, drawn in 2005 for the author.

COURTESY JOSE VIGOA.

erage, and I believe we——" The radio crackles. An urgent message: "Shots have been fired in the parking lots."

"Pat, we have a report of shots fired," Zinke tells Fischer.

"I'm on my way."

It is 6:34 a.m.

The police arrive in force, but Jose and his crew have vanished. The gangsters, with their $155,523.20 in loot, drive to yet another "lay-off" car parked at an apartment complex east of the Strip, switching to the third vehicle used that day. By then the Bellagio and Las Vegas Boulevard are overrun with Metro patrol, detective, and crime lab vehicles.

Other than a parked car at the Holiday Inn Boardwalk garage with some paint traces, there will be no significant forensic evidence left behind at the hotel. The crime scene is clean as a whistle. But there will be something else left behind, which makes the police ecstatic.

For the first time in two years, the police are the hunters and, although he doesn't know it yet, Jose Vigoa is the prey. "The gunmen might as well have left their passports and wallets behind on the front counter," Alamshaw tells a superior. "We don't need fingerprints or shell casings——

Brian Zinke, the supervisor in the gaming surveillance control who began directing video coverage of the Bellagio robbery as it unfolded, a key break in the case.

COURTESY MGM MIRAGE GROUP AND BELLAGIO HOTEL.

the bad guys are starring in their own movie, and I've got the title: *Do Not Pass Go; Go Directly to Jail!*"

Even now security officials are reviewing the surveillance footage and discover it is astonishingly good. Excellent resolution. Full color. Vigoa and his crew also are taped on high-end Pelco cameras as they arrive at the cage, when Oscar and Luis vault the counter, and as the crew ransacks the drawers. There are head-on, side, and overhead cameras. There are close-ups, medium shots, and long shots. The gang's departure, from various angles and from within and without the hotel, has been recorded.

Stephen G. Koenig, vice president of security for the Bellagio, is at home when the robbery unfolds. Koenig, a burly six-foot-two, 220-pound executive, who unlike many security managers on the Strip is not an ex-cop or FBI man, throws on blue jeans and a T-shirt and is heading to the hotel when he learns that shots have been fired at his men. He floors the accelerator and races to the hotel. "The first thing that crosses my mind is to make sure everyone is okay," he said of that day. "One of the things we teach our folks is don't get hurt during this. Ensure the safety of our customers and our employees. We don't want any heroes. We don't want people tracking these guys. We employ a kind of SWAT technique, including suspect location and observation techniques." Hotel security agents are trained to stay with the criminals, report their location by radio—but not to engage. "Rather than everybody rushing to the cage itself, you just go out to the peripheral, and you just wait for the description to be broadcast," Koenig said.

The head of security immediately screens the video. It is outstanding, Koenig realizes, and Alamshaw and his detectives are asking for dubs of the surveillance video and they are asking *hard*. Koenig agrees to allow the police to screen the footage, but he is reluctant to release footage to the media. The detectives want the video aired on local television stations. Koenig pauses. Handing out casino crime footage is considered bad public relations. Las Vegas is supposed to be the world's safest tourist destination, according to the city's high-powered publicity machine.

Alamshaw and his captain, Greg Jolley, lobby hard. The next day the tape is released. "It was a tough decision," Koenig said. "Here it is, the robbery video playing on the news, and they say, 'Look, the Bellagio just got robbed,' and of course a person like me in my job would say, 'Oh my God, I wish this would go away, we just got robbed of one hundred fifty-six thousand dollars.' " But Koenig knew the stakes. "Giving out the video doesn't tarnish our reputation. It means we are willing to go out there and catch you no matter what the cost. We just get stronger over it. We use it as training material."

THE GANG TOOK exactly two minutes to complete the main robbery. The change booth took fewer than fifty-two seconds and was on the escape route anyway. Total robbery time, including the jog to the getaway car, was just under three minutes. The robbery netted $155,523.20, although Vigoa would claim proceeds in excess of $200,000. However, the gang overlooked a greater sum of money stacked in a counting room at the rear of the main cage. Cisneros and Suarez were scarcely twenty feet from an area known as the "soft room," where at least $2 million was sitting neatly on a table in bundled piles of hundreds, fifties, and twenties. The door to the counting room was unlocked at the time of the robbery, a police source said.

Chapter 27

JOURNEY'S END

At 6:48 on the same Saturday morning, the phone began ringing at the west end home of Lieutenant John Alamshaw. Cindy Alamshaw was accustomed to her husband's telephone calls at all hours and rolled over to grab another hour's sleep. Alamshaw was up and about, drinking coffee and thinking of his dark red 1968 Camaro Super Sport and maybe a little weekend tinkering in the garage.

A patrol sergeant from the Southwest Area Command brought first word of the Bellagio heist: three suspects, two shots fired, two hits on a moving vehicle. Alamshaw took a deep breath. That wasn't a local homeboy or a crystal meth addict. *They* were back. Alamshaw's cell phone began to ring again, playing the theme from Sergio Leone's spaghetti Western *The Good, the Bad and the Ugly,* and the lieutenant also felt his pager vibrate. Alamshaw looked at the house phone: Two lines were blinking red. One of Alamshaw's robbery detectives from the task force was on the phone, and he sounded almost giddy.

"Do you feel lucky?" the detective asked.

"What is this, a Clint Eastwood movie?" Alamshaw snapped, not in the mood for banter.

"Come on, John, do you feel *lucky?*"

"Well, if you're about to retire early and leave town, then I'll feel lucky. Or maybe my test results came back negative, and your sister's going to be okay."

"Lieutenant, wait till you see what we've got."

"I hope three dead gangsters with third eyes," Alamshaw said. But he could feel the detective's excitement coming through the telephone wires, and it didn't sound like bad news at all.

"L.T., the surveillance video is fantastic. Like a movie. We put the footage on the air, and we've *got* 'em. Frontal shots of the leader. Some kid in the surveillance room tracked the gang all the way to their getaway van. Zoomed in on the plate. He ought to win an Oscar."

The surveillance video was the key to ending this nightmare, Alamshaw knew. And the detectives would have to move fast. *They're not done yet. They're in town, probably counting the money right now and packing up for another strike.* But would the hotel give up the tape? Acquiring surveillance footage of a major crime from a Las Vegas hotel had not been a foregone conclusion in recent years, especially when Metro dealt with the newer, more upscale hotels. In the old days, casinos were happy to give up their surveillance footage, such as it was. Then came the big corporations, the lawyers, and new rules. Often it took an administrative subpoena to shake loose crime video, and that took time.

Alamshaw slammed his clenched fist on the kitchen countertop. The coffee mug toppled over, rolled into the stainless steel sink, and shattered.

We need the video and we need it now.

Moments later Alamshaw spoke to Detective Bob Rogers on the phone. "I've been saying this from the beginning," he told Rogers. "These people are going to grow bolder and more and more violent as they go along. With each success, we are guaranteed there will be another heist and there will be more casualties."

"Do you think they're going to go to ground for a while?" a detective asked.

"No. I think they're planning another major hit right now."

Alamshaw knew and respected the Bellagio's Steve Koenig. The hotel executive was sharp, Alamshaw observed. Koenig would not need a lecture on what might happen if the gang continued its assault on the Strip. Koenig had personally overseen the design and installation of the Bellagio's security system. Now it had been tested.

After an anxious twenty-four hours, Alamshaw got the news. Yes, Metro could release certain *portions* of the tape to the media, Koenig said. However, the hotel did not want to air footage of the gunmen jumping over the low counters. That vulnerability to thieves would be remedied as soon as possible with the construction of a cage with bars on the windows, but in the meantime, let's not ask for more trouble. On Sunday, June 4, the hotel handed over the video. By Monday afternoon it was playing on every television station in town.

Vigoa was about to have his fifteen minutes of fame and a good deal more. The phone began ringing at Sandy Slate Way. "Vigoa, dude, you're on TV . . . Hey, chico, how come you still in town? You're all over the news, my man . . . Vigoa, what the hell you doing in Las Vegas? I can even see your fuckin' gun on the channel five news, hombre. Turn on Fox news, I can see you. You gotta go, bro."

Vigoa had no intention of going anywhere. Vigoa was convinced the police were clueless as to his identity even after he failed to wear a proper disguise—that stupid baseball hat was worthless—and despite the hundreds of cameras following his every move. "This time, at the Bellagio, I used a different approach," he explained. "No masks, no Ninja costumes. I was too relaxed after the birthday party at Luis's house. I exposed my face too easily, and this mistake put me right on the news. Even then I still had plenty of time to disappear after seeing my face again and again on the daily news and after receiving phone calls from friends. It took four days for the FBI and police to receive a call from my parole officer. In my mind, this only proved what I thought to be true: The police were, as I liked to call them, 'the stupids.' "

ON MONDAY, JUNE 5, Alamshaw and other robbery detectives, including partners Bob Rogers and George Sherwood, crowd into the robbery section's cramped screening room to watch the Bellagio surveillance footage. Although Alamshaw is viewing a second-generation VHS tape, the images are clear enough; the Bellagio has spent its $5.5 million in electronics wisely.

The tape, the single most important piece of evidence in the long-running case, begins with a wide shot of Vigoa at the main cashier cage. He wears a white ballcap and a dark blue athletic jersey. The first angle is from the left as Vigoa leans casually on the counter. It is apparent that he is talking to someone behind the counter. It may be his crew, or it may be cashiers. Vigoa slowly turns his head to each side as he scans the casino. He casually walks three paces east toward the main entrance and then returns to the middle of the counter. His appearance is unexceptional; he could be just another customer waiting for a friend or killing time.

A new angle, from the right, reveals that Cisneros and Suarez have jumped over the counter. Vigoa turns to his left and looks into the camera. He's still talking. To the left of the frame, there's a glimpse of Cisneros looting the drawers. Vigoa is still talking when the gangster swings his head to the left and looks straight into the camera. He swivels to the right for four seconds, then turns again to look directly at the hidden camera. It is clearly Vigoa. The detectives notice the oversize, distinctive sunglasses and a large square watch on his left wrist.

One of the detectives starts to chuckle. "This is too fucking cool, dude."

At 28:41 Vigoa helps Cisneros loot the change booth. Vigoa places one large stack of currency on a counter to his left and then resumes loading money into the black bag. At 28:50 Oscar leaves the booth while Vigoa tries to pry open a cabinet in the left corner of the booth. At 28:57 Vigoa departs the booth.

"Watch this," Detective Bob Rogers says. "It's priceless." Four seconds pass, and suddenly there's Vigoa again—he comes back and grabs the package of currency he left behind. The next shot is of the three men running from right to left through valet parking in front of the hotel's main entrance. Vigoa is in the lead, passing a bush at 29:38. Luis is second at 29:42. Cisneros, with his heavy bag of swag, comes in third at 29:45. At 29:50 we see the getaway car, a teal Dodge caravan. Almost on cue, the camera zooms in to capture the license plate number. The detectives yell and break into applause.

Alamshaw's men scramble to make copies of the tape. The lieutenant writes a press release to go with the Bellagio video. That evening the robbery video begins airing on local television stations in the form of news bulletins. Now the police must wait for the public to respond. If there is a hit, will the identification be made in time? Or will the airing of the video send the crew to ground?

PEDRO DURAZO, VIGOA's federal probation officer since 1996, and possibly the man in the justice system who knows him best, was too busy to watch the news bulletins or the evening newscasts. Pedro's workdays were longer than he could ever remember. A probation officer typically carried a caseload of forty felons in the 1980s and 1990s. By the time of the Bellagio robbery in 2000, Pedro was routinely handling seventy to seventy-five felons at any given time. "That's hurting the system," the veteran civil servant decried.

At five foot eight, 160 pounds with black hair, graying temples, and a thoughtful, pleasant face, Durazo conveyed the air of someone who took his work in stride, who was conscientious in fulfilling his duties but who didn't take his work—and its inevitable disappointments—too personally. With two degrees from the University of Nevada, Durazo was nobody's fool.

When Vigoa emerged as the prime suspect in the two-year casino spree, there were the inevitable questions about the effectiveness of the probation system. How could Vigoa commit nine robberies and buy houses, cars, and jewelry without arousing Durazo's suspicion? And what about Vigoa's complaint that a zealous Durazo appeared at his job sites and informed employers of his drug-dealing past?

"That's basically true," Durazo said. It was the probation supervisor's duty to inform others of Vigoa's past if the Cuban failed to do so himself, Durazo said, and any probation officer who failed to enforce this regulation would not be doing his duty. The principle is called third-party risk. The probation system, when it releases a felon early, is obliged to protect the citizenry, which is the third party at risk, because the citizenry might come into close contact with the violator and become another victim. When a convicted felon with a history of violence is released into society, many people share the risk: landlords, roommates, employers. "When it comes to a roommate, for example, we have to make sure they know who they're living with," Durazo said.

To qualify for early release, the felon agrees to notify others of his background. This is a condition of release. "If the violator leaves something out in telling about his past, I fill them in," explained Durazo. "For example, if he has stolen from his landlord in the past, I will tell his new landlord that." Durazo admits that this procedure handicaps the felon when he seeks work, but that is the price a convicted felon must pay. These were not unwritten rules or policies enforced on a whim. The felon signs a contract with the U.S. government that includes a clause known as provision 13:

> The defendant shall notify third parties of risk that may be occasioned by the defendant's criminal record or personal history or characteristics and shall permit the probation officer to make such notifications and to confirm the defendant's compliance with such notification requirement.

Vigoa did in fact sign such an agreement.

—

BY TEN O'CLOCK Monday night, Vigoa's employment problems are the last thing Durazo has on his mind. It has been another twelve-hour day. The "clients" keep rolling in. Some survive the transition to the outside; most do not. Tonight Durazo is working late preparing an arrest warrant for a felon who has violated his parole on an unrelated case. At some point close to eleven, weary of the paperwork, Durazo starts channel surfing.

"As I'm doing my work, I'm real cognizant of casino robberies, anything to do with casinos. I'm reading a document, and I hear something that attracts my attention. I glance at the TV." There he is: Vigoa. "I had his face basically memorized, and, sure enough, that was him."[1] Unless he had a twin brother, this had to be Vigoa. The probation officer began scanning channels and catching other newscasts. He managed to see two more reports.

Durazo decided to wait until Tuesday morning to alert police. The probation officer, suspecting that Vigoa might have been implicated in the Ross double homicide, would not sleep well tonight. Tossing and turning, Durazo remembered the first time he heard of Vigoa. In late 1996 an appeals court agreed to drop all weapons charges against Vigoa and release him halfway through his nineteen-year sentence. Usually the U.S. Probation Office was to be notified thirty to sixty days in advance before a felon was scheduled to report to a specific probation office. This notice, including a package containing the offender's criminal records and prison file, was necessary to give the staff sufficient time to conduct a pre-release investigation of the new client.

"During this stage we go out and investigate the family and inspect the new residence of the subject," Durazo said. "We let people know what his background is. We gather additional information about just about everything. The probation staff reviews the client's institutional history, reads his progress reports, runs a DMV check, and updates the felon's criminal history." On rare occasions, a newly released offender would show up unannounced at the probation office because of a bureau-

---

[1] The hotel produced a copy for the police from its original, creating a second-generation tape. The police then made their own copies for the television stations, thereby creating a third-generation tape. It is possible the television stations went to a fourth generation during their editing. With each succeeding generation, the tape lost color and resolution.

cratic error or case overload. This person was called a walk-in. Probationary managers do not like walk-ins. They confuse the system and leave the probation officer with an information void at the outset of the relationship.

Vigoa was a walk-in. On December 16, 1996, he strolled through the front door of the probation department's downtown office. After waiting ninety minutes in the lobby, Vigoa was assigned to Durazo, who handled difficult cases involving major felonies.

As Durazo drifted in and out of sleep early Tuesday morning, he remembered the wiry, lean Cuban with the heavy eyebrows, piercing eyes, and respectful demeanor. Vigoa was a Marielito, but he was unlike any Marielito the probation officer had ever met. *Always a gentleman,* Durazo recalled. *Good posture. Well educated. Carried himself like that. Called me "Mr. Durazo." Never lost his cool. Always respectful. Like an officer in the army who is well trained and very sharp.*

Vigoa stood out. "The typical Marielito is a hard man who has lived a life of abuse; you can tell that right away," Durazo observed. "Vigoa had no tattoos. He was clean-cut. That's why I thought he was military. He had a very military bearing. He was well dressed and well mannered."

But still, even granting that Durazo carried a heavy probation caseload, how could Vigoa hoodwink his probation officer so completely and for so long? "He was a model offender," Durazo said. "Very open with me. From the information we had, he was very candid. He was very meticulous. He took his time when he spoke. I could see he was thinking."

Early Tuesday morning, the federal probation officer called Brett Shields. Durazo told FBI agent Brett Shields he had been watching the Bellagio video. "I'm 90 percent sure it's Vigoa," Durazo said.

"You need to get to Metro robbery right away," Shields said. "They'll show you the whole tape. I'm coming over too. I know Vigoa. I arrested him nine years ago when he was selling dope."

The misspelled name on the anti-flowchart: Vigoa. The Marielito who controlled the storage lot where the MGM license plate was stolen: Vigoa. The convicted felon who refused to talk to Gordon Martines and the PSU officers after the MGM heist and slipped away, never to be interviewed again: Vigoa. The brother-in-law of Pedro Duarte, implicated in the Desert Inn robbery: Vigoa. Pedro Durazo's polite offender on supervised release, claiming to be destitute but secretly living large in a well-furnished home on Sandy Slate Way and flashing rolls of hundred-dollar bills to realtors and furniture salesmen: Vigoa.

Shields urgently called Alamshaw. The two lawmen were excited. "Our blood was up," Alamshaw said. "We were on fire."

Shields arrived first at the detective bureau on Charleston Boulevard. With Alamshaw and George Sherwood in the screening room, Shields watched the Bellagio footage for the first time. Preoccupied by an FBI inspection, Shields had not seen the television coverage. The tape was played.

"That's Vigoa," Shields said a minute into the tape. "That's one of our prime suspects who has been on our board the whole time on this thing. We've got his photo down at the off-site where the task force meets. Let me go get it. I'll show you exactly, and you can make up your own mind."

"Go!" Alamshaw said.

Shields returned an hour later with the photo taken off the wall from the task force office. "You know how when you have static electricity on the screen?" Shields recalled. "I took the photo, stuck it up on the screen, and everyone's like, 'Oh my God, that's him.' " The video frame on the television monitor was paused on a shot in which Vigoa looked into a hidden surveillance camera on the side of the main cage. It's the same angle as in the older still photograph from Shields that was stuck on the side of the monitor. The images were almost identical.

Durazo arrived and screened the footage. Durazo finally looked up and sighed. "That's Vigoa."

"Are you 100 percent sure?" Alamshaw asked.

"Almost. The tape is a little blurry in places. Let's say I'm 90 percent."

Alamshaw called Koenig, the Bellagio security chief. "Can we come over and look at the original master tape?"

"Not a problem," Koenig said. "We'll have it ready."

At the hotel Durazo and Shields took a second look. The original video was sharp, bright, and clear.

Durazo nodded vigorously. "I'm 100 percent sure this is Vigoa. One hundred percent."

"Then let's take him down," Alamshaw said.

Alamshaw summoned both robbery squads, consisting of six detectives per unit plus a sergeant. Alamshaw tracked down Jutta Chambers, his Henderson counterpart: "*Now* you can say an arrest is imminent," Alamshaw said.

Jutta laughed. "I'm not saying a damn thing until we have this guy locked up!" She then alerted detectives Gerald Collins and Ed Newman—the lead detectives on the Ross murders—and told them to get ready to rumble.

Alamshaw mobilized SWAT, his old unit, and placed the elite police combat unit on alert. "We're coming heavy," Alamshaw told his men, and the room stirred as though a stiff breeze had blown through an open window. Detectives began to check their weapons. No one noticed that DuVall, the thirty-six-year-old robbery sergeant, was sitting at his desk with his head bowed. An evangelical Christian, DuVall silently prayed. He asked God to protect all the policemen as they searched for Vigoa. "I prayed nobody would get hurt," DuVall said. "I prayed for everyone's safety, including Vigoa."

But where *was* Vigoa? After four days of television coverage, was the Cuban even in town? And if so, how to flush him out after so much publicity? Alamshaw decided to attack on two levels: Durazo would page Vigoa and summon him to an instant meeting; under the rules, Vigoa had to comply. Durazo was hopeful this would work, as Vigoa always had answered his pages promptly. While waiting for Vigoa to return Durazo's call, the detectives, backed by armored vehicles and all the firepower local agencies could muster, would raid Vigoa's known residences on Boulder Highway and Sandy Slate Way.

Durazo paged Vigoa shortly before three in the afternoon. As Durazo waited for Vigoa to answer, the detectives streamed out of the Charleston Boulevard bureau, climbed into their unmarked Monte Carlos, and headed east for the freeway and a twenty-minute trip south to Vigoa's purported residence off Boulder Highway near the well-known Sam's Town hotel and casino. Alamshaw led the first strike force. If the detectives were lucky, Vigoa might be found in the storage yard. Otherwise the plan called for the detectives, supported by a SWAT team, to make a felony-vehicle stop once Vigoa was spotted by surveillance teams in motion throughout the city.

THE METRO MANTRA in preparing for a high-risk felony arrest is, "Let's hope for the best and plan for the worst." It is a wise creed, as Alamshaw's strike force is about to discover. In the sprawling countywide hunt for Vigoa, nothing goes according to plan. Alamshaw and his men, complete with an armored car, raid the storage yard but discover Vigoa is not there. They are searching the decrepit trailer when Durazo calls. Vigoa has answered the page. He has used a business phone at a Midas Muffler Shop at 2620 Windmill Parkway in Henderson. Detective Ed Newman, one of the task force members, races to the muffler shop. Within fifteen minutes he is at the Windmill scene and broadcasts a terse, excited signal: "He's here!"

The Midas Shop is about three miles to the south of the storage yard. "The cavalry is coming," Alamshaw tells Newman. "Try to stay with Vigoa. Whatever else may happen, don't lose sight of the suspect!"

At one point Newman thinks he's been spotted by Vigoa as the two men make eye contact. But then Vigoa turns away and begins arguing with the service manager, who is nervous and sweating heavily. The manager knows that Vigoa is a dangerous fugitive, but he's agreed to help the police by delaying the muffler replacement in an effort to keep Vigoa on the premises.

Vigoa begins to get the old itchy feeling of being watched by the enemy—but then his cell phone rings. It's Luisa, his wife. She's on her way to pick him up and is just around the corner.

Afterward, Vigoa will recall the moment:

"June 7, 2000, was a warm day, normal for that time of the year. However, the heat that I could feel was a different kind. I didn't want to leave town. I was concentrating on our final job, the big truck from the central bank that I wanted to hit later in the week. I wanted to get rid of the weapons used to kill the two guards [in Henderson] and told Oscar to see they were destroyed or taken out of town. Oscar told me he was going to drive down to Mexico and exchange the weapons for dynamite and high explosives. It was not a bad idea. We already had twenty-seven pounds of high-grade TNT and C-4 that already was ordered to use in our last job on the three-axle truck.

"On June 7 I got off early from my job in a beauty supply warehouse. I drove my truck over a speed bump a little too fast and heard a loud noise—I had broken the muffler. Around two-thirty I went straight to a Midas Muffler Shop, where I waited around until they could put the truck on a lift and begin the work. At about three-thirty, I received a call on my beeper from my parole officer. This was the only way he could reach me because of the story I told: As far as my parole officer was concerned, I lived in a small room in a trailer on Boulder Highway without a phone that I rented for one hundred ninety dollars a month—what I called my roach coach.

"That day, unfortunately, was Lucky Police Day, and everything turned out to be on their side. I made the mistake to respond to the beeper call from my parole officer from the Midas Muffler Shop. I don't know why I answered the beeper, but mistakes like that become like echoes— once you make just one, it comes back at you in waves, one after another. The police traced the call back to the shop and told the employee to delay repairing my car for as long as possible. A few minutes later, I started to notice strangers walking by the shop and cars parked with people inside. The police didn't approach because they didn't know if I had my weapons with me."

At about four o'clock, Vigoa notices a bull-necked middle-aged man with reddish hair watching him from a nearby car. It is Newman. Vigoa contemplates walking up to the visitor and confronting him, perhaps with one of the tire irons so plentiful in the shop. But then he hears a horn honk. Pulling into the driveway is Luisa in the Pathfinder. A little round face peers out of a side window. It is Maria, age twelve, who smiles and waves to her father. Vigoa gets behind the wheel.

"They are moving!" a voice crackles on Alamshaw's radio. The detective lieutenant, alone in a dark green Monte Carlo, spots the Pathfinder and realizes there's a woman and child in the vehicle. As the Pathfinder eases into traffic on Pecos Road, a major north-south street that runs through Henderson and Green Valley, Alamshaw pulls alongside the SUV and takes a quick look at the driver. Alamshaw's assignment is to move in front of Vigoa and then stop. A white van with six SWAT team members is supposed to pull behind Vigoa's SUV tightly, almost bumper to bumper, and block any further movement, in what is called an I formation.

The SWAT van stops ten yards behind Vigoa's Pathfinder just before the intersection of Pecos and Patrick Lane, leaving room for Vigoa to maneuver. Vigoa slams the SUV in reverse, narrowly misses backing into the SWAT vehicle, and then speeds forward. The policemen spring out of their van brandishing MP-5 submachine guns and order Vigoa out of the vehicle. Vigoa's response is to swerve around Alamshaw and race off, leaving six SWAT officers standing in the street holding their MP-5s, to the astonishment of other drivers.

Newman and his partner are among the first cars to peel out after Vigoa. When Vigoa begins to skillfully weave in and out of traffic, Newman and his partner find themselves trapped in the dense traffic. The SWAT team is also gridlocked.

The FBI's Brett Shields pulls alongside Vigoa at a choke point where traffic is slowing down. Vigoa stares boldly at the FBI agent. Shields glares back. "I'm showing him that I am FBI, and pointing at my light and everything, and he's just saying, 'Who are you?' and just keeps going. I'm in the vehicle right behind him. We go from Pecos all the way up to Tropicana. We take the right on Tropicana. He gets onto the freeway right there, onto the 95. We are now in Las Vegas five o'clock traffic. We are along the center median concrete barrier going in excess of one hundred miles an hour. We've got Men at Work signs flying over my cars, vehicles to the right of us."

For Sherwood, one of the lead detectives, it will be a day of surprises. Sherwood expects this to be a routine arrest. Vigoa is with his wife and daughter. Sherwood makes a quick call to his wife, Sharon, at home. "Hey, everything's going smooth. I'm not going to be too long. I'll call you back. We're just getting ready to take him down." Sherwood tosses his cell phone onto the seat. Suddenly the routine stop becomes a full-blown high-speed chase. The cell phone slides off the seat, and the redial button is accidentally activated. At home, Sharon answers the phone. She can hear the roar of a car engine—it sounds like it is going fast—and urgent transmissions among police. She recognizes her husband's voice. Sharon shakes her head; another one of George's pranks. "Hello, hello, George, is that you?" Sharon asks. She starts to rebuke George for being such an idiot, but then she realizes this is not a gag. Anxious for her husband, she will stay on the phone and follow the pursuit from beginning to end.

"I had a little Ford Taurus," Sherwood recalled. "It was going about 105 and rattling. Finally some patrol units get involved and were helping us. We go off the freeway onto Sunset, which is extremely busy. Vigoa has a good knowledge of the town and city."

Alamshaw guns the Monte Carlo, its six-cylinder engine whines, and suddenly the lieutenant is alongside Vigoa once again. "He cuts around me, hauling ass, so I go after him," Alamshaw recalled. "I'm alone, and I'm pissed." A Metro supervisor, believed to be Captain Mike Ault, breaks into the radio traffic. He wants the chase called off or at least reduced in intensity. Let the helicopter track the suspect. The risk of a serious accident involving an innocent bystander is too great. Alamshaw refuses. "This suspect is wanted for multiple counts of murder," he says adamantly. Now Alamshaw is placing his career and pension on the line.

"I knew if anyone was hurt as a result of the chase, it would come down to me and me alone," he reflected. "We had a hundred men on this operation. The suspect was wanted for multiple counts of homicide. I was concerned Vigoa might kill an innocent person, or kill a cop who stops him for a minor traffic violation and doesn't know who he is. We had to catch him here and now."

The police helicopter is next to be heard with a bulletin: The air space over the region of the chase has been closed to all air traffic. There will be no other flights or aircraft permitted into the area until the emergency has ended and the pursuit is over.

Just as Vigoa reaches the rear end of a Federal Express truck, and when it seems there is no place left to go, he spins the SUV's steering wheel sharply to the right and guns the engine. His wife cries out. Narrowly missing the right rear bumper of the delivery truck, Vigoa pulls off Pecos Road and careens into a fast food lot. The SUV rocks back and forth, and Vigoa nearly loses control. Customers scatter.

Alamshaw, Sherwood, and Shields continue in hot pursuit, with Alamshaw calling for more black-and-white patrol units to join the chase. The vehicles are now roaring east on Tropicana. The SWAT team, jammed up in traffic, is no longer part of the chase. Alamshaw realizes the danger immediately. *I have no real heavy firepower with me. If this guy pulls out an assault rifle, I'm gonna get smoked.*

Vigoa can hear the helicopter overhead. He thinks briefly of speeding to the Galleria Mall on Stephanie, a block from the Ross robbery scene, and then smashing the SUV into the mall, tearing through stores and mowing down shoppers like the scene from the *Blues Brothers* movie. *That would fuck up their chase.* He discards the idea as too dangerous to his wife and child. Unarmed and heavily outnumbered, Vigoa begins to realize that he is fast running out of options. But there is still hope: Vigoa notices that the longer the chase continues, the fewer police units are in pursuit. The others find themselves trapped in traffic.

"Without a doubt I had been in worse situations before," said Vigoa later. "I was not going to give up that easily in any case. Oh, did I wish I was armed at that moment. I didn't care how many there were and what their special weapons and tactics may have been; let them fight me, and I would deal with them all. I was angry, very angry at that moment. I regretted the fact I wasn't driving my big Chevrolet Silverado so I could crash the truck against other cars and kill as many as I could. Or that I didn't have my Russian grenades to throw as I fought to the death. I know one man is no match for all the cowards of the world, and I knew the police already had two to three hours to get ready and create all their road blocks, but I would have lost them easily if not for the fact they had all this time to get ready."

There are many near collisions, as well as other problems. Alamshaw glances at his dashboard and sees that the needle on the water temperature gauge is climbing. The engine cannot take the combination of high RPMs and desert heat much longer. "I turn off my air-conditioning so I can stay in the pursuit without my vehicle overheating," he recalled. "But because I have to maintain radio contact, I am forced to roll up my windows. It is hot."

Alamshaw alerts Henderson and Metro patrol units that it's time to move in. They've got to seal off all avenues of escape, drive Vigoa off the road and disable his vehicle. Otherwise, this chase has gone too far. The captain may have been right; some innocent person will get hurt.

"We go through a couple of red lights," Alamshaw said. "Heavy, heavy traffic. Vigoa turns into an industrial park, and there's a sidewalk and then a grassy knoll of about twenty-five feet that runs along the street. He goes up, into the air, over the sidewalk, over the grassy knoll, and into the parking lot, a drop of about two feet. Sherwood was right behind him and couldn't make the quick turn, so I make the turn, go over the grass, and wind up airborne like in *The Dukes of Hazzard*. All four wheels spin in the air and then come crashing down. The only thing I did was bust a headlight."

Abruptly Vigoa makes another radical move. Near a major intersection, he pulls off the street, drives over a sidewalk, and roars up a small, grassy incline. For a moment it appears the SUV is going to roll. It's a reckless move, but it seems to confuse the police. Alamshaw flies over the mound and chases Vigoa through the lot.

Sherwood decides to outflank Vigoa and intercept as he exits the parking lot. "They're chasing him around the back side," the detective said. "Well, I said, you know what? I'm going to catch this guy coming out the front and put myself back as the primary unit. I go up this alley, and he's coming down the alley, and it's the classic meet-me-in-the-alley game of chicken. I was going to head-on him, and the only thought I had at the second that I was trying to make the decision of whether to ram him head-on was that if I hit my head or something goes wrong, and he gets to guns before I do, I'm in big trouble. So I kind of waited for him to pass, and as he passed me, I turned left as hard as I could right into his car."

The pit maneuver sends Vigoa and his SUV spinning out of control. Sherwood thinks the SUV is about to roll. Instead the Pathfinder flies over the curb, speeds across six lanes of traffic, and heads into the Taco Bell parking lot.

Once again the police are forced to regroup. The chase is eleven minutes old. The scene at the corner of Sunset and Mount Vista is one of sirens, skidding tires, shrieking brakes, and roaring engines. Units of every possible description, including black-and-white Metro patrol cars, detective sedans, and blue Henderson police vehicles, race in every direction—and even in circles—trying to anticipate Vigoa's next move. Helicopters buzz the scene, adding to the noise and frenzy. For a moment it appears that Vigoa might have done the impossible, scattering his pursuers in a dozen directions and creating mass confusion. But then, two years and thirteen days after the first robbery attempt by Vigoa and his crew, it is over.

After bolting across six lanes of heavy traffic and avoiding a major collision, Vigoa tries to recover and break the wall of police cars by charging down Sunset Road in one more burst of speed. But he loses control again and slams into a large tree in front of the Taco Bell at 44125 East Sunset Road, in Henderson.

At 4:51 p.m, an unidentified detective, possibly Sherwood, begins broadcasting a running play-by-play of the pursuit's climax:

"Vehicle is going back to Sunset—he just hit . . . He just piled into the tree in front of the Taco Bell. White male, black shirt, he's running westbound by the Taco Bell . . . White male, he's running westbound by the Taco Bell just east of [*inaudible*] . . ."

Vigoa sprints behind the Burger King toward the Village Santa de la Paz apartment complex at 4375 East Sunset. "He's running!" voices shout into the radio.

There's a foot chase. Vigoa scales a six-foot-high wall and sprints down a sidewalk with Sherwood, Rogers, DuVall, Frank Hernandez of narcotics, and at least two SWAT officers in hot pursuit. There's a brief scuffle on the ground. It will take five policemen to bring Vigoa to heel, Sherwood relates: "Detective Rogers and I come around the corner right as the wrestling match is on, so we jumped in, and we ended up wrestling with him for a couple minutes. He was surprisingly strong."

Hernandez, who is Cuban-American and speaks a Cuban dialect, remembers the takedown as more like wrestling than a boxing match. "We were grappling. In my nearly thirteen years as a policeman, I can recall very few instances when you actually exchange blows with a suspect. It's more about getting on top and gaining control." As Vigoa is forced to the pavement, detectives and uniformed cops are yelling, "Stop resisting, you're under arrest! . . . Stop resisting, you're under arrest!" Hernandez remembers it sounded like a chorus.

"*Fuego! Fuego!*" Hernandez yells at Vigoa, who is now struggling under four large men. Literally, *fuego* means "put out the fire." In this case, it also means stop resisting, the game is over, the fire is out. Vigoa responds, "But *Cubano,* I haven't done anything, I didn't do nothing. What's this all about?"

"We handcuffed him," Sherwood recalled. "We stood him up."

Alamshaw and Shields now join the group. Vigoa is marched to the wall, hoisted over, and then sat on the ground by Alamshaw as police search the Pathfinder. The tactical radio channel, strangely silent for the past thirty seconds, now comes alive:

"All three suspects are in custody," Alamshaw broadcasts. "Everything is code 4." (There is no longer an existing emergency.)

Ed Newman and Gerald Collins arrive. The two Henderson detectives peer into the damaged Pathfinder resting against the tree. Inside they find an ashen-faced Luisa and a trembling Maria. They are unhurt but frightened. Newman turns to say something to his partner when both men hear the screech of brakes and a loud noise. Someone screams.

Gawking at the crime scene, a woman driver has taken her eyes off the road and rammed another car. Her air bag deploys, and she's knocked out cold. Her head is hanging out the window. "The funny part was that we did this long chase at very high speeds, and nobody got into an accident," Newman recalled.

More police and FBI units arrive. The arrest becomes part circus, street carnival, rubbernecker's wet dream, police buff's fantasy. Sirens yelping. Spectators running. Look at all the cops! Patrol cars, detective units, FBI sedans, SWAT trucks, fire engines, and EMS units block the streets, creating a monstrous traffic jam of honking horns and befuddled motorists. Here comes a network news satellite truck! More television vans and reporters swarm like locusts. Cops string yellow tape around Vigoa's Pathfinder. Grim FBI men inspect the area.

As sirens wail and the crowd of onlookers grows even larger, a distraught woman and her sobbing daughter are led to a patrol car: Vigoa's wife and child. And then—there he is, the man of the hour, expressionless, trying to maintain a semblance of dignity. Vigoa squats on the grass in handcuffs. He is surrounded by a circle of detectives and FBI agents. Alamshaw walks up, and the detective and Vigoa talk briefly. Then Brett Shields approaches.

Vigoa begins to yell at the police. What he actually says at this heated moment in his thick Cuban accent and while out of breath is in dispute. Alamshaw and Shields insist Vigoa boasted he was invincible. Alamshaw remembers Vigoa screaming, "I am the man! I am the fucking man, and

The KVVU-TV studios were a block from the crash scene after the high-speed chase. Its Fox affiliate news photographer captured the arrest of Jose Vigoa, who is seen handcuffed on the ground in a dark shirt.

COURTESY KVVU-TV, CHANNEL 5, LAS VEGAS.

FBI Special Agent Brett Shields, on far left, grabs the dark T-shirt of Jose Vigoa and pulls him toward a waiting detective car. As a rookie agent a decade earlier, Shields was part of the team that arrested Vigoa for drug trafficking.

COURTESY KVVU-TV, CHANNEL 5, LAS VEGAS.

you can't touch me!" Shields recalls hearing the same outburst. The FBI agent walks up to Vigoa. He introduces himself politely and shows his FBI credentials. "I am the FBI," Shields says. "We can't touch you? Well, we touched you before. We will touch you again."[2]

In handcuffs, Vigoa is lifted off the ground by Alamshaw and led to a police car. For a brief moment, his head turns as something on the highway catches his eyes. A large armored car, the size of a tractor-trailer, slowly drives by the arrest scene, escorted by a gray unmarked van transporting three uniformed men with sidearms. Bank security guards. There are two more guards in the big truck, and they gawk at the commotion like everyone else. Vigoa recognizes the ten-wheeler. This was to be his last score, $100 million, the target he would blow to atoms with hidden

[2] Vigoa claims that he actually said, "I am a man. I am not an animal. Treat me like a man." Frank Hernandez, the Cuban-American Metro officer who witnessed the arrest, supports Vigoa's story. "He said, 'I'm not an animal, treat me like a man, like a man.' He had a real thick accent, kind of like Tony Montana, and some of these guys may not have understood him."

The chase ended when Vigoa drove his SUV into a tree. His wife and daughter were not injured.

COURTESY KVVU-TV CHANNEL 5, LAS VEGAS.

C-4 plastique. The guards are unaware this arrest has possibly saved their lives. On the Brink's radio between truck and van, the supervisor tells his men to keep their eyes on the road and quit rubbernecking. "It's probably some knucklehead from a casino who stole an old lady's bucket of quarters."

Hernandez will accompany Vigoa on the ride to the robbery bureau. At first the thirty-year-old narcotics detective will try to calm Vigoa and build a Cuban-to-Cuban rapport, but Vigoa is incensed that a Cuban, of all people, would be working with the police. "You can't be a Cuban, no way you're a Cuban," Vigoa berates Hernandez.

"Yes, I am Cuban," Hernandez says. "I was born in Los Angeles, but my parents are both from Cuba, and this is what I do."

"So what's this all about?" Vigoa asks.

"It's alleged you're involved in some robberies; the robbery detectives want to talk to you," Hernandez said, carefully leaving out any reference to homicides. Let the robbery detectives drop that bombshell. Vigoa explodes. He calls Hernandez a *maricón,* an offensive term for homosexual, and questions the detective's manhood. Hernandez has had enough. He berates Vigoa: "You know what? You're an embarrassment as far as Cubans go. Cubans come to this country, and they work hard, like my parents, and this is what you come out here to do. To commit crimes."

Hernandez is fascinated by Vigoa's fast-changing temperament and techniques of intimidation. "Vigoa speaks really fast, his brain operates at a rapid rate, and he processes information really quick. Before I would even finish my statement, he'd be firing back right away. He's an intelligent person. He is well educated. He can be placid while he's talking to you, and we had these little windows where we could be talking reasonably. And then, boom, here comes another dose of psychotic anger, and every man to Vigoa is a coward and a queer, and he makes all these comments, and then he is very adversarial."

At the detective bureau, the police begin their interrogation. Vigoa shakes his head. "I don't know nothing, I don't know nothing. I don't know what you're talking about." The detectives mention the name of Oscar Cisneros. Vigoa looks up attentively. Hernandez remembered that "Vigoa lit up a little bit." Sherwood then tells Vigoa of the Bellagio video.

Vigoa nods. "I want to talk to a lawyer."

The detectives say, "Sure, you're entitled to a lawyer, but the best thing is to talk to us now, because all we have is one side of the story, and some of the facts we don't know, and it could be a misunderstanding, you know?"

Vigoa smiles. "Where's my fucking lawyer?"

Chapter 28

THE RAIDERS

t six o'clock Wednesday evening, with the media swarming over the Taco Bell crash site, Detective Sergeant Robert DuVall and Sergeant Frank Hernandez transported Jose Vigoa to the Metro robbery offices on Charleston Boulevard. DuVall told Rogers and Sherwood the night's plan: The detectives would interview Vigoa, then "book Vigoa on the pursuit charge" and let the prosecutors and cops sort out the major felonies later. "Keep him in jail," DuVall ordered. "He goes nowhere."

As the detective car pulled away with the robbery unit's prize prisoner in the passenger seat, John Alamshaw took a deep breath. The most exhilarating and certainly one of the most dramatic moments of his career called for celebration—and maybe a couple of stiff drinks—but the job

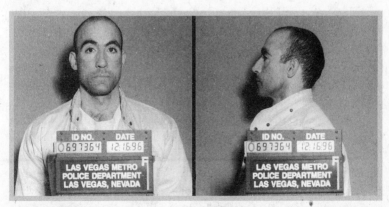

Mug shot taken of Jose Vigoa in 1996, five weeks after his release from federal prison. An attempt by the INS to deport Vigoa back to Cuba failed, and Vigoa was permitted to reside in Las Vegas on probation after claiming to be a political refugee.

COURTESY LAS VEGAS METROPOLITAN POLICE DEPARTMENT.

was not yet done. Like the others, the lieutenant was still in what cops call an altered state, an adrenaline-fueled condition caused by the 100-mile-per-hour chase, foot pursuit, and arrest. The chase was dangerous. But the next stage, in which the police set out to execute search warrants on the homes of Vigoa and Oscar Cisneros, could be even more so.

Based on affidavits and the actual search warrant prepared by Bob Rogers, George Sherwood, Richard Beasley, and Brett Shields, the Honorable James C. Mahan, district judge for the Eighth Judicial District Court, Department XII, signed the warrant on Wednesday, authorizing police to raid the 5690 South Boulder Highway trailer supposedly used by Jose as a primary residence and Vigoa's home at 8952 Sandy Slate Way. The warrant also authorized the search of Vigoa's 1992 red Chevrolet pickup truck and the 1999 Nissan Pathfinder driven by Luisa. According to the document, police could make "entry without officers announcing themselves, because of Jose Manuel Vigoa's history of violence."

There would be no further briefings. The raids would be immediate, supported by still more SWAT units, and would include representatives of all three agencies. They were to gather at a fire station. Alamshaw would lead the storage yard raid. The Cordelle Drive home of Oscar Sanchez Cisneros, which also served as the residence of three of his brothers, would be searched by agents Beasley, Wenko, and Rice; detectives Newman, Collins, and Wellman of Henderson; and Bob Rogers of Metro.

The searches were essential to proving the charges against gang members. The police had Vigoa in custody and high-quality color video that *appeared* to show Jose robbing the Bellagio—or someone who looked like Jose, according to Durazo and Shields. But defense lawyers would argue that the suspect in the video wore a cap and large sunglasses. "Our job is only beginning," Alamshaw said to DuVall. "From here on, a half dozen defense lawyers will be scrutinizing everything we do."

Evidence. There was some, but it was incomplete and disconnected. By the time of Vigoa's capture, the police had blood DNA from the Ross homicides. The question was, whose blood? The detectives had shell casings from the Desert Inn, Ross, and the Bellagio. Metro technicians had recovered a spent slug from the tire of the Bellagio security van, while hotel security guards managed to find the bullet and casing from the second shot in the parking lot. There was the water bottle from the Desert Inn heist that gave up multiple strands of DNA. But there were many gaping holes in the investigation.

After two years of recovering stolen getaway cars, the police had virtually nothing to connect the vehicles to any member of the gang. The Thrifty Car Rental investigation had gone nowhere despite a full-blown grand jury investigation. There would be no ballistic breakthroughs if the police and FBI were unable to locate the weapons used by the Vigoa crew. Also, three of the gang members were still at large. Alamshaw was certain that news of Vigoa's apprehension was even now spreading through the Cuban community and the Vegas underworld. In the worst case, they may be holed up in a fortified location, heavily armed and ready for all-out battle. The police would have to move fast.

VIGOA'S SANDY SLATE home, located west of South Maryland Parkway, was the first target. The police arrived. SWAT officers made a fast and nonviolent entrance into the home, moved Luisa and the daughters outside, and conducted a preliminary walk-through to secure the dwelling. The police noticed new furniture, three computers, and a jar of casino chips in one of the daughter's bedrooms.

Sherwood looked in a bedroom closet and noticed a carpet edge curled up in a corner. This was a telltale sign. He ripped up the carpet and discovered a trap door. "Crap just started flying out of the closet," DuVall recalled. "This was a major find. Underneath the trap door in the master bedroom closet, we found a ton of everything, including one hundred twenty-five thousand dollars in cash buried in a hole in the floor. That's why the carpet was up. He had a hole in the upper floor of his house, and that's where he hid his cash, chips from each of the first three casino robberies—all in a Sparkletts water bottle. You know how people keep their change in a bottle. I thought perhaps these were the chips they were using to case the place, because the majority of the chips in this Sparkletts bottle were from the MGM, the Desert Inn, and the Mandalay Bay."

Once it is established that the target dwelling does contain contraband and evidence, the police were more aggressive. The search party also found clothing, sunglasses, a white ballcap, and a custom-designed wristwatch. They had seen it all before—on the Bellagio tape.

BUT ALAMSHAW IS worried. The elaborate raid at the South Boulder Highway storage yard, employing armored vehicles and resembling a full-scale military assault, has produced no evidence. The search of the Sandy Slate home uncovers money but no weapons. Jose has asked for a lawyer.

The Cisneros house at 6553 Cordelle Drive is the next logical target, but there is a problem. There is no search warrant because police believe they lack probable cause at this point. Oscar Sanchez Cisneros, the only non-Cuban and non–family member in Vigoa's crew, is not only a participant in every shooting, he is the front man for Vigoa's financial dealings. The Cisneros family has lived in Las Vegas for three years. It is known that Cisneros made regular trips to Mexico and might bolt at any moment.

A new plan was hatched. Beasley would shadow Cisneros. "We gotta keep him in pocket, we gotta talk to him," Beasley told Alamshaw and Shields.

Beasley followed the young Mexican to the other side of town. Cisneros, his girlfriend, and his parents were house hunting. While the Cisneros family members inspected a home, the FBI men listened to the chase on the radio. Just as the pursuit of Vigoa was terminated, Oscar walked out of the house.

"Let's do it," Beasley said. He and Agent Larry Wenko approached Cisneros and flashed their identification. They conducted a quick patdown. No weapons. The FBI agents gave Cisneros the news: Vigoa has been captured. He is on his way to jail.

Cisneros smiled. "Okay."

"We'd like to search your house," Beasley said.

"Okay," Cisneros shrugged.

Beasley would remember the moment: "Oscar was very cordial, very friendly, no issues. So I pulled out an FD26—a search warrant. I pulled it out right there in front of the car, and he signed it. I said, 'Would you like to ride with me?' and he said, 'No, I'd rather ride back with my family.' I told him he was not under arrest and tried to build some kind of rapport with him. So we said, 'Okay, we'll just follow your dad's van.' En route Brett Shields called me and said be careful: There were a couple of guys around Cisneros's house. They turned out to be just brothers, but we didn't know if they were part of the robbery crew. We didn't know who they were. We called and had some guys meet over there at the house, and when we turned the corner, they were already there."

Once the house was cleared, the FBI agents and Cisneros entered and sat down at the dining room table for a chat. Other agents and detectives began a room-by-room search. Beasley would recall Cisneros as being relaxed and friendly. At about six-thirty, the first formal interview with a Vigoa crew member was under way.

The interrogation at the dining room table would last four hours. The tone would be courteous and civil at all times. Although under stress themselves—one small mistake might destroy the case—the agents and detectives were patient and calm. They also tape-recorded the conversation. When the machine failed, Cisneros loaned Newman a battery from his pager.

"We know a lot more than what you think we know," Newman told Cisneros. Often police make such a claim to intimidate the suspect when in fact they know little, but Newman was telling the truth. The police were aware that Cisneros was fronting for Vigoa in a variety of transactions and that the young laborer enjoyed remarkable surges of cash flow after the MGM, Mandalay Bay, and other jobs. The FBI and police also knew that Cisneros closely resembled the big guy in the Bellagio video vaulting over the cashier's counter.

Another standard ploy, a favorite of prosecutors for generations, features the train of justice that was about to leave the station with all the good people on board. Cisneros could jump on the train and become a cooperating witness and part of the prosecutor's team. Or Cisneros could be left standing at the station like some poor dumb schmuck, surrounded by angry cops and facing the wrath of an indignant criminal justice system.

"You need to give us the truth here," Beasley continued. "You need to come clean with exactly what's going on so we can go and tell the prosecutor, here is *exactly* what happened." The FBI warned that police even then were interviewing Vigoa. "What is he going to tell them about you?"

For another hour the interrogators pressed forward. They would appeal to Cisneros's sense of family, point out that he had no serious criminal record other than a bust for soliciting a female vice cop for prostitution, and that the young man had so much to lose. It wasn't all contrived. The policemen realized Oscar was just a soldier, a kid from Mexico who had fallen in with dangerous people, and he was in very serious trouble.

"Oscar, you seem like a decent guy," Beasley said. "You got a wonderful family. Your girlfriend seems very nice. You got a nice pickup out there. An awful lot just to throw away."

At first Cisneros was unmoved, banking on the fact that the police would find nothing at the house. But just when it appeared Cisneros would stonewall the detectives, there was a breakthrough.

"Do you have any money here in the house?" Beasley asked.

"Yeah," Cisneros replied. "He gave me some money last week."

"Jose gave you money last week?" Beasley said.

"Yeah."

Newman snapped to attention. Beasley knew this was important but maintained a steady voice and demeanor.

Q: How much?
A: I don't know. It's a bag like this. I don't know how much.
Q: Why did he give you money?
A: For favors. He wants us to do a favor, to get a loan for his car and the house, and I don't have no money right now.

Money in a bag—Jose's money—given to Oscar at the time of the Bellagio robbery.

Oscar broke into a sheepish smile, shrugged, and said he wanted to stop. "I don't wanna talk no more."

On the second floor, the search continued but without results. Agent Wenko began to wonder: Could the Vigoa crew have cleaned out the house this quickly? Or was the Cisneros home clean to begin with because of the other family members in residence? The search appeared over, but neither the FBI man nor the Henderson detective believed the house to be clean. There were guns in this house, Wenko believed. Detective Todd Wellman had the same edgy feeling. Something was here. There was no need for the two men to talk about it; the search would continue. Back in the closet, Wellman was on his knees and Wenko was standing. The FBI agent saw something catch the light. He bent over. Brass hinges. Wellman pulled back the carpet to find a door beneath the rug. "It was as wide as the closet door and very well built," Wenko said.

At eight o'clock Wellman walked downstairs to the dining room. He gave Beasley and Newman a quick briefing. Beasley turned to Oscar. "What are we going to find in the bags?" he asked.

The young Mexican bowed his head. "The guns and everything," Cisneros said.

Newman studied Cisneros's face. "He had a look that said, *I'm fucked*."

Beasley tried to remain calm and expressionless, though it wasn't easy. "It was one of those electric moments."

The FBI agent told Cisneros the secret closet has been found, and it was time for Oscar to step up and tell the truth. "What's going to be in there?" Beasley asked again. Cisneros shrugged. The FBI man stood up. "Oscar, you are under arrest. You have the right to remain silent. Anything you say may be held against you . . ." When Beasley finished, Cisneros was read the Miranda warnings in Spanish by a Hispanic agent.

Beasley's cell phone began to ring. Other cell phones went off. Alamshaw and the detectives at the Sandy Slate house were calling. They too had hit the jackpot: The robbery detectives had found a hidden safe in an upstairs bedroom and a cache of money. Gambling chips from the robbed hotels were in jars all over the house, and his men were jubilant. It was raining evidence.

A stunning breakthrough in the case is captured in this police photo: FBI Special Agent Larry Wenko discovers a trap door in the upstairs master bedroom of Oscar Cisneros's home.

COURTESY CLARK COUNTY DISTRICT ATTORNEY.

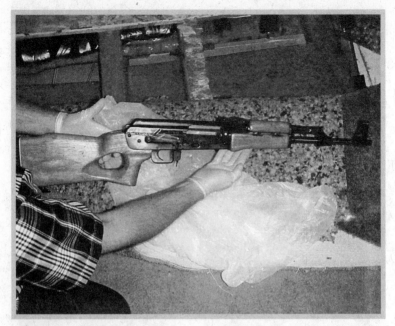

Jose Vigoa's Chinese-made AK-47 copy, found in the secret compartment.

COURTESY CLARK COUNTY DISTRICT ATTORNEY.

Detective Newman noticed Cisneros's right knee. There was a fresh scar. It appeared to be from a puncture wound about the size of a quarter. "What happened there?" Newman asked.

"I fell off the ladder at work," Cisneros said.

"A *ladder?*" Newman broke into a malicious grin. "Never seen a ladder do that!"

Beasley examined the scar. *A ladder my ass,* he thought. *It's a bullet wound—a through-and-through bullet wound.*

"How 'bout that scar on the *inside* of the leg; what happened there?" Newman asked.

Oscar sighed. "A bullet. I got shot."

Beasley would remember the moment for years to come. "I looked at Ed, and Ed looked at me, and we didn't say anything, and it was like a lightning bolt between us," he recalled. "He was involved, but now we've identified the man who took the bullet at Ross. We're on our way. Because he'd told us he didn't want to answer any questions right now, we just kind of backed off and went outside in front. We were like, 'Oh my God, can you believe he said that?!' We called the guys at Sandy Slate, and they were very happy about that too. After about one half hour after that statement, we started at him again, then he decided he would talk to us. Laid it out from the MGM to the DI then to the Ross then to the New York–New York then to the Bellagio."

Beasley has a theory as to why the young Mexican suddenly opened up. "I think he realized which direction the whole thing was going. At one point we mentioned the death penalty. I told him that was a real possibility in this case. Also told him that Jose Vigoa could be over at his house telling everything that happened, and if he is, hopefully it is true. Hopefully it's not Oscar who set this whole thing up. It turned out, obviously, Vigoa *didn't* say anything, but we didn't know that, Cisneros didn't know that. It was in his best interest to talk to us, and it was in the best interest of his family; the girlfriend was pregnant with his child at the time."

Henderson detective Monique Panet-Swanson and Metro crime scene analyst Peter Schellberg recorded the items seized from the hidden room in the Cisneros house. In the State of Nevada's Application and Affidavit for Arrest Warrants, Chief Deputy DA David Roger described the evidence found beneath the trap door. On the right side of the master bedroom closet floor, Wenko found a plastic bag containing $24,000 in currency clipped in denominations of one, five, ten, and one hundred dollars. "These bills were bundled in the same manner as the currency found at Jose Manuel Vigoa's house on Sandy Slate Way. This was also the exact manner the money was bundled at the Bellagio cage," Roger declared.

Underneath the trap door, Wenko also found a large black duffel bag containing a white ballcap with the words "National Champions FSU" emblazoned on the front—the same cap Vigoa wore during the Bellagio robbery. There was also the dark blue Wilson athletic shirt seen in the robbery, several pairs of black gloves, and six pairs of sunglasses. Also found were baseball caps similar to those worn by Cisneros and Suarez in various robberies. Wenko found a bulky black plastic bag. Inside were two body armor vests. One of the vests was damaged by two apparent gunshots to the back. There also was a pair of black sweatpants wrapped around five pry bars. Two of the bars had red handles. Observed Roger, "In a Bellagio surveillance tape, Luis Suarez is seen prying open the cashier cage drawers with a red-handled pry bar."

Next to come out of the secret room was a brown canvas bag. Wenko found three dark-colored ski masks inside. Then the jackpot: a Smith &

Wesson .38 revolver taken from Kyle Carney, one of the guards who was robbed at the Mandalay Bay hotel heist. Metro firearms examiner Torrey Johnson tested this revolver and concluded it was the weapon fired at Gary Prestidge during the Ross firefight.

Also found in the secret room was a Smith & Wesson .40-caliber semi-automatic wrapped in a black cloth towel, also stolen from Carney at the Mandalay Bay. Other weapons clattered from the duffel bags, including a chrome Ruger P-85 9 mm semiautomatic pistol, similar to the one used in the Bellagio robbery; a black Glock model 21 .45-caliber semiautomatic handgun, registered to Cisneros and later proved to be used at the Desert Inn shoot-out; and a chrome-plated .357 Ruger revolver, stolen during a residential burglary in August 1998.

Finally, there was a Norinco MAK 90 assault rifle carefully wrapped in multiple plastic bags and secured by gray duct tape. This was the rifle Vigoa fired at the Desert Inn and used to kill Prestidge and Sosa during the deadly Ross gunfight. Virtually the entire Vigoa arsenal was under the closet floor. Other weapons seized included a second MAK 90 automatic rifle; two Vyatskie Polyany VEPR .308 rifles, believed to be a Russian sniper's weapon; and more than a thousand rounds of Russian-made ammunition.

And when they unpacked all of the duffel bags and got to the bottom of the hidden room—a man could stand inside it and be up to his shoulders—they came across something else that would give detectives and agents a chill, especially when they learned later that Jose had special plans for this material. From the FBI 302 report of June 7, 2000: "At approximately 10:38 p.m., agents and detectives searching the house located a device which could have been a bomb. For safety reasons the house was evacuated, and elements of the bomb squad were called to respond to the residence. At that point, HPD detectives took custody of Oscar Sanchez Cisneros, eventually transporting him in the vehicle of Las Vegas Metropolitan Police Department detective Bob Rogers."

The police found multiple explosive devices and additional gray and brown powder to make additional "fireworks," as Jose liked to call them. There was enough explosive material to blow up a large-size armored truck, should one care to do so.[1]

---

[1] In 2006 Jose Vigoa told me that most of the explosives were stored elsewhere and not at the Cisneros house. "That would have been too dangerous; we could have blown ourselves up real easy." The missing containers of C-4 and TNT were never recovered.

A celebratory victory photo of detectives and FBI agents after the chase, raids, and arrests. L-R: Front row: FBI agent Brett Shields, Sergeant Lori Crickett, Sergeant Robert DuVall, Detective Gordon Martines, Detective Steve Popp, and Detective John Hanover. Second row: Detective Al Garris, Detective Jeff Hutchinson, Detective Steve Devore, Lt. John Alamshaw, and Detective George Sherwood.

COURTESY LAS VEGAS METROPOLITAN POLICE DEPARTMENT AND JOHN ALAMSHAW.

AFTER SORTING THROUGH material at the Sandy Slate house, Alamshaw conducted a late-night press conference in his usual straightforward but wary fashion. Not everything could be told; there were at least two dangerous men still on the loose, Pedro Duarte and Luis Suarez.

John liked most reporters; a few he found arrogant and provocative. One such reporter, Glen Pruitt of the *Las Vegas Review-Journal,* was about to ruin the highpoint of John's police career.

"I worked through the night on the day of Vigoa's arrest and all through the next day, about thirty-three hours straight. I got home somewhere around five o'clock the next day," Alamshaw said. When he returned home, there was a message from Pruitt on the detective's un-listed home phone. Pruitt wanted an interview. "How did you get my number?" Alamshaw asked. The reporter revealed he had obtained

Alamshaw's home address from voting records, went to the mailbox phone, and left the message as a visitor might do. Alamshaw said he was tired, Pruitt should have been at the press conference with everybody else, and there would be no interview that evening.

"Pruitt then said, 'I know where you live, and I want to come there and interview you,'" John recalled. "I said, '*Don't come here.*' I said, 'If you come to this house, I would not take kindly to it.' He said, 'Is that a threat?' I said, 'No, I'm just telling you not to come to my house.'"

The reporter complained to his editors that he had been physically threatened and that the very freedom of the press was at stake if cops could bully journalists. A senior editor called the sheriff. The sheriff referred the matter to the under sheriff, the number-two police official, who contacted Alamshaw, gravely related the complaint, listened to John's version of the story, and said there would be a meeting between Metro and the newspaper to clear the air. John thought the matter was closed.

"Well, that wasn't good enough for Glen Pruitt," Alamshaw said later. "He contacted internal affairs and opened up a complaint. It was like double jeopardy." The department assigned a detective to the case who interviewed both the lieutenant and the reporter and then filed an official report. Alamshaw was cleared. (Contacted repeatedly, Pruitt refused to be interviewed in connection to this incident.)

It had been quite a week. John and his men had captured one of the most dangerous killers in the history of Las Vegas, had recovered more than $100,000, confiscated a lethal cache of firearms and explosives, obtained a confession from one of the gunmen, assembled valuable forensic evidence for Dave Roger, prevented a catastrophic attack on a large armored truck—and the robbery lieutenant in charge of the investigation found himself under investigation. No one would have blamed the earnest, conscientious Alamshaw had he asked for time off to heal his wounds, or perhaps sulked around the office for a few weeks.

That was not to be. There would be two more jolts in the case, and the shock waves would leave the detectives and FBI agents stunned and reeling.

Chapter 29

OSCAR'S CONCERT

After the dining room table interview on the evening of June 7, 2000, a weary and distraught Oscar Cisneros was transported to the detective bureau on Charleston Boulevard. Shortly after midnight, Bob Rogers of the robbery section and Ed Newman of the Henderson police conducted a second interview. Now they would flesh out Cisneros's story, fill in the details, look for contradictions, and develop further leads. They also sensed something about the character of their prisoner during the four-hour session on Cordelle Drive, a quality they would not find in any other gang member.

The twenty-three-year-old Mexican was not hard core, despite having been present at two homicides, as many attempted murders, and six armed robberies—and also, it is believed that Cisneros shot Chuck Fichter at the Desert Inn. Nor was he the sharpest knife in the drawer, Rogers, Beasley, and Newman agreed, but Cisneros did show remorse. The detectives knew he had something more to say, something he *wanted* to say, and it was just a question of letting the young man come face to face with his own conscience.

From 12:35 a.m. until two in the morning Thursday, Oscar Cisneros sang, and he sang loudly. Vigoa would later call it Oscar's Great Concert. A transcript of the second interview, conducted by Bob Rogers and Ed Newman, has survived. Rogers begins by establishing that this is a voluntary confession.

Q: Okay. All right, tell me in your own words what's happened on some of these other ones. I want to get your side of the story. I think it will be beneficial for you to talk to us about it.

A: Okay.

Q: Start at the beginning, that's always easier.

A: Okay.

Q: What was the first one?

A: The MGM Grand.

Q: MGM Grand?

A: Yeah.

Q: Okay. All right, tell me what happened.

A: [*A heavy sigh*] We go the casino . . . We wait for the guards, and then when they go out to the car, we take the bag out of [their] hands, and we do it.

Q: When you say guards, were they guards for the hotel?

A: Just two guards. Ah, one was security guard for the hotel, and two guards for the car.

Q: For the what?

A: The car.

Q: The car?

A: Yeah.

Q: Oh, so it was an armored car?

A: Uh-huh.

At this point Rogers, who has studied the case carefully, feigns ignorance. This works on multiple psychological levels: First, it suggests that maybe things aren't so bad after all—the police are groping in the dark. Also, it gives Cisneros a chance to help the detective and perhaps even bond with the police. "Help me out here," the detective seems to be saying. By pretending not to know details of the case, the detective also sets a trap for Cisneros. The more he lies, and is caught at lying, the greater the policeman's advantage.

Q: Okay, I'm not too familiar with these cases, so bear with me if I ask you a lot of questions.

A: Okay.

Q: Ah, so, do you remember the name of the armored truck?

A: Ah, yeah, Brink's.

Q: Brink's, okay. And who was with you on that?

A: Jose.

Q: Jose?

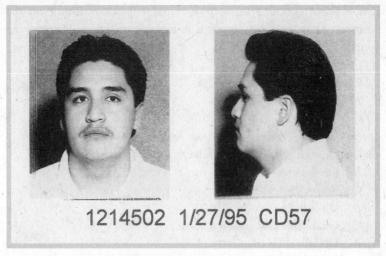

1214502 1/27/95 CD57

Oscar Cisnero's police photograph from an earlier 1995 arrest for soliciting a police decoy posing as a prostitute.

COURTESY LAS VEGAS METROPOLITAN POLICE DEPARTMENT.

A: Yeah.

Q: And who else?

A: I don't know his name.

Q: Is he a friend of Jose's?

A: Yeah.

Q: But what made you do it? Do you have a gambling problem, or what?

A: No. We're still working, but don't have that much money.

Q: Just easy money. Okay, paint me a picture. Did the three of you drive to the San Remo in a white truck?

A: No, when [name indecipherable] went to the casino, he's suppose to get outside and be waiting for us in his truck, the white truck. And then he's never there, so, Jose and me, we were running to the front to the San Remo and get inside the parking lot, the parking, the closed parking. And, we wait for him.

This is something the police didn't know—the story of the missing getaway driver who is supposed to be waiting outside.

Next the detectives zero in on the weapons used in the robbery. This is an important detail: proving the gunmen were armed. Identifying the weapons. Showing they were used in multiple robberies. Determining the pistols were loaded.

Q: What kind of gun was it?

A: .45s.

Q: What brand?

A: Glock.

Q: Okay. Is it yours, are you the registered owner?

A: I'm the owner.

Q: You're the owner?

A: Uh-huh.

Q: Okay. Was it, ah, was it loaded?

A: Loaded, what's that?

Q: Was there bullets in it?

A: Yeah.

Q: There were bullets in it. Okay. What kind of a gun did, ah, Jose have?

A: He had a Glock .45, and I had one, a .357.

Q: Oh, maybe I misunderstood. Did he have the Glock?

A: Yeah.

Q: He had your gun?

A: Uh-huh.

Q: Okay. So are you saying that he had a gun in each hand?

A: Uh-huh.

They move on to the Desert Inn shoot-out. Once again Cisneros identifies Vigoa as his partner. He describes a short but fierce gun battle as though talking about a trip to the supermarket. It is almost as though "me and Jose" are the victims, waylaid by armed guards who unexpectedly open fire. This will be a recurring theme of both Oscar and Jose: We didn't want trouble. We just wanted the money. The only reason we fired our weapons was to defend ourselves.

Q: Okay. What happened then, I'm not familiar with this one either . . .

A: Yeah, when we, we waiting outside of the casino.

Q: Outside of the casino.

A: Yeah, by the side door, we stay inside of the [*unintelligible*] and everything, when those guys came, we get out and we told them, don't move. And those guys shot the guns and everything.

Q: Oh, they shot their guns?

A: Yeah, those guys.

Q: Who are these guys, guards?

A: Yeah, the guards.

Q: Oh, what did he have? What kind of gun did he [Jose] have?

A: He have a MAK 90.

Q: Wow, MAK 90 or MAK 9?

A: Ninety.

Q: Ninety. What is that?

A: It's a big kind of gun, it's a new one.

Q: How much did that cost?

A: Two thousand.

Q: Okay. Ah, what gun did you have at the Desert Inn?

A: My .45.

Q: The Glock again?

A: Yeah.

Q: Okay, did you shoot it?

A: I shoot it.

Q: So, in your mind, you were protecting yourself?

A: Yeah.

Q: Yeah. Okay. That says something about you, doesn't it, that you're—you're not a bad guy, right?

A: I just went for money.

Q: Okay.

A: Just so I wanted the money, nothing else.

Q: You're not a violent person?

A: No.

Q: Is Jose?

A: He, he. He's not, because he's had a chance to kill those guys, 'cause he's got a big gun.

Q: Hum.

A: And he didn't do it.

Q: Okay. What was the next one after the Desert Inn?

A: Well, that's the Mandalay Bay.

As the interview unfolds, Rogers begins to realize why the investigation moved in fits and starts during its two years and why the case took so long to gain momentum: The police were never certain it was the same gang until late in the crime spree. Every job was different in at least one significant aspect.

There will be six pages of interview before Rogers and Newman get to the crime that horrified Clark County. Importantly, the detectives do not alter the pace or their tone of voice. Beasley appears to be in no hurry, as if each crime was merely an account to be duly noted, recorded, and stored away for future reference. One can imagine, however, that Rogers's blood pressure is rising when he asks about the violent deaths of Gary Prestidge and Richard Sosa outside the Ross Dress for Less on March 3, 2000.

But first, a little interrogation guile. Rogers pretends not to know what's next on the crime calendar:

Q: Okay. What about—what was the next one?

A: The other one was . . . the one on Ross.

Q: Ross.

A: Yeah.

Q: Yeah. That was a bad one, huh?

A: Yeah.

Q: Yeah, tell me about that one.

A: We start looking up everything around, you know, at all the, the places, and who gets money and, and everything like a week, week and a half before that.

Q: Oh, you were looking at it?

A: Yeah, I was looking at it.

Q: Now, whose idea was it to go from the armored trucks in casinos to go to a shopping center? Wasn't that different?

A: Yeah. Because, uh, the casinos got too many people inside.

Q: What, what casinos?

A: All the casinos, too much security.

Q: So you wanted to do something different.

A: Yeah.

Q: Okay.

A: Not the same thing.

Q: Okay. Whose idea was that to do something different?

A: Both.

Q: Both. Okay. Was it you, Jose, and Luis again?

A: Yeah.

Q: Luis. Okay. Just the three of you.

A: Yeah.

Q: Yeah. What, what went wrong?

A: Ah, when we get out the car, the guy that was outside, we told him don't move, and he move and he start shooting.

Q: Oh.

A: And then, ah, Jose, Luis, the one behind me, he shoot him because he shoot my leg first time.

Q: Oh, now you got, you got something in your calf, huh?

A: Yeah.

Q: Wow. Is that where you got shot?

A: Yeah.

Q: Is there a mark on the other side of your calf?

A: [*Both men talking at same time*].

Q: Wow. Lucky you didn't get hurt worse, huh?

A: Ah, yeah.

Q: Yeah, what happened then?

A: When the guards were outside [we were] inside the car, they walking, and we got out to the van, and then I told him don't move, and, ah, he was walking and had a gun right here. His, uh, thing right here, and he, he stopped, but he want—he tried to move back to do like this. [Cisneros demonstrates Gary's maneuver with the money bag and pistol.] When he turn around like this, he shooting away right here. So I, ah, Jose, Luis, one behind me, he start shooting too, and, ah, I was hurt and everything, and I go inside the car.

Q: Did you guys get anything? Any money?

A: I, I don't know because I just go straight to the car. Hurt and everything.

Q: Yeah.

A: So, I leave to the . . .

Q: Just the three of you again on this—

A: Yeah.

Q: Hmmm, ah, what about the other guard? I think—wasn't there two that were hurt or something?

A: Yeah, was two.

Although there can be little doubt that Cisneros learned of Sosa's killing at some point, if only from Vigoa as the crew fled the scene, it is possible the Mexican is telling the truth at this point. Wounded and in pain, Cisneros was limping back to the maroon Intrepid when Vigoa opened fire on Sosa.

Q: Did you go anywhere, get treated? Doctor?
A: No.
Q: No. It just heal itself. Is that the first time you've been shot?
A: Yeah.
Q: Wow. You had to be scared, huh?
A: Oh, yeah.

The detectives have precisely what they want: Vigoa, Cisneros, and Suarez at the Ross. All three men participating in an armed robbery with deadly weapons. Admission of a gunfight. Cisneros appears to be suggesting Luis Suarez got off at least one shot, but that fact remains in dispute—Vigoa claims it was Cisneros who shot Gary Prestidge.

The Bellagio is the next topic. Under Nevada law, the state may charge a robbery suspect with multiple counts relating to a single crime depending on how many victims are involved. For example, if there are four employees in the cashier's cage when Cisneros vaults the counter, Cisneros will face four counts of armed robbery, as will Suarez and Vigoa. If the police can nail down the Bellagio robbery, through Cisneros's testimony and the casino tape, they can put away the gang for life.

Detective Rogers is one of the primary investigators on the Bellagio robbery. He was called to the casino, saw the tape, and helped plan the subsequent raids. Yet he acts like he's never even *heard* of the hotel, much less the robbery and shooting.

Q: Okay. What was—what was the next one after that?
A: The Bellagio.
Q: Bellagio? Didn't that just happen? Bellagio? That was—when was that one?
A: Sa-Saturday, Saturday.
Q: Yeah, Saturday. What time was that?
A: Six, six-thirty in the morning.

Q: Okay. I think I've seen . . . ah, I've seen the tape, but I can't remember. There's a couple of guys that jumped over the counter.

A: Yeah.

Q: Was—was one of those you?

A: Me and Luis.

Q: You and Luis. Okay. Same thing. Were you guys wearing . . . You remember your clothes, hats, gloves?

A: Yeah, I can remember that. They have a blue, a blue . . .

Q: What, what gun did you have?

A: The one we take it from, uh, the guards, the Brink's, at the Mandalay Bay.

Q: Okay.

A: That one was . . .

Q: That was the—that was—Where's that at now?

A: It's a .40 [caliber]. Oh, *where* is it?

Q: Yeah.

A: This is in my house.

Q: Okay. So that, that's a .40 caliber?

A: Yeah. Smith & Wesson.

Q: Okay. And then after you robbed the cage, you guys ran out to the, to the van.

A: Yeah.

Q: Oh, how'd you guys get the money out? I mean, the other ones, you know, with guards and bags and stuff, how'd you guys get the money? Was it—I'm assuming the drawers were locked. Did you guys have keys to the lock or—?

A: No. We have a big . . . like tools.

Q: Tools?

A: Yeah.

Q: Oh.

A: And break it. Just break it and then take all the money.

Q: Did that open the drawers in the change booth too?

A: Yeah.

Q: Anything happen on the way there? Anything unusual?

A: Yeah. When we go driving, that's, ah, a van that stop in the street when, when we leaving. These two men are inside, but

> I don't know if it's police or security or I don't know, because those guys going behind, behind us.

Q: Uh-huh.

A: And [Jose] got a gun and shoot two times to stop them.

Q: Uh-huh. Would that be your Glock that he shot?

A: Yeah.

Q: Who was driving the van?

A: I'm driving.

Q: You were driving?

A: I was driving.

Q: And Luis is in the back?

A: Yeah.

Q: Okay. What happened when he shot? Did he hit the guy?

A: No, no. Just, uh, he shot for [them to] stop.

Q: Oh, just to scare him.

This admission, that they fired at a hotel guard, is crucial—it opens the door to a charge of attempted murder. Cisneros believes he has robbed a single hotel on one Saturday morning, nobody was hurt, and he faces one charge of robbery. In fact, under the law there were eight victims: four behind the counter, one in the change booth, and three in the security van. Cisneros faces eight major felony charges.

Rogers reports the good news to Alamshaw. The two-year crime spree is over. There have been more than 1,500 armed robberies during the first six months of the year, and many have been given only a cursory investigation because of the Vigoa raids. Alamshaw smiles as he drives home in his unmarked Monte Carlo after a round of drinks at the Big Dog's cop bar off West Sahara Boulevard. It's late at night when the lieutenant gets home. He is too wound up to go inside where his wife and children sleep, so he sits in the driveway in his car and listens to Eric Clapton's "Wonderful Tonight" on a cassette. It is a balmy and cloudless June night. At two in the morning, stars in the big Nevada sky shine brilliantly. The old feeling, two decades gone, returns. Las Vegas is a great place to be a cop. The job is still exciting and worthwhile even if so much has changed. Alamshaw laughs out loud. He can feel all the tension, frustration, anxiety, and uncertainty of two years begin to recede.

There's no way for the detective to know that the party is barely getting started. In the weeks and months to come, Pedro Duarte will set up a video camera in his living room, point the lens at his front door, and taunt the police to come arrest him. Vigoa will prove nearly as menacing in jail as he was on the street. Oscar Cisneros will stun authorities and turn the neatly organized case into chaos. And Luis Suarez, the only gang member to flee Nevada, will spring a surprise of his own.

ON AUGUST 26, 2000, three months after the capture of Jose and Oscar, Luis Suarez walks into the Henderson Police Department. He is accompanied by his girlfriend Caridad Farray, who made the initial telephone call to police setting up an appointment. Detective Gerard Collins, one of the primary detectives on the Ross double homicide, will conduct the interview. Collins will be assisted by Officer Orestes Guerra, who speaks fluent Spanish and serves as a translator when needed.

At first cocky and confident, Suarez tells Collins he knows the police are looking for him, and he can't understand why. Suarez insists that he had a fight with Caridad and went to Tampa Bay, Florida, early in May. Therefore the rumors about him being involved in the Bellagio heist are false.

Unlike the Cisneros interviews, where the taciturn Mexican spoke slowly and had to be prodded along, Suarez can't stop talking. At six foot one and 245 pounds, he is the biggest of the Vigoa crew, a powerfully built man who dwarfs Collins, who is five foot ten and 175 pounds. Suarez talks rapidly, repeating over and over that he knows nothing about the robberies and only heard about them on Tampa TV. Collins listens and makes a note of the news story reference. *A local TV station in Florida wouldn't cover the Bellagio caper,* Collins thinks.

It's not logical, Suarez complains: If he participated in the Bellagio caper or any other major robbery, then why doesn't he have any money? Would someone please explain why Suarez was so broke that he and his family are unable to pay their phone bill? Suarez says he is a housepainter and handyman. He came to Las Vegas in 1993 and had a few legal problems after he was caught selling cocaine. He says he knows Jose Vigoa but only because Jose's wife is Caridad's sister. He's attended a few weekend parties among the Cuban family members. He barely knows Oscar Cisneros. He never worked for Jose. He portrays himself as a hardworking Cuban who supports five children, only one of which is his own. He would never hurt another human being.

Collins listens patiently. Finally, after a ten-minute harangue by Suarez, Collins breaks in and asks sharply, "Were you ever involved in the shooting or robbery at Ross?"

Suarez answers quickly, "No, I don't know anything. That's why I'm here, because they say somebody is accusing me." Suarez continues to claim he's never been around guns. This is a serious gaffe. Suarez apparently is unaware that Collins has his file from the older narcotics arrest. On February 7, 1995, Metro detectives searched Suarez's apartment at 489 Calcaterra Circle in Las Vegas. They found rock cocaine, $1,385 in cash—and an M1 rifle.

Jose and Oscar are in jail, Collins reminds Suarez, and they have named him as their confederate. "Why are they saying that you are involved in these robberies and these shootings?" Collins asks.

"That's the big problem that I want to find out," Suarez replies. "Why are they involving me if I never hung out—I have never hung out with him. [Jose] would come to my house . . . There would be the party, the dinner, and he would go. With the other guy, I had never talked, and I have nothing to do with him."

Collins informs Suarez that the police have found handguns, assault rifles, boxes of ammunition, baseball caps, sunglasses, sports jerseys, body armor, clothing, ski masks, gloves, explosives, and every imaginable item used in the crime spree—especially in the Ross and Bellagio robberies. "Would your fingerprints be on any of those?"

"I don't know—no, nothing, nothing! I don't have anything to do with that."

Collins mentions the Bellagio surveillance video. "I can recognize Jose. I can recognize Oscar," the detective says. "And the third guy looks a lot like you."

Suarez sticks to his story. "I promise you, I don't have anything to do with that. They are getting me involved."

Collins comes on hard. "You know those two men that you guys killed?"

"No, not me. I haven't killed anybody!"

"This is the time to tell me now, because if it goes to court—there's no more."

"But, sir, what would I say? I haven't done anything. I will say it fifteen thousand times, I didn't do anything."

"Why would they pick *your* name out?" Collins sneers, shaking his head.

"That's what I would like to know!"

Caught up in the moment, Officer Guerra lobs in a question of his own: "And why is your face in that video?"

"This is not true!" Suarez protests.

The gloves are off. This is no longer a friendly meeting in which a good citizen steps forward to correct an unfortunate police mistake. Luis Suarez is *el sospechoso primero* (the prime suspect). And now Suarez *knows* he's not going home tonight or possibly for a long, long time. The look on Collins's face is cold and hard when he asks the next question.

"Do you love your kids?"

"Sure."

"So did Richard Sosa," the detective snaps.

Detective Collins leaves the room. A moment later the door to the interview room opens. Detectives Bob Rogers and George Sherwood of the Las Vegas Metropolitan Police Department enter the cubicle and place Luis Suarez under arrest for the Bellagio robbery. He is driven to jail and a reunion with Jose and Oscar.

On April 3, 2001, Detective Collins and Special Agent Brett Shields of

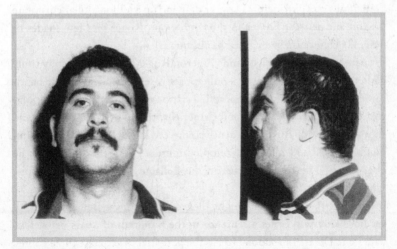

Police ID photograph of Luis Suarez taken August 26, 2000, after the Cuban turned himself in to Henderson detectives.

COURTESY HENDERSON POLICE DEPARTMENT AND LAS VEGAS METROPOLITAN POLICE DEPARTMENT.

the FBI will travel to Tampa, Florida, to examine Suarez's alibi. It does not check out. The address provided by Suarez for his stay in Florida does not exist. As Collins later explains in a court document, "One phony address he gave us would have been right in the middle of Tampa Bay."

AS VIGOA, CISNEROS, and Suarez settle into the grim routine of life at the Clark County Detention Center at 330 South Casino Center Boulevard, two blocks south of the famous Golden Nugget hotel and casino, the powers of Las Vegas want maximum punishment and no-quarter vengeance for the brazen two-year crime spree. The old mob founders of Las Vegas had a saying: "Robbing a casino owned by the boys wasn't in the cards." Now the new corporate owners, ruthless in their own way, and with considerably more money invested on Las Vegas Boulevard, intend to reinforce that maxim.

Stewart L. Bell, in his last term as district attorney, selects David Roger, his protégé and chief deputy, to lead a team of crack prosecutors from the major crimes unit. Roger is a good choice. A Nevada native, thirteen-year veteran of the DA's office, and a career prosecutor (he joined the DA's office in 1987 after clerking for a district court judge), he is as meticulous as a Philadelphia lawyer drawing up a billion-dollar corporate buyout and a street fighter in the courtroom. Roger sees few shades of gray. He believes in swift, hard punishment.

After the arrest of Vigoa and Cisneros, Roger's strategy is to buy time, gather more facts, and create a bulletproof case. His colleague, the handsome, Dutch-born Frank Coumou, a star prosecutor in the major violators unit, will charge Vigoa and Cisneros with the Bellagio robbery and shooting, develop further evidence connected to the Ross and Desert Inn gunfights, *and* add murder, attempted murder, and other charges as he goes along. The focus will be on the Bellagio, Desert Inn, and Ross, where gunfire takes place.

Because there are at least eight alleged victims at the Bellagio, a guilty verdict likely will bring a sentence in the hundreds of years per defendant. The Desert Inn shoot-out has the potential to generate three counts of attempted murder by itself and three more counts of armed robbery. Another hundred-year sentence per accused is possible if the defendants are found guilty of the Desert Inn attack. The district attorney's office will deploy at least eight prosecutors and investigators on the case, in ad-

dition to the FBI agents and Metro detectives who will ~~~~~
leads and surveil Suarez and Duarte, who will remain ~~~~~

Vigoa, of course, is not talking. Even when c~~~~~
neros's confession, shown photographs from the Bellag~~~~~
color 8 × 10 glossies in close-up—even when told the guns, body ~~
and white baseball cap have contributed decisive ballistics and DNA data,
he denies everything.

If Vigoa's stonewalling is expected, it is his choice of counsel that will
surprise. Still smarting from the disastrous 1990 drug trial and the halfhearted, rambling defense of Kevin Kelly (Vigoa claims the lawyer
charged him more than $300,000), the Cuban asks for a public defender.
Vigoa intends to preserve his assets, including hundreds of thousands of
dollars believed buried or hidden out of state. Vigoa vows: "This time the
lawyers will get nothing!"

A public defender instead of a high-powered criminal lawyer—a curious choice considering that Vigoa may be on trial for his life.[1] The best
high-profile criminal lawyers tend to be uniformly aggressive and sharp
witted, skilled at manipulating the media, and adroit at confusing jurors
in the face of hard evidence. Selecting a public defender is a crapshoot.
There are career public defenders who are little more than overburdened,
burned-out bureaucrats, lawyers with little stomach to go nose-to-nose
with high-powered, well-funded prosecutors. To be fair, there are public
defenders who are first-class defense lawyers dedicated to equal justice
under the law. These men and women forgo lucrative private practice because they believe the poor have a right to quality representation.

Drew Christensen, who will represent Vigoa, is one of the good ones.
A tall, amiable thirty-eight-year-old major crimes attorney with an excellent reputation among other lawyers, Christensen will do more than provide able counsel. Christensen will fight hard to save Vigoa's life.

Christensen has no inferiority complex. The public defender's office is
a noble and important institution, he believes, and justice should not be
about a man's net worth. A Texas-born military brat and the son of an air
force surveillance pilot, he grew up on bases around the world. He has no
problem tracking down witnesses at midnight in the toughest part of
town. The six-foot, one-inch, 195-pound lawyer does not hesitate to
meet face to face with killers, rapists, and the worst of mankind as part of

[1] Jose's dilemma was how to access his hidden loot and how to pay a criminal lawyer without the funds
being seized.

Public Defender Drew Christensen, who fought to spare Jose Vigoa the death penalty.
COURTESY DREW CHRISTENSEN.

his normal routine. He will stand alone in a courtroom and take on a battery of cops and assistant district attorneys without losing his calm and good humor.

Christensen recognizes the state's strategy: "What the state said was, there was a pattern of conduct among the Vigoa crew," Christensen said. "With the evidence they found both at Vigoa's house and the Cisneros house—the guns and the bounty of the crimes—the state felt it could pretty much prove that Cisneros and Vigoa, and possibly the others, committed a number of these robberies. Through the evidence, the state believed they had them dead to rights on the Bellagio. Now, at the Ross itself, they couldn't prove Vigoa was there. What they were arguing to the judge and the jury was, if it walks like a duck and quacks like a duck, it's a duck."

As he calculated the number of felony counts from only two of the robberies, Christensen saw the trap engulfing Vigoa and Cisneros, and any others who might be found guilty in the two-year crime wave. "The Desert Inn shooting will create multiple counts of attempted murder," he told Vigoa. The Bellagio had numerous counts of attempted murder and robbery. Jose is looking at one thousand years even if we win the murder and death sentence case."

A few blocks north on the seventh floor of the district attorney's office at 200 South Third Street, Roger orders a study of cell phone calls made among Vigoa and his crew. A new financial analysis will be undertaken by Detective Bob Rogers that will track the stolen money as it is spent. Torrey Johnson, of Metro's ballistics unit, will tie the weapons found at Oscar's house to shell casings and slugs left behind at the Desert Inn, Ross, and Bellagio. The Cisneros confession will provide the foundation for an expanded and more focused investigation as the police and prosecutors build their case and "prove up" each allegation. David Roger plans other unpleasant surprises for Christensen and his client. Along with prosecutors Roger Cram, Frank Coumou, Thomas Leen, and a very pregnant Pamela Weckerly, Roger will use the grand jury with devastating effectiveness—some will say ruthlessness—summoning Cisneros's mother, father, and brothers before the panel, as well as Luisa Vigoa, Vilma Duarte, and even the young Vigoa children, a move that raises eyebrows even among cynical courthouse lawyers.

Roger is unapologetic. "I wanted to bring Vigoa's family members in to testify, and I did that for a couple of reasons. One, to eliminate Vigoa's alibi, Suarez's alibi, and Duarte's alibi. I also wanted to put a little pressure on the family. I thought that Vigoa's wife probably was the matriarch of the family, and if I could put some pressure on her, perhaps somewhere down the road Vigoa would fold. It was a real crapshoot because in all my years of prosecuting, I've had very few people of Cuban descent either roll over on other defendants or plead guilty in court. It seems like the people I've dealt with are fighters, and they go to the mat on their cases."

Vigoa and Suarez claim to be at the all-night birthday party at the Suarez home for nineteen-year-old Jenny Cruz, a cousin of Caridad Farray. One by one the family members are grilled. They differ as to when the party started, how long it lasted, who was there for what period of time, and when the celebration ended. The alibis of Suarez and Vigoa slowly disintegrate.

Some of the exchanges between the prosecutor and the children have survived in grand jury transcriptions. There's Maria Vigoa, a seventh-grader, prodded by the prosecutor to admit that her father lived at the Sandy Slate Way home. Without her parents or a family member present, and confronted by a skeptical, relentless chief deputy district attorney, the child holds her ground. Jose didn't live at the house, she states. "My mom didn't want him to live with us, if you know what I mean." Maria testifies that her parents are ordinary and hardworking people living "a normal life" without much money. "Then explain the $100,000 we found in your house," Roger fires back. The girl says she knows nothing of the money and never saw such wealth.

Maria was the girl in the car during the high-speed car chase that led to her father's arrest. She tells the jurors she pleaded with her father to run away because she thought the pursuers were carjackers, killers, or worse. Throughout her ordeal Maria is polite and appears at peace with her conscience.

Anna Vigoa, eighteen, is next. Because of her age, the gloves will be off. There is nothing subtle about her grand jury examination.

Q: Have you reviewed any of the police reports in this case?
A: I try not to.
Q: Have you seen any of the evidence in this case?
A: I also try not to.
Q: But you're saying that your father is innocent?
A: Right.

Anna will be grilled in detail about family finances, about the Bellagio surveillance tape, and about Jose's presence at Jenny Cruz's birthday party. Her father left the party only briefly to buy more supplies. "We ran out of soda. He was gone for, like, twenty minutes."

Q. You said you thought your father was a good man?
A. Yes. I know he's a good man.
Q. Why did he go to prison for seven years?
A. Because he did something he wasn't supposed to.

Anna is asked if there's anything else she wants to say. Yes, the young woman says. "I think that everybody is, is—what's the word—innocent until proven guilty. So I believe he should be given a fair trial, and if he's proven guilty, then I think he should receive whatever you're going to give him, but I think you should give him a fair trial and not play dirty."

A juror asks what Anna means by playing dirty. She recites the beating of Suarez in his cell, an incident with Duarte in jail, and how Maria was handcuffed and held at gunpoint by police after the wild chase.

Another juror calls Anna a liar. "Now, you speak to me with forked tongue, it sounds like, okay?" the juror says.

Anna replies that she doesn't understand the question.

"When someone is suspected of cold-bloodedly killing two men and shooting two other guards," the juror lectures, "how do you think you should treat them?"

Without missing a beat, Anna answers. "The person that is suspected, yes. Not a kid. Not a kid that's a *little* kid. I wouldn't do that to a *little* kid."

Eleven-year-old Belladonna Vigoa is the third child to be questioned. Most of the interview concerns a letter Belladonna wrote two years earlier to the Spirit of Christmas, the politically correct local version of a letter to Santa Claus. In the letter the child, then nine, asks Santa to help the family by letting her Dad win the lottery so he would not have to do the things he was doing. It is an innocent and plaintive letter about a family in crisis. Maybe Dad is struggling financially, maybe Mom and Dad are having terrible fights because of the financial stress, or maybe Dad is a killer with an AK-47 and a cache of explosives.

"In your letter to Spirit of Christmas, you said that your father was getting mean," says Roger.

The little girl answers softly and does her best to protect her father. "But he never hurt anyone," she says.

By October 2000, four months after the arrests of Vigoa and Cisneros, the DA's office was determined to pursue a death penalty case.[2] By themselves, Cisneros's two taped confessions could not be used in court against Vigoa because of his Sixth Amendment protection and his right to confront his accuser—you can't cross-examine a tape recording. Cisneros would have to testify in Vigoa's presence. But how to make this happen?

ONE PERSON WHO isn't ready to hop aboard the DA's famous train of justice is Jose Vigoa. He will give the detectives nothing before or during his transport to the Clark County Detention Center. "VIGOA IS UN-

---

[2] Under Nevada law, multiple killings, or placing others in peril during a murder, are considered aggravated circumstances, a condition for the death penalty.

BREAKABLE," he writes from jail. "I don't have nothing to say to the police except FUCK YOU ALL."

Vigoa is booked into the Las Vegas jail, officially known as the Clark County Detention Center, or CCDC, on June 7, 2000, without incident. He is given a physical examination and is found to be in good health. Vigoa considers the Clark County Detention Center nothing more than a "little vacation" with three square meals a day, free television, air-conditioning, a private room, "and wonderful security." That's fine with the police and prosecutors; they consider Vigoa's cooperation no longer necessary. The government has the Cisneros confessions in hand, they expect him to repeat the admissions in open court, and the remaining gang members have been identified. Pedro Duarte is defiant and remains in Las Vegas, openly taunting the police. Spotting a team of FBI agents conducting surveillance, he drives by, grins, waves, and yells, "Catch me if you can!"

AT FIRST VIGOA is treated like an ordinary inmate and mingles with the general population. Later he is assigned to the seventh floor and a housing unit known as closed custody, the second-highest level of isolation. Vigoa will be allowed out of his cell once a day for exercise and will be allowed to make phone calls. The amount of his free time will depend on his behavior.

Even in these tightly controlled circumstances, Vigoa begins to agitate and sow discord in an overcrowded facility where approximately 450 unarmed correction officers are outnumbered by as many as 2,800 inmates, a roughly 6-to-1 ratio at times. An elite unit charged with transporting Vigoa to court will resign en masse in a dispute over his guarding. Vigoa will be suspected of ordering the beatings of informants and child molesters and making contact with outside gang members. He will embark on multiple hunger strikes. He will develop dossiers on key jail personnel through outside contacts and subtly conduct his own interviews with staff while secretly sketching a detailed blueprint of the facility. At least one custody officer is so unnerved by his encounter with Vigoa, he asks to be taken off the floor where the Cuban is housed. Vigoa uses coded language in his correspondence. The guards learn that wherever Vigoa is moved within the facility, he counts the precise number of steps from one location to the other.

Despite his reversal of fortune, Vigoa conducts himself, a supervisor says, like a colonel in the midst of his regiment. "You don't get the feeling you're talking to an inmate who's facing the death penalty and is locked up in a cage; you think you're talking to your superior," a jail sergeant recalled.

Sergeant Kristy Crawford, an eleven-year custody officer who is head of STING (Security Threat Intelligence Networking Group), the jail's gang intelligence unit, notices Vigoa's militarylike bearing and awareness of environment. The petite platoon sergeant knows that he will be a challenge, but he won't be the first hard case to set foot inside the CCDC building, and he won't be the last. A single mom, a second-generation Metro officer, and the daughter of a retired deputy chief, Sergeant Crawford is a pioneer in her field—one of the first women in Nevada to enter the correction ranks and to survive the harsh masculine environment of a big-city jail. Crawford became a correctional officer in 1989 and accepts the fact that the jail is one of the most dangerous workplaces in Nevada. The correctional officer, or CO, is always being tested. "I like the psychological challenge. The job is about outthinking the other guy. That's how you beat these people, with your mind, not with your fists." Vigoa will prove to be an excellent subject for Crawford's explorations.

"My gang-intel people were very concerned about his demeanor. I could see why. When Vigoa talked to you, he was not giving you information, he was obtaining information. And the average officer in here couldn't grasp that. I would catch officers up there bullshitting with him. I said, like, what do you not *get*?"

One day, Crawford remembers, Officer Dante Tromba of SERT (Special Emergency Response Team) was assigned to take Vigoa to court. Tromba entered the cell.

"Stand up, turn around, and face the wall," he said.

Jose smiled and looked the CO "dead in the eye" and then looked down.

"Those are nice new boots, Officer Tromba. You bought them last night at American Shoe."

Tromba was stunned. Vigoa was right.

By late summer of 2000, Crawford and her staff begin to receive warnings from Metro and Henderson police. The correction officers learn that Vigoa is believed to be either former police or military. She believed the report. "We were told he was either SWAT or military trained—high military, as in a ranger or Green Beret. Just watching him on the videotape when he entered the casino, you could see the way he would survey the area, the way he carried his body, almost in a stealthlike mode. And then there was his shooting ability. At one point in the investigation, they thought he was a law enforcement officer. Gordon Martines came to the jail about once a week. He said they thought their suspect was either a SWAT officer or certainly had a military background because of his precision in shooting. When he made his getaway from one of the casinos, he was traveling at a high rate of speed and discharging a firearm backward toward the vehicle chasing him with enough accuracy to blow out the tire. This shocked everyone."

BY OCTOBER CISNEROS is feeling the heat. He tells his jailers that he has been warned that he will never make it to his trial and if he even agrees to testify, then his mother, father, and three brothers will be killed as well. It is believed this threat came directly from Vigoa, who has never

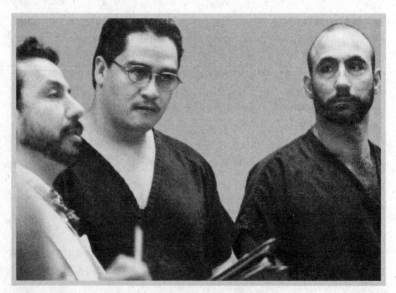

During preliminary hearings, Oscar Cisneros and Jose Vigoa sat together in court. This was soon prohibited as prosecutors and jailers attempted to separate the two suspects.

COURTESY LAS VEGAS REVIEW-JOURNAL. PHOTO BY GARY THOMPSON.

denied the allegation. The lawyers for both sides know that Cisneros already is a target for assassination because of his two confessions and the fingering of Vigoa and Suarez, but there can be no hope for leniency, no chance for a plea bargain, or any other consideration unless he gets on the witness stand, points his finger at Vigoa, and gives up his former partner.

The DA has great power, but Cisneros has leverage too. From the DA's vantage point, Oscar will make a superstar witness after proper preparation, and his testimony will almost guarantee the death penalty for Vigoa and possibly Suarez if it can be proven that the two Cubans were at the Ross.

Cisneros's public defender, Phillip Kohn, will visit his client in early October to review the case and explain his options. In their time together, Kohn finds Cisneros lucid and hopeful. But after the lawyer leaves, Cisneros is alone in his cell. What to do? These are matters far beyond the understanding of a twenty-three-year-old laborer. Cisneros writes a letter on the night of October 6, 2000, to the U.S. Immigration and Naturalization Service, better known as the INS.

> I'm being held at the Clark County Detention Center with no bail. I would like to be deported back to Mexico ASAP. I understand that being deported I will not be able to return to the United States.

The proposal to the INS is a preposterous notion. "Writing to the INS made no sense," Kohn said. "That was not going to happen. They were not just going to take his deposition and ship him off to Mexico. That was impossible." While the proposal has no chance of success, it makes clear Cisneros's desperation.

At 3:45 a.m., on the fifth floor of the Clark County Detention Center, Correction Officer Scott Keiser, working the graveyard shift, begins serving breakfast to inmates of the D module on the upper tier of the fifth floor. Calvin Weston, an inmate worker with a history of misdemeanors, is helping the guard serve a breakfast of eggs, bacon, and coffee. This is a high-security unit that houses major felons and those in protective custody, and all meals are delivered to the cells. Those on the fifth level are allowed out of their cells only one hour a day and do not have contact with other prisoners.

The two men reach 5-D23, the cell of Cisneros. The one-man cell on the upper level of the fifth floor is a model of bureaucratic efficiency and skillful use of space. As one walks through the door, the toilet and sink are immediately to the right. Next to the toilet is a small desk area along the wall, although there's barely enough room to write a letter. The bed, with a glass window overhead, runs east to west on the north wall. D23 has been recently retrofitted with new air vents that have only quarter-inch holes to prevent inmates from hanging themselves.

"Chow," the correction officer says.

Weston, the trustee, places the tray into the slot but notices no movement or sound in the cell.

"Here's your tray," Weston says.

Procedure requires the inmate to take the food and shove back the empty tray from the previous meal. Weston looks into the cell. "He's hanged himself!" Weston shouts to the correction officer. "He's got something around his neck. Oh, Lordy. He's hanging there!"

Keiser looks into the cell. Cisneros appears to be standing to the right of the cell door near the toilet. For a moment he appears normal. Then Keiser looks again.

"Officer Toyota! Officer Toyota!" Keiser shouts, summoning Randy Toyota, another correction officer who is serving breakfast on the tier below. Keiser sounds the alarm as other inmates awaken and begin shouting.

"Code 99!"

"Code Red 405!"[3]

The cell is opened. Cisneros is found hanging by strips of a bedsheet tied to an air vent in his cell. Toyota uses a seat-belt cutter to sever the sheet. Cisneros is informally pronounced dead in the cell by nurses from the jail's medical unit. His body shows signs of rigor mortis, which suggests that he committed suicide before midnight. When the makeshift bedsheet noose is removed, his advanced rigor causes him to remain in a standing position with his feet on the floor, his head tilted forward and chin resting on his chest. It is a macabre sight.

Cisneros is an important man in death, and the Metro homicide unit is given the case. Sergeant Kevin Manning and detectives Dave Mesinar

[3] Code 99 is a medical emergency; code 405 denotes emergency radio silence and suicide.

COLLISION | 319

and Michael J. Franks will visit the cell and conduct a murder investigation. Crime scene analysts Larry Morton and Joe Matvay inspect and photograph the cell, body, and potential evidence. They will find nothing unusual or suspicious. Two inmates in Cell 5-D22, next to Cisneros, are interviewed. Christopher Buck and Greg Robertson assert they were unaware of who was in the next cell and heard or saw nothing unusual that night. The next morning an autopsy is conducted by Dr. Sheldon Green of the Clark County Medical Examiner's Office. Green finds recent ligature marks around Cisneros's neck but no other trauma to the body, no drugs that might have weakened or disoriented him, and no sign of any struggle. Green rules that the cause of death is asphyxiation due to strangulation—a suicide.

The next day, October 9, 2000, public defender Phil Kohn contacts Detective Mesinar. Kohn advises that the public defender's office had Cisneros evaluated by a psychologist. The psychologist said Cisneros was *not* suicidal, Kohn tells the detective pointedly.

"In my dealings with Oscar I never saw him depressed in any way, and I never suspected or anticipated suicide," Kohn says later. "I've had a number of clients commit suicide, and every one of them was predictable—absolutely predictable. I certainly saw no sign whatsoever that Oscar was despondent, suicidal, or depressed."

Immediately the attention focuses on Jose. "Cisneros was housed right above Vigoa," recalled Jay McCauslin, a member of the elite SERT team. "They were on different floors, but one room above and below each other, so they were able to communicate through the vents. There was some kind of a mix-up where Cisneros was housed."

No one from the jail staff, district attorney's office, or Metro will ever tie Vigoa to the death of Cisneros. In May 2003 Jose will discuss the suicide at length. He is asked whether he sent a message to Oscar promising ruthless retaliation unless the Mexican took his own life. "Here is the law," Jose explained patiently. "If you don't have the balls to stay in the thing the right way, the honorable way, don't get in! Right? If you're going to do what Oscar did, *don't get in!* Who snitched on me and hurt me? A rat, right? And he also hurt my family. If I am in this world, and I snitch on you, it means I don't care about my family to begin with. Do you understand me? Oscar learned that a man should die before becoming a coward and a snitch. He died for his honor and his family. Even though he screwed up, he gained my respect in the end for cleansing his honor as he did."

But was Vigoa involved in the death? He gives a cryptic answer: "When Oscar decided to kill himself, I was in the general population on the seventh floor, 7-D, also in cell twenty-three, and one floor above Oscar."[4]

---

[4] The fifth floor is double tiered, which means Oscar actually would have been housed on the *sixth* floor. If Jose was in 7-D23, he would have been directly above Oscar and able to communicate through vents, pipes, or other means. This has not been established by any official body, however, although John Alamshaw was told this story by a custody officer.

Chapter 30

JOSE: OSCAR DID THE RIGHT THING

Everybody feels sorry for poor Oscar Cisneros. Well, let me tell you my side of the story.

For two years Oscar was one good friend with courage to do whatever he was told to do, and he proved himself several times. I have to recognize that merit now. Yet I knew all along that Oscar would break up if he got in trouble with the law. Most people, no matter how hard or stand-up they are, will crack when it is time to face the law. Good examples are the Mafia. They can be very hard when they're in the gang, but once they get arrested, they go straight to the witness protection program and become a bitch for the feds, betraying their own mother if necessary because they're afraid to do a few years.

Oscar understood perfectly our way of life and the code we enforced when it came to snitches. I learned about Oscar snitching as soon as I entered the CCDC. While I was in the holding tank, I was watching one of Las Vegas's local news channels, and according to what I heard, I knew immediately Oscar was snitching. Actually, even before I was in the tank, while I was being transported to CCDC by Rogers, the Metro detective, I heard bits and pieces of information over the police radio about plan B. Based on what they were saying, and some confidential information they already knew, I knew Oscar was singing.

At the jail I saw one scared Oscar. It was not the Oscar I knew. He was totally different. I looked straight into his face, and I saw his shame, fear, and embarrassment. His courage and strong spirit had crashed. Even though I didn't know all the details, he had crossed far over the line, and there was no turning back. I realized the police probably wanted me to know this and see Oscar in this sad state—this is an old police trick. The police were betting that once I knew about Oscar's concert, then maybe I will start to sing too and try to outdo Oscar with my squealing and treachery. But no, that is not Jose's way.

Oscar allowed the FBI and police to lie to him, and to spin many fictions. I went to court with Oscar two and three times, and that's where I learned what was being said. We talked briefly during a hearing. Oscar told me of his conversations with the police. I was disgusted, but I kept my cool. "They will let me go back to Mexico if I testify," Oscar said, all excited. I realized this was his big foolish hope and stupid dream: Oscar thought he could play with the pigs and go home with no problems at all. Two people dead, and he was in the gunfight, was shot in the leg, shot at the kid guard, shot the man at the Desert Inn—and just like that, he gets to go home![1]

"Oscar, you're a fucking idiot," I said, trying to warn him. "They are using you and lying to you."

"Well, I already made two statements, but I told them I won't testify in court," Oscar said.

"Yeah, sure, Oscar," I replied, before the cops saw us talking and quickly separated us. I had no illusions about what Oscar intended to do. The cops were playing him real good.

I knew Oscar was going to give in to the DA, like most cowards (or fools) do, but I was doing my homework also. I told everybody at the jail, on every floor, that Oscar was a snitch. And I was in the cell above him. Did you know that? I was right above him. I think there were more than 2,600 inmates in jail that day, and I wind up right above Oscar. Think about that. Just don't ask me how or why.

Of course the cops promised Oscar he could go free, they promised him all kinds of things, he believed them, and they tricked him, and they helped kill him. Everybody blames me for Oscar's death. They say that if Oscar doesn't take his own life then I'll see that he and his family are wiped out. But I didn't put Oscar in that position. Why don't you talk to the police if you want to blame someone? And, man, Oscar was not *only* talking. That would be bad enough. Fuck, Oscar was singing and playing all the instruments in the band! He was driving around the city with the pigs showing houses of friends of mine. What the DA didn't know was

---

[1] Vigoa is right in one key respect: The DA's office had no intention of making a deal with Cisneros that would allow the Mexican to go home in exchange for his testimony and other cooperation. Police and FBI investigators deny making such an offer.

that Oscar Sanchez Cisneros knew who I was and what I am capable of doing when my rules are broken. Man is born a man with honor. During his years in this life, he must represent his honor. When this honor is gone, there is only one solution. That is exactly what Oscar Sanchez Cisneros did: He *killed himself* without sacrificing other innocent lives, including his family. Luckily Oscar Sanchez Cisneros decided to take his own life in a long and no-turning-back journey on October 8, 2000, at about 3:30 to 4:00 a.m. in a single cell number twenty-three on the fifth floor, "D" side, in this segregation unit nicknamed the Hole.

Some keep getting back to Oscar and his father and his mother and his brothers and, oh my, oh my, would I really kill them all *and* Oscar to keep Oscar from testifying in court or as punishment if he did. *Did you think I was too intelligent and civilized for that kind of beastlike behavior?* Well, think about it. I had a wife and three children. When Oscar starts to sing, what about my wife and children? What about their lives, which have been so devastated? What about the families of the other men and their children? What happens to them? Do they not matter?

I am saying that when Oscar killed himself, he did the right thing and restored a little bit—not all, but a little bit—of his honor. As he left this place, holding his one-way ticket in his hand, I think I know what happened; I think he knew the truth. The cops put Oscar at the end of that bedsheet. Oscar had to know in that final moment of life, the cops will fuck you every time.

Chapter 31

JOSE IN BONDAGE

In the aftermath of Cisneros's death, the hammer fell on Vigoa, and it fell hard and fast. Vigoa had impudently attacked the lifeblood of Las Vegas, its casinos, he had exposed the city's vulnerabilities, and the system had been cheated out of the death penalty because of Cisneros's elimination. There would be payback.

Lieutenant Scott Karkos, who later ran for sheriff, recalled an urgent conference where the tension was palpable. "They said we have this very high-risk inmate; they didn't tell me his name or anything else. I was told the court personnel weren't pleased with what they called a lack of security that our section put on this guy. The truth is, it wasn't our fault—we didn't have any information on the guy, either. None of us knew his background." The meeting included top brass from both Metro police and the custody division, as well as U.S. marshals, SWAT representatives, and a court administrator. There were two deputy chiefs from patrol, Karkos recalls. The jail was represented by Captain Henry Hoogland, Captain Mikel (Mike) Holt, and Karkos.

The message was clear: "We will put a bullet in his head if Vigoa tries to escape," a deputy chief told the group. "That's how serious this guy is."

There were briefings in which Vigoa, thanks to the FBI, was identified as a former Cuban officer who was educated and trained in the old Soviet Union. The district attorney's office, stunned by Oscar's purported suicide, was contacted by the FBI and given the same report. Deputy DA Frank Coumou was one of those briefed: "During my prep work, I was told Vigoa was involved in the Cuban Army and that he had been trained and educated in the Soviet Union."

John Alamshaw found himself back on the case as part of a planning committee for security outside the jail. He learned that District Court Judge Kathy Hardcastle wanted absolute assurance that she would be safe, that the trial would not be disrupted, that there be no trucks filled with C-4 plastic explosives driving through courtroom walls and blowing the judge and her attendants to smithereens. Alamshaw pointed out that in the history of the jail, no one has ever tried to break *into* the facility, but breakouts during court appearances had been attempted. "We had intelligence there was going to be an escape plan put into place during the court proceedings and that Vigoa probably contacted others to help him escape," Alamshaw said. "We had information that some people were going to shoot out the windows where Vigoa was. He'd break those windows, and he'd be able to climb down from his cell window. We figured whoever was going to do that might have automatic or semiautomatic weapons—we were pretty concerned about that."

FOR DREW CHRISTENSEN, an already sprawling case was fast turning into a circus. The public defender feared the abuse of his client by a vengeful, frightened system that the normally mild-tempered attorney would compare to a "police state" in media interviews. "Once Cisneros committed suicide, security changed," Christensen recalled. "Prior to that my contacts with Jose, and my visits to the jail, and his court appearances, were no different from any other client I ever represented. And then suddenly everything went crazy."

Vigoa was moved to a high-security lockdown tier,[1] and the next time he went to court for a preliminary hearing, Christensen was horrified. In full view of the press, two twelve-man SWAT teams have been deployed and even brandish submachine guns inside the courtroom. School buses are parked around the courthouse to serve as barriers. Snipers are deployed on rooftops. Armed helicopters hover overhead. SWAT officers wearing camouflage battle dress and carrying assault rifles patrol the sidewalk. Inside the courtroom, the walls are lined with grim-faced cops. All that's missing are tanks to block the intersections and barricades erected at stoplights.

---

[1] The housing units include: second floor, isolation; third, women; fourth, women; fifth, administrative segregation; sixth, administrative segregation; seventh, close custody; eighth, close custody (a step down from segregation); ninth, close custody; east end, medium custody.

The intense siegelike security does not go unnoticed. The media arrives in force. The rumors are almost as sensational as the truth. One unverified report suggests Vigoa's crew and possibly even some former Cuban and Russian commandos flown in from the Caribbean are going to storm the building in an all-out military assault and recapture their leader. Another incendiary story, possibly triggered by leaked police documents, tells of a plot to crash through the doors of the courthouse with an explosive-laden vehicle—after all, didn't they find bombs at one of the Vigoa houses during the raids?

More accurate is the information that Alamshaw compiles. One source tells of a sniper outside the jail with a high-powered rifle. At a pre-designated time, possibly synchronized with a jail uprising, the gunman will shoot out the window of Vigoa's jail cell. Using a rope made of bedsheets, Vigoa will climb out of his fifth floor window and rappel down the wall while gunmen pour automatic fire into the open window.

After Cisneros's suicide, jailers searched the Mexican's cell and found escape plans for Cisneros and Vigoa. No one, including Phil Kohn and Cisneros's own legal staff, believed the inexperienced Mexican capable of planning a breakout. Whether by an overhead vent, or in some other fashion, Cisneros was communicating with Vigoa and possibly other gang members.

Crowds gather around the courthouse. Television news trucks jockey for position and begin broadcasting live. But what the reporters don't know is what's happening beneath their feet. A tunnel located under South Casino Drive connects the jail to the courthouse. The tunnel is cleared. A squad of SWAT and SERT[2] officers moves down the passageway, with two more officers pushing a strange-looking contraption that appears to be half wheelchair and half metal cart, something seemingly created by an asylum's welder. *Clank-clank-clank:* Vigoa is wheeled through the tunnels and then pushed and pulled by the police—*boom-bang-bing*—up the stairs to the back hallways and holding pens of the courtroom.

At the sight of his client, Christensen is stunned. Decorated with chains, belts, shackles, irons, and a stun belt, the Cuban looks less Tony Montana and more Hannibal Lecter. "They had his face masked with belts and different things locked on his head and over a black pillowcase

[2] SERT is the Special Emergency Response Team. These officers remove violent inmates in what is called cell extraction. They also deal with disturbances, riots, and transporting high-risk inmates.

kind of hood so he could not see where he was," Christensen recalled. "He was tied down to a wheelchair-looking device. But the way they pushed the wheelchair was to lean it back so they were wheeling him on two wheels with his legs and arms strapped in." Christensen is outraged at this treatment and immediately protests to the court.

A journalist later asked David Roger about Vigoa's right to a fair trial. How could anyone select a jury in the first place after this kind of intense pretrial spectacle? What about potential juries witnessing the doomsday excitement and Metro's dramatic wall of steel? "We never got to that point," the future district attorney said unperturbedly. "The only people that might be prejudiced by all the security would be jurors in a jury trial, and this case never went to trial."

There would be other incidents and examples of controversial behavior on the part of authorities.

On February 26, 2001, Vigoa and Suarez are banned from physically attending a hearing scheduled before Judge Hardcastle and are ordered to appear by video hookup from the jail. There was no legitimate concern of disruptive behavior by either defendant—Vigoa and Suarez had appeared in earlier hearings and preliminary proceedings without incident.

On June 20, 2001, defense lawyers question whether a fair trial is possible because of the dramatic, and widely publicized, security measures. "It has the potential to taint jurors," Christensen says. It is disclosed that Vigoa is wearing an electric stun belt while in court. Although fatalities from such units are rare, the shocks are said to be excruciatingly painful, causing the victim to lose control of his bowels and bladder.

On July 16, 2001, an indignant Vilma Farray Duarte, wife of Pedro Duarte, appears before the grand jury and asks Roger why her husband and others are being subjected to what she calls "torture." She claims that Suarez has been beaten, stripped of his clothing, and left without a blanket for days in his cell.

Witnesses in a grand jury proceeding are not permitted to have an attorney present. Alone, Vilma Farray Duarte will face David Roger, the formidable chief deputy DA and the fourteen members of the grand jury. Vilma will be defiant and outraged, demanding the alleged brutality stop.

"You guys should see him," Vilma says of her husband. "He's tied, his legs and his arms, when he goes to court. Do you know what they do when he goes to court? Do you know? When my husband goes to court, they got him chained with electricity, where if he moves he would shit or pee. They don't do that to animals. They don't do that to animals, why to them?"

On August 15, 2001, Rolando Larraz of the *Las Vegas Tribune,* a weekly tabloid newspaper with circulation in the Latino and African-American communities, became the first journalist to interview Vigoa. The resulting story produced an eye-catching front page headline:

Vigoa High Security Violates His Rights

In the interview, Vigoa denied his guilt and claimed that the police routinely listened to his conversations with his attorneys. He accused his probation officer, Pedro Durazo, of bias against Cubans because he believed his estranged wife once had an affair with a Cuban man. Vigoa repeated charges that Luis Suarez was beaten and thrown nude into his cell for waving at him when they accidentally passed each other on the same floor.

On November 30, 2001, Vigoa is discovered by his lawyers dazed and disoriented after an apparent blow to the head. He is unable to communicate or understand where he is, the lawyers tell the court. It is later determined that Vigoa was hit on the head—the explanations for the injury differed—and then thrown nude into his cell without a mattress or blanket.[3] On December 3, 2001, codefense attorney Stephen Immerman, complains of Vigoa's "inhumane treatment." Judge Hardcastle takes no action and orders the proceedings to continue on schedule. When it is pointed out that locking Vigoa in his cell nude and without a mattress or blanket is a rather unusual treatment for a concussion, officials say Vigoa was on a suicide watch. His lawyers scoff at this lame explanation. Other sources say Vigoa talked back to a guard and was beaten.

The treatment would intensify. A few days after a fight in his cell with guards, Vigoa was taken to court. Scott Karkos recalled another incident: "We strapped him in the restraint chair, we put earmuffs on him, goggled him so he couldn't see anything, gave him the whole nine yards, and on the way up, we warned him and said, 'Don't try to move, we're going to be carrying you up some stairs, and if you start doing things, we're going to drop you.' Well, we're probably three-quarters of the way up the stairs, and he jerked, being a smart-ass, and we dropped him briefly, and he let

---

[3] The official explanation for the November 30 incident, when Vigoa is discovered by his attorneys to be incoherent, is that the Cuban defendant "slipped in the shower and hit his head."

out a little yelp, and he didn't like that very much. We didn't have a problem with him after that."

Over time Vigoa began to treat the grotesque bondage as a badge of honor. "There was a special steel-wheeled cart, brand new, the paint was fresh," he wrote from jail. "This cart was made especially for Vigoa. It was a steel-wheeled cart pulled by the SWAT officers with no weapons around me. I was seated in this seat every time that I was in court. I wore leg shackles, and an electric belt that was normally fifty thousand watts or volts. One time I wanted to see if this shit really worked, and I fought with the SERT team officers while on restraint, and they tried to activate it, but it didn't work that day, so I have the electric belt with another belly chain. My hands were inside some special mittens that were kind of like tube shaped. These mittens are like the kind of gloves that a woman might wear to pull hot stuff out of the oven. This is to prevent me from removing a gun from the police hosts.

"There were also some special dark eyeglasses that did not allow me to

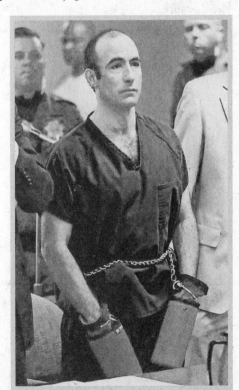

As proceedings
unfolded in 2000 and
2001, security
measures, including the
wearing of custom-
made "mittens" by
Jose Vigoa in court,
intensified.

COURTESY LAS VEGAS
REVIEW-JOURNAL.
PHOTO BY GARY THOMPSON.

see my way around and to see all the security measures. All this becomes a normal routine. Court days were like Hollywood. The entire courtroom was full of news media, with cameras everywhere. It was a complete theater for the Clark County deputy DA, David Roger, who was running for the Clark County district attorney."

In Vigoa's mind the feverish spectacle merely validated his long-held views that all governments were false and contrived, that justice was manipulated by the powerful, and that politics—twisted, corrupt, and perverse politics—ruled all. But he also considered the system weak and vulnerable—hadn't he proved all that with steel and blood up and down the Strip and in Henderson?—and he would play his role until it came time to make his next move.

In his darkened cell late at night, Vigoa chanted the Spetsnaz mantra learned twenty-two years earlier: "Before you die, the last thing you will see is my shadow." He believed that fortune favored the bold and that, in the end, you controlled your own destiny no matter how desperate the circumstances.

And he planned to prove it.

Chapter 32

JOSE'S EARLY CHECKOUT

Vigoa knew that some battles were certain to be lost. And he was enough of a jailhouse lawyer to know that even without Cisneros's testimony, the DA would have a strong case against the gangsters. Maybe the DA's men couldn't place Vigoa at the Ross, but the Bellagio appeared to be a slam dunk for the prosecutors. And the Bellagio charges meant hard time, or what Vigoa called "an elephant sentence."

Vigoa could count. Between the Bellagio and Desert Inn crimes—*without* the Ross, MGM, New York–New York, and Mandalay Bay robberies—District Attorney Stewart Bell and his chief deputy, David Roger, had the legal authority to file four attempted murder charges, seven armed robbery counts, and a smorgasbord of felony charges, including evading the police during the high-speed chase, conspiracy to commit armed robbery, conspiracy to commit burglary, child endangerment, violation of probation, possession of a firearm by an ex-felon, and discharging a firearm out of a motor vehicle.

Vigoa was forty years old at the time of his arrest. He faced a minimum of one hundred years from the Bellagio and the Desert Inn jobs alone, and the DA made it clear the other charges would come in time. Police arrested Suarez on August 26, 2000, and on June 18, 2001, detectives scooped up Duarte, who declined to cooperate and went into isolation and twenty-three-hour lockdown along with his cohorts. The authorities, not to mention the powers that be in Las Vegas, intended to cut Vigoa no slack at all.

It was time to talk deal.

At the outset of 2002, Drew Christensen and David Roger began crafting a plea bargain agreement that would spare the state the expense of a trial and protect the good citizens of Nevada from the audacious Cuban for all time. The deputy DA would not seek the death penalty, a major concession likely to be controversial when it reached survivors of Gary Prestidge and Richard Sosa. Also, the state would not prosecute Luisa Farray Vigoa, Vilma Farray Duarte, or any other family member, nor would it seek economic retribution. In return, Vigoa would plead guilty to forty-six felonies—which were outlined in a 131-page brief by Roger—and would agree to a combined sentence of more than five hundred years. There would be no possibility of parole; Vigoa would spend the rest of his life in a maximum-security prison.

It appeared that the long episode of crime and punishment finally had played out. But when Alamshaw learned of the proposed plea bargain, he thought something was odd. "That didn't sound like Jose at all. He was hard core. I was completely surprised."

Christensen, for one, was relieved. For all the time he spent fighting to save his client's life, the public defender never thought this day would come. He too felt that wasn't Vigoa's style. Christensen thought that for all the passion Vigoa showed in accepting his fate, he might have been buying a used car. But there was a good reason for Vigoa's serenity. The

Facing either the death penalty or life in prison without parole by early June 2002, Jose Vigoa had one more card to play.

COURTESY LAS VEGAS REVIEW-JOURNAL. PHOTO BY GARY THOMPSON.

lawyers could talk all they wanted, but Jose Manuel Vigoa Perez wasn't through quite yet. He had one more card to play.

It is known today from his journals that Vigoa was happy to do business with the chief deputy district attorney and agree to this and agree to that and sign a piece of paper, or a hundred pieces of papers, surrendering his freedom for all time, doing whatever the hated authorities wanted, playing the game with those he called the "stupids," "homo faces" and "dick eaters" of the American criminal justice system and pretending that, yes, the crazy Cuban, too hard even for Fidel, finally had been beaten down, was rolling over, whipped like a mangy dog with three legs.

Vigoa would play his part for the time being. The Americans would make Jose wear their ridiculous black hoods and tunnel mittens and have him ride around in a metal cart that had to be propped up on two wheels (he always hoped the heavy wheels would lop off some idiot guard's foot), and the guards would throw him into a freezing cell without clothes, and Jose could take it, JOSE COULD TAKE IT (as he wrote in his diary in large, bold letters), and the whole fucking jail knew that JOSE WAS THE FUCKING MAN, and no animal, coward, or snitch without honor. Give me the fucking paper and tell me where to sign. And sure, Jose would be happy to walk into Kathy Hard-ass-Castle's courtroom— or should we say, *wheel* into the lady's chamber—and bow his head and make tears in his eyes, and say, oh, oh, oh, Jose has been a bad little boy, and now he's going to Pay His Debt to Society.

In his private moments, Vigoa laughs darkly. He agrees to the DA's terms because at that moment, based on Vigoa's plan for his future, they mean nothing. Vigoa has decided to check out early and stiff the DA and his minions.

THE CUBAN HAS been cutting through the window of cell block 5-C1 since early April with a homemade tool provided by another inmate under the nose of heavy security. By the afternoon of June 3, 2002, the job is nearly complete. Vigoa has made a six-inch-by-six-inch hole in the wall and is making rapid progress in expanding the breakthrough now that he's penetrated the glass itself. Freedom is very close. Vigoa writes later:

> *I knew that the stainless-steel mirror frame used in the jail was strong enough to cut through the metal plates that were welded to the window.*

Also, I thought of using Vaseline not only to work more quickly, but also to reduce the amount of noise I made while I was cutting the metal. But the jail didn't sell Vaseline in the inmate store, or canteen, as it was called, but there was a blue grease called "hair dress" that worked as well. At that time I don't want to remove my cell mirror out of the place yet in case that I really need it. It was not an easy task to remove that frame. No inmate ever was able to remove that complicated frame out of the mirror, I was later told.

That frame would be my main tool. The problem that I had was the special police SERT officers in charge of me and watching closely. My cell was inspected very frequently and real good. These officers are trained to perform this check-down routine better than anyone. I had decided to make a plan against all those odds. By now I have all the metal frames inside my cell already cut in pieces, and also I cut these two metal plates in no time like a knife on hot butter. I have two welded metal plates already cut, but this was not enough. I must develop a special technique to lock these two metal plates from inside so the window remained looking normal, and the metal plates must also remain strongly attached to the window frame very nicely.

I had my good and trusted people to look out for me while I worked. I also made some cardboards and painted them black. I started to work on the rest of the window frames as well, including the very special hard glass that the jail had. I discovered the glass is over an inch thick, and it is fabricated like a sandwich, with hard plastic layers inside. There were five layers of glass and four plastic sheets sandwiched together—not an easy task, but not impossible. I started to cut the window main frame and over time, many days, I wind up with a huge hole inside the window.

By June 2, 2002, I was four hours away from being finished. I had the entire outside map. By all details I was on the fifth floor, approximately thirty-five feet to the garage roof that's inside the county jail. From that roof to the outside street and concrete sidewalk was another twenty-eight feet, a piece of cake! I was ready to jump to these thirty-five feet as well as the other and final twenty-eight feet to the street over the entrance of the county jail. This is where the police cars park, and all newly arrested prisoners enter this door. In front of these doors were two electrical steel "rolling doors," and on top of those doors are cameras to observe the new incoming cars, but none of this presented any serious obstacles to me. I considered it done.

On June 3, 2002, I was ready to touch down, to take off from the Clark County Jail at nighttime. It was to be a good and final gift from me to all the law enforcement people, not to mention publicity for the DA and something to keep the news people busy. But something unexpected and unplanned happened. A friend of mine got caught with prison-made wine. The police asked me if they could come into my cell for one second because someone got caught with wine, and the police wanted to know if I had some. They looked around, and they didn't find nothing. I had been working that day on the window, doing my last work, but I did not have the metal plates attached very well or disguised, because the cell search was so sudden, and I was so close to checking out—and the new correction officer without experience discovered my work by accident. It was one lucky shot.

The official story adds another twist. The damage to the window was not spotted from within, it was detected from outside the jail—and from five stories above. Sergeant Neal Kelso and Officer Richard Forbus of the CCDC were heading home at 4:45 p.m. when Forbus, after reaching the parking garage, glanced down at the outside wall of the Detention Center. Something was not quite right—there was a ripple or aberration in the red brick façade of the building. A reflection from the sun? A water leak? Pigeon droppings? Officer Forbus squinted and looked again. Sergeant Kelso took a look too.

"Oh shit."

"Is that what I think it is?"

"Call it in—*now!*"

According to Lieutenant Scott Karkos, it took two inspections before jailers on the cell block discovered the escape attempt even after being called. "They [Kelso and Forbus] called the module officer to take a look at the window to see if it was damaged, and it seemed okay. The person who reported it said, 'NO, there's something wrong,' and they went back and checked it again, and discovered it had been breeched."

Armed SERT officers charge into Vigoa's cell with weapons drawn. Normally they do not carry weapons, but now the custody officers suspect the hole is made not for escape—because of the fifty-foot drop to a roof below—but to smuggle weapons into the jail so that Vigoa can lead an insurrection and escape during the upheaval. "The hole was large enough where he could have smuggled in a gun and other material,"

Karkos recalled. "We went down with our weapons and started securing the area. We began looking to see what he might have smuggled in."

Vigoa, however, would dispute this theory. He intended to make a rope crafted from his sheets and blankets, he claimed, and to accomplish the jailbreak would have outside help. He would rappel down the wall and use other means to soften the fall.

The guards are ordered to tear Vigoa's cell apart, inch by inch. The officers disassemble the stainless-steel toilet and find four openings in the concrete wall behind the sink and toilet assembly. Three of the holes connect to the plumbing behind the sink; the bottom opening is for the toilet's flush pipe, also called a "down" pipe.

"We've got something here," one of the guards says sharply. The supervisors take a look. The caulking around the base of the toilet has been removed and replaced with soap. Hidden inside the space, underneath and behind the toilet, is a manila folder containing a hand-drawn blueprint of the jail—and more.

From the official Metro investigation:

> Captain Mikel Holt recovered a detailed handwritten map [of the facility and escape route] entitled "Top Secret, Destroy Immediately." Forbus recovered a handwritten letter from Carlos Torres in Spanish and handwritten pages entitled "DG1 Cuba Intelligence," outlining various weapons from Russia, Afghanistan, Saudi Arabia, Turkey, Austria, etc. Also contained in these handwritten documents were plans to release poisonous gas in Florida during hurricane season. Vigoa also gave accounts of him being in federal prison and knowing terrorists in relation to Middle Eastern Muslim countries and Islamic countries. These documents, along with the two pieces of cardboard which were joined together and painted black, resembling the sheet metal panels in Vigoa's cell, were all impounded.

The documents subsequently are forwarded to the FBI and to U.S. intelligence services. Other than the papers found in the cell, there is no evidence connecting Vigoa to any known active terrorist group acting against the interests of the U.S. or its government.

Sergeant Kristy Crawford of the jail staff describes what happens next: "We then did something with Vigoa we had never *ever* done in this institution—we moved him once a week so that his counterparts couldn't find him or talk to him through the ventilation systems or send messages through inmate workers. We ultimately—and I think this shocked even him—put Vigoa in the female isolation unit. We have never, ever housed a male inmate in a female housing unit before. And about every two days, we'd switch him to another room and then another room."

Chapter 33

JUDGMENT

Finally it was time for Vigoa to settle accounts with the State of Nevada. On August 16, 2002, Vigoa appeared before Judge Hardcastle for the last time.

No one ever thought it would end this way: quietly, somberly, in a hearing that lasted barely twelve minutes. There were no demonstrations or untoward incidents. Vigoa sat erect and attentive as usual, looking straight ahead with an intense, studied expression like a man trying to solve a difficult mathematical problem that's just beyond his grasp. Eight members of the city's SWAT team and the jail's Special Emergency Response Team stood along the courtroom walls or directly behind Vigoa and attorney Drew Christensen. Vigoa wore mittens, heavy chains, and the notorious 50,000-volt stun belt.

Gary Prestidge, Sr., the father of the slain guard at the Ross Dress for Less robbery, was the only speaker. He read from a prepared statement to a hushed courtroom, occasionally looking up at Vigoa.

> I am a father appealing for justice. On March 3, 2000, I realized every parent's nightmare. I received the one phone call a parent never wants to receive. On that day my son, Gary Prestidge II, was violently murdered by ruthless criminals.
>
> That was the day my son and I died. You see, when you take the life of a father's only son, you also take the life of the father. Not only has it destroyed my life, it has destroyed my family as well. Each day I pray that I be taken soon, for I can no longer live with the pain. I no longer have a reason to live. My son was my whole life.

On August 16, 2002, Gary Dean Prestidge, Sr., told a hushed court of his pain and loss after the murder of his son. The father of the young guard slain at the Ross wept as the sentence was read.

COURTESY LAS VEGAS REVIEW-JOURNAL. PHOTO BY CLINT KARLSEN.

As a father I was blessed. I was proud to call him my son and best friend. Gary and I spent most of our free time together. We had a very special father-and-son relationship. He once said to me, "Dad, I'll never leave you." He was right. For he will be in my heart and my memory forever. I only wish I could hold him one more time and tell him all the things that I forgot to say. On our last day together, our parting words were "I love you, bud," and "I love you too, Dad." That's the last time I saw him. Just a few hours later he was gone.

The District IV Parole and Probation Department made its recommendation next. There was nothing ambiguous about parole and sentencing investigator William D. Chickering's presentence report:

The fact that the defendant pled guilty to forty-three felony and three gross misdemeanor offenses in the instant case, including the murder of two people, speaks for itself. The Division believes that the defendant is a long-term, accomplished, and hardened criminal with no evidence of remorse for the crimes he has committed and with no contrition whatsoever for the two murdered victims. He went ahead with the crimes, coolly and rationally, for the purpose of enriching himself, with no sense of humanity for

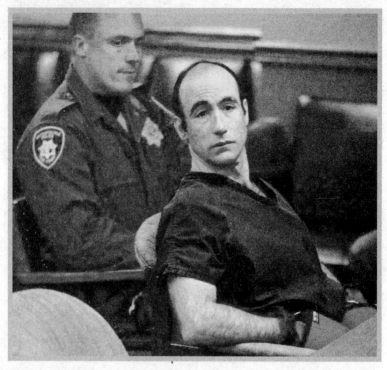

Jose Vigoa, who would be guarded by teams of SWAT officers during preliminary hearings, appears in court after the death of Oscar Cisneros.
COURTESY LAS VEGAS REVIEW-JOURNAL. PHOTO BY CLINT KARLSEN.

the deaths and injuries he caused. Sentencing to prison for the maximum term is recommended, without reservation.

Alluding to Vigoa's prenegotiated guilty plea, David Roger spoke for the prosecution. "We are grateful that Jose Vigoa will never walk the streets of Las Vegas again . . . He is one of the most dangerous criminals in the history of Clark County."

One last time the court reviewed the guilty plea and asked Vigoa if he understood its terms and significance. This was a moment of some drama and uncertainty: A previous sentencing hearing had turned into chaos when Vigoa refused to accuse Duarte and Suarez during his allocution, the guilty party's formal address to the court in which he admits wrong-doing and outlines details of the crime. The lawyers had scrambled to re-

**David Roger, Clark
County District
Attorney**

vise the document. This time Vigoa agreed to enter a plea of guilty under oath to all forty-six counts, including two counts of first-degree murder. He would be sentenced to life without the possibility of parole on the two murder counts. All sentences would run consecutively. Vigoa would be given the maximum penalty on each count allowed by law. But according to the plea agreement, he would not have to turn against friends or family to save his own skin.

> The State will urge the U.S. Attorney's Office to not file charges arising out of this case against Defendant and his wife Luisa Vigoa. The State will not file perjury charges against Luisa Vigoa and her children. The State will not file further charges arising out of the instant conspiracy unless other murders are uncovered by law enforcement. The State agrees that it will not call Jose Vigoa as a witness in any proceedings concerning his accomplices . . .

> The State agrees that Defendant's affidavit will not be used against Pedro Duarte or Luis Suarez in any proceeding in which Defendant is not a witness.

***Moments after his sentencing on August 16, 2002, Jose Vigoa
is led away.***

Judge Hardcastle then asked Vigoa if he had anything to say. In clear, barely accented English, Vigoa apologized for the suffering he had caused and then added, "But I cannot erase the past."

Judge Hardcastle sentenced Vigoa to four terms of life without parole, for a total of more than five hundred years.

Suarez and Duarte will travel different routes during their long and anxious journey through the corridors of southwest Nevada justice.

After the high-speed chase of Vigoa in June, Suarez disappeared for six weeks. The police believed he fled the state. Then Suarez abruptly resurfaced in Las Vegas and was arrested by Metro detectives Sherwood and Rogers after surrendering to Henderson detective Gerald Collins.

Suarez eventually negotiated a plea bargain through attorney Peter Christiansen, expecting a modest sentence after the Nevada Department of Parole and Probation recommended a sentence of two to seven years for the Bellagio robbery. Since Suarez already had served five years in the Clark County Detention Center awaiting trial, he hoped to be released on parole almost immediately. Then came the legal system's version of a

Pedro Duarte waves to his wife during the only full-scale trial relating to the Vigoa robberies and homicides.

COURTESY LAS VEGAS REVIEW-JOURNAL.

hidden trapdoor. Judge Hardcastle, noting that many people were put at risk during the Bellagio heist, and perhaps aware that Suarez was not charged for the Ross killings even though police said he was there, sentenced the Cuban to six to fifteen years.

Pedro Duarte was perhaps the least culpable of all the gunmen, according to his lawyer, Mike Cristalli. The getaway driver at the MGM Grand and Desert Inn robberies, Duarte was not present at the Ross double homicide or at the Bellagio, Mandalay Bay, New York–New York, or Thrifty crimes. Police believe Duarte quit or was fired by Jose after the DI heist when Duarte left his red truck at the Vagabond Motel, a blunder that eventually led the police to the Vigoa-Farray crime family.

Duarte remained free for more than a year after Vigoa's apprehension. Arrested on June 18, 2001, Duarte rejected a negotiation plea and decided to slug it out in trial. The state's case suffered a midtrial disaster when prosecutor Roger Cram called John Thornburg, a California correction officer and tourist who witnessed the gang's getaway from the Vagabond Motel parking lot after the Desert Inn heist. Thornburg was the state's star witness. He was standing thirty feet away from gang members when they arrived in the Isuzu Rodeo, jumped out, and switched to a pickup truck. Now he had to identify Pedro Duarte, who sat at the defense table wearing headphones and in street clothes. Duarte sat next to Cristalli, who clearly was not Hispanic, did not require a translator, and wore a brown pin-striped suit with a light brown shirt and tie.

"Do you see that person in the courtroom today?" Cram asked.

"No, I don't," the witness said.

There was a rustle in the courtroom. Undaunted, the prosecutor believed that Thornburg's view was obstructed. "Can you see around me with this equipment here?"

The judge interjected and spoke to the witness helpfully: "If you need to step down, you may do so."

Cram tried again. "Okay. Would you please point to that person and identify a piece of clothing that they're wearing?"

Now standing scarcely ten feet from Duarte and Cristalli, the state's pivotal witness pointed directly at Cristalli. There was a gasp.

Second-chair prosecutor Pam Weckerly, who was preparing for another witness at the prosecution's table, froze. "I was taking notes, and I was looking down at what I was writing. I heard Roger ask the witness to describe what Duarte was wearing, and I heard the description, and in my head, I was like, that's what Cristalli is wearing, and that's not Duarte. It was just a horrible, sinking feeling, and to Roger's credit, I'd say he handled it as best he could."

Cram tried a third time. "Okay. Do you see two individuals at this table? Are you referring to this table here, one of the individuals at this table?"

"Yes."

Cram stood opposite Cristalli.

"And which one are you referring to: the person seated here where I'm at, or the person next to him?"

Thornburg again pointed to the defendant's lawyer. "I felt like someone had just unloaded a shotgun blast into my stomach," Cram said. "I did not know what to do, so I just, well, somehow we went on, because here is my only eyewitness to this case that can identify Mr. Duarte, and he's just picked out the defense attorney."

Cooly Roger Cram would move on, blitz the defense with forensic evidence and try to regain the momentum in the eight-day trial. But the young six-foot-four-inch, 200-pound prosecutor, a Mormon and former high-school All-American basketball player, couldn't believe his witness had balked at identifying the defendant. "That," he said, "was the worst moment in my life."

After the witness fiasco, Cram focused on forensic evidence, the DA's best friend. "Circumstantial cases are the strongest cases we can have," he explained. "We had all the independent facts. The strongest facts begin with Duarte's truck being found at the Vagabond. His fingerprint is on the back of the cold (stolen) plate, his DNA is found on the water bottle in the back of the getaway SUV that was driven to the Vagabond, you have his ridiculous alibi, you have phone calls placed between himself and Vigoa, and then there was the crazy stuff that happened afterward. Vigoa and Cisneros were arrested, and within two days Duarte sets up a video camera at his front door because he knows they are going to be coming for him. He wanted to record them entering his home."

Cram gave a strong and detailed closing argument emphasizing that circumstantial evidence. This was no ordinary gang of misfits, he reminded the jury. These were deadly professionals who tried to kill two human beings for money by ambushing an armored car.

Cristalli, in his final argument, pointed out that the state's own witness could not identify Duarte as one of the three men switching vehicles. The state's case is bogus, he argued, because it is based on the testimony of the confused witness. We don't even know if there was a getaway driver, because it was Thornburg, utterly unreliable, who said there were three men, the lawyer asserted. Cristalli's close was powerful, repeating over and over the phrase "reasonable doubt." Duarte was waving to his wife and smiling at the defense table, believing he would beat the charge and become a free man at trial's end after two years in jail in segregated lockdown.

The other prosecutor was thirty-seven-year-old Pamela Weckerly, a pretty, five-foot-seven-inch, auburn-haired deputy DA with a UCLA law degree. Earlier in the year, the trial had been delayed when Weckerly gave birth the day before it was due to begin. A nine-year veteran, who was appearing in her first high-profile trial, Weckerly was a member of the crack murder team and would deliver a powerful rebuttal argument.

During deliberations the jury was at first divided. In its initial vote, five of the twelve panelists decided that Duarte was not guilty. After two days of deliberation, however, the jurors determined that even if Duarte did not pull the trigger in the Desert Inn robbery and engage in the furious firefight, under the law he was criminally liable for all that occurred during the heist.

Pedro Duarte was convicted of conspiracy to commit robbery, two counts of attempted murder, three counts of attempted robbery, and one count of possession of a stolen vehicle. On September 17, 2003, Judge Hardcastle sentenced him to prison for a term of sixteen to seventy years.

Chapter 34

THE MIDNIGHT EXPRESS

At midnight on August 24, 2002, SERT members from the Ely State Prison in east-central Nevada rumble into Las Vegas in a caravan of three vans. Jose Vigoa is sitting at a small desk writing a letter when his cell door opens, and he hears the familiar command to stand up, turn around, and face the wall. Vigoa's belongings are quickly packed. He is then placed in leg irons, handcuffs, mittens, and the stun belt. A black hood is slipped over his head, as though Vigoa were heading for the gallows. He is not, and Vigoa knows what is next.

Under heavy security, from both the jail and the prison, Vigoa is taken to the middle vehicle by the prison SERT members, also known as the "boom squad"—and to inmates, the "dick eaters." Along with the armed men in all three vans, there are two dogs. The caravan leaves promptly at midnight, heading northeast into the steaming black night. This late at night, the temperature still hovers at 100 degrees.

There is no conversation in the van. The prison SERT guards appear bigger and even more intimidating than the ones at the county jail. Out of habit Vigoa keeps track of the trip by counting to himself, measuring time, estimating the speed of the SUV, and listening to sporadic radio traffic among SERT members.

Gradually the brutal desert heat begins to wane as the procession climbs up the mountains of central Nevada. The caravan rolls past Crystal Springs, past the Humboldt National Forest, past the Great Basin National Park, over Connor's Summit at 7,722 feet. Vigoa's ears pop. He can feel the cool, refreshing mountain air.

Although the black hood remains on, Vigoa will feel the welcome rays of the sun at dawn, a sensation he has been denied for more than two years

The Ely State Prison, Nevada's toughest prison. The facility is four hours by car north of Las Vegas.

PHOTO BY JOHN HUDDY.

because of his punitive CCDC lockdown. From the time elapsed, the reduced speed of the van, and the noise of traffic, Vigoa realizes they are passing through a town and correctly discerns this is Ely, Nevada.

Thirty minutes later the vehicles wind down a hill into a valley, pass through a gate, and enter a secured area surrounded by watchtowers and men with rifles. This is Ely State Prison, a maximum-security facility built a decade earlier and believed to be escape proof. It is considered one of America's toughest prisons. This is where Vigoa is sentenced by the State of Nevada to serve multiple life terms without parole.

Jose Vigoa is home.

Lieutenant John Alamshaw, after a Metro career of twenty-four years and two months, retired on December 29, 2005, as a Las Vegas police officer. Alamshaw is now working in private security investigating major crimes and can be seen from time to time driving down the Las Vegas Strip on his black Harley-Davidson.

Drew Christensen continues to fight the good fight on behalf of indigent defendants for the public defender's office. Christensen is now chief deputy public defender and focuses on capital cases, including murder.

David Roger was elected district attorney in 2002 and reelected in 2006. Frank Coumou is now chief deputy district attorney, while Pamela Weckerly is a member of the DA's elite murder case unit. Roger Cram is now in private practice at the law firm of Vannah & Vannah.

Stephen Koenig continues as vice president of MGM Mirage resorts. Brian Zinke, the alert surveillance operator at the Bellagio hotel, is now director of surveillance at the New York–New York Hotel & Casino, one of the MGM Mirage hotels.

Detective Gordon Martines ran for sheriff in 2002 but received less than 1 percent of the vote. He ran again in 2006 but dropped out for lack of funds. Martines continues as a robbery detective and remains sharply critical of the department.

Bob Rogers and George Sherwood are assigned to the elite homicide unit of the Las Vegas Metropolitan Police Department.

Jutta Chambers, the first female officer of the Henderson Police Department, has been promoted twice since the Vigoa crime spree. She is now a deputy chief, the first woman to hold that position.

Donald Bowman, the Brink's guard and ex-marine who resisted

fiercely during the Desert Inn robbery, continues to work for Brink's. His partner Charles Fichter now works in security for the U.S. government at Las Vegas's McCarran International Airport.

Special agents Brett Shields, Rich Beasley, Larry Wenko, and Lee Zechter continue at the Las Vegas office of the FBI.

At the Armored Transport company, known today as AT Systems, it is now a firing offense to tamper with the driver's barrier door or engage in the practice of double hopping (in which both driver and messenger leave the truck to speed up the delivery run). Armored trucks today are kept in guarded garages when not in use. John Zamora, the former branch manager, is back in Las Vegas as a driver and warehouse man for a document shredding company.

Pedro Duarte and Luis Suarez are serving time at the Nevada State Prison at Indian Springs, a maximum-security prison northwest of Las Vegas. Duarte has appealed his conviction, arguing improper contamination of DNA evidence.

Si monumentum requires circumspice. If you seek his monument, look around you. Since the Vigoa robbery spree, major Las Vegas Strip hotels have eliminated "friendly" open-cage counters and now employ bars, bulletproof glass, or other barriers at the cashier's cage. Vegas police have produced a color video on how casino employees should respond to an armed robbery and suggest techniques for "freezing" the crime scene.

Jose Vigoa continues to reside at the Ely State Prison in a sixteen-foot-by-six-foot one-man cell. He was originally classified as a high-risk prisoner (HRP) and placed in a twenty-three-hour lockdown mode. HRP prisoners are not permitted contact with other inmates, take their food in their cells, and are allowed one hour of solitary exercise each day in a seventy-five-foot-by-fifty-foot yard. HRP imprisonment is the most severe form of isolation allowed by law and continues to be challenged in courts as inhumane. On October 23, 2003, Vigoa was moved from the HRP wing to administrative segregation, a less restrictive status. On October 22, 2004, he was upgraded to general population status and given additional food, canteen, shower, and work privileges.

However, in 2005 he was transferred back to the HRP block, where he now resides. Jose Vigoa has appealed this status.

From Ely, Nevada, to Havana, Cuba

*M*ay 7, 2003.

The car heater is cranked up to seventy-eight degrees, but I am shivering. It is midmorning in the high country of central Nevada, sixty miles west of the Utah border, and a freak May blizzard has moved in to catch me by surprise. As the spring storm blankets the small town of Ely, Nevada, under three inches of snow, I turn north in my rented Lincoln on Lackawanna Road, a two-lane state highway known locally as "the prison road." There are no other cars to be seen and no sounds other than the crunching of tires on ice and the thumping of windshield wipers. The sky is gray and darkening as the snow softly pelts the car. It is eerily quiet and desolate. Not even a jackrabbit or bird can be seen along this road, as if they too know where Lackawanna Road leads. The hours pass more slowly in White Pine County, as some of its more notorious residents up the prison road might attest.

The trip from Las Vegas to Ely is four hours—enough time to reflect on the journey and why I am here. Thirty-seven years ago, while still a student at Ohio State University, I began my career as a cops and courts reporter for the *Columbus Dispatch,* my first job in an exciting and often tumultuous media career. After a dayside shift on the city desk, I would return to the deserted newspaper at night, take an unmarked press car, and cruise the city while listening to the police scanners, hoping to beat the cops to the crime scene.

Eventually I moved on to the *Miami Herald* to write a column and later became a network show runner in New York and Washington, DC, producing NBC and CBS programming with presidents, tycoons, generals, world leaders, and movie stars. I spent a summer with Federico Fellini, drank with Janis Joplin, sparred with Burt Reynolds, produced documentaries on hero cops and corrupt police alike, aired two network interviews with Charles Manson, and worked on my first feature film. But always I would remember the raw drama of the street. Lieutenant John Alamshaw was right. We live our happy little iPod and Big Mac lives without realizing that just beneath the surface lurks random tragedy and unspeakable horror.

So here I am, driving high into the Nevada badlands, back on the police beat, having come full circle. In the summer of 2001, while producing a documentary called *Vegas Cops,* I heard rumors about a violent gang that raided the Vegas Strip with AK-47s, violating a long-standing tradition that no one touched a heavily guarded Las Vegas casino. Surprisingly, the national media had overlooked the story.

The Nevada Department of Corrections initially turned down my request to interview Jose Vigoa, who was classified a high risk prisoner (HRP). But with the intervention of a tough but fair warden named E. K. McDaniel, and help from Vigoa's lawyer, Drew Christensen, I eventually received approval. John Alamshaw told me to be careful. "I know you've met bad people as a journalist, but remember, I've dealt with criminals all my adult life," the detective said. "Jose Vigoa is the most dangerous man I've ever met, and I've been a policeman for twenty-four years. Your trip may be a waste of time. He told us absolutely nothing."

FOURTEEN YEARS EARLIER, surveyors from the department of corrections built the most isolated high-security jail in America in northeast Nevada. They knew what they were doing. White Pine County, population 9,600, is an isolated fuel stop surrounded by rugged black mountains that rise from the earth as if an angry glacier tore through the region, tearing up the earth in spite and pushing the terrain to 6,500 feet above sea level so that snow in May is not so strange after all.

Yet, like the desert to the south, there is more here than meets the eye. Life endures, even flourishes, and there is constant change and elegant surprise. The bristlecone pine trees on the mountainside are said to be four thousand years old, among the oldest living things on earth. A glacier sits atop a 13,000-foot mountain in a nearby basin, and there's an ice blue lake at 10,000 feet that's a sight to behold. In the mid-nineteenth century, a stream of humanity came to this land in search of gold, silver, and copper. Today the gold, silver, and most of the state's wealth can be found 245 miles south in Las Vegas.

I'M NEARLY THERE. Ten minutes out of Ely, I drive up a slight hill and head straight for a huge boulder that appears to block my path. Abruptly the state highway veers sharply through the Hercules Gap, and there it is, down below, in a small, snow-covered valley ringed by mountains: the Ely (pronounced "E-lee") State Prison, Nevada's toughest maximum-security facility. Fifty acres of retribution (but not always rehabilitation). All of this seems fitting—the wintry vista in May, gray sky, and the unsettling silence—in harmony with what man has built in this remote corner of east-central Nevada. The state prison is literally the end of the road. No one has ever escaped from Ely.

Moments later Jose Manuel Vigoa, inmate number 73847, shuffles into the prison's small courtroom wearing an orange jumpsuit, chains and manacles from waist to toe, and a shy, toothy grin. The Hannibal Lecter image is a good one—all that's missing is the fiberglass face mask. Two large guards wearing blue extraction unit jumpsuits and helmets with Plexiglas shields and football-style bars stand behind the Cuban. Vigoa welcomes his visitors. "You see, they take good care of me," Vigoa quips. "I even have bodyguards."

A first look at Vigoa: sad brown eyes, shaven head, broad shoulders, olive complexion with a slight jailhouse pallor, long, pointed ears that curl upward, and sharp predator's teeth. In the small prison courtroom, the guards insist on remaining in the room throughout the interview. I do not argue. Drew Christensen, the public defender, will remain for part of the interview (and future encounters).

Until this very moment Vigoa has refused to talk to police, prosecutors, or even his own lawyers about either his drug crimes or the casino violence. Now Vigoa tells his story in detail and in hurried bursts; his English is only fair, but I grew up in Cuba and am familiar with the Cuban dialect. "You have the questions," he smiles. "And I have the answers."

That he does, along with other claims. Vigoa admits to the five major casino robberies, the Ross murders, and the Sunset Station heist that puzzled police for years. He confides he was about to rob a Brink's truck outside a Henderson bank when he accidentally fired his AK-47 rifle, blew out the rear window of the van, and was forced to abort. The discharge, blamed on a "jealous mistress," or hair trigger, was never reported. Tragically, the armored car robbery in front of the Ross Dress for Less was the backup target. Had the rifle not fired outside the bank, the double homicide might never have occurred.

Vigoa claims to have planted listening devices in unguarded armored trucks. Vigoa reveals an attempted robbery at the Venetian Hotel but says it was broken off when a change attendant alerted security. Vigoa confirms his plans to attack the three-axle, ten-wheel super-armored car on its way to Los Angeles. This job was scheduled the day after his arrest. He intended to use a shaped charge to rip through the vehicle's armor. "My idea was to set explosives under the van," he says. I point out many people would have died. "This is war," he says.

War. The word comes up often. Vigoa will describe the more violent crimes in enthusiastic detail, like a general poring over old battles. But the real breakthrough occurs when Vigoa talks about life before Las Vegas. Indeed, the boy nicknamed Manolo was a child of the revolution. He was a toddler at the time of the Bay of Pigs, three years old during the Cuban Missile Crisis, and eleven years old when the Cubans began dispatching troops to faraway lands. At the age of thirteen, Vigoa says he was sent to the Soviet Union for schooling, and when he was seventeen, he began military training. Vigoa relates he was commissioned a second lieutenant a year later and was selected for a Spetsnaz unit.

Vigoa describes battles in Afghanistan and Angola. The war stories are not heroic but emphasize survival. The descriptions, cynical and self-deprecating, tell of governments run amock; of small, vicious wars in "dung heap places"; of murderous aggressors and equally murderous partisans; and wars without rules or boundaries. This will be Vigoa's recurring theme and, in a sense, his justification for his criminal acts: "I am what you and countless other despots, warlords, bungling politicians, and hypocritical leaders have made me. I had so many beautiful dreams when I came to America. Now look at the mess I am in. Justice? America has the greatest legal system in the world. If you are rich."

THE TONE OF OUR FIRST and subsequent interviews is businesslike and even cordial. But when Vigoa compares the Ross gunfight and tragic deaths to war, I interrupt. "Robbing people at gunpoint is not war," I say. "Robbing people at gunpoint for self enrichment and then shooting them when they resist is murder."

Vigoa's face darkens. He gives me a hard look, and we lock eyes. There's a long pause, and then he sighs. "You're right, it's not war," Vigoa says. "Well, maybe a little bit like war. In war we kill not only soldiers but innocent people too. But sometimes a man has no choice." Vigoa is still stunned that guards at the Desert Inn and Ross store risked their lives for someone else's money.

In our third interview, I casually mention to Vigoa that I hope to go to Cuba to find his mother and sister and visit his old neighborhood. A week later I receive a letter that includes the address of Hilda Perez, Vigoa's mother, and directions to the little town of Caimito del Guayabal.

THE FLIGHT FROM Nassau to Havana will take barely an hour. As the Cubana turboprop turns southwest, I flip through a confidential psychiatric report ordered by Vigoa's defense lawyers. Vigoa is neither a sociopath nor a psychotic, the psychologist concludes in the June 29, 2002, evaluation.[1] He does have an elevated level of anxiety and paranoia, but that's to be expected in his line of work. Jose is judged antisocial and manipulative by the shrink. However, Jose has a conscience, a moral code, and the ability to love others. Jose is the product of extreme childhood deprivation and high levels of stress.

"Despite Mr. Vigoa's narcissism, antisocial traits/behavior, and paranoia, he is able to bond and connect," the psychologist continued. "I was fortunate to meet his oldest daughter. She has a tremendous amount of love and respect for her father. She discussed how her father was very active in the household and interacted with all three of his daughters in a positive venue. Mrs. Vigoa also discussed how her husband, despite his activities, was a decent man. As illustrated, some bonding is evident. Mr. Vigoa also discussed how he enjoyed his criminal activities. He reported that it was a thrill in regards to planning and carrying out his capers. This

[1] The psychologist met with Vigoa five times and also conferred with Luisa and his oldest daughter. Tests included the Wechsler Adult Intelligence Scale, the Wechsler Memory Scale, the Wide Range Achievement Test, the Minnesota Multiphasic Personality Inventory, a Personality Assessment Inventory, and the Millon Clinical Multiaxial Inventory.

indicates that Mr. Vigoa exhibits strong inclinations toward crimes not only for financial gain, but also because it reinforces his sense of mastery and control (narcissism) . . ."

The report went on to explain that Jose was the product of an affair between a married wealthy lumber company owner and the town beauty, a free-thinking young woman with a bohemian outlook: Hilda, Vigoa's mother. The lovers did not marry, although the relationship continued. Jose suffered pneumonia and other medical complications at birth and nearly died until his biological father intervened and arranged medical care. He also suffered a fractured skull at the age of nine after falling out of a banana tree and has suffered headaches ever since.

THE AIRCRAFT ENGINES throttle back. I look off to the left, and there she is: *hermosa Cuba*. I, too, have a personal link to the island. I grew up in pre-Castro Cuba, at the U.S. Naval Base at Guantanamo Bay, with my parents, my brother, Norman, and two sisters, Anne and Virginia. For eleven years Norman Walter Huddy, my father, ran the base telephone system. I visited much of the interior of Cuba, including the city of Guantanamo and the waterfront village of Caimanera. I saw firsthand the conditions in Cuba under the U.S.-backed Batista dictatorship. They were harsh and degrading.

Moments later we're on Cuban soil. I am sharply interrogated by a female customs agent but eventually passed through. I walk into the main terminal lobby and into the able hands of Jorge Luis Quesada, a bright and funny young travel agent who will be my guide for the next four days. "We don't have communism, we don't have socialism—we have Fidel-ism," he quips during our drive to Caimito.

After an hour's trip into the countryside west of Havana, we find a neighbor who remembers a boy named Manolo. I recognize this as Jose's nickname among family members. We learn that Mrs. Perez is visiting Norma, her daughter in the nearby town of Bauta. Off we go, in our Czech-made four-cylinder rental car. We eventually pull onto a narrow street lined with modest but livable one-story cinder-block homes. We find the address, and I knock on the door.

And there she is. Hilda Perez is a tall woman with jet black hair and younger than I expected. (Vigoa described his mother as about eighty, she says she is seventy-four.) Holding her arm is her daughter, with a fair complexion and blond hair—Norma, Vigoa's forty-two-year-old sister. I explain that I am a writer from Los Angeles who knows Jose. I do not elaborate about Vigoa's troubles because I assume they already know. I am invited inside. The living room is furnished with lawn furniture and is adjacent to a dining room and a small bedroom. The home, with a telephone, television set, and electric fan, is comfortable and clean.

Her son Manolo nearly died at birth, the mother says, but the great crisis came when Manolo's father died suddenly of cirrhosis of the liver. Yes, he owned a lumber mill and was prosperous before the revolution. But the mill was taken by the government. Manolo was only four and overwhelmed by his father's death. The little boy suffered a mental breakdown and was hospitalized. "He was very affected by his father's death," Mrs. Perez explains. "The sadness was too much for him. He was treated by doctors for several months."

There were five children: Juan Pedro Sanchez, the oldest, Alberto Sanchez Perez, Jose, (nicknamed Manolo), Norma Perez, and Enrique Perez. Hilda worked in an orange grove and the family was destitute. At times, they nearly starved. The U.S. embargo devastated the Cuban economy.

Abruptly, Hilda asks about her son. "Where is Manolo living now, in Las Vegas or with you in Los Angeles?" My guide's eyes widen. Jorge mouths the words, *She doesn't know, what should I say?*

"Your son is living near a town called Ely, Nevada," I reply. "I've seen him a number of times. He's helping me write a book about his life in America." I do not mention murder, prison, four life sentences, twenty-three-hour confinement, and Hannibal Lecter bondage.

Mrs. Perez is silent, and there are no further questions. Her face shows absolutely no emotion. I change the subject and ask if either Hilda or Norma has any old family photographs. Aside from the fact that they lived in a shanty for many years before the government provided a house of cinder blocks, and a hurricane blew away what little home they had, the truth is that they have no pictures of Manolo or the family. They were too poor. They never took any photographs. They never had a camera. I am embarrassed that I asked the question. I might as well have asked to see their Learjet.

I ask Hilda about Vigoa's military service. She shakes her head. "*No es*

A street in the village of Caimito del Guayabal, Jose Vigoa's hometown west of Havana.

PHOTO BY JOHN HUDDY.

permission." It is not permitted. By now I've decided to inform the family of Vigoa's imprisonment. While Hilda and Jorge talk, I ask Norma to join me on the porch.

"Manolo is in serious difficulty with the police," I say. "He's healthy, he's being treated humanely, but he's in trouble."

"What kind of trouble?" Norma asks. Her eyes well with tears.

"He's in prison," I say.

Norma begins to sob. "I knew something had happened. I thought he was dead. We suddenly stopped hearing from him five years ago. Every night I pray to God that Manolo is alive somewhere, that he is all right, but I know in my heart something bad has happened."

On the ride back to Havana, Jorge is unusually quiet. We pass through the countryside with its towering royal palms, banana trees, sugarcane fields, cattle ranches, cowboys on horseback, and endless groups of school-children in neat blue and brown uniforms, as though Cuba were one big Catholic school. The countryside is green and lovely. As we travel east on the straight divided highway, there are few cars on the road in the countryside, but I begin to realize in fact Cuba is a realm of endless conveyances. Men on bicycles. Mopeds. Motorcycles with sidecars. Russian jeeps. Trucks that serve as buses for the rural folk. The ubiquitous bicycle taxis with sinewy young men pedaling customers from street to street and even town to town. There are horses pulling carts, brand-new air-conditioned Volvo buses for the tourists, subcompacts from Eastern Europe, and, of course, those famous American cars from the 1950s.

Cuba has a transportation problem, in part because of the embargo, in part because it cannot afford fuel. There's a uniquely Cuban solution in place: It is a mark of good citizenship to pick up strangers. Although guides driving tourists are theoretically exempt, Jorge slams on the brakes when two attractive young women step out from the curb and wave. They are joined by a young man with a guitar, and they happily squeeze into the rear of the little car. It turns out they're musicians on their way home from a gig. I tell them that many years ago I was the entertainment editor of the *Miami Herald* and was the paper's critic for film and pop music. "Maybe you will review us for the *Miami Herald*," the pretty girl with the Hard Rock Cafe T-shirt laughs. As is true throughout my trip, there is not a hint of animosity because I am an American. I am treated with kindness, and there is no government interference. Ten miles down the road, we drop off the singers. They will walk the four miles home without complaint.

Jorge and I pass a billboard with a picture of a beaming Fidel Castro looking off to the side. Fidel wears the expression of a man watching his grandchildren arrive for a family picnic. Underneath Fidel's image are the words *Vamos Bien*. Translation: We're doing well.

ONE IMPORTANT QUESTION remained unresolved after a week in Havana. While in Caimito, I asked neighbors about Vigoa's travels as a youth and reputed military service. One woman said that Manolo, at about thirteen, began disappearing for extended periods of time, and no one knew where he was. Another said he returned to Cuba after such an absence and promptly left for the U.S. on the Mariel boatlift. One woman thought Manolo had problems with the police and may have been in jail. Another said he was fascinated by the Russians and their military equipment and was befriended by a high-ranking Russian officer and spent much of his time on a nearby Soviet base before being sent to Russia.

The Cuban government has never confirmed or denied Vigoa's account of his military service or responded to written requests for information, although if Vigoa had been a serving officer in the Cuban army, it is unlikely the Cubans would claim him in view of his criminal history.

Lieutenant Alamshaw and his men believe Vigoa's story. "Here's this guy yanked off into the military, led this deprived military life, and was forced into battle," George Sherwood, the detective, said. "He comes to the United States, the land of opportunity, and can't seem to make it. He's working piss-ass construction jobs and wants better for his life. He can't do it by legal means, and he reverts to his training and what he's good at." Sherwood points to the Bellagio video. "I was convinced that he was either military or police just by the manner in which he moved, the manner in which he carried his weapon. He had a tactical hold on his firearm for close quarters."

Peter Brookes, a retired CIA operative, said Vigoa's claims are consistent with the historical record. "It all sounds very plausible to me. Cuba was a client state of the Soviet Union. The Russians brought people to the Soviet Union all the time. And yes, there were foreigners serving with the Soviet Union military and Spetsnaz." Brookes says the Vigoa story, in which a highly trained special forces officer reinvents himself as a gangster, is not uncommon. "Look at the situation in Russia," Brooks says. "All the KGB guys who lost their jobs—what do they do? They put their field craft to a new use. It's called the Russian Mafia. These skills are very transferable. If you can't find a respectable occupation—well, it's like what happened to your Cuban."

Brian Latell, the CIA expert on Cuba who served as national intelligence officer for Latin America from 1990 to 1994 and whose Cuba expertise spans thirty years, confirms that young Cubans were educated and trained in the Soviet Union during the period cited by Vigoa, and that the Cubans did aid the Russians in multiple military excursions.

"It sure sounds like he was in special operations or special forces, although he might also have been military intelligence or part of the Ministry of Interior in intelligence," Latell told me.

Wayne Smith, the former Havana mission chief for the U.S. State Department, said that between 1960 and 1985, thousands of Cuban youths studied and trained in the Soviet Union, and, yes, during the boatlift, hundreds of agents flooded the U.S. "He may not have been a deserter at all," one retired operative said. "That part of his story I would question.

He may have been a sleeper agent sent to the U.S. in the chaos of the boatlift. That would be my bet."

It has been confirmed by the FBI and INS that Vigoa entered the U.S. on the Mariel boatlift. Coast Guard accounts verify that there was a sudden storm of near-hurricane intensity that struck the Florida Straits at the time of Vigoa's passage. A Coast Guard cutter was forced to cut a towline to smaller boats because of dangerous sea conditions.

Could Vigoa have been an active agent? After his attempted escape on June 3, 2002, police discovered documents in Vigoa's cell. Despite jail surveillance, Vigoa managed to dislodge his stainless-steel toilet, remove the caulk, insert secret documents into the wall beyond the commode plumbing, and then recaulk the toilet. Police found notes on biological warfare, chemical poisons, and plots to blow up a Florida nuclear power plant. The contents of this cache of documents are being disclosed here for the first time.[2]

"The poison gas is concentrated," a document in Vigoa's handwriting says. "It comes in a heavy-duty steel pipe or tube with hundreds of PSI compressed [*unintelligible*] chemical. It has an elaborate detonator that works with a clock that starts opening the escape valve slowly. When the valve gets to opening [*unintelligible*], it releases a cloud of clear poison that mixes with the wind. This gas can spread over hundreds of miles in the direction the wind blows. Once this deadly chemical expands in the air, it works like nuclear radiation in a chain reaction of thousands of feet per second."[3]

Vigoa also reveals the plot to explode the Florida nuclear plant. "The time was set by the hurricane season in Florida . . . because of the powerful winds."[4]

Vigoa's ability to dismantle a toilet in his jail cell while under twenty-four-hour surveillance is considered significant. "That's sophisticated tradecraft," former Central Intelligence Agency case worker and author Robert Baer said. "An ordinary criminal wouldn't have that kind of skill and training."

The real-life intelligence agent who inspired the George Clooney

[2] At the request of authorities, and for reasons of national security, I have edited the documents.
[3] The jail staff has confirmed that Vigoa did not have access to books dealing with any of these subjects and that his cell was searched regularly, and the contents reviewed and inventoried.
[4] Another paper includes a list of military officers by name in South American countries who allegedly traffic in narcotics, weapons, and money laundering. They appear under the heading "La Compra de Missiles S.A.7.8.10."

character in the Warner Bros. spy thriller *Syriana*, Baer offered another possible explanation for Vigoa's trip to America: Vigoa was a deeply planted sleeper agent "who eventually went wrong, as many do."

Baer continued: "That makes perfect sense. All along, the KGB and the GRU had to worry about providing detailed cover for their agents. So why not take somebody who you trust and who has been trained for stay-behind operations and send them in on the boatlift? That's what I would have done if I had been a Russian case officer in Havana."

Another tantalizing clue comes from Vigoa himself. In describing his arrival at Mariel Harbor and the harrowing boat trip on the *Lady Lee* to Key West, he talks at length about Roberto, the intelligence agent who teaches Vigoa how to enter the U.S. without being caught and who plays a prominent role as Vigoa's companion and protector on the trip itself.[5]

Was there really a Roberto? Or was Roberto actually Jose Manolo Vigoa? Vigoa asserts he came to America on a whim, but that strikes me as wholly out of character—Vigoa is many things, but not whimsical. Baer makes perfect sense. I believe that Vigoa was in fact the Cuban intelligence agent on the boat and that he created that character to provide a clue as to his real reason for entering the U.S. amid the chaos of the boatlift. Vigoa was a spy who later became dazzled and corrupted by the allure of Las Vegas.

"Keep in mind that Cuba is not the U.S. Not anyone can go out and buy a high-powered assault rifle to shoot deer," Baer, a twenty-year veteran of the CIA, said. "Firearms are restricted to the police and military. So where did Jose Vigoa learn his shooting skills? I don't think there's any other explanation. He's had military training."

ON RETURNING TO Las Vegas in 2006 for a final round of interviews, the questions everyone from police to FBI agents wanted to know were the ones I considered every time I sat across from Vigoa or read thousands of pages of journals and correspondence provided by the Zelig-like gangster who went from dedicated Marxist mercenary to hard-charging capitalist in the blink of an eye.

Who is the real Jose Vigoa?

Revolutions, wars, invasions, and retreats, the man seemed to be

---

[5] The first-person Vigoa chapters, assembled and edited by the author, include Vigoa statements from prison interviews, correspondence, and signed reports.

everywhere. Roberto or Jose. Spetsnaz or spy. Marxist or capitalist. Loving father or brutal killer. Vigoa seemed to be a multitude of characters. So many layers, so many veils, so many twists and turns. I'm convinced Vigoa is neither a psychopath nor a sociopath. The murders of Gary Dean Prestidge and Richard Sosa were ruthless and brutal, and I have done my best to convey the spirit of the guards' admirable lives, but dismissing Vigoa as a mad-dog killer is too easy. Vigoa is bright, resourceful, loyal, enterprising, and energetic. He has a moral code. Vigoa believes his soul to be a battleground for the forces of good and evil, and that fate and random events can tip the scale at any moment. He cites the union strike that triggered his drug dealing, the abuse of his child at the day-care center, the alleged vendetta of the FBI in the Jose Diaz case, his inability to find employment after his 1996 release from prison because of provision 13, as occasions when he turned, or was pushed, to the dark side.

Under different circumstances, Vigoa might have been a successful businessman or high-ranking officer or an engineer building highways. This was not to be. The fierce gales that buffeted his life from the day he was born never subsided. First there was the Castro Revolution that challenged the mighty American Empire but placed Cubans in the bull's-eye. Then the retaliatory American embargo against Cuba that left the Vigoa family near starvation. The Cold War was no media catchphrase if you were Cuban—everyone on the island faced the threat of nuclear annihilation or invasion by those Americans "with the monster faces." Long before 9/11, Vigoa says he found himself in a life-or-death struggle with Islamic fundamentalism and the mujahideen. The rise of African nationalism put Vigoa in harm's way once more in the most vicious kind of proxy war and counterrevolutionary conflict.

Vigoa rode the tsunamis of history. The fact that he washed ashore in Las Vegas, like a Roman legionnaire dropped into a Galleria Mall, might be considered ironic, even amusing, except for the deaths of Gary Dean Prestidge and Richard Sosa, and the escalating violence of the Vigoa crew and its leader's thirst for the "rush" of action. Vigoa insisted after the Ross slayings that he intended to kill no one. "That wasn't me!" he exclaimed. That's probably true, but such a sentiment will give little comfort to the families and loved ones left behind.

But if the Ross violence wasn't Vigoa, then what was? The Cuban's answer is plain enough: "When I couldn't get a decent job, when I couldn't provide for my wife and three daughters, I resorted to the only

364 | AUTHOR'S NOTE

training I had—leading men in combat." The dubious morality of such a career choice aside, this much rings true: Clearly Vigoa received extensive military training before he crossed the Florida Straits. Authorities also believe he may have received high-level training in intelligence and counterinsurgency warfare.

And something else: Vigoa is right. He may be serving life terms in a harsh twenty-three-hour lockdown tier, but there will be other soldiers of the empire, trained either by the West or the East, by the insurgents or the occupiers, and they are coming our way.

"Jose Vigoa is an example of the criminal to be most feared in the future," Sheriff Bill Young said. "We in American local law enforcement know exactly how to deal with the homegrown street thug but are way behind the curve with the foreign born and trained, who are smart and not committing crimes because they are addicted or need money for drugs. We're seeing more and more of these types in Vegas, particularly from the Middle East, Israel, the Baltic states, and South America. Their values are far different from ours, and the ruthless side they display leaves many American cops stunned. Many of these guys have military backgrounds and are sophisticated and well read. It's going to take a concerted effort on our part to effectively deal with the Jose Vigoas of the world."

The story of Jose Manuel Vigoa Perez, it turns out, is very much a story of our times.

Please turn the page for a chapter not published in the hardcover edition of **STORMING LAS VEGAS.**

It is February 2000.

On the heels of stealing twelve vehicles from a Thrifty lot and just weeks away from the fateful clash with two armored-car guards in front of a Ross department store, Jose Vigoa's crew is planning another heist—one that goes curiously awry. . . .

A week after Valentine's Day in February 2000, on a cloudy, rainy day, a new silver Plymouth Voyager minivan with stolen Arizona license plates, late of the Thrifty Car Rental agency, pulled into the parking lot of the Nevada State Bank at Olympic and Green Valley Avenues in Henderson. Six weeks after the brazen theft of twelve vehicles at the Thrifty lot, the Vigoa gang was back in action. Today's mission: hit a Brink's truck in front of the bank.

The gang had removed the rear seats from the van the day before the robbery. Oscar and Jose then taped precisely measured black construction paper, the kind children use in school to make Halloween and other decorations, over the long, tall windows on the sides of the van. They placed empty cardboard boxes behind the driver compartment to obscure the gunmen in the main cabin should anyone look inside through the windshield. They removed the lights from the interior domes so that when the door was open there was no illumination.

At 10:33 A.M. the van slipped into a parking slot near the front door of the bank. Oscar drove and sat in plain view, pretending to study his checkbook while Jose and Luis squatted in the back. "We don't want to be too early 'cause the police patrol the banks out here and the banks watch their own parking lots," Vigoa said. "Not too soon, not too late."

Jose, Oscar, and Luis remained hidden in the van and waited for the armored car, due to arrive between 10:35 and 10:45, according to Jose's previous surveillance. In accordance with Vigoa's rules, the Nevada Bank offered multiple escape routes, excellent concealment from the street, and the likelihood of making good money, as much as $500,000.

"Our job is not to kill anybody or even fire our guns, but if the guards resist, we'll give them all the bullets they want," Vigoa said.

The very mention of resistance reminded Jose of the Desert Inn debacle, and his face darkened. And there was one other nagging detail:

"Oscar, you still got that fucking .38?"

Oscar grinned sheepishly and patted his jacket where the revolver was concealed.

"Well then, you must have lots of confidence, muchacho, 'cause you only got six rounds in that little pistol. Hope we don't have no bullshit heroes today."

Bullshit heroes was a term Jose invented after the Desert Inn shoot-out with guards who stood their ground. Jose felt his blood pressure spike.

"The .38 won't jam on me," Oscar said mildly. "I like revolvers. No problems because you don't have no . . ."

Boom!

A deafening explosion from inside the cabin rocked the van. A tremendous retort and the sound of breaking glass. Oscar jumped in his seat so high his head slammed into the truck's ceiling. Oscar clung tightly to the steering wheel, his mouth agape, his ears ringing, his eyes looking frantically about. *Oh no, not again.* The big Mexican began checking his body for gunshot wounds and blood. His ears began to throb. His ears began to *hurt.*

An accidental discharge. Someone's weapon had gone off inside the cabin.

Jose stared accusingly at his rifle, the cause of the gunfire. He looked like the errant shortstop who had just booted a routine ground ball and stared indignantly into his glove. Jose called the AK-47 "my jealous mistress" because of its light, sensitive trigger. Impatiently fidgeting with the weapon, he had "launched one out the back window," he later explained.

A fine white haze filled the van. The two men squatting on the floor in the rear cabin held their ears and cursed prodigiously.

The smell of cordite, sour and pungent, was intense, almost sickening. The cursing continued.

"Fuck!"

"Oh, shit!"

"Conjo!"

Outside the van, the front door of the bank opened. A dark-haired and buxom teller peered out and looked around. *What was that noise?*

In spite of himself, Oscar stared at the woman's tight black sweater before realizing the young woman with the big round eyes was looking back at him. Oscar shrugged. *Yo no se.* The teller smiled and went back inside. *A car backfire.*

More confusion within the van as the men began squabbling:

"Oscar, you hit?"

"No, I don't think so."

"Everybody okay?"

"What the fuck, Jose!"

"My goddamn jealous bitch, she bit me again."

"No, shit."

Luis looked around.

"Jose. The rear window don't look no good."

Jose sighed heavily. Half of the glass had been shot away; another sheet dangled over the bumper. A mess. Peevishly Jose crawled over and pulled the strip of safety glass from the frame.

The bank door opened again. The branch manager, young, balding, and babyfaced, looked around. He saw Oscar and frowned. The manager went back inside.

"Let's get out of here," Vigoa said.

"Oscar!"

"*Si.*"

"Just start the engine and slowly back out. You're not in a hurry. Don't look at nobody. Don't break any laws. The roads are wet. No accidents."

"Okay."

As the Voyager pulled away, Jose rolled down a window, pulled back a corner of the black construction paper, and listened for any shouts or screams that might indicate that the stray round had hit some hapless civilian. Jose also listened for sirens.

He heard nothing but the sound of traffic and a distant barking dog. To this day, no one has found a stray bullet lodged in a wall or vehicle. The gunfire in front of the bank was never reported to police.

As the Voyager retreated cautiously down a side street, Jose heard a familiar sound, one he had listened to many times in the preceding weeks as the gangster shadowed armored trucks around the suburb. It was the clanking, clutch-shifting noise of a heavy armored vehicle coming up the street. Vigoa looked out as a squat Brink's truck passed by in the opposite direction heading for the bank. 10:40 fucking A.M. Right on schedule.

In the armored truck neither of the guards noticed the strange-looking Plymouth Voyager with the blacked-out windows when the two vehicles passed each other.

Another gun accident in the middle of a job.

Eighteen months earlier, while fleeing the Desert Inn robbery, the getaway truck racing out of the Vagabond Hotel accelerated too quickly, Jose's Norinco MAK 90 assault rifle slid to the back of the truck bed and discharged when it slammed into the tailgate. The round ripped through the cabin, tore through Oscar's sleeve, and narrowly missed hitting the Mexican.

Now this fiasco. Embarrassing. The crew leader who worried about the character of his team during desert training now could blame only himself for ruining the Nevada State Bank job by failing to obey the most basic rule of firearm handling: One is taught to wrap one's finger *around* the trigger guard and never make contact with the trigger itself unless the shooter intends to fire *at that moment*.

But Jose liked a hair trigger because he felt it worked better when you went to full-automatic fire. "I've had accidents like this before with jealous rifles that have hair triggers," Jose said nonchalantly, as if the near disaster were of no consequence and even amusing. "I like my guns like that—they're good for fast shooting."

This time, however, there would be no three-month wait between jobs. Perhaps this is why Jose treated the incident so lightly. Jose was ready to strike again and quickly. He explained later:

"I had been watching two other armored trucks for weeks operating in the same area, and I had enough information to develop a plan in a matter of days. It was just a case of switching locations. I knew where to place the getaway cars, what escape routes to use, and how to attack the guards. A piece of cake."

The backup target was Armored Transport vehicle 3280 on what the company designated run number 5. A last-minute replacement on the truck, filling in for a sick Kevin Prokopich, was young Gary Dean Prestidge, pleased to be taken out of the stuffy, stressful vault and placed back on the street with all the action.